SEVEN PAULINE LETTERS

SEVEN PAULINE LETTERS

Peter F. Ellis

THE LITURGICAL PRESS
Collegeville, Minnesota

2nd printing, September 1984

Nihil obstat: Robert C. Harren, J.C.L., *Censor deputatus.*

Imprimatur: ✝George H. Speltz, D.D., Bishop of St. Cloud. March 3, 1982.

COVER DESIGN BY ANN BLATTNER. ADAPTED FROM A WOODCUT BY HANS HOLBEIN THE YOUNGER, CA. 1524.

Library of Congress Cataloging in Publication Data

Ellis, Peter F.
  Seven Pauline letters.

  Bibliography: p.
  1. Bible. N.T. Epistles of Paul—Commentaries.
I. Title.
BS2650.3.E44   227'.077   82-15252
ISBN 0-8146-1245-8 (pbk.)   AACR2

To Judy,
my heart's delight

Contents

Preface

This book flows from an almost lifelong love for the great Apostle to the Gentiles and from fourteen years of teaching his eloquent and deeply theological letters. The aim of the book is to study the mind of Paul as it developed and matured theologically during the course of his ministry from 51 to 58 A.D. and thus share with him his continually deeper penetration of soteriology, Christology, and the relationship of each of these to the Father's plan of salvation for the world.

The outline of the book follows, as far as it is ascertainable, the chronological development of Paul's mind as that development is deducible from the seven letters acknowledged by all to be authentically Pauline: 1 Thessalonians, 1 and 2 Corinthians, Philippians, Galatians, Romans, and Philemon.

The approach of the book is ancillary to the aim. It deals with the man, his medium, and his message. Chapter I deals briefly with the man—Paul's background, travels, ministry, and the critical events of his career; and with his medium—the letters: their format, nature, dating, and principles of interpretation. Chapters II-VII deal extensively with Paul's message: his parousiac theology in 1 Thessalonians (Chapter II); his soteriology and Christology in 1 Corinthians, Philippians, 2 Corinthians, and Galatians (Chapters III-VI); and his concept of the cosmic Christ and justification by faith for all in Romans (Chapter VII).

The format of the commentary section of the book follows three steps. First, a brief introduction to each letter, stressing the audience and the literary format of the letter. Second, the Revised Standard Version (RSV) text for each successive section or division of the letter. Third, a commentary, concentrating on the literary and theological sense of the text. Since the complete text of each letter is given, the book can be used conveniently without a Bible.

The book is meant for all serious students of the Pauline letters. Professional Scripture scholars will recognize some new literary discoveries dealing with Paul's manner of presenting his material. They will also recognize and be able to evaluate the new insights into Paul's mind that result from these and other discoveries. Undergraduate students should find the book a difficult but rewarding companion for a one- or two-semester course. Serious study groups will find the book a challenging and provocative spur to theologizing beyond the call of duty.

The notes and bibliography have been put at the end of the book to prevent cluttering the text. The Revised Standard Version text has been used because it is more faithful to the original Greek than other modern translations and because, as a consequence of this greater fidelity to the original, it makes it much easier for the reader to recognize and enjoy Paul's regular use of an A-B-A' form of chiastic parallelism in the presentation of his material.

At the conclusion of writing a book there is much to be thankful for and many to thank. My gratitude goes first to Paul; then to Fr. Stanislaus Lyonnet, S.J., of the Pontifical Biblical Institute in Rome, whose enthusiasm for Paul's realism deepened my growing interest in the great Apostle; then to my Redemptorist confreres, Fr. William Biffar, Fr. Matthew Meehan, and Fr. Joseph Rowan; and finally to my students in the Graduate School of Religion and Religious Education at Fordham University, whose response to Paul and his message have made my years of teaching there a continuous challenge and a continual delight.

Peter F. Ellis

Fordham University
August 1, 1981

Abbreviations

CBQ   *The Catholic Biblical Quarterly.* Washington 1939–.

ITQ   *The Irish Theological Quarterly.* Dublin 1906–22, 1951–.

JAAR   *Journal of the American Academy of Religion.* Missoula, Mont. 1933–.

JBC   *The Jerome Biblical Commentary.* Edited by Raymond E. Brown, S.S.; Joseph A. Fitzmyer, S.J.; Roland E. Murphy, O. Carm. Englewood Cliffs, N.J.: Prentice-Hall, 1968.

JBL   *Journal of Biblical Literature.* Boston 1881–.

NAB   The New American Bible

PG   *Patrologia Graeca.* Edited by J. P. Migne. 161 vols. Paris, 1857–66.

RSV   The Holy Bible: Revised Standard Version

TS   *Theological Studies.* Woodstock, Md. 1940–.

Chapter I

PAUL AND HIS LETTERS

Letters are revealing and tell much about the writer. This is particularly true in Paul's case, and whoever reads his letters, especially 1 and 2 Corinthians, Galatians, and Philippians, will learn more about Paul than about any other figure in early Christianity. The letters tell what Paul was thinking, what he was doing, where he was traveling, how he felt about Jesus and the work of spreading the gospel, what he thought about both his friends and his enemies, and, most important, how his mind functioned theologically. They provide historical sources of the first rank about early Christianity and about the Apostle who did more than any other man to spread the message of Jesus to the Gentile world. The letters provide a great deal of information about Paul, but in addition to the autobiographical material in the letters, there is also a fair amount of biographical material about Paul in the Acts of the Apostles (cf. Acts 13–28). Since autobiographical material has considerably greater historical value than biographical material,[1] we will begin with a summary of the autobiographical material in the letters and then say something about the biographical material in the Acts of the Apostles. In either case, there is no substitute for reading the actual sources.

The autobiographical material

In Gal 1:11–2:14, Paul gives a rapid rundown of his life up to approximately 50 A.D.,[2] mentioning his conversion (1:11-12; cf. 1 Cor 9:1; Acts 9; 22; 26); his pre-conversion life as a persecutor of the Church (1:13; cf. Phil 3:5-6); his time spent in Arabia and his return to Damascus (1:17); his first visit to Jerusalem three years after his conversion (1:18); a period of time spent in Syria and Cilicia, probably at Antioch and Tarsus (1:21); a second trip to Jerusalem fourteen years later (2:1); and finally his confrontation with Peter at Antioch (2:11).

The reader should note that Paul does not indicate whether the fourteen years mentioned in Gal 2:1 are to be reckoned from the time of his conversion or as following upon the three years spent in Arabia and Damascus before returning to Syria and Cilicia. It is because of the uncertainty of reckoning the starting point of these fourteen years that there are such differences in the chronologies of Paul's life. If it is assumed that the meeting in Jerusalem between Paul and the other leaders of the Church took place about 49 A.D., and the fourteen years are reckoned backward from the time of the meeting, then Paul's conversion can be dated to the year 35 A.D. But if the fourteen years are reckoned as following upon the three years mentioned in relation to Paul's first visit to Jerusalem (Gal 1:18), then his conversion would have to be dated seventeen years earlier, sometime in 32 A.D. If the latter date is more accurate, Paul was already persecuting Christians and was himself converted to Christianity within two years of Jesus' resurrection!

When Paul's survey of his life in Galatians is compared with the account of his life in the Acts of the Apostles, the differences are notable and demand an evaluation of the historicity of Acts. Galatians, for example, speaks of only two trips to Jerusalem before 49 A.D.; Acts speaks of three and possibly four trips (cf. Acts 9:26; 11:30; 12:25; 15:4). One must ask: Is Acts a more complete account, and did Paul fail to mention one or two trips prior to the meeting in Jerusalem mentioned in Acts 15:4, or is the author of Acts mistaken? Recent studies suggest that the latter solution is correct and that the biographical material in Acts should be subjected to a more critical scrutiny than has been customary up to modern times.

The biographical material in Acts

R. H. Fuller[3] and others[4] cite favorably the emphasis of recent study on Luke as a theologian and the consequent de-emphasis of Luke as a historian. Fuller adopts the view of E. Haenchen,[5] which may be summarized as follows. First, Luke's work is consciously literary, and Acts is a theological work artistically composed for purposes primarily of edification and apologetics. Second, the eight Petrine and nine Pauline speeches in Acts are Luke's, not Peter's or Paul's, compositions. Third, the author of Luke-Acts is not a companion of Paul or even a contemporary but a Christian theologian-historian who looked back upon Paul from the sub-apostolic age and probably wrote his two-part work as late as 85 to 100 A.D. Thus, the consciously literary aspect of Acts — especially the author's composition of the speeches, his use of summaries, and his structuring of the material to show the spread of the gospel from Jerusalem to Samaria, to Antioch, Greece, and finally Rome — has led scholars, not to a rejection of Luke's historical testimony, but to a more critical evaluation of it. Recent study of Acts, according to R. H. Fuller, has led to the following methodological conclusions:

> Where Paul and Acts contradict each other, Paul must be followed. . . .
> Acts can be confidently used only when: (1) it tallies with the Pauline data;

(2) it offers supplementary data which are otherwise compatible with the Pauline information. . . . The only legitimate procedure today is the reverse of the usual order: to start from the data of Paul and then fit the data of Acts, after critical assessment, into the Pauline scheme.[6]

Such an assessment of Luke makes it difficult to work out a critically acceptable chronology of Paul's life and letters. The following is suggested as a "working," not a critical, chronology.[7]

Paul's birth	c. 1 A.D.
The resurrection	30
Paul's persecution of Christians	31–32
Paul's conversion	32 (35?)
Paul in Arabia (Transjordan) and Damascus	32–35
Paul's first trip to Jerusalem	35
Years spent in Tarsus (?) and Antioch	35–48
First missionary journey (Acts 13–14)	48
Second trip to Jerusalem (Gal 2:1; Acts 15)	49
Second missionary journey (Acts 15:36–18:22)	50–52
Eighteen-month stay at Corinth (Acts 18:11)	51–52
At Antioch for about a year (Acts 18:22-23)	53
Third missionary journey (Acts 18:23–21:17)	53–57
Three-year stay at Ephesus (Acts 19:10)	54–57
Arrest and imprisonment in Caesarea (Acts 23:31-33)	58–60
Voyage to Rome and imprisonment in Rome (Acts 27–28)	60–62

Paul's background—Jewish or Hellenistic?

The question of Paul's background is important because every individual is conditioned by his environment and influenced by his training and education. The mind conditioned by a Hellenistic environment and education will approach and express theological teaching in a manner different from a mind conditioned by a rabbinic environment and education. The interpreter has to take these differences into consideration in interpreting a theologian's writings. Since environment and education are factors of such broad and variegated influence, it cannot be a question of Jewishness to the exclusion of Hellenism, or Hellenistic influence to the exclusion of rabbinic influence, but a question of degree. Was Paul predominantly Jewish and rabbinic in the cast of his mind or predominantly Hellenistic?

The question admits of no simple solution. A. Schweitzer interprets Paul in almost exclusively Jewish terms.[8] C. G. Montefiore, on the other hand, interprets Paul as a Jew of the dispersion practically untouched by the rabbinic Judaism of Palestine and familiar only with the watered-down Judaism of the Diaspora.[9] Without attempting to explain the complicated factors of the solution, the conclusion more recently proposed is that Paul was predominantly Jewish and rabbinic in his cast of mind rather than Hellenistic. This conclusion has been proposed by J. Bonsirven,[10] W. C. van Unnik,[11] and W. D. Davies.[12] Davies concludes his opening chapter with the statement:

> Only an examination of the basic elements in Pauline thought can reveal whether Paul was rooted in Rabbinic Judaism or not, and it is to such an examination that we shall apply ourselves in the following pages. It will not be our purpose to give a complete statement of Pauline theology but, beginning with his conception of sin, we shall endeavor to show that in the central points of his interpretation of the Christian dispensation Paul is grounded in an essentially Rabbinic world of thought, that the apostle was, in short, a Rabbi become Christian and was therefore primarily governed both in life and thought by Pharisaic concepts, which he has baptized "unto Christ."[13]

According to the testimony of his letters, Paul was proud of his Jewish heritage and claimed to have been not only a Pharisee but a strict and uncompromising defender of Pharisaism and its teachings. In Gal 1:13-14, he says: "For you have heard of my former life in Judaism, how I persecuted the church of God violently and tried to destroy it; and I advanced in Judaism beyond many of my own age among my people, so extremely zealous was I for the traditions of my fathers." In Phil 3:5-6, Paul speaks of himself as "a Hebrew born of Hebrews; as to the law a Pharisee, as to zeal a persecutor of the church, as to righteousness under the law blameless" (cf. also 2 Cor 11:22).

The thesis that Paul's rabbinic background and education were the predominant though not the only influence on his mind is not unimportant. If it is true that a man generally thinks and writes according to the categories of the culture that formed his mind and emotions, then the principal key to the interpretation of Paul's letters will be found in his knowledge and use of the Old Testament and in his propensity for rabbinic forms of theological argumentation and literary presentation. Practically speaking, such a conclusion means that more often than not Paul's mind is to be interpreted against his background in Jewish culture rather than against the cultural and philosophical background of Hellenism.

Critical events influencing Paul's theological development

All the critical events that influenced Paul's theological development during the thirty or more years of his ministry can neither be known nor adequately analyzed. Certain events, however, when considered against Paul's background as a Pharisee, would appear to have served as catalysts in the development of his new theology as a Christian rabbi.

In some cases the events can be deduced from the differences between Paul's thinking as a Pharisee and his thinking as a Christian. In a few cases the events can be deduced from data in Paul's letters. More often than not the events are deduced from the tone of Paul's arguments and from the reactions of his audience. Since the critical events are for the most part mirrored in Paul's reaction to them in his letters, we will list them according to their probable chronological order as they appear behind the façades of the letters.

a) Paul's vision of the risen Christ — *the* critical event;
b) the naïve expectation of an imminent second coming of Christ;
c) the rejection of the resurrection of the body by the Greeks at Corinth;
d) Paul's close brush with death at Ephesus and his realization that Christian existence is to be patterned on the suffering life of Christ;
e) Paul's encounter with false apostles at Corinth, which leads him to a more profound concept of apostleship and its relationship to the cross;
f) a controversy with Jewish Christians about the Mosaic law and Christian liberty, which forces Paul to theologize in depth on the relationship between faith and justification;
g) the Jews' rejection and the Gentiles' acceptance of the gospel, which leads to the falling together of the theological data in Paul's mind to bring home to him an understanding of the place of the cosmic Christ in the Church and in the Father's plan of salvation history.

For some appreciation of the impact of these critical events on Paul's mind and emotions, the reader should consider the events in relation to what Paul already believed as a Pharisee prior to his meeting with the risen Christ on the road to Damascus.

With regard to Paul's vision of the risen Christ, the reader should remember that Paul as a Pharisee already believed in resurrection of the dead.[14] It was a Pharisaic doctrine with Old Testament roots in Dn 12; 2 Mc 6-7; Wis 1-4. The Pharisees believed not only in the fact of a bodily resurrection but in the resurrection of the dead as a sign of the coming and completion of God's promised kingdom. Paul's vision of the risen Christ did not initiate but rather confirmed his Pharisaic belief in the resurrection of the dead. What Paul's vision of the risen Christ meant to him, however, went far beyond a simple confirmation of his belief in resurrection; it convinced him that Jesus was sent by the Father, that Jesus was the Messiah, and that with Jesus' resurrection there had begun the beginning of the end — the turning point of all history, the time when God would fulfill his messianic promises to Israel and the world. J. Jeremias expresses the impact of the resurrection on Paul and on the early Christians as follows:

> At first glance, to attempt to discover what the appearances of the Risen Lord meant to the first witnesses in *terms of immediate experience* seems

quite hopeless, as our sources are decades removed from the events and the Easter accounts have been elaborated and reshaped in a number of respects in the interim. Nevertheless, a hypothesis may be ventured *if one begins from the thought of the time.* Judaism did not know of any anticipated resurrection as an event in history. There is nothing comparable to the resurrection of Jesus anywhere in Jewish literature. Certainly there are mentions of raisings from the dead, but these are always resuscitations, a return to earthly life. Nowhere in Jewish literature do we have a resurrection to *doxa* (glory) as an event of history. Rather, resurrection to *doxa* always and without exception means the dawn of God's new creation. Therefore the disciples must have experienced the appearances of the Risen Lord as an eschatological event, as a dawning of the turning point of the worlds.[15]

Paul's naïve expectation of an imminent second coming of Christ flowed from his understanding of Jesus' resurrection as the sign and guarantee that God was about to bring to consummation his plan for the salvation of the world. How soon this would happen neither Paul nor anyone else in the early Church knew, but they all expected it to happen shortly. And Paul himself felt for a good while that he would be alive for the second coming of Christ (cf. 1 Thes 4:16-17; 1 Cor 15:51-52). The parousiac fever of the early Christians is not easy to understand but it was very real. It affected Paul in his early preaching and is evident in all his letters, especially 1 Thessalonians, 1 Corinthians, and Philippians.

In all probability, the early Christians' parousiac expectations arose from their reading of apocalyptic literature. Apocalyptic literature (Daniel is the best example) has many peculiarities (see pp. 30–32), but nothing is more peculiar about apocalyptic literature than its emphasis on the suddenness of God's coming to destroy his enemies and reward his friends. In all likelihood, the emphasis on "suddenness" in the apocalyptic literature was transferred to the work of Christ. Since he had not "completed" his work of victory over the forces of evil in the world—or so it seemed, since the same forces inimical to God were still at work—the early Christians and Paul fully expected him to return shortly and clean up all unfinished business. It was only as the decades passed without Christ's return that the early Christians learned that there was more to Christ's second coming than a mere squaring of accounts with the forces of evil. In the earliest decades, the years when Paul preached and wrote his letters, parousiac fever ran high and strong (cf. 1 Thes 4:16-17; 1 Cor 15:51-52).

The rejection of bodily resurrection, as opposed to "soul" resurrection, by the Greeks and early Gnostics caused Paul to defend the bodily resurrection of Christians. Paul's own background as a Jew led him to think of the person as a body-person. The Greeks thought of the person as made up of two principles: soul and body. They considered the body the prison of the soul. This led them to reject the teaching of the resurrection of the body.

Paul's response to their objections is found in 1 Cor 15 and in parts of 2 Corinthians.

Paul's close brush with death at Ephesus, reflected in Phil 1:12-26 and 2 Cor 1:8-11, had a double effect on him: it made him realize that he might not be alive for the parousia and that following Christ meant more than sharing in his victory – it also meant sharing in his sufferings and death. This latter realization was the more significant. It led Paul to a more profound conception of Christian existence and its relationship to the passion, death, and resurrection of Christ. Growth in Christ meant sharing in Christ's sufferings. This is a central theme of Philippians and 2 Corinthians.

Paul's encounter with false apostles at Corinth led him to reflect on the purpose and meaning of apostleship and on the characteristics that distinguished the true from the false apostle. He came to realize that an apostle was called not only to preach Christ but to pattern his life on the life of the suffering Christ, and thus to preach with his life the central message of the gospel. He expounds his conception of "the true apostle" in 2 Corinthians.

To understand Paul's controversy with Jewish Christians about law, liberty, and justification by faith alone, the reader has to remember that there very likely was a time when Paul himself, as a strict, practicing Pharisee, defended justification by observance of the law. His devotion to the law as law, however, shriveled when he came to realize that man is justified by faith and is freed from the law by Christ. Not all Jewish Christians saw this as clearly as Paul did. When Paul himself first realized the difference and the significance of justification by faith as opposed to justification by works, we cannot know. He had no doubts about it, however, by the time he came to write Philippians, Galatians, and Romans.

Paul's Pharisaic belief that Gentiles could be saved only by and through their entrance into the Jewish religion must be taken into consideration if the reader is to understand the impact upon Paul of the Gentiles' acceptance and the Jews' rejection of the gospel. How early he realized that it was the Gentiles as a group and not the Jews as a group who were accepting the gospel, we do not know. At some point in his career, probably in the middle fifties, Paul was forced to accept the fact that "the first (the Jews) would be last and the last (the Gentiles) first." Once he had accepted that, he began to theologize anew on the Father's plan of salvation. This led him to the synthesis we find in Romans, the most profound and the most theologically important of all his letters.

The format of Paul's letters

Paul expressed his theology in letter form. An understanding of the format and style of letter writing in the first century A.D., therefore, should help the reader to interpret Paul's letters. Since the little letter to Philemon[16]

is typical of first-century letters in format and serves to focus attention
upon much that is helpful for the understanding of Paul's letters in
general,[17] we shall quote it as a whole and then concentrate on the individual parts.

Address and greeting (vv 1-3)

[1]Paul, a prisoner for Christ Jesus, and Timothy our brother, to
Philemon our beloved fellow worker [2]and Apphia our sister and Archippus
our fellow soldier, and the church in your house: [3]Grace to you and peace
from God our Father and the Lord Jesus Christ.

Thanksgiving (vv 4-7)

[4]I thank my God always when I remember you in my prayers, [5]because I
hear of your love and of the faith which you have toward the Lord Jesus
and all the saints, [6]and I pray that the sharing of your faith may promote
the knowledge of all the good that is ours in Christ. [7]For I have derived
much joy and comfort from your love, my brother, because the hearts of
the saints have been refreshed through you.

Message (vv 8-20)

[8]Accordingly, though I am bold enough in Christ to command you to
do what is required, [9]yet for love's sake I prefer to appeal to you—I, Paul,
an ambassador and now a prisoner also for Christ Jesus—[10]I appeal to you
for my child, Onesimus, whose father I have become in my imprisonment.
[11](Formerly he was useless to you, but now he is indeed useful to you and
to me.) [12]I am sending him back to you, sending my very heart. [13]I would
have been glad to keep him with me, in order that he might serve me on
your behalf during my imprisonment for the gospel; [14]but I preferred to do
nothing without your consent in order that your goodness might not be by
compulsion but of your own free will.
    [15]Perhaps this is why he was parted from you for a while, that you
might have him back for ever, [16]no longer as a slave but more than a slave,
as a beloved brother, especially to me but how much more to you, both in
the flesh and in the Lord. [17]So if you consider me your partner, receive him
as you would receive me. [18]If he has wronged you at all, or owes you anything, charge that to my account. [19]I, Paul, write this with my own hand, I
will repay it—to say nothing of your owing me your own self. [20]Yes,
brother, I want some benefit from you in the Lord. Refresh my heart in
Christ.

Conclusion and final greeting (vv 21-25)

[21]Confident of your obedience, I write to you, knowing that you will do
even more than I say. [22]At the same time, prepare a guest room for me, for
I am hoping through your prayers to be granted to you.
    [23]Epaphras, my fellow prisoner in Christ Jesus, sends greetings to you,
[24]and so do Mark, Aristarchus, Demas, and Luke, my fellow workers.
    [25]The grace of the Lord Jesus Christ be with your spirit.

Paul's letters, as is now evident from comparisons with Greco-Roman and Jewish letters of the first century, followed the format in vogue at the time. The format consisted of four parts:

a) **The address and greeting (vv 1–3),** containing the name of the sender followed by the name of the addressee, whether an individual or group, followed by a greeting-wish, usually expressed by Paul in the words: "Grace (*charis*) to you and peace (*eirēnē*) from God our Father and the Lord Jesus Christ" (v 3).

b) **The thanksgiving and prayer (vv 4–7),**[18] containing an expression of gratitude and prayer to God, expressed in a long periodic sentence whose function, as P. Schubert says, is to "focus the epistolary situation, i.e., to introduce the vital theme of the letter."[19] In Philemon, the use of the thanksgiving to focus the epistolary situation is found in v 6: "and I pray that the sharing of your faith may promote the knowledge of all the good that is ours in Christ." Presumably the "good" that Philemon can know is the good of forgiving Onesimus.

As an aid to interpretation, the thanksgiving is valuable for the evidence it gives by anticipation of Paul's purpose in writing as well as for its function in setting the tone the letter will take. This is true of the thanksgiving in Philemon; it is generally true also of the longer letters as well, but it is not always so clear.[20]

c) **The message or body of the letter (vv 8–20),** containing usually both doctrine and exhortation, i.e., both the theoretical and the practical. The doctrinal part is the heart of Paul's message. The exhortation or ethical part usually flows from the doctrinal part. In the earlier letters (1 Thessalonians, 1 and 2 Corinthians, Philippians), the two are generally intermingled; in the later letters (Galatians and Romans), the doctrinal part occurs first (e.g., Gal 1–4; Rom 1–11) and is followed by a section dedicated to practical advice and exhortation (e.g., Gal 5–6; Rom 12–16). If one can speak of a doctrinal element in so short a letter as Philemon, it would be contained in v 16, where Paul refers to Onesimus as "a brother" in the Lord. Paul's exhortation to Philemon flows from the relationship of Christians as brothers in the Lord. It runs throughout the letter but is most evident in vv 8–9, 20–21.

d) **The conclusion and final greeting (vv 21–25),** containing personal news, requests, regards to friends, and a blessing. The blessing-wish is usually in the words: "The grace (*charis*) of the Lord Jesus Christ be with your spirit," or some such words (v 25 and cf. 1 Thes 5:28; Phil 4:23).

The nature of the letters

Whether Paul's letters are truly letters in the usual sense of the term or literary pieces using the format of letters is of some significance because in both ancient and modern times a distinction has been made between the personal and the literary letter. The distinction is clear enough when it is a question of a purely private letter or a public, literary letter such as a papal encyclical. In other cases — and this is the situation of most of Paul's letters — it is the degree of privacy or personalness that determines whether the letter should be considered purely private, a letter to a single group, or a letter to many groups, which is for all practical purposes the same as an encyclical.

Philemon is the closest to a purely personal letter among Paul's letters, but even Philemon is addressed to more than one person (Paul mentions in his address, in addition to Philemon, two other persons, Apphia and Archippus, as well as the Christians who meet at Philemon's house). The other letters are relatively personal to particular groups, and Paul's personal touch is evident in his references to common experiences and personal friends (see especially the concluding sections of the letters). Many consider Romans a literary rather than a personal letter, on the grounds that Paul wrote it to be read not only at Rome but in all the churches.

The chronology of Paul's letters

A chronology of the letters is important because it is difficult to study the theological development of Paul's mind unless one can date the letters and thus demonstrate the progress made by Paul from one letter to another.[21] Dating them, however, is difficult.

The letter to Philemon helps to focus the problem. Paul three times speaks of himself as a prisoner (vv 1, 9, 10) and in v 22 asks Philemon to prepare a room for him, on the chance that he may soon be released from prison. This is all the internal evidence available for dating the letter; there is no external evidence whatever.

If Paul had been in prison only in Rome toward the end of his life, it would be easy to date the letter, since we know with some certainty from Acts 28:16ff that he was a prisoner in Rome for approximately two years near the end of his life (between 60 and 64 A.D.). According to Acts 24:22-27, however, Paul was in prison in Caesarea for two years (c. 58-60). There is, in addition, circumstantial evidence to suggest that he was in prison for a time during his stay in Ephesus (cf. 1 Cor 15:32; 2 Cor 1:8-11). Finally, there is Paul's personal testimony to his many "imprisonments" (2 Cor 11:23). His references to himself as a prisoner in Philemon, therefore, do not help in dating the letter.

No more helpful is Paul's possible reference to his old age (Phlm 9).[22] The reference suggests that the letter was written late rather than early in Paul's apostolic life. But Paul was already an old man, at least by first-century standards, when he was preaching in Ephesus (c. 54-57) and could as easily have considered himself an old man from 54-57 as he could from 58-62, the years of his imprisonments at Caesarea and Rome. In fact, since all his letters were written between 51 and 58 A.D., when he was probably in his fifties, there is no time in that period when he might not have considered himself "an old man."

The only additional internal evidence for dating Paul's letter to Philemon would appear to be Paul's request for a room in Philemon's house (v 22). Since Philemon probably lived in the neighborhood of Colossae (cf. Col 4:17), the request would be more reasonable coming from Paul in Ephesus (a two-day journey from Colossae) or in Caesarea (some three hundred miles away) than from Paul in prison in Rome (some eight hundred miles away). On the same internal evidence, Fitzmyer dates Philemon to Paul's imprisonment in Rome,[23] and Feine-Behm-Kümmel to his captivity in Caesarea.[24]

Similar problems arise with the dating of Paul's other letters. Leaving aside the discussion of the evidence, the following dates seem reasonably close to the mark and will serve as a working hypothesis:

1 Thessalonians	51 from Corinth
1 Corinthians	54 from Ephesus
Philippians	56 from Ephesus
2 Corinthians	57 from Macedonia
Galatians	58 from Corinth
Romans	58 from Corinth

Number and grouping of the letters and lost letters

Of the fourteen letters attributed to Paul, only seven are unanimously accepted today as authentic: 1 Thessalonians, Galatians, Philippians, 1 and 2 Corinthians, Romans, and Philemon. Three letters are debatably authentic: 2 Thessalonians, Colossians, and Ephesians. Three are very doubtful: 1 and 2 Timothy, Titus. One is certainly not authentic: Hebrews. The letters are commonly grouped as follows:

The **early letters:** 1 and 2 Thessalonians (51–52 A.D.).

The **great letters:** Galatians, 1 and 2 Corinthians, Romans (54–58 A.D.) – so called because of their doctrinal importance.

The **captivity letters:** Philippians, Colossians, Ephesians, Philemon (59–64 A.D.) – so called because presumably written from prison.

The **pastoral letters:** 1 and 2 Timothy, Titus (undatable but very late).

Some of Paul's letters (referred to in 1 Cor 5:9 and 2 Cor 2:4) are presumed to have been lost. It is possible, but not likely, that parts of them have been conserved by editing and interpolating them into 1 or 2 Corinthians.[25] Paul's extant letters derive from the peak period of his ministry (c. 51–58 A.D.). Letters written previous to and following upon this period have been lost. It is safe to presume that Paul wrote purely private letters that have not survived.

How to get to the heart of a Pauline letter

Since most letters represent one side of a dialogue carried on in writing over a distance rather than face to face, the more one knows about the life situation of the parties to the dialogue, the more one can reasonably expect to understand the dialogue. The best preparation for understanding Paul's letters, therefore, is a familiarity with his life and with the life situation of the early Christians in Asia Minor, Greece, and Rome to whom Paul wrote.[26]

The next best preparation is to read the letters as letters, keeping in mind that in basic form and psychology Paul's letters do not differ from letters written today. Thus, his practice of hinting at or anticipating in the thanksgiving the central concern that has prompted him to write the letter is not unlike the common practice today of carefully phrasing the opening of a letter in order to set the stage for the more important subject matter of the body of the letter.

Paul's practice of using a theoretical or dogmatic exposition as a preparation for the solution of a practical problem should help the reader to discover a link between the doctrinal instruction and the ethical exhortation. The reader should attend carefully to the problem Paul faces and then analyze his solution of the problem in relation to the doctrinal points he makes in leading up to his solution.

The reader should remember that problems dealt with in one letter lead in later letters to more nuanced solutions and to a consequent deeper penetration of the earlier theological teaching. Paul's solution to the problem of the parousia and the resurrection in 1 Thessalonians, for example, is followed a few years later by the deeper penetration of the resurrection in 1 Corinthians and Romans. Also, it is possible to discern a development of Paul's theology of faith and justification from his initial exposition of the problem in Gal 2:15–3:29 to his final, masterful exposition of the same problem in Rom 1–11.

Finally, the reader should realize that Paul's letters have both the advantages and the disadvantages inherent in communication by letter. They have all the spontaneity, sincerity, warmth, and interest of personal communication, but at the same time they have the brevity, tentativeness, and incompleteness so typical of letters. Unlike literary works, letters cannot be revised or re-edited; all the writer can do is write another letter. It is for this reason that we have a second letter to the Corinthians and a more nuanced and more profound version of Galatians' argumentation on faith and justification in Paul's later letter to the Romans. Paul's situation as a letter-writer-theologian is well expressed by Bultmann:

> Paul did not theoretically and connectedly develop his thoughts concerning
> God and Christ, the world and man in an independent scientific treatise as

a Greek Philosopher or a modern theologian. He only developed them fragmentarily (except in Romans), always broaching them in his letters for a specific and actual occasion. Even in Romans, where he expresses them connectedly and with a degree of completeness, he does so in a letter and under the compulsion of a concrete situation. These facts must not be allowed to lead one to the false conclusion that Paul was not a real theologian, nor to the notion that to understand his individuality he must be regarded, instead, as a hero of piety. On the contrary! The way in which he reduces specific acute questions to a basic theological question, the way in which he reaches concrete decisions on the basis of fundamental theological considerations, shows that what he thinks and says grows out of his basic theological position—the position which is more or less completely set forth in Romans.[27]

Chapter II

THE
FIRST LETTER OF PAUL TO THE
THESSALONIANS

The first letter to the Thessalonians was written in 50 or 51 A.D., twenty years before the earliest Gospel (Mark) and only twenty-one years after the resurrection. It is the earliest individual part of the whole New Testament.

Paul had entered Europe for the first time on his second missionary journey (Acts 15:36–18:22), stopping off successively at Philippi (Acts 16:11-40), Thessalonica (Acts 17:1-9), Beroea (Acts 17:10-15), Athens (Acts 17:16-34), and finally Corinth (Acts 18:1-18), where he settled down to preach and teach for a full year and a half.

While still at Athens, Paul heard that his new Thessalonian converts were being persecuted by their gentile countrymen (1 Thes 2:14-15). Unable himself to return, Paul sent Timothy to assist and strengthen them (1 Thes 3:1-8). When Timothy returned with news of the situation in Thessalonica, Paul sat down and wrote 1 Thessalonians.

The letter contains Paul's reminiscences of his stay in Thessalonica (2:1-12), his wish to visit the Thessalonians again (2:17-3:13), sundry expressions of gratitude, encouragement, and exhortation *(passim),* and brief discussions of the Thessalonians' most pressing problems. These problems, as the letter demonstrates, were almost all the result of the Thessalonians' feverish expectation of Jesus' imminent return in glory to judge the world and bring it to its end. Believing that time was short, some were ignoring the commandments, feeling that they might as well enjoy themselves in the little time left before the end of the world (cf. 4:1-12). Others were worrying about the fate of those Christians who had already died, fearing that since they had died before the parousia, they would not rise with Christ at his coming and live forever (cf. 4:13-5:11). Lastly, some were suffering from a parousiac lethargy, living in idleness in the belief that work was a waste of time when the end was so close. All in all, they were victims, one way or another, of parousiac fever.

Division of the letter

The letter has three parts, each divided into three sections according to an A-B-A′ format, with the material in A′ reflecting back in a loose but studied manner to the material in A. This, as we shall see, is Paul's typical format for composing his letters.

Part I (1:1–2:16): Thanksgiving for the success of the gospel in Thessalonica

    (a) Address and **thanksgiving** (1:1-10)
      (b) Paul's apologia for his apostolic preaching (2:1-12)
    (a′) A second **thanksgiving** (2:13-16)

Part II (2:17–3:19): Personal news

    (a) Paul's desire to **revisit** Thessalonica (2:17-20)
      (b) Timothy's mission to Thessalonica (3:1-8)
    (a′) Paul's desire to **revisit** Thessalonica (3:9-13)

Part III (4:1–5:28): Instructions on living a Christian life

    (a) **Exhortations** and warnings (4:1-12)
      (b) Resurrection and the parousia (4:13–5:11)
    (a′) **Exhortations** (5:12-28)

Paul's A-B-A′ pattern for presenting his material has been noticed by a number of authors.[1] J. Murphy-O'Connor describes it as follows: "He starts with one topic, then shifts to another, and finally returns to the first but with a slight difference."[2] Paul uses it regularly not only in 1 Thessalonians but in 1 and 2 Corinthians, Philippians, Galatians, and Romans as well. Recognition of the pattern here and elsewhere solves many of the problems that have disconcerted interpreters of Paul's letters. As we shall discover, sections of Paul's other letters that commentators wish either to change around or to eliminate as later interpolations are readily explained as integral to the letters and make excellent sense when seen as part of his A-B-A′ pattern.

Part I (1:1–2:16): Thanksgiving for the success of the gospel in Thessalonica

Parallel structure

    (a) Address and **thanksgiving** (1:1-10)
      (b) Paul's apologia for his apostolic preaching (2:1-12)
    (a′) A second **thanksgiving** (2:13-16)

[In the text that follows, the words in boldface type in section (a) indicate those words and expressions to which Paul will return in section (a′). Since Paul uses this A-B-A′ format in almost all of his letters, the reader is advised to pay careful attention when words are in boldface type in the text.]

Text

(a)   1:1 Paul, Silvanus, and Timothy, to the church of the Thessalonians in God the Father and **the Lord Jesus** Christ: Grace to you and peace.

²**We give thanks to God** always for you all, constantly mentioning you in our prayers, ³remembering before our God and Father your work of faith and labor of love and steadfastness of hope in our Lord Jesus Christ. ⁴For we know, brethren beloved by God, that he has chosen you; ⁵for **our gospel came to you not only in word,** but also in power and in the Holy Spirit and with full conviction. You know what kind of men we proved to be among you for your sake.

⁶And you **became imitators** of us and of the Lord, for **you received the word** in much **affliction,** with joy inspired by the Holy Spirit; ⁷so that you became an example to all the believers in Macedonia and in Achaia. ⁸For not only has **the word of the Lord** sounded forth from you in Macedonia and Achaia, but your faith in God has gone forth everywhere, so that we need not say anything. ⁹For they themselves report concerning us what a welcome we had among you, and how you turned to God from idols, to serve a living and true God, ¹⁰and to wait for his Son from heaven, whom he raised from the dead, Jesus who delivers us from **the wrath to come.**

(b)   2:1 For you yourselves know, brethren, that our visit to you was not in vain; ²but though we had already suffered and been shamefully treated at Philippi, as you know, we had courage in our God to declare to you the gospel of God in the face of great opposition. ³For our appeal does not spring from error or uncleanness, nor is it made with guile; ⁴but just as we have been approved by God to be entrusted with the gospel, so we speak, not to please men, but to please God who tests our hearts. ⁵For we never used either words of flattery, as you know, or a cloak for greed, as God is witness; ⁶nor did we seek glory from men, whether from you or from others, though we might have made demands as apostles of Christ. ⁷But we were gentle among you, like a nurse taking care of her children. ⁸So, being affectionately desirous of you, we were ready to share with you not only the gospel of God but also our own selves, because you had become very dear to us. ⁹For you remember our labor and toil, brethren; we worked night and day, that we might not burden any of you, while we preached to you the gospel of God.

¹⁰You are witnesses, and God also, how holy and righteous and blameless was our behavior to you believers; ¹¹for you know how, like a father with his children, we exhorted each one of you and encouraged you and charged you ¹²to lead a life worthy of God, who calls you into his own kingdom and glory.

(a′)   ¹³**And we also thank God** constantly for this, that when **you received the word of God** which you heard from us, you accepted it not as the word of men but as what it really is, **the word of God,** which is at work in you believers. ¹⁴For you, brethren, **became imitators** of the churches of God in Christ Jesus which are in Judea; for you **suffered** the same things from your own countrymen as they did from the Jews, ¹⁵who killed both **the Lord Jesus** and the prophets, and drove us out, and displease God and oppose all men ¹⁶by hindering us from speaking to the Gentiles that they may be saved—so as always to fill up the measure of their sins. But God's **wrath has come** upon them at last.

Commentary

(a) Address and thanksgiving (1:1-10)

1:1 Silvanus, and Timothy. Silvanus (Silas) was Paul's companion on his second missionary journey after his split with Barnabas (Acts 15:36-40). Timothy was the son of a Jewish Christian mother and a gentile father. He also accompanied Paul on his second missionary journey (Acts 16:1-5) and served as his go-between with the Thessalonians when Paul himself could not visit them (1 Thes 3:2).

Grace . . . and peace. Paul uses this greeting-wish in all his letters, with "grace" signifying salvation and all that it embraces, and "peace" signifying the fullness of life and joy inherent in its Hebrew equivalent, *shalom.*

1:2 We give thanks to God. Paul's thanksgiving section (vv 2-10 and their parallel in vv 13-16) prepares the ground for the letter as a whole by complimenting the Thessalonians, thus predisposing them to accept his exhortations and warnings, and also by hinting at the topics he will discuss in the body of his letter: (1) the "labor" of faith, hope, and love that will enable them to make progress in their Christian life (vv 3-4); (2) the success of the word of God among them (vv 5-9); (3) the second coming of Jesus (the parousia) and the problems it has caused (v 10).

1:3 work of faith and labor of love and steadfastness of hope. Faith and love are central to the Christian life (cf. 1 Cor 13:13). The words "work" and "labor" suggest that Paul has in mind, not just theological virtues considered abstractly, but practical virtues. In view of the parousiac lethargy that has persuaded some of the Thessalonians to give up work and live in idleness, there is a hint here, supported by Paul's later appeal to his own example (cf. 2:9), that he is preparing the ground for his later warnings against idleness (cf. 4:11; 5:14).

1:4-5 we know . . . he has chosen you; for our gospel came to you . . . in power. Paul does not attribute the conversion of the Thessalonians to his own preaching but to the power of the Holy Spirit working in their hearts to bring them to accept the message of the saving gospel. Thus, the work of conversion is not the work of man but of God, and the preacher of the gospel is only God's instrument (cf. 2:13 and see 2 Cor 2:14-4:18).

1:6-8 you became imitators of us and of the Lord. Paul, like Jesus, suffered for preaching the word of God. Now the Thessalonians in a similar way are suffering some sort of persecution for their faith at the hands of their pagan colleagues (cf. 2:14-15).

1:9 how you turned to God from idols. This remark indicates that the Thessalonians were for the most part converted pagans rather than converted Jews. It has been suggested, since the cult of Dionysus was strong in Greece, that the converted Thessalonians had hitherto belonged to that cult.[3]

1:10 to wait for his Son from heaven. More than any other single line in the letter, these words highlight the atmosphere of feverish expectation that has gripped the Thessalonians since they first heard the gospel from Paul. They are waiting for Jesus' return from heaven—some with a mentality of parousiac free-for-all (cf. 4:1-12), some in confusion and disappointment over the fate of their deceased relatives and friends who died before the glorious coming of Jesus (cf. 4:13–5:11), and some in the thrall of a parousiac lethargy that has reduced them to a *cui bono* disdain for day-to-day work (cf. 4:11; 5:14). What Paul means by the coming of Jesus from heaven will be discussed in 4:14–5:11.

(b) Paul's apologia for his apostolic preaching (2:1-12)

2:1-2 our visit to you. Paul's reminder of the opposition he encountered when he preached at Thessalonica and Philippi (cf. Acts 16:16–17:9) prepares the way for his defense of his preaching in vv 3-12.

2:3-6 our appeal does not spring from error or uncleanness. Paul contrasts his motives for preaching the gospel with those of the many traveling teachers and philosophers who not infrequently took advantage of their audiences' credulity either to make money from them or to enhance their own reputations. Paul's defense is probably in reply to accusations of trickery and greed made against him by his opponents either at the time he preached the gospel to the Thessalonians or more probably in the period that followed his visit there. It is possible that some of the news Timothy brought back on his return from Thessalonica was that such charges were being made against Paul.

2:7-8 gentle . . . like a nurse taking care of her children. The simile speaks for itself and provides a poignant description of the warmth and depth of Paul's concern for his fellow Christians.

2:9 For you remember our labor and toil. When Paul speaks well of himself, as he does here and elsewhere (cf. 1 Cor 9; 2 Cor 2:14–6:1; Phil 3:2-16; Gal 1-2), it is not, as is sometimes supposed, because he is conceited or insecure but rather as a subtle means of instructing his converts. Here he may very well be reminding the Thessalonians how he "worked night and day" in order to jar the complacence of those indulging their parousiac lethargy by refusing to work at all (cf. 4:11; 5:14, and see 2 Thes 3:6-12).

2:10-11 You are witnesses. Paul can call upon the Thessalonians as witnesses to the integrity of his life and the disinterestedness of his ministry among them. He was, as he says, "like a father with his children." In short, whatever his opponents say about him, the Thessalonians know from their own experience of Paul that it is not true.

(a') A second thanksgiving (2:13-16)[4]

2:13 And we also thank God . . . for this. A second thanksgiving is unusual in a Pauline letter but is justified here on the basis that Paul has found a special reason for additional thanksgiving, namely, the way the Thessalonians received the word of God: "not as the word of men but as what it really is, the word of God, which is at work" in them.

2:14 imitators of the churches of God in Christ Jesus which are in Judea. Paul expands here what he had already alluded to in vv 4-6. He is convinced that the word of God is at work in the Thessalonians because they are experiencing the same persecution from their countrymen as the churches in Judea, where Jewish Christians were persecuted by the synagogue authorities for their belief in Jesus. Paul presupposes that one of the criteria for discerning the true from the false is that the false persecutes the true. Thus, persecution proves that the Thessalonians have really believed in the gospel.

2:15-16 who killed both the Lord Jesus and the prophets, and drove us out. The words "drove us out" are the key to this bitter attack against Paul's fellow Jews. He is against them not only because of their opposition to Jesus and the prophets but because their opposition to his preaching (cf. Acts 14–28 *passim*) hinders him "from speaking to the Gentiles that they may be saved." It is for this reason that Paul says they "displease God and oppose all men" (v 15b). They are, in short, enemies of the gospel, which is good news for all men. Why Paul should compare the pagan Thessalonians who are persecuting their fellow Christian Thessalonians to the Jews is clear. Both the Jews and the pagans are making themselves obstacles to the spread of the gospel and therefore to the salvation of all men. It is not clear, however, why the pagan Thessalonians are persecuting their Christian fellow countrymen. Since opposition from the entrenched incumbent party, whether social, religious, or political, is hardly something new, one may reasonably suspect that the pagan adherents of the Dionysian cult or some other pagan cult might exert pressure against companions who were deserting them to join the new Christian religion.

Part II (2:17–3:19): Personal news

Parallel structure

    (a) Paul's desire to **revisit** Thessalonica (2:17-20)
      (b) Timothy's mission to Thessalonica (3:1-8)
    (a') Paul's desire to **revisit** Thessalonica (3:9-13)

Text

(a)   2:17 But since we were bereft of you, brethren, for a short time, in person not in heart, we endeavored the more eagerly and with great desire to see you face to face; [18]because **we wanted to come to you** — I, Paul, again and again — but Satan hindered us. [19]For what is our hope or **joy** or crown of boasting before **our Lord Jesus at his coming**? Is it not you? [20]For you are our glory and **joy.**

(b)   3:1 Therefore when we could bear it no longer, we were willing to be left behind at Athens alone, [2]and we sent Timothy, our brother and God's servant in the gospel of Christ, to establish you in your faith and to exhort you, [3]that no one be moved by these afflictions. You yourselves know that this is to be our lot. [4]For when we were with you, we told you beforehand that we were to suffer affliction; just as it has come to pass, and as you know. [5]For this reason, when I could bear it no longer, I sent that I might know your faith, for fear that somehow the tempter had tempted you and that our labor would be in vain.

     [6]But now that Timothy has come to us from you, and has brought us the good news of your faith and love and reported that you always remember us kindly and long to see us, as we long to see you — [7]for this reason, brethren, in all our distress and affliction we have been comforted about you through your faith; [8]for now we live, if you stand fast in the Lord.

(a′)   [9]For what thanksgiving can we render to God for you, for all the **joy** which we feel for your sake before our God, [10]praying earnestly night and day that we may **see you face to face** and supply what is lacking in your faith? [11]Now may our God and Father himself, and our Lord Jesus, **direct our way to you;** [12]and may the Lord make you increase and abound in love to one another and to all men, as we do to you, [13]so that he may establish your hearts unblamable in holiness before our God and Father, **at the coming of our Lord Jesus** with all his saints.

Commentary

(a) Paul's desire to revisit Thessalonica (2:17-20)

2:17-18   with great desire to see you face to face. Paul's desire to revisit the Thessalonians is clear here and in what follows. What is not clear is why he himself could not revisit them and had to send Timothy in his place (3:1-3).

Satan hindered us. Whatever it was, Paul blames it on Satan. Since sickness and other evils were routinely attributed either to sin or to Satan, it is possible that Paul could not revisit them because of illness (cf. 2 Cor 12:7). It is equally possible that he was about to begin his evangelization of Corinth, only twenty miles south of Athens, and was too busy to make the long trip north to Thessalonica. In any event, he wants to make it clear that he sent Timothy only because he himself was hindered from going.

2:19-20   crown of boasting before our Lord Jesus at his coming. Paul's mind is very much set on the second coming of Jesus (cf. 1:10; 4:13ff), and he looks upon his work of evangelization in Thessalonica as a reason, humanly speaking, for boasting at the final judgment. In 1 Cor 3:5-9, he readily admits the secondary nature of his work: "I planted, Apollos watered, but God gave the growth," but he nonetheless is perfectly confident that his work of evangelization is a legitimate human boast (cf. Phil 2:16; 4:1; 2 Cor 1:14).

(b) Timothy's mission to Thessalonica (3:1-8)

3:1-5 we sent Timothy. Paul already knew, either from what had happened while he was still at Thessalonica or more likely from news he had received since arriving in Athens, that the Thessalonians were suffering persecution for their faith (cf. 1:6; 2:2, 14). He had evidently warned them that they would have to suffer for their faith (v 4) but was still worried enough about the firmness of their commitment to Jesus to send Timothy to support them in their afflictions.

3:6-8 now that Timothy has come to us from you. Timothy rejoined Paul in Corinth (cf. Acts 18:5), and his report was good: the Thessalonians were standing fast in the faith. But, as chs 4–5 will show, the Thessalonians were not without problems. It was evidently Timothy's report about these problems that induced Paul to write his letter.

(a′) Paul's desire to revisit Thessalonica (3:9-13)

3:9-10 what thanksgiving can we render to God for you? Paul is grateful for the good news Timothy has brought, but he still prays to be able to see the Thessalonians "face to face" (cf. 2:17) in order to "supply what is lacking" in their faith. What is lacking in their faith will be the subject of his exhortations in chs 4 and 5.

3:11-12 may our God and Father . . . and our Lord Jesus, direct our way to you; and may the Lord make you increase and abound in love. Paul's prayer is meant as a further preparation for his subsequent exhortations in chs 4–5.

3:13 that he may establish your hearts unblamable in holiness. In 4:1-12, Paul will take up the subject of holiness in relation to the Christian life. His use of the word here provides the immediate transition to the exhortations that follow. The reader should note that in section (a′), such words and phrases as "joy" (cp. 3:9 with 2:20), "face to face" (cp. 3:10 with 2:17), and "at the coming of our Lord Jesus" (cp. 3:13 with 2:19) serve as parallels to section (a) and thus form an easily recognizable inclusion-conclusion.

Part III (4:1-5:28): Instructions on living a Christian life

Parallel structure

(a) **Exhortations** (4:1-12)
  (b) Resurrection and the parousia (4:13-5:11)
(a′) **Exhortations** (5:12-28)

Text

(a)   4:1 Finally, **brethren, we beseech and exhort you in the Lord Jesus,** that as you learned from us how you ought to live and to please God, just as you are doing, you do so more and more. ²For you know what instructions we gave you through the Lord Jesus. ³For **this is the will of God,** your sanctification: that you abstain from immorality; ⁴that each one of you know how to take a wife for himself in holiness and honor, ⁵not in the passion of lust like heathen who do not know God; ⁶that no man transgress, and wrong his brother in this matter, because the Lord is an avenger in all these things, as we solemnly forewarned you. ⁷For God has not called us for uncleanness, but in holiness. ⁸Therefore whoever disregards this, disregards not man but God, who gives his Holy **Spirit** to you.

⁹But concerning love of the brethren you have no need to have any one write to you, for you yourselves have been taught by God to love one another; ¹⁰and indeed you do love all the brethren throughout Macedonia. But **we exhort you, brethren,** to do so more and more, ¹¹to aspire to live quietly, to mind your own affairs, and to **work** with your hands, as we charged you; ¹²so that you may command the respect of outsiders, and be dependent on nobody.

(b)   ¹³But we would not have you ignorant, brethren, concerning those who are asleep, that you may not grieve as others do who have no hope. ¹⁴For since we believe that Jesus died and rose again, even so, through Jesus, God will bring with him those who have fallen asleep. ¹⁵For this we declare to you by the word of the Lord, that we who are alive, who are left until the coming of the Lord, shall not precede those who have fallen asleep. ¹⁶For the Lord himself will descend from heaven with a cry of command, with the archangel's call, and with the sound of the trumpet of God. And the dead in Christ will rise first; ¹⁷then we who are alive, who are left, shall be caught up together with them in the clouds to meet the Lord in the air; and so we shall always be with the Lord. ¹⁸Therefore comfort one another with these words.

5:1 But as to the times and the seasons, brethren, you have no need to have anything written to you. ²For you yourselves know well that the day of the Lord will come like a thief in the night. ³When people say, "There is peace and security," then sudden destruction will come upon them as travail comes upon a woman with child, and there will be no escape. ⁴But you are not in darkness, brethren, for that day to surprise you like a thief. ⁵For you are all sons of light and sons of the day; we are not of the night or of darkness. ⁶So then let us not sleep, as others do, but let us keep awake and be sober. ⁷For those who sleep sleep at night, and those who get drunk are drunk at night. ⁸But, since we belong to the day, let us be sober, and put on the breastplate of faith and love, and for a helmet the hope of salvation. ⁹For God has not destined us for wrath, but to obtain salvation through our Lord Jesus Christ, ¹⁰who died for us so that whether we wake or sleep we might live with him. ¹¹Therefore encourage one another and build one another up, just as you are doing.

(a′)   ¹²But **we beseech you, brethren,** to respect those who labor among you and are over you **in the Lord** and admonish you, ¹³and to esteem them very highly in love because of their **work.** Be at peace among yourselves. ¹⁴And we exhort you, brethren, admonish the idle, encourage the fainthearted, help the weak, be patient with them all. ¹⁵See that none of you repays evil for evil, but always seek to do good to one another and to all. ¹⁶Rejoice always, ¹⁷pray constantly, ¹⁸give thanks in all circumstances; **for this is the will of God in Christ Jesus for you.** ¹⁹Do not quench the **Spirit,** ²⁰do not despise prophesying, ²¹but test everything; hold fast what is good, ²²abstain from every form of evil.

²³May the God of peace himself sanctify you wholly; and may your spirit and soul and body be kept sound and blameless at the coming of our Lord Jesus Christ. ²⁴He who calls you is faithful, and he will do it. ²⁵Brethren, pray for us. ²⁶Greet all the brethren with a holy kiss. ²⁷I adjure you by the Lord that this letter be read to all the brethren. ²⁸The grace of our Lord Jesus Christ be with you.

Commentary

(a) Exhortations (4:1-12)

4:1-2 we . . . exhort you . . . just as you are doing, you do so more and more. Paul's exhortations deal with how the Thessalonians "ought to live and to please God," but he first assures them that they are doing well and need only to make progress in what they are doing. These remarks should be considered as a softening-up of his readers, since in what follows Paul discusses serious lapses in Christian morality.

4:3 this is the will of God, your sanctification. In 3:13, Paul spoke of holiness (*hagiōsynē*). Here the word "sanctification" (*hagiasmos,* a derivative of *hagiōsynē*) picks up the same theme and relates it directly to abstaining from immorality. The nature of the immorality is the subject of vv 4-8. For Paul, sanctification signifies the spiritual and moral process whereby a person learns to live a life worthy of his or her calling to commitment to Jesus and the Kingdom.

4:4-8 that each one of you know how to take a wife for himself in holiness. In the Greek, the import of these words is much less clear. The RSV translates it as here but gives another translation—"how to control his own body"—in a footnote; and the NAB gives a third possible translation: "each of you guarding his member in sanctity." The different translations flow from the ambiguity of the Greek, which uses the word "vessel," a word that could mean "wife" as above, or "body" as in the RSV footnote, or "member" (a euphemism for the sexual parts) as in the NAB. The NAB translation "member" would imply personal unchastity. The RSV translation "wife" would imply adultery. No certain solution is possible, but the context, especially in v 6, would seem to favor the translation "wife," and the nature of the immorality as adultery. Underlying such immorality, one may suspect a devil-may-care attitude toward sex in view of the fact that the end of the world was considered near.

4:9-10 But concerning love of the brethren. In 3:12, Paul had prayed: "May the Lord make you increase and abound in love to one another and to all men." Here Paul speaks specifically of love of the brethren (*philadelphia*) — a special love, it would seem, for members of the community. His remark that the Thessalonians have been "taught by God" may be an allusion to Jer 31:34, where Jeremiah spoke of all being "taught" by God in new covenant times, or it may be a reference to how God himself taught them to love by sending his only-begotten Son to die for them. Thus, the actual teacher could be either God the Father or Jesus.

4:11-12 aspire to . . . work with your hands. This may be a simple exhortation to give good example to others. The words "work with your hands," however, suggest that some have given up working. In view of the fact that the letter says so much about the second coming of Christ (cf. 1:10; 2:16, 19; 3:13; 4:13–5:11; 5:23) and in view of the fact that Paul warns the "idlers" in 5:14, we think it probable that Paul is out to combat parousiac lethargy — the natural tendency to give up work on the basis that any labor was wasted effort when the second coming and the end of the world were so near.

(b) Resurrection and the parousia (4:13–5:11)

Paul deals here with two matters that are troubling the Thessalonians. First, they are concerned for their friends and relatives who have died already. Second, they would like to know when the end is coming. These are concerns we do not share in the same way as the Thessalonians did. We shall have to say something, therefore, about (1) the problem itself; (2) the cause of the problem; (3) Paul's solution to the problem; (4) a solution to Paul's solution to the problem; (5) Paul's normative theology; (6) the influence of apocalyptic literature on the early Christians.

4:13 But we would not have you ignorant, brethren. Timothy, as seems probable, reported to Paul that the Thessalonians feared that their dead relatives and friends would miss out on the second coming and that the Thessalonians were running a high parousiac fever in the belief that the second coming was due to take place in a very short time. Paul deals with the first problem in 4:13-19 and with the second in 5:1-11.

The cause of both problems, it would seem, was Paul's own preaching. He had shortly before evangelized the Thessalonians. If they were filled with a feverish expectation of the second coming, it almost had to be because Paul himself had preached to them that it was imminent.[5] This is confirmed by the fact that in his response Paul takes for granted that he himself will be alive at the parousia. His words can hardly be interpreted in any other way: "For this we declare to you by the word of the Lord, that *we who are alive,* who are left until the coming of the Lord, shall not precede those who have fallen asleep" (4:15). In 1 Cor 15:51, he implies the same: "Lo! I tell you a mystery. We shall not all sleep, but we shall all be changed . . . ." It is further confirmed by the fact that Paul speaks in a similar way about the imminence of the parousia in his other letters (cf. Phil 1:23-24; 3:20-21; 2 Cor 5:1-10; see also 2 Thes 2:1-3).

In short, the earliest Christians, including Paul himself, expected the second coming of Christ to take place within the short span of their own lifetime. The corrective influence of time and the reaction of all four Gospels softened this expectation but never quite removed it, as is evident from the apocalyptic discourses in Mt 24, Mk 13, and Lk 21. That Paul should have thought the second coming imminent seems strange to us. It would not have seemed strange, however, to either Jews or Christians in the first century A.D. Jewish theories of the time held that with the advent of the Messiah there would come also the end of the world. Apocalyptic writers harangued their readers about the imminence of the end of the old world, the advent of the new age, the resurrection of the dead, the coming of the Messiah and of the reign of God.

These theories and the apocalyptic atmosphere in which they flourished influenced Paul and the early Christians. The Messiah had indeed come. He had been raised from the dead. The reign of God had arrived! It was only a matter of time, therefore, before God would complete his definitive conquest of the forces of evil in the world. Then all who believed in Jesus would share with him in the resurrection from the dead and in the glorious victory of the reign of God in the world. It is in the light of such thinking that 4:13-18 should be interpreted.

4:15 we who are alive . . . shall not precede those who have fallen asleep. Paul asserts this "by the word of the Lord," but there is no such saying recorded in any of the Gospels. It has been suggested that the saying comes from a New Testament prophet speaking in the name of Jesus, just as the Old Testament prophets spoke in the name of Yahweh. Paul's words "we who are alive" leave no doubt that he expected to be alive for the parousia.

4:16-18 For the Lord himself will descend from heaven. Four points are important for understanding Paul's bizarre description of Jesus' second coming: (1) the meaning of *parousia;* (2) Paul's use of the term as a metaphor; (3) Paul's use of the metaphor against an apocalyptic background; (4) the difference between the medium and the message of apocalyptic literature.

1) *Parousia* is a Greek word having the general meaning of "presence." A sentence from a papyrus letter illustrates the sense of the word: "The repair of what has been swept away by the river requires my presence (*mou tēs parousias*)." From Ptolemaic times, the word took on the quasi-technical sense of the "visit" of a king or some other person of great authority.

Another papyrus letter illustrates this more technical sense of the word by making a reference to "the eighty artabae of wheat for the supplies imposed in connection with the king's visit (*pros tēn tou basileōs parousian*)." Since Paul is describing the coming (*parousia*) of Christ in glory, the full technical force of the word should be taken into account for its meaning and for the connotation it would have for his readers.

2) Paul's use of the "visit" (*parousia*) of the king in relation to the second coming of Christ can be understood as a metaphor from a comparison of Paul's description of Christ's parousia in 1 Thes 4:15-18 with Josephus' description of Titus' victorious entry into the city of Antioch. The suggested parallels are in bold type:

When the people of Antioch learned Titus **was coming** to the city, their joy was such that they could not rest within the walls until he came. Instead they **went out to meet him,** going a distance of more than thirty stadia. Not only the men went, but a **multitude** of women also, with their children, and **when they saw Titus coming,** they stood on either side of the road saluting him with their hands raised. They brought him to the city with **acclamations of all sorts,** and while they applauded him, they did not cease to ask that the Jews be expelled from the city.[6]	For this we declare to you by the word of the Lord, that we who are alive, who are left **until the coming of the Lord,** shall not precede those who have fallen asleep. **For the Lord himself will descend from heaven** with a cry of command, with the **archangel's call, and with the sound of the trumpet of God.** And the dead in Christ will rise first; then we who are alive, who are left, shall be caught up together with them in the clouds **to meet the Lord in the air;** and so we shall always be with the Lord. Therefore comfort one another with these words.

St. John Chrysostom's use of the visit (*parousia*) of the emperor to clarify Paul's words in 1 Thes 4:15-18 shows that in the early centuries of Christianity there was no great difficulty in understanding the analogy of the triumphal procession:

> When a city receives the emperor, the high dignitaries and those who are in his favor go out from the town to meet him, while the criminals are kept within the walls under guard, to await the emperor's sentence upon them. Likewise, when the Lord comes, those who are in his grace will go up to meet him in the air, while sinners and those whose consciences are darkened by many evil deeds will remain on earth to await their judge.[7]

3) What Paul has done in 1 Thes 4:15-17 is to combine the well-known triumphal procession with the mythological symbolism he was familiar with from apocalyptic literature. From the triumphal procession he has taken the elements of the festive day: the coming together of the multitude, the going out of the elect to meet Christ coming in triumph, the sound of the

trumpets, and the joy of the resurrected who will be with the Lord unceasingly. From apocalyptic symbolism he has taken the mythological themes of the Son of Man coming on the clouds of heaven (Dn 7:13-15), the angelic trumpets announcing the judgment of all mankind, the victory of the resurrected elect, the "Day of the Lord," the "suddenness" of the coming of the Day of the Lord, and the warnings to be prepared.

4) The solution to Paul's "solution" of the Thessalonians' problem is to realize that he is speaking metaphorically. From beginning to end, Paul's language remains metaphorical and apocalyptic. When the metaphor of the triumphal procession and the apocalyptic language are positively demythologized, the message that emerges is relatively simple.[8] God, through Christ, has effectively conquered the forces of evil. The day will come when Christ will punish the wicked and reward the good. The elect will rise from the dead and be with the Lord forever.

There remains, of course, the task of still further demythologizing in a positive manner the meaning of the "coming of Christ" and "the Day of the Lord," the mode of the resurrection, the manner of rewarding the good and punishing the wicked, and the inscrutable element of timing in relation to a transcendent God who nevertheless works immanently, for the most part, in the history of mankind.[9]

For Christians whose God is a God of love and whose Lord is a Lord of life, the overtones of the metaphor of the conquering king whose goal is victory, power, and self-aggrandizement are obviously not only distasteful but repugnant. All metaphors limp; apocalyptic metaphors hobble. They need desperately the crutches supplied by St. John's more refined conception of the work of the Father and the Son in the world of mankind: "For God so loved the world that he gave his only Son, that whoever believes in him should not perish but have eternal life. For God sent the Son into the world, not to condemn the world, but that the world might be saved through him" (Jn 3:16-17).

5:1 But as to the times and the seasons. In apocalyptic literature, the last days were viewed as not only imminent but foreordained, as if God had set up a calendar of events for the termination of world history. Paul's remarks are meant to divert the Thessalonians from idle and mischievous speculation about the date of the parousia to something far more important —their spiritual preparation for that day whenever it arrives.

5:2-3 the day of the Lord. The expression goes back as far as Amos the prophet (cf. Am 5:18) and is a code word in apocalyptic literature for the day when God will intervene in world history to bring about the fulfillment of his plan of salvation. In the New Testament, it is another way of speaking about the parousia, the second coming of Christ (cf. 4:15-17). The similes "like a thief in the night" (cf. Mt 24:43) and "as travail comes upon a woman with child" (cf. Is 13:8; Jer 6:24; Hos 13:13) function here, as in all apocalyptic literature, to impress upon readers the imminence of the end and the need to be prepared. It is this latter theme that concerns Paul, as the following verses indicate.

5:4-5 But you are not in darkness. The central theme and truth of apocalyptic literature is that there is an ongoing conflict in this world between the forces of good and the forces of evil. This struggle is what is meant by God versus anti-God, Christ versus anti-Christ, the light versus the darkness. To tell Christians that they are not in darkness is to remind them that they belong to the forces of good in the great battle.

5:6-7 So then let us not sleep. To keep awake and to be sober means to be upright as children of the light (cf. Jn 12:36; Lk 16:8; Eph 5:8), who know the truth and live by the truth, in contrast to the sons of darkness, who love the darkness and refuse to come to the light that is Christ (cf. Jn 3:18-21).

5:8 since we belong to the day. The exhortation to put on the moral armor of faith, hope, and charity is Paul's way of describing metaphorically the manner in which Christians defend themselves in the great battle between the forces of evil and the forces of good.

5:9-10 salvation through our Lord Jesus Christ, who died for us. This is the earliest mention of the redemptive nature of Jesus' death in the New Testament and indicates that it was part of the Christian tradition already in the fifties. Paul will say more about it in 1 Cor 1–2 and in Rom 5:1-21; 6:1-11; 8:31-39.

5:11 build one another up. The building metaphor refers to the growth in Christ-life of the individual Christian and the Christian community. Paul uses the building metaphor regularly throughout 1 Corinthians and expresses in 1 Cor 8:1 what he understands to be the dynamic underlying all efforts at "building up": "Knowledge puffs up, but love builds up" (cf. also 1 Cor 3:5-16 and 13:1ff).

In what Paul says about the "day of the Lord" in 5:1-11, it must be remembered that for the primitive Christian Church, the fact of the ultimate victory that would come about with the second coming of Christ was foreordained. Only the time was a matter of debate. In thinking that it was imminent, even in their own lifetime, Paul and the early Christians were mistaken. The whole of 5:1-11, however, is significant because it shows that while Paul "felt" that the second coming was imminent, he refused to put a date to it. He insists rather on its suddenness and on the need to be prepared for it. In this he is the same as the evangelists, who refused to put a date to the second coming but at the same time insisted that Christians should always be prepared for it (cf. Mt 24–25; Mk 13; Lk 21:5-36).

Paul's normative theology in the whole of this apocalyptic section (4:13–5:11) is as simple as it is unsophisticated. He asserts that Jesus died and rose (4:14), that he died for us (5:10), that "God will bring with him

[Jesus] those who have fallen asleep [died]" (4:14), that there will be a second coming (*parousia*) of Jesus (4:16), and that whatever the interval between the first and the second coming of Jesus, Christians must work not only with their hands but in the context of a life lived out of love and manifested in works of love for others (1:3; 2:9; 4:11-13).[10] It should also be remembered that because of the nature of Paul's mythological, apocalyptic language, it is impossible to deduce anything about the nature, the time, or the manner of the second coming.[11]

(a') Exhortations (5:12-28)

5:12-15 But we beseech you, brethren. The rapid stream of admonitions in 5:12-22 flows from Paul's exhortation in 5:11 to "build one another up" and continues the exhortation theme he had begun in 4:1-11, the parallel of this section. It is not clear who those are "who labor among you and are over you in the Lord." They are evidently people who have positions of leadership in the community, but whether or not they constitute some kind of an incipient hierarchy set up by Paul is a matter of pure speculation.

5:16-18 Rejoice . . . pray . . . give thanks. This staccato-like burst of exhortations puts in a nutshell the cachet of Paul's spirituality. He will develop it at length in his letter to the Philippians.

5:19 Do not quench the Spirit. Paul is probably referring to the charismatics in the community. However much he later qualifies his enthusiasm for charismatics (cf. 1 Cor 12 and 14), his advice here is to allow them freedom.

5:20-22 do not despise prophesying. Paul probably means the charismatic gift of inspirational preaching, a gift he valued highly (cf. 1 Cor 14). His advice to "test everything" refers to the content of the preachers' exhortations and cautions the hearers not to be carried away by the charismatic enthusiasm of the preachers—advice as relevant now as it was then.

5:23 spirit and soul and body. These are not three elements that make up a human person. In the Semitic mind, the human person is a unity that can be viewed from three different points of view: one's relation to God (spirit); one's principle of life or vitality (the soul), a principle similar to that of all living beings; and one's body. Paul does not share the Greek view of man as constituted of a spiritual soul and a material body. When Paul uses the word "soul," he is not thinking of a simple, spiritual, indestructible component of the human person; for him, "soul" means the animating principle by which the human being breathes, lives, and functions.

5:27 that this letter be read to all the brethren. Since not all could read, Paul insists that his letters be read aloud so that his message will reach all in the community. In all probability, it was this reading aloud in the liturgy that brought about the inclusion of Paul's letters in the canon of the New Testament.

EXCURSUS: APOCALYPTIC LITERATURE AND ESCHATOLOGY

In a certain sense, the rash of books in the seventies on what has been called "the theology of hope" represents a throwback to the parousiac fever of the early Christians. Both look to the future, to the end and the end-time, but with a significant difference. The early Christians were concerned about the imminence of the end, or *eschaton* (end in the temporal sense). Theologians of hope are concerned about the end as a goal (end in the sense of the Greek word *telos*). Their concern about the future is not so much about the future in itself as about the guidance and the teleological dynamism the future provides for shaping the face of the present. For the theologians of hope, the end (*telos*) is a beacon that illuminates the direction the present should take and a lodestone that galvanizes and focuses the immanent energies the present provides. These differences between the modern "beacon" theology of hope and the parousiac fever of early Christianity are significant. But the modern theology of hope is nonetheless firmly based on the parousiac theology of early Christianity.[12]

The immediate catalysts of the theology of hope have been the writings of Dietrich Bonhoeffer, the "God is dead" literature, and the "secular city" literature. The immediate catalysts of early Christianity's parousiac theology were the apocalyptic literature, eschatology, and, superlatively, the resurrection of Jesus from the dead. We shall say more about the resurrection in our treatment of 1 Corinthians. For the present we shall have to say something about apocalyptic literature and eschatology. Since the two are closely associated in the Sacred Scriptures and frequently deal with the same subjects — the kingdom or reign of God, messianism, and the idea, the philosophy, and the theology of history — it is advisable to consult works dealing with these subjects and with such apocalyptic writings as Daniel, Joel, and Revelation.[13]

The apocalyptic literature[14]

Apocalyptic literature concentrates on one aspect of Israel's covenant theology, namely, the certain and effective success of the covenant-King's implementation of his plan for the salvation of Israel and the world.[15] Apocalyptic literature borrows from the traditions that preceded it. It takes up the design of history elaborated in the salvation histories and in messianic theology, the element of judgment in the prophetic discourses, and the general wisdom goal of synthesizing everything in a grand plan. Out of all these, apocalyptic forges a new literary form.

The new form has distinctive characteristics that flow, for the most part, from the literary devices adopted to express the new viewpoint, from the psychological situation of the authors and their audiences, and from the theological traditions out of which the apocalyptic viewpoint was born.

From the biblical literature as a whole, but particularly from Amos, Isaiah, Ezekiel, Joel, Zechariah, and perhaps from Persian mythology, the apocalyptic authors drew such literary characteristics as the following: (1) symbolism—names, numbers, beasts, colors, etc.; (2) an extensive angelology; (3) bizarre descriptions of cosmological upheavals; (4) a systematized presentation of historical events; (5) pseudonymity; (6) esotericism; (7) the repetition of the same basic message through the presentation of grand symbolic tableaus.

From the psychological situation of the authors and their audiences—a situation of frustration and disillusionment induced by captivity, persecution, and politico-religious crisis in general—the form acquired such secondary characteristics as the following: (1) an invincible confidence in God; (2) an indomitable faith in the inspiration of the Sacred Scriptures; (3) a refined appreciation for the superiority of the true faith; (4) a heightened and sometimes blind hatred for the forces of evil, both in the individual moral sphere and in the misguided materialism of the dominant political powers.[16]

From the prophetic tradition,[17] the wisdom tradition,[18] and the post-exilic theological emphasis on the transcendence of God, the form drew what may be considered its four primary and essential characteristics: (1) an overall concern with eschatology;[19] (2) a deterministic outlook on history; (3) a relative or mitigated dualism; (4) a transcendentalism that expects everything from God and almost nothing from man.

As a literary medium, apocalyptic is the strangest, and to some persons the most repulsive, of literary forms. Its message, however strange the medium, is nevertheless basically simple. It is expressed succinctly in the words of John's Gospel: "You will suffer in the world. But take courage! I have overcome the world" (Jn 16:33). Even in so brief an apocalyptic message as 1 Thes 4:13–5:11, this is the message behind the medium.[20]

It is not easy to like apocalyptic literature, and one may be inclined to ignore it out of hand. But its importance is great.[21] One cannot really understand the New Testament in depth without a knowledge and appreciation of apocalyptic literature. C. E. Braaten is emphatically correct when he says: "The New Testament is a literary occurrence largely within the medium of apocalyptic. This is the gist of what Albert Schweitzer was saying; it is the meaning of Ernst Käsemann's dictum: 'Apocalyptic was after all the mother of all Christian theology.'"[22]

Apocalyptic theology is "visionary" theology. Its *visions are artificial* and sometimes even repulsive, but its *"vision" is genuine.* It envisions the hope of the world for a guaranteed happy outcome to history. It believes in a God who can and will overcome the forces of evil. It hopes for the best at all times and especially in the worst of times. Its interpretation of history past, therefore, is not pessimistic. Its prognosis of history future is emimently optimistic, because it sees history from the end-time back. And the God who is at the end is the God who was in the beginning, a God the inspired theologians know is a God who cares.

Eschatology

We moderns do not expect an imminent end of the world. We look to a long future, plan ahead, take out insurance, get degrees. Our governments have five- and ten-year plans. They try to forecast rises in population and the need for more food, power, and transportation. We do this without worrying that all the planning will be nullified by a sudden termination of the world and life as we know them.

It was not so for the early Christians. They were under the influence of apocalyptic literature and its overall conviction that the existing world order would soon come to an end. They were, in short, rabidly interested in what we call "eschatology" — the study or science or investigation of the "end," either in a chronological or a teleological sense of the word.

Eschatology, of course, neither begins nor ends with the apocalyptic literature. It is central, however, to the message of apocalyptic, and no other literature so focused Israel's and Christianity's attention on eschatology as effectively and permanently as apocalyptic.[23]

The reader who wants to get the "feel" of this early and almost paranoiac addiction to eschatology that existed from 200 B.C. to 100 A.D. can do so with ease by reading the apocalyptic section of the book of Daniel (chs 2, 7–12). In Dn 2, the author opposes the kingdom of God to the kingdom of this world and predicts the final victory of the kingdom of God through the intervention of the symbolic messianic "stone from the mountain." In Dn 7 and 8, the same opposed forces are symbolized respectively by "beasts" and by the Son of Man, and the same outcome is predicted. Dn 9 focuses Israel's attention on the certainty and imminence of victory over the forces of evil by giving a symbolic interpretation of the seventy years of exile predicted by the prophet Jeremiah in 605 B.C. Dn 10–12 does the same, concentrating, however, on the historical events immediately preceding the end.

In Daniel and in all apocalyptic literature, the reader's attention is continually directed to the future and to the "end" or "end-time." We shall speak therefore about the meaning of the term "eschatology," the development of the concept of the end-time, and the various theological views of the "end," or *eschaton,* in the Old Testament and the New Testament.

The term "eschatology"

"Eschatology" comes from the Greek term *eschaton* (Hebrew: *aharit*), meaning "the last or furthest off," "the end."[24] Since the "end" is relative to what one is considering, it is possible to speak of (1) individual eschatology

—the end for the individual person, which traditionally entails an explanation of death, judgment, heaven, and hell; (2) national eschatology—the end of an era, e.g., the end of the Old Testament era or the end of Israel as a nation; (3) eschatology of the kingdom of God in the world—the end of the era of the domination of evil and the beginning of the reign of God in individual hearts (realized eschatology) and in society (the parousia); (4) cosmic eschatology—the end of the physical universe, either absolutely or as it was known during the reign of sin in society; (5) immanent eschatology —the end brought about by forces within the world (human in the main but assisted by the divine); and transcendent eschatology—the end brought about by God intervening in the world independently of all human cooperation or effort; (6) absolute or terminal eschatology—the end of history as a time-sequence and the beginning of eternity for the world and for the kingdom of God.[25]

The development of eschatology as a concept

Before and outside of Israel, almost all pagan thinkers saw "history" as a cyclic movement of events. Understanding and projecting the gods as the forces behind natural phenomena, they conceived history to be, like the phenomena of nature, cyclically patterned. In Israel, the dynamics of revelation broke the cyclical pattern of historical thinking by introducing three new factors: (1) the concept of promise and fulfillment; (2) the concept of the kingdom or reign of God in the kingdom of Israel and in the world as a whole; (3) the belief in the intervention of a "God who acts" to bring about the fulfillment of his promises and the realization of his reign or kingdom on earth.

These three factors led Israel's theologians to a linear view of history. This view in turn focused the attention of Israel's theologians on the "end" of history, conceived first as a goal (*telos*) and eventually in a temporal sense as end or *eschaton*. The goal, or *telos,* of history was generally and variously conceived to be the effective reign of God in the world of men, first in covenanted Israel and then in the world as a whole through the intermediacy of covenanted Israel. This basic *telos* is aptly expressed in the words of the Our Father: "Thy kingdom come. Thy will be done *on earth as it is in heaven.*" It is summarized in apocalyptic language by St. Paul in 1 Cor 15:22-29. Eventually attention came to be centered on the time of the *telos.* This came about as a result of Israel's subjection to successive pagan political powers in the post-exilic age. The rule of the pagans over God's covenanted people led Israel's theologians to ponder agonizingly the question raised by the psalmist: "How long, O God, is the foe to scoff? Is the enemy to revile thy name for ever?" (Ps 74:10; cf. also Pss 44 and 73).

Apocalyptic literature then attempted to answer this question by asserting in its own bizarre manner: (1) that God would intervene directly and decisively to conquer the forces of evil that were holding back the realization of his reign in the world of men; (2) that this intervention would come relatively soon; and (3) that it would entail the end of the reign of the forces of evil in the world and the beginning of the reign of God. Finally, the New Testament asserted that in and through the passion, death, and resurrection of Jesus, God had intervened, had decisively defeated the forces of evil, and had initiated the effective reign of God in the world.[26]

The development of eschatological thinking

The Yahwist, in the tenth century B.C., is the earliest of Israel's theologians to think eschatologically (cf. Gn 2-3; 49:1, 8-12; Nm 24:14, 17-19). His emphasis is on the future. Since Gn 2 is no longer considered an attempt to describe what happened historically but rather a description of what the Yahwist envisioned as the state God intended in the future for mankind, it may be considered the Yahwist's imperfect concept of what God has planned for mankind when "the seed of the woman" has eventually conquered the "seed of the serpent." If this is so, it means that the Yahwist, in his mythological description of the "beginning-time," was in reality giving his eschatological conception of the "end-time."

The Yahwist's promises in Gn 49:1, 8-12 and Nm 24:14, 17-19 appear to speak directly about David and do indeed have him in the foreground, but they are introduced as prophecies dealing with "the end of the days" (cf. Gn 49:1 and Nm 24:14); and since they were written after the time of David (in the reign of Solomon, c. 950), they give every indication of referring to the end-time envisioned in Gn 2. The paradisiacal colors of Gn 49:8-12 support this view. Finally, it should be noted that the Yahwist's eschatological thinking is in an immanent rather than a transcendent vein. He envisions the end-time and its realization as brought about in some way by the response, and therefore the activity, of God's covenanted people.

In the eschatological thinking of the prophets, it is doubtful if Amos' prophecies concerning "the day of the Lord" for Samaria can be considered truly eschatological, except in the limited sense of the end of an era. His introduction of the terminology "the day of the Lord," however, is important because it focuses attention on the future and comes to be favored by the prophets and the New Testament authors as terminology when speaking about eschatology. *The day* of the Lord will eventually be the same as the parousia in the language of some New Testament authors. Genuine eschatological thinking can be found in the prophets, e.g., Is 2:2-4; 2:9-22; 11:1f; Zeph 1:2ff; 3:8; Jer 25:3-38 and the new covenant texts (31:23ff; 32; 33); Ez 37 and his prophecies concerning the messianic age; Is 54; 60–62 and throughout Deutero-Isaiah wherever there are references to a new exodus and a new creation.

In the apocalyptic vein and with a view of eschatology that is more transcendent than immanent, some post-exilic prophets and apocalyptists focus on the certainty of God's conquest of the forces of evil and upon the imminence of the "last days": (1) the great battle in Ez 38-39; (2) the little apocalypse of Is 24-27; (3) the great battle and the judgment in the valley of Jehoshaphat in Zech 12-14; (4) the conquest of the forces of evil in the end of the days in Jl 3-4; (5) the great battle and the conquest of the forces of anti-god in the book of Judith; (6) the imminent coming cf the kingdom of God in the book of Daniel.

The influence of apocalyptic and eschatology on the New Testament is evident from the earliest (1 Thes) to the latest (Rv) of the canonical books.[27] It is equally evident in the intermediate literature—the Gospels. Mark, in 70 A.D., contains an apocalyptic discourse (Mk 13). Matthew and Luke, some ten or fifteen years later, have even more elaborate apocalyptic discourses (Mt 24-25; Lk 21:5-36). In John's Gospel, both apocalyptic and eschatology are muted. But they have not been reduced to silence (cf. Jn 15:18–16:33). And in the book of Revelation, at the end of the first century, the earlier urgency and impatience sound again, however hesitantly and resignedly, in the prayer "Amen, come, Lord Jesus" (Rv 21:20).[28]

In the New Testament, the eschatological horizon shifts perceptibly. In 1 Thes, the parousia is undatable, but the horizon is almost within reach. In the Gospels of Mark and Matthew, the parousia is still undatable, but the horizon is farther away. In Luke and especially in John, the horizon has receded significantly, and the parousia is hardly more than a blur in the distance. It is obvious that the early and eager hopes of Christians have been disappointed. A more stoic attitude has replaced the parousiac fever and the eschatological impatience of the apocalyptic-minded early Christians. Imminent eschatology, apart from the occasional seizure of millenarianism, has seen its day. Hope abides, but it needs new expression.

The new expression is perhaps clearest in John's Gospel, where the attitude toward the *eschaton* and the parousia is expressed in what has been termed "realized eschatology." Speaking of the parables, C. H. Dodd says:

> They use all the resources of dramatic illustration to help men to see that in the events before their eyes—in the miracles of Jesus, his appeal to men and its results, the blessedness that comes to those who follow Him, and the hardening of those who reject Him; in the tragic conflict of the Cross, and the tribulation of the disciples; in the fateful choice before the Jewish people, and the disasters that threaten—God is confronting them in his kingdom, power and glory. This world has become the scene of a divine drama, in which the eternal issues are laid bare. It is the hour of decision. It is realized eschatology.[29]

Joachim Jeremias goes a step further than Dodd. In attempting to express the new attitude toward the *eschaton* that Dodd sees intimated in the parables, Jeremias replaces the term "realized eschatology" with the perhaps more accurate term "self-realizing eschatology."[30] With this term Dodd concurs.[31] Jeremias says:

> In attempting to recover the original significance of the parables, one thing above all becomes evident: it is that all the parables of Jesus compel his hearers to come to a decision about his person and mission. For they are all full of the "secret of the Kingdom of God" (Mark 4:11), that is to say, the recognition of "an eschatology that is in process of realization."[32] The hour of fulfillment is come, that is the urgent note that sounds through them all. The strong man is disarmed, the forces of evil are in retreat, the physician has come to the sick, the lepers are cleansed, the heavy burden of guilt is removed, the lost sheep has been brought home, the door of the Father's house stands open, the poor and the beggars are summoned to the banquet, a master whose grace is undeserved pays his wages in full, a great joy fills all hearts. God's acceptable year has come. For he has been manifested whose veiled kingliness shines through every word and through every parable — the Savior.

The problem, however, remains. Realized eschatology and self-realizing eschatology describe the attempts by the inspired theologians of the New Testament to come to grips with the fact that Christ did not return either as expected or when expected. Ultimately, then, the question is thrown back not just to the disappointed expectations of the primitive Christians and the perhaps ambiguous preaching of Paul in 1 Thessalonians and 1 Corinthians that added to those expectations, but to the preaching and expectations of Christ himself.[33] C. K. Barrett has posed the question and the problem in almost agonizing terms:

> The teaching and activity of Jesus were directed towards a future, which appears to have included his death; did it include also the resurrection, and the founding of the Church? Was the future he envisaged the future that happened in the days, the years, the centuries after the first Easter Day? What sort of continuity, if any, exists between Jesus and the Church? Was his preaching of the kingdom fulfilled or falsified in the Christian mission? Most of the problems of New Testament scholarship were posed by Loisy in a dozen words when he wrote, "Jesus foretold the kingdom, and it was the Church that came." It is a familiar but important fact that whereas the word *basileia* (kingdom) is one of the most common and characteristic in the gospels, the word *ekklesia* (Church) occurs in only two passages, both exposed to severe critical doubt and objection. Does this fact suggest that the hopes of Jesus were disappointed? that he looked simply for the super-natural establishing of the kingdom of God in power, and not for the con-tinuing existence, in the conditions of this world, of a human community?[34]

The questions posed by eschatology in the New Testament are not always answerable, but they are important. Harvey Cox has observed: "In the coming decade . . . it will certainly be eschatology, our understanding of Christian promise, which will require the application of the best theological thought," and ". . . our new thinking in eschatology will require a relentless reappraisal of all our other doctrines, for eschatology is not just one item on the agenda of theological deliberation; it provides the perspective from which all else must be understood."[35]

Some questions that should be asked are not always easy to answer. Did the New Testament theologians and even Christ himself, with his human intelligence, ever fully escape or transcend the apocalyptic atmosphere of their era? Did the evangelists truly deduce a realized eschatology or even a self-realizing eschatology, or have modern interpreters foisted upon them attitudes and concepts historically foreign to them?

Did St. Paul, in the course of his theological development from 1 Thessalonians to 1 Corinthians to Romans, progress from an apocalyptic-transcendent orientation toward man, the *eschaton,* and the parousia to a more immanent, anthropocentric, and humanist orientation toward the *eschaton* and the parousia? Does his "Son of Man" or "second Adam" theologizing represent a development from his earlier and more transcendent theologizing in 1 Thessalonians and perhaps even 1 Cor 15 to a more immanent, humanistic, but nonetheless abidingly transcendent theology in Rom 1–8?[36]

Ultimately, is it not true, as Moltmann says, that "the decisive question is, whether 'revelation' is the illuminating interpretation of an existing, obscure life process in history, or whether revelation itself originates, drives, and directs the process of history; whether consequently, as Barth has asked, revelation is a predicate of history, or whether history has to be understood as a predicate of the eschatological revelation and to be experienced, expected and obediently willed as such"?[37]

That history made by man is to be the predicate of revelation is perhaps the ultimate extrapolation of Irenaeus' seminal anthropological dictum: "The glory of God is man fully alive." Man is "fully alive" when he knows his God-given powers, is given scope to use them, uses them with the fullest freedom, and orders their use by his vision of the future. Man fully alive "gives glory" to God when he uses the powers God has given him, as God would use them, for the purpose for which God would use them, and with recognition of, and gratitude for, the gift of freedom that ultimately and truly endows him with the power to be "fully alive." That it is through Christ, with Christ, in Christ — the man-God "fully alive" — in the unity of the Holy Spirit that all glory and honor are given to the almighty Father of all is the passionate conviction of Paul and the central message of the New Testament as a whole.[38]

Chapter III

THE
FIRST LETTER OF PAUL TO THE
CORINTHIANS

Paul wrote at least four letters to his unruly converts at Corinth.[1] He founded the church there around the year 51A.D., and he wrote the letters during the last part of his three-year stay at Ephesus (54–56), only four or five years after his initial visit to Corinth.[2]

According to Acts, Paul spent a few months at Philippi (Acts 16:11-40), a few months at Thessalonica (Acts 17:1-8, 16-34), and finally arrived in Corinth, where he stayed for a year and a half before going to Ephesus (Acts 18:1-19:1). His year and a half in Corinth is dated between 50 and 52 A.D.

The time-sequence is important for two reasons. First, the fact that Paul preached at Corinth so short a time after preaching at Thessalonica makes it probable that in both cities he preached substantially the same message about the parousia and the resurrection. This explains why in both letters he has to deal with problems intimately associated with the parousia and the resurrection. It may also indicate that Paul's treatment of the parousia and the resurrection at Thessalonica and Corinth was inadequate, since whatever he taught was so quickly misinterpreted and had to be corrected.

Second, however much time Paul spent at Philippi and Thessalonica (and a few months rather than a few weeks is more probable[3]), the fact that he spent a year and a half at Corinth indicates the importance he attached to establishing a Christian foundation in that city. With a population of approximately one half million,[4] it was a port city on the isthmus that connected the Adriatic with the Gulf of Corinth on the Aegean Sea. It was a trade center and the meeting place for national and international travelers. It had been the seat of the Roman governor of the province of Achaia since the year 27 B.C.

The problems

Paul's information about the problems in the Corinthian community came to him from a woman named Chloe (1:11), from a letter written to him by the community (7:1ff), and from three visitors from Corinth— Stephanas, Fortunatus, and Achaicus (16:15-18).

According to Chloe, the community was breaking up into rival factions. Groups were following and extolling individual teachers and theologians. As Paul put it: "What I mean is that each one of you says, 'I belong to Paul,' or 'I belong to Apollos,' or 'I belong to Cephas,' or 'I belong to Christ'" (1:12 and cf. 4:5). As Paul understood it, the danger was that for many of the Corinthians the teaching of rival theologians about Christ was becoming more important than Christ himself. Paul deals with this problem in chs 1:10–4:21.

In chs 5-6, Paul tries to deal with some scandalous behavior that is all the worse because the community not only tolerates but condones it—a man living with his own stepmother (5:1-13); Christians bringing other Christians before pagan courts (6:1-11); and Christians claiming "All things are lawful for me," including fornication with prostitutes (6:12-20).

In chs 7-15, Paul gives his solutions to problems presented to him in a letter. In ch 7, he answers questions about marriage, sex, and celibacy; in chs 8-10, he deals with questions about eating meat sacrificed to idols; in ch 11, he gives advice on women's dress (11:1-16) and scolds the Corinthians for the scandalous way they celebrate the Eucharist (11:17-34). In chs 12-14, he answers questions about the evaluation and function of the charismatic gifts. In ch 15, he refutes the claim of some in the community who are saying "there is no resurrection of the dead" (15:12).

What is difficult throughout the epistle is not so much in understanding Paul's solutions to problems as in accurately identifying the kind of thinking and teaching that gave rise to the problems.

Exegetes have tried for centuries to understand just what kind of thinking led the Corinthians to gather into rival factions around one teacher or another (chs 1-4), and to promote fornication and prostitution on the one hand (6:1ff), and on the other to pursue either asceticism in conjugal sexuality or celibacy in place of marriage (7:1ff).

The mind-set behind the eating or not eating of meat sacrificed to idols is easier to understand (chs 8-10), but the thinking behind the problems of women's dress (11:1ff), of the scandalous way of celebrating the Eucharist (11:17ff), of the evaluation and function of the charismatic gifts (chs 12-14), and the astounding claim that "there is no resurrection of the dead" (15:1ff) is to this day quite unclear.

To understand the thinking that led to these problems, we shall have to say something about Paul's opponents—the kinds of thinkers and teachers who were propounding the theories that underlay these problems.[5]

Paul's opponents

In trying to identify Paul's opponents at Corinth, there are three major possibilities to be considered: (1) philosophizing Greek Christians; (2) Greek and Jewish Christians influenced by at least incipient Gnostic theories; (3) fanatic enthusiasts who believed that Christians, by right of faith and baptism, were already in this life confirmed in a state of being similar to the state of being of the exalted Christ in heaven. None of these is easy to understand, but we shall try to describe them.

Philosophizing Greek Christians

The Greeks at Corinth were not the easiest people in the world to understand, especially for a Jew like Paul. At best, they were open-minded, uninhibited, curious; at worst, they were pleasure-seeking, sophisticated, snobbish, and overly intellectual. Because of their intellectual history from the time of Socrates on down through Plato, Aristotle, and the whole sweep of renowned Greek philosophers, they were inclined to give first place to the intellect, intellectual achievements, and whatever pertained to the field of the theoretical. Because of their pagan background and their domestication and demythologization of the pagan gods, they were inclined to countenance a good degree of immorality in general and sexual immorality in particular. While not amoral and antinomian, they were inclined to be more humanistic than religious, and their attraction to ethics was more intellectual than God-fearing. Apart from the Stoics among them, they were not overly concerned with the integration of truth and the practice of what the truth demanded in an ethically orientated life.

Paul's background as a Pharisee would have inclined him not to be overly sympathetic to the intellectualist, anthropocentric Greek mentality. But the influence of Christ on Paul's anthropology and especially Paul's Adamic "image and likeness of God" view of man did give him a certain qualified sympathy with the Greek love of freedom and the Greek propensity for glorifying man and his God-given powers. On the other hand, Paul's Pharisaic bent of mind was unabashedly theocentric, and at no time in his career did he ever bow to the prevailing intellectualist and anthropocentric bent of mind so characteristic of the average Greek.

Ultimately, for the Greeks the mind was everything. For Paul, the intellect was important, but it was subordinate to the moral law and to the will of him who had created both mind and body. Paul would have said with Irenaeus: "The glory of God is man fully alive." The Greeks would have said: "The glory of man is man fully alive." The same Paul who said "For all things are yours . . . and you are Christ's; and Christ is God's" (3:21-23) also said: "'Knowledge' puffs up, but love builds up" (8:1). The Pharisaic Jew and the Greek humanist were worlds apart. It was the genius of Paul that he bridged the two worlds and prepared the way for eventual integration.

In 1 Corinthians, Paul clashes with the intellectuals on a number of points: first, the Greek exaltation of mind over matter, intellect over will, and both over the integration of truth with moral life; second, the Greek attitude toward sexual morality; third, the Greek attitude toward the resurrection of the body.

An inkling of Paul's confrontation with the intellectual Christians is his emphatic denunciation of human wisdom in 1 Cor 1-4 and his insistence on the "wisdom of the cross." A perhaps clearer indication of the confrontation is found in 1 Cor 15, where Paul has to argue against those who say "there is no resurrection of the dead." Whatever the precise thinking behind the rejection of the resurrection of the dead (see p. 111), it is clear that on one point at least, the Greeks would have disagreed with Paul on the resurrection, namely, the question of the physical resurrection of the body. The disagreement is described at the end of Luke/Paul's sermon in Acts 17, where Paul concludes with the words: "and of this he has given assurance to all men by raising him from the dead." The Greek reaction to the idea of man being raised from the dead is then described by Luke: "Now when they heard of the resurrection of the dead, some mocked." The Greeks mocked because, as L. Cerfaux points out:

> The more a Greek thought religiously—either as philosopher or as a mystic
> —the more he took fright at the idea of the resurrection, for the resurrection was directly opposed to his hopes. The cultured Greek world never
> forgot the teaching of the dying Socrates. He who loved the exercise of his
> intelligence before all else, cherished the hope of finding it in full bloom
> when he came to Hades (Plato, *Phaedo,* 693-840). This Greek hope and
> Christian hope are diametrically opposed, for the former is based on the
> liberation of the body, while the latter has the resurrection as its foundation. The Orphics and Pythagoreans were in agreement that the
> philosopher purifies his soul in this life and frees it from the shackles of
> passion, pleasure and pain, that is to say, from the bonds of the body.
> Death is the magnificent occasion of total liberation. . . . On this account
> the teaching of St. Paul was received coldly. . . . It was not the possibility
> of the miracle which was called into question here, for at Corinth, as elsewhere, there was no doubt that God could reanimate a corpse; but why
> reanimate a corpse which had fallen into decay?[6]

Incipient Gnostics

In addition to opposition from the philosophical front, Paul encountered what has been called the Gnostic front. It is supposed by many that much of Paul's argumentation is directed against the teachings of Christian converts who had been infected either before or after their conversion by early Gnostic ideas and theories.[7]

Paul is believed to be attacking Gnostic ideas when he speaks about the true as opposed to the false *gnosis* or wisdom in 1 Cor 1-4; when he attacks the easy attitude toward fornication and general immorality in 1 Cor 5-6; when he discusses marriage and celibacy in 1 Cor 7 and antinomianism in 1 Cor 8-10; and especially when he argues with his opponents at Corinth about the fact of the resurrection and the nature of the resurrection body in 1 Cor 15.

Some of the tenets of Gnosticism[8] that may be reflected in the ideas attacked by Paul in 1 Corinthians are the following: (1) the material world is the creation of a wicked demiurge and is inherently evil; (2) in every person there is a spark of divinity or spirit that has been captured and imprisoned by the material world and cannot be saved unless a savior brings saving *gnosis* (knowledge); (3) the key to release from the oppression of matter is a *gnosis* (knowledge) that brings persons into union with the divine principle of which they had originally been part.

Whether Gnosticism as a full-blown philosophy and religion developed before, during, or immediately after the age of primitive Christianity (c. 30-70 A.D.) is debated.[9] What is certain is that Gnosticism flourished from the middle of the second century A.D. and in the course of the centuries planted the seeds for such deviations as Docetism, Manichaeism, Beghardism, Jansenism, and perhaps even Puritanism. It is the mother of many heresies and deviations, philosophically impossible but ideologically dynamic. As W. Schmithals says: "Gnosis is not theory but power, salvation, deliverance, freedom; it is simply blessedness. Gnosis is gospel. Gnosis is to the Gnostic what *pistis* (faith) is for Paul; indeed it is more, in that *elpis* (hope) is superseded, and *agapē* (love) has become unimportant. Anyone who possesses Gnosis (knowledge) is free."[10]

The effects of Gnosticism on the moral life flow from the Gnostic attitude toward matter. Since matter is evil, the creation of a wicked demiurge, the Gnostic's attitude toward matter, and the material body in particular, can be ambivalent. He may shun matter because it is evil and express his hatred of matter by asceticism, particularly in relation to marriage and sexuality; or he may feel that his *gnosis* (knowledge in the sense of secret, liberating knowledge) has freed him from the influence of evil matter. In the latter case, the Gnostic may embrace libertinism, on the score that once freed by saving *gnosis* from the evil principle of matter, matter itself becomes either neutral or indifferent, and the body and its passions may be indulged without moral qualms. Paul's quotation of his opponents' words in 1 Cor 6:12 and 10:23 ("All things are lawful for me") may be a nuanced reference to this libertinistic Gnostic attitude.

Fanatic enthusiasts

Enthusiasm for Christ and the gospel ran high in Corinth—much of it healthy, some of it suspect, some of it perverted and destructive of the gospel and the community.

Despite Paul's later criticism of the Corinthians' exaggerated evaluation of "knowledge" (chs 8–10) and of certain charismatic gifts (chs 12 and 14), there is no reason to doubt his sincerity when he tells the Corinthians: "I give thanks to God always for you because of the grace of God which was given you in Christ Jesus, that in every way you were enriched in him with all speech and all knowledge" (1:4-5).

The Corinthians truly were "enriched with all speech and all knowledge." As for knowledge, they could boast of such teachers as Paul himself, Peter, and Apollos, the Alexandrian. As for charismatic gifts, they could boast of apostles, prophets, teachers, miracle-workers, healers, administrators, tongue-speakers, and interpreters of tongue-speech (cf. 12:27-29; 14:26-33).

This was all to the good, and no doubt many of the Christians looked to Christ crucified as their model and exercised their charismatic gifts as God's gifts given for the building up of the community in love. But there were others who did not warm to the memory of a crucified Lord, who gloried rather in the reputation of their teachers, who boasted, "All things are lawful for me" (6:12) and claimed an extremely liberal code in relation to morals, who gloried in and inexplicably proclaimed their conviction that "there is no resurrection of the dead" (15:12).

It is difficult to discover the mind-set behind such ideas. Some of it could be traceable to Greek intellectualism, some to incipient Gnosticism, some perhaps to over-excited apocalyptic imaginations. A possibly more fruitful explanation would be to trace it to an exaggerated and myopic exaltation theology.

The earliest Christians believed that Jesus died, was buried, rose from the dead, and was exalted to the right hand of the Father in glory. How all this applied to them as followers of Christ, however, was not clear.[11] Would they have to die before being raised and exalted like Christ? The Thessalonians, and probably even Paul himself at the time he wrote to them, did not think so. Would the end come soon, and with it the parousia or second coming of Christ in glory? Paul, when writing to the Thessalonians and probably during most of his life, thought that the end would come before his death. Some early Christians expected it to come so imminently that they gave up working and had to be scolded by Paul for making themselves a burden on the community (1 Thes *passim*). Had the end already come, and were Christians who believed in Christ and who had been baptized already enjoying, at least in the spirit, the exalted condition of the risen Christ? Some, it would seem, were thinking along these lines.

When Paul contrasts his way of thinking with the Corinthians' way of thinking in 1 Cor 4:8-13, the Corinthian way is almost the exact opposite of Paul's crucifixion theology. Paul says:

Already you are filled! Already you have become rich! Without us you
have become kings! And would that you did reign, so that we might share
the rule with you! For I think that God has exhibited us apostles as last of
all, like men sentenced to death; because we have become a spectacle to the
world, to angels and to men. We are fools for Christ's sake, but you are
wise in Christ. We are weak, but you are strong. You are held in honor, but
we in disrepute. To the present hour we hunger and thirst, we are ill-clad
and buffeted and homeless, and we labor working with our own hands.
When reviled, we bless; when persecuted, we endure; when slandered, we
try to conciliate; we have become, and are now, as the refuse of the world,
the off-scouring of all things.

One must ask, what kind of thinking would account for early Christians
feeling that they were "filled . . . rich" and had "become kings" with no
help from Paul? And what can be inferred from Paul's reaction: "Would
that you did reign, so that we might share the rule with you"? "Would that
you did reign" implies at least that they think they already reign! In some
strange way, these people considered themselves already risen, already exalted, and already reigning with Christ in glory.[12] It should be noted that
Paul's question in 1 Cor 15:12, ". . . how can some of you say that there is
no resurrection of the dead?" would be answered by people of this mind-set
very logically. There is no resurrection of the dead because they consider
themselves already risen.

In the exaltation theology of the Corinthians, the problem seems to lie in
a warped eschatology. For them, what was eschatological had already happened; the parousia and the judgment had already taken place, and they,
possessed of the Spirit, already had a part in the exalted Christ without
following in the way of the cross. As H. Conzelmann puts it: "The Corinthians misjudge the situation: Between the present and the 'goal' there inter-
venes the parousia and the judgment, which they in their spiritual self-
assurance believe they have behind them."[13]

With such a mind-set, one can understand the exuberant enthusiasm of
some of the Corinthians. No wonder they have little concern for the
crucified Christ (1:10ff) — they believe they belong to and enjoy the preroga-
tives of the exalted Christ! No wonder they can say, "All things are lawful
for me" (6:12) — the time of testing, trial, and judgment is past (4:8-13)! No
wonder they can say, "There is no resurrection of the dead" (5:12) — they are
already resurrected and reigning with the exalted Christ!

If this is the mind-set of at least some of the Corinthians and their
teachers, then their problem, as at Thessalonica, is one of a misguided
eschatology. To solve their problem, Paul will have to make clear to them,
as Mark does in his Gospel for a later generation, that the way of the cross
comes first, then the judgment, then the other last things. He will have to
teach them first that "the wisdom of the cross" is "the foolishness of God"
(1:17-4:21) and that it is a foolishness they will have to understand. It is in

this vein that his irony in 4:10 makes sense: "We are fools for Christ's sake, but you are wise in Christ."

He will have to instruct them in the correct understanding of freedom, agreeing with them that "all things are lawful for me," but "not all things are helpful" (6:12), and reminding them that "knowledge puffs up, but love builds" (8:1).

Most of all, when he speaks about the resurrection, he will have to insist that just as death preceded resurrection and exaltation for Christ, so it must precede for Christians. In short, he will have to teach and emphasize, as he does throughout the letter, that there can be no exaltation if there is no cross, that the cross is the way to the exaltation, and that true wisdom lies in understanding the cross as the wisdom of God.

Not in defense but in mitigation of what seems to be the fanaticist enthusiasm of the Corinthians, it should be remembered that they had an admirable awareness and dynamic appreciation of the meaning of Christ's resurrection for the world. An important "end" had come. They truly were living in a "new age." The Christ-event was indeed the pivotal event of all history, and they were living in the white, white light of that event. If they were a little blinded, it was not all that bad a blindness.

What was needed by these fanatics and what Paul supplied was not a dimming of the light but a clearer perception of what it meant, namely, that the end had already come, the new age had already arrived but it had not yet fully arrived. Between the Christian and the resurrection, there was still, as there was for Christ himself, the cross. Paradigmatic for Christians was the tradition Paul preached to the Corinthians, namely, "that Christ died for our sins . . . , that he was buried, that he was raised . . . ." (1 Cor 15:3-4). It is the overall aim of 1 Corinthians to correct the eschatological enthusiasm of the Corinthians by setting right the eschatological sequence: the cross first, then the resurrection and exaltation.

Outline of 1 Corinthians

Introduction (1:1-9): Greeting and thanksgiving

Part I (1:10-4:21): Teachers and the cross as true wisdom

    A (1:10 2:5): The problem: teachers, the cross, and wisdom
    B (2:6-16): Apparent digression: Mature Christians understand the wisdom of the cross.
    A' (3:1-4:21): Advice concerning teachers

Part II (5:1-6:20): Scandals in the community

    A (5:1-13): Sexual immorality
    B (6:1-11): Lawsuits among Christians
    A' (6:12-20): Sexual immorality

Part III (7:1–14:40): Paul's reply to the Corinthians' letter

(1) 7:1-40: Celibacy and the Christian life

A (7:1-16): Marriage, celibacy, and divorced Christians
B (7:17-24): A general rule for all
A' (7:25-40): Practical advice concerning celibacy

(2) 8:1–11:1: Freedom, conscience, and meat sacrificed to idols

A (8:1-13): The problem: eating food sacrificed to idols
B (9:1–10:22): Apparent digressions
A' (10:23–11:1): Practical solution to the idol food problem

(3) 11:2-16: Men's and women's hairstyles

(4) 11:17-34: Community and the Eucharist

A (11:17-22): The Lord's supper is ignored.
B (11:23-26): The supper is "in remembrance" of Jesus' death.
A' (11:27-34): The solution of the problem

(5) 12:1–14:40: Charismatic gifts and the community

A (12:1-31): Criteria for evaluating the gifts
B (13:1-13): Apparent digression: Love is the fundamental criterion.
A' (14:1-40): Practical advice for charismatics

Part IV (15:1-53): The resurrection and the resurrection body

Part V (16:1-24): The collection, travel plans, farewell greetings

Introduction (1:1-9): Greeting and thanksgiving

Text

1:1 Paul, called by the will of God to be an apostle of Christ Jesus, and our brother Sosthenes, ²to the church of God which is at Corinth, to those sanctified in Christ Jesus, called to be saints together with all those who in every place call on the name of our Lord Jesus Christ, both their Lord and ours: ³Grace to you and peace from God our Father and the Lord Jesus Christ.

⁴I give thanks to God always for you because of the grace of God which was given you in Christ Jesus, ⁵that in every way you were enriched in him with all speech and all knowledge— ⁶even as the testimony to Christ was confirmed among you— ⁷so that you are not lacking in any spiritual gift, as you wait for the revealing of our Lord Jesus Christ; ⁸who will sustain you to the end, guiltless in the day of our Lord Jesus Christ. ⁹God is faithful, by whom you were called into the fellowship of his Son, Jesus Christ our Lord.

Commentary

1:1-3 Paul, called by the will of God to be an apostle of Christ Jesus, and our brother Sosthenes. Paul uses the same basic pattern to introduce all his letters: first, his own name as sender, and the name or names of those with him; second, the name of the recipients; third, a brief greeting. His emphasis on his call to be an apostle is probably in view of the fact that there were some at Corinth who contested his apostleship (cf. 4:1-5, 14-21; 9:1-7). Sosthenes' identity is unknown; he may be the Sosthenes mentioned in Acts 18:17.

1:4-9 I give thanks to God. Paul's thanksgiving focuses on the themes of the letter: knowledge, the charismatic gifts, and the parousia—all of which are related to the troublesome situation in the community. Paul thanks God that "in every way [the Corinthians] are enriched in [Jesus] with all speech and all knowledge" (v 5), but, as he will point out later, "Knowledge puffs up, but love builds up" (8:1). He thanks God that the Corinthians "are not lacking in any spiritual gift" (v 7a), but in chs 12 and 14 he will criticize those who grossly overvaluate certain of the gifts, especially the gift of tongues. His reference to the Corinthians waiting for "the revealing of our Lord Jesus Christ" (vv 7b-8) indicates clearly enough that both Paul and the Corinthians are still running a high parousiac fever. In 1 Cor 15, however, Paul will speak at length about the relationship between the resurrection and the parousia, and will insist that resurrection for Christians is still something in the future.

Part I (1:10-4:21): Teachers and the cross as true wisdom

Paul's argumentation in 1:10-4:21 is arranged in chiastic form, i.e., he begins with a general treatment of his problem, which lies in the Corinthian teachers' failure to understand the cross as wisdom (section A: 1:10-2:5); then he moves on to what appears to be a digression—a discussion of mature versus immature Christians (section B: 2:6-16); and he concludes by returning to the themes of 1:10-2:5, giving practical solutions and advice concerning teachers, the cross, and true wisdom (section A': 3:1-4:21). It is the same A-B-A' format Paul used in 1 Thessalonians. He will use it regularly throughout 1 Corinthians, where it is especially clear in chs 5-6; 7; 8-10; 11:17-34; 12-14. Besides using the A-B-A' format because he considers it artistic and believes it helps his readers, Paul argues in this way for a purpose. By using such a subtle theological and psychological line of argumentation, he gets his point across clearly and at the same time spares the feelings of the troublesome Corinthian teachers and their overenthusiastic followers. In this particular case, Paul's chiastic format constitutes a powerful argument for the unity of everything he says in 1:10-4:21. In the outline that follows, it should be noted that in each of the three sections of 1:10-4:21, Paul's words about wisdom are always in the middle.

Parallel structure of 1:10-4:21

A (1:10-2:5): The problem: teachers, the cross, and wisdom

(a) Reputedly wise **teachers** are causing disunity (1:10-17).

    (b) But true **wisdom** is found only in the **cross** (1:18-25).

(a') When Paul **taught,** he **taught** the wisdom of the cross (1:26-2:5).

B (2:6-16): Apparent digression

    (a) **The wisdom Paul teaches** (2:6-7)

        (b) Description of **wisdom** (2:8-12)

    (a') **The wisdom Paul teaches** (2:13-16)

A' (3:1-4:21): Advice concerning teachers

    (a) The function of **teachers** (3:1-17)

        (b) A reprise of the **wisdom**-folly of the **cross** (3:18-23; cp. 1:18-25)

    (a') A reprise of the function of **teachers** (4:1-21; cp. 3:1-17 and 1:10-17)

We have shown the parallel structure of 1:10-4:21 in order that the reader may see it as a whole and as a unity. It is perhaps the most elaborate use of parallelism in all of the Pauline epistles. Similar but less elaborate parallel structures will be found in 1 Cor 12-14 and throughout Galatians. We shall now take each section of 1:10-4:21 and analyze it separately, keeping in mind that each section is a part of the larger unit.

A (1:10-2:5): The problem: teachers, the cross, and wisdom

In the three subsections that make up section A, Paul deals successively with the immediate problem in Corinth: (a) the division of the community into factions following one or the other prestigious teacher (1:10-17); (b) the only source of true wisdom—the cross (1:18-25); (a') the wisdom Paul himself preached when he first came to Corinth—the wisdom of the cross (1:26-2:5). It should be noted that what is not said about the divisive teachers in 1:10-17 is said implicitly in 1:18-2:5, where Paul implies that if the teachers in Corinth concentrated on the preaching of the cross as he himself did, there would not be factions in the community.

Text

(a)   1:10 I appeal to you, **brethren,** by the name of our Lord Jesus Christ, that all of you agree and that there be no dissensions among you, but that you be united in the same mind and the same judgment. [11]For it has been reported to me by Chloe's people that there is quarreling among you, my **brethren.** [12]What I mean is that each one of you says, "I belong to Paul," or "I belong to Apollos," or "I belong to Cephas," or "I belong **to Christ.**" [13]Is **Christ** divided? Was Paul **crucified** for you? Or were you baptized in the name of Paul? [14]I am thankful that I baptized none of you except Crispus and Gaius; [15]lest any one should say that you were baptized in my name. [16](I did baptize also the household of Stephanas. Beyond that, I do not know whether I baptized any one else.) [17]For Christ did not send me to baptize but to preach the gospel, and **not with eloquent wisdom,** lest the **cross of Christ** be emptied of its **power.**

(b) ¹⁸For the word of the cross is folly to those who are perishing, but to us who are being saved it is the power of God. ¹⁹For it is written, "I will destroy the wisdom of the wise, and the cleverness of the clever I will thwart." ²⁰Where is the wise man? Where is the scribe? Where is the debater of this age? Has not God made foolish the wisdom of the world? ²¹For since, in the wisdom of God, the world did not know God through wisdom, it pleased God through the folly of what we preach to save those who believe. ²²For Jews demand signs and Greeks seek wisdom, ²³but we preach Christ crucified, a stumbling block to Jews and folly to Gentiles, ²⁴but to those who are called, both Jews and Greeks, Christ the power of God and the wisdom of God. ²⁵For the foolishness of God is wiser than men, and the weakness of God is stronger than men.

(a′) ²⁶For consider your call, **brethren;** not many of you were wise according to worldly standards, not many were powerful, not many were of noble birth; ²⁷but God chose what is foolish in the world to shame the wise, God chose what is weak in the world to shame the strong, ²⁸God chose what is low and despised in the world, even things that are not, to bring to nothing things that are, ²⁹so that no human being might boast in the presence of God. ³⁰He is the source of your life in Christ Jesus, whom God made our wisdom, our righteousness and sanctification and redemption; ³¹therefore, as it is written, "Let him who boasts, boast of the Lord."

2:1 When I came to you, **brethren,** I did not come proclaiming to you the testimony of God **in lofty words or wisdom.** ²For I decided to know nothing among you except Jesus **Christ** and him **crucified.** ³And I was with you in weakness and in much fear and trembling; ⁴and **my speech and my message were not in plausible words of wisdom,** but in demonstration of the Spirit and **power,** ⁵that your faith might not rest in the wisdom of men but in the **power** of God.

Commentary

(a) Reputedly wise teachers are causing disunity (1:10-17).

1:10-11 I appeal . . . that all of you agree and that there be no dissensions among you. The main problem at Corinth was that the community was dividing up into contentious factions, some following one teacher, some another.

Chloe's people. Chloe is unknown, but some of her friends have brought the news to Paul in Ephesus about the breakup of the community.

1:12 each one of you says, "I belong to Paul." This is the boastful slogan of one faction in the community; the other slogans represent other factions. The Apollos faction followed Apollos, a convert Jew from Alexandria (Acts 18:24–19:1). The Cephas faction probably appealed to the teaching of Peter, the "Rock," and may represent the strict law-abiding Jewish Christians of Jerusalem. The faction that had as its slogan "I belong to Christ" is hard to identify but probably represented a group that followed an exaltation theology and looked to Christ as the Lord of glory who had brought them to glory even in this life. There seems to have been a group in the community who claimed a mystic relationship to Christ himself and excluded all others (cf. 4:8-13). In 3:1–4:21, where Paul again discusses teachers, it is clear that the dissensions are caused by groups that boasted allegiance to certain prestigious teachers; for example, in 3:21, Paul says: "So let no one boast of men"; and in 4:6 he says: "I have applied all this to myself and Apollos for your benefit, brethren, that you may learn by us to live according to scripture, that none of you may be puffed up in favor of one against another."

1:13 Is Christ divided? Paul's question is best understood in the light of his teaching that the community is the body of Christ (cf. 3:16-17; 6:15; 10:17; 12:12). Different factions imply different parts of the body of Christ (the community), as if he had been divided up.

Was Paul crucified for you? This and the following question about baptism are to be answered in the negative. Everything flows from the fact that it was Christ who was crucified for them and that it was into his body that they were baptized when they became Christians (cf. Rom 6:3ff). Christ is central, and all in the community are one in him (cf. 10:17). Paul will deal with his own function and the function of teachers in general in 3:1–4:21, where he will refer back to what he has said here.

1:13c-16 were you baptized in the name of Paul? The point of Paul's remarks about baptism is not to demean the importance of baptism but to emphasize the relationship of baptism to the cross. By baptism Christians have become one with Christ and his body, the Church. Who baptizes is of no consequence. Paul may be attacking here a view of baptism imported into Christianity from the pagan mystery religions – the view that baptism creates a special relationship between the baptizer and the baptized. Against this Paul insists that baptism is into Christ and into him crucified. Only the cross gives meaning to baptism, not the one who baptizes. Paul also may be intimating that people baptized by him have no right to boast of special privileges of any kind in the community. If there really was a "Paul faction," these remarks may well have been intended to warn its members that they could not appeal to him to support their faction.

1:17 not with eloquent wisdom. The gospel does not need the forensic and oratorical skill of its preachers. It has its own intrinsic power (cf. 1:18; 2:1-5; Rom 1:16).

(b) But true wisdom is found only in the cross (1:18-25).

1:18 the word of the cross is folly to those who are perishing. In 1:18-25, Paul goes to the heart of the problem in Corinth by contrasting true wisdom with false wisdom. By false wisdom he means either the human wisdom of the philosophers or perhaps the so-called saving "knowledge" or "wisdom" of the Gnostics. Comparing 1:18-25 with its chiastically balanced counterpart in 3:18-23, the reader will find the two mutually complementary and enlightening. Since the cross represents the self-sacrifice of Christ in obedience to the will of the Father, it follows that those who understand wisdom as obedience to the will of the Father will no longer put their confidence in knowledge as such, even the highest theological or philosophical knowledge.

1:19 I will destroy the wisdom of the wise. Paul deals with wisdom in three key passages: 1:18-25; 2:6-15; 3:18-23. None is easy to understand, but a consideration of Paul's opponents, a comparison with a similar situation at Philippi, and some idea of what wisdom meant to Jews and Jewish Christians will go a long way toward clarifying Paul's understanding of wisdom.

The reason for Paul's forthright emphasis on the cross as wisdom is that his opponents at Corinth have been indulging in a gross over-intellectualizing of the faith in one way or another. They could be philosophical-minded Greek Christians who were scorning the crucifixion as rationally foolish (1:22) and the resurrection of the corpse as simply unworthy of belief (15:1-34). Or they could be incipient Gnostics who were claiming they were already saved either through their knowledge of Christ or through baptism as a rite that conferred upon them "saving knowledge." Finally, they could be believers in an exaltation theology who were claiming they already shared with Christ his triumph and all that went with it. Whatever they held and taught, it did not correspond to the wisdom of the cross and to the emptying of self that wisdom called for.

In another but different situation of disunity at Philippi (cf. Phil 2:2, 12 and cp. with 1 Cor 1:10-12), Paul urged the Philippians to be of one mind with Christ in their abandonment of self-interest (cf. Phil 2:6-11). In Phil 2:7-8, Paul understands the mind of Christ to be such that he "emptied himself, taking the form of a servant, being born in the likeness of men. And being found in human form he humbled himself and became obedient unto death, even death on a cross."

In both Phil 2:6-11 and 1 Cor 1-4, where Paul talks about wisdom and the cross, he is talking not so much about the crucifixion as an example to be imitated as about a "state of mind." The mind of Christ is to do fully the will of the Father, even if it means going to the cross. This is wisdom. It is a moral, not an intellectual, disposition.

More important than a consideration of Paul's opponents and a comparison with the situation at Philippi is an understanding of what wisdom meant to Paul as a Jew. In the wisdom tradition of the Old Testament, to which Paul as a Jew was heir, wisdom was not primarily a matter of knowledge. It was the art of living successfully and happily, and neither of these could be achieved unless a person did the will of God. As the wisdom writers put it: "The beginning of wisdom is fear of the Lord." By "fear of the Lord" they meant obedience to the will of God.[14] Thus the obedient man is the wise man and vice versa.

In Paul's mind, although he does not bother to say it in 1 Cor 1-4, the cross is wisdom, because by accepting the cross, Christ did the will of the Father perfectly. The cross is the wise plan of the Father, because the Father planned that humankind should be saved through the obedience unto death of his Son rather than through any purely human endeavor, however intellectually brilliant or impressive.

1:20-21 the world did not know God through wisdom. The meaning of these words is best understood in the light of Rom 1:18ff, where Paul indicts the philosophers because, even though they have the rational capacity to recognize the existence of God from the evidence of creation, they nevertheless refuse to accept what their reason, through creation, tells them about God.

1:22-24 For Jews demand signs and Greeks seek wisdom. By demanding signs, Paul probably refers to that skeptical attitude toward faith that looks for physical certitude before trusting God (cf. Jn 4:48; 6:25-30; 20:24-29). Paul, however, is concerned here not so much with the Jews demanding signs as with the Greeks seeking wisdom. His topic is precisely: What is the true nature of wisdom? He will speak, therefore, of four different and opposed kinds of wisdom: (1) the wisdom of the philosophers (1:21), which is man-centered, leaves God out of consideration, and is therefore bad; (2) rhetorical wisdom (1:17-2:4-5), or the art of persuading by clever speech, which is sometimes used against the truth and in defense of error, and is frequently therefore also bad; (3) wisdom that is capable of discerning from the evidence of creation the existence and goodness of God, which is good wisdom; (4) that wisdom which is God's overall plan for man's salvation through the sending of the Son to the cross (1:21-25; 2:6-16), which is the highest wisdom. In 1:18-25, the contrast is between the first and the fourth kind of wisdom.

Whether his opponents are philosophizing Greek Christians, Gnostic Christians, or exaltation-theology Christians, Paul's answer is the same: the cross represents God's wisdom and power. The power of the gospel to save is precisely in the preaching of the crucified Christ.

1:25 For the foolishness of God is wiser than men. The cross seems foolish, but it is God's wise way. Substantially, Paul does nothing more than state the central motif of Phil 2:6-11 — that the "mind" of Christ was to be obedient to the will of the Father even unto the death of the cross — and call this death a manifestation of the wisdom of God. He does not explain how it is wisdom. He takes for granted that Christians who have the Spirit and the mind of Christ (2:16) will be able to understand this wisdom. It will not be until Rom 1-8 that Paul will attempt to explain how the passion, death, and resurrection of Jesus constitute the wise plan of the Father.

Paul's argument presupposes the Old Testament understanding of wisdom as fear of the Lord, i.e., obedience to the will of God. It also presupposes faith. Since his opponents have faith, however misguided their ideas about the faith, he is able to appeal to them. Against opponents without faith and without an understanding of the Old Testament concept of wisdom as fear of the Lord, his whole argumentation about the cross being God's wisdom would have made little sense.[15]

(a') When Paul taught, he taught the wisdom of the cross (1:26–2:5).

1:26-31 consider your call, brethren. Paul's argument is not flattering to the Corinthians. He argues from what they can testify to from their own experience, namely, that those in Corinth who accepted the message of the cross in the beginning were the poor and the unlettered, not the intellectuals. They must admit, therefore, that their acceptance of the gospel did not depend upon their intellectual abilities but upon the inherent power of the preached message of the cross. There is no reason, therefore, for boasting (vv 29-31). It is probable that Paul refers to the boasting about teachers that he warned against in 1:12-17.

2:1-5 lofty words or wisdom. Paul repeats what he said in 1:17. He argues from the Corinthians' own experience. They must remember that when Paul first taught them, he did not sway them to accept the faith by means of persuasive language or by what they understand as rhetorical wisdom. He quite simply preached the humanly foolish message of the cross. On the basis of this message, they believed.

in demonstration of the Spirit and power. Paul attributes the effectiveness of his preaching, not to rhetorical wisdom, but to the influence and power of the Spirit working in the hearts of believers (2:4-5).

B (2:6-16): Apparent digression: Mature Christians understand the wisdom of the cross.

Parallel structure

(a) **The wisdom Paul teaches** (2:6-7)
(b) Description of **wisdom** (2:8-12)
(a') **The wisdom Paul teaches** (2:13-16)

Text

(a)   2:6 Yet among the mature **we do impart wisdom,** although it is **not a wisdom of this age** or of the rulers of this age, who are doomed to pass away. [7]But **we impart** a secret and hidden **wisdom of God,** which God decreed before the ages for our glorification.

(b)   [8]None of the rulers of this age understood this; for if they had, they would not have crucified the Lord of glory. [9]But, as it is written, "What no eye has seen, nor ear heard, nor the heart of man conceived, what God has prepared for those who love him," [10]God has revealed to us through the Spirit. For the Spirit searches everything, even the depths of God. [11]For what person knows a man's thoughts except the spirit of the man which is in him? So also no one comprehends the thoughts of God except the Spirit of God. [12]Now we have received not the spirit of the world, but the Spirit which is from God, that we might understand the gifts bestowed on us by God.

(a') [13]And **we impart this in words not taught by human wisdom** but taught by the Spirit, interpreting spiritual truths to those who possess the Spirit. [14]The unspiritual man does not receive the gifts of the Spirit of God, for they are folly to him, and he is not able to understand them because they are spiritually discerned. [15]The spiritual man judges all things, but is himself to be judged by no one. [16]"For who has known the mind of the Lord so as to instruct him?" But we have the mind of Christ.

Commentary

(a) The wisdom Paul teaches (2:6-7)

2:6 among the mature we do impart wisdom. Even though Paul talks about a wisdom for the mature, he is not giving a superior or even a hidden wisdom that he has not previously taught; instead, he is indirectly accusing the Corinthians of being immature. His argument is that mature Christians understand the wisdom of the cross because they have the Spirit and the mind of Christ (cf. 2:13-16). Since the Corinthians cannot seem to grasp the importance of the cross, it follows that they cannot really be mature. They are acting like children (cf. 3:1ff), who are incapable of adult nourishment. As Conzelmann says, "The division between believers of a lower and higher order arises from the fact that the addressees do not conform to the true status conferred on them (3:1ff)."[16] To the degree that the Corinthians do not grasp the importance of the cross as wisdom, they are incapable of understanding Paul's message.

(b) Description of wisdom (2:8-12)

2:8 they would not have crucified the Lord of glory. Paul speaks here about the cosmic effects of the crucifixion; he is not speaking about a new wisdom but about a new dimension of the wisdom of the cross. His thesis is that if the "rulers of this age" had known the mystery of the cross—that through the crucifixion they would be defeated—they would not, for very obvious reasons, have crucified Jesus. This conclusion proves that the wisdom Paul preaches for the mature is not a superior or hidden teaching but the same wisdom of the cross he spoke about in 2:6-7 and 1:10–2:5.

2:10 God has revealed to us through the Spirit. Paul expresses the same idea in a different way: those who understand the wisdom of the cross are the spiritually mature because they have been instructed by the Spirit of God, who alone knows the wisdom of God and communicates it to believers.[17] The spiritually mature are those who have the mind of Christ as expressed in Phil 2:6-11 (cf. 2:16).

(a') The wisdom Paul teaches (2:13-16)

2:13 And we impart this in words not taught by human wisdom. With the repetition of "we impart," Paul returns to the language and theme of 2:6-8 (a). He will now explain how it is that *mature* Christians understand the cross—the wisdom of God: it is because they are taught by the Spirit and have "the mind of Christ."

2:14-15 The unspiritual man. Paul again expresses the difference between mature Christians who understand the wisdom of the cross and immature Christians who do not. If the Corinthians are not led by the Spirit, they do not understand the mystery of the cross and vice versa (cp. vv 14-15 with 1:18-19). The teaching of the mystery it entails is esoteric only to the degree that it is understood by those taught by the Spirit and not understood by the rulers of this age (vv 6 and 8) and by those like them.[18]

2:16 But we have the mind of Christ. The mind of Christ (cf. Phil 2:5-7) was concerned with self-sacrifice through death on the cross for others. Mature Christians have the same mind-set (the cross) as Christ. Immature Christians have the mind-set of the "rulers of this age." They are unspiritual.

A' (3:1–4:21): Advice concerning teachers

Parallel structure

> (a) The function of **teachers** (3:1-17)
> > (b) A reprise of the wisdom-folly of the cross (3:18-20)
> (a') A reprise of the function of **teachers** (3:21–4:21)

Text

(a)   3:1 But I, brethren, could not address you as spiritual **men,** but as **men** of the flesh, as **babes in Christ.** [2]I fed you with milk, not solid food; for you were not ready for it; and even yet you are not ready, [3]for you are still of the flesh. For while there is jealousy and strife among you, are you not of the flesh, and behaving like ordinary **men?** [4]For when one says, "I belong to **Paul,**" and another, "I belong to **Apollos,**" are you not merely **men?**

[5]What then is **Apollos?** What is **Paul? Servants** through whom you believed, as the Lord assigned to each. [6]I planted, **Apollos** watered, but God gave the growth. [7]So neither he who plants nor he who waters is anything, but only God who gives the growth. [8]He who plants and he who waters are equal, and each shall receive his wages according to his labor. [9]For we are fellow workers for God; you are God's field, God's building.

[10]According to the commission of God given to me, like a skilled master builder I laid a foundation, and another man is building upon it. Let each man take care how he builds upon it. [11]For no other foundation can any one lay than that which is laid, which is Jesus Christ. [12]Now if any one builds on the foundation with gold, silver, precious stones, wood, hay, stubble—[13]each man's work will become manifest; for **the Day will disclose** it, because it will be revealed with fire, and the fire will test what sort of

work each one has done. [14]If the work which any man has built on the foundation survives, **he will receive a reward.** [15]If any man's work is burned up, he will suffer loss, though he himself will be saved, but only as through fire. [16]Do you not know that you are God's temple and that God's Spirit dwells in you? [17]If any one destroys God's temple, God will destroy him. For God's temple is holy, and that temple you are.

(b)   [18]Let no one deceive himself. If any one among you thinks that he is wise in this age, let him become a fool that he may become wise. [19]For the wisdom of this world is folly with God. For it is written, "He catches the wise in their craftiness," [20]and again, "The Lord knows that the thoughts of the wise are futile."

(a′)   [21]**So let no one boast of men.** For all things are yours, [22]whether **Paul** or **Apollos** or **Cephas** or the world or life or death or the present or the future, all are yours; [23]and you are **Christ's;** and **Christ** is God's.

4:1 This is how one should regard us, as **servants** of Christ and stewards of the mysteries of God. [2]Moreover it is required of stewards that they be found trustworthy. [3]But with me it is a very small thing that I should be judged by you or by any human court. I do not even judge myself. [4]I am not aware of anything against myself, but I am not thereby acquitted. It is the Lord who judges me. [5]Therefore do not pronounce judgment before the time, **before the Lord comes,** who will bring to light the things now hidden in darkness and **will disclose** the purposes of the heart. Then every **man will receive his commendation from God.**

[6]I have applied all this to myself and **Apollos** for your benefit, brethren, that you may learn by us to live according to scripture, that none of you may be puffed up in favor of one against another. [7]For who sees anything different in you? What have you that you did not receive? If then you received it, why do you boast as if it were not a gift?

[8]Already you are filled! Already you have become rich! Without us you have become kings! And would that you did reign, so that we might share the rule with you! [9]For I think that God has exhibited us apostles as last of all, like men sentenced to death; because we have become a spectacle to the world, to angels and to men. [10]We are fools for Christ's sake, but you are wise in Christ. We are weak, but you are strong. You are held in honor, but we in disrepute. [11]To the present hour we hunger and thirst, we are ill-clad and buffeted and homeless, [12]and we labor, working with our hands. When reviled, we bless; when persecuted, we endure; [13]when slandered, we try to conciliate; we have become, and are now, as the refuse of the world, the off-scouring of all things.

[14]I do not write this to make you ashamed, but to admonish you as my beloved **children.** [15]For though you have countless guides **in Christ,** you do not have many fathers. For I became your father **in Christ** Jesus through the gospel. [16]I urge you, then, be imitators of me. [17]Therefore I sent to you Timothy, my beloved and faithful child in the Lord, to remind you of my ways **in Christ,** as I teach them everywhere in every church. [18]Some are arrogant, as though I were not coming to you. [19]But I will come to you soon, if the Lord wills, and I will find out not the talk of these arrogant people but their power. [20]For the kingdom of God does not consist in talk but in power. [21]What do you wish? Shall I come to you with a rod, or with love in a spirit of gentleness?

Commentary

(a) The function of teachers (3:1-17)

3:1-3 But I, brethren, could not address you as spiritual men. In 2:6-16, Paul had almost reduced the Corinthians to the status of the immature. Here he mitigates his language and simply says that they have been acting like children. They have shown they are only children in Christ by their manner of concentrating on certain prestigious teachers rather than on the cross and the self-sacrifice it calls for.

The "jealousy and strife" associated with factions in the community came from boasting about and from concentrating on such prestigious teachers, as Paul had already implied in 1:10ff. He will have to show them, therefore, the relative unimportance of teachers, whether it be himself or Apollos or any other teacher. This will be the burden of his remarks in 3:5-21.

3:5-9 What then is Apollos? The relationship between the community and its teachers is expressed first and foremost in the word "servants." The teachers are the servants of the community. The service is then described in metaphorical language, first as the work of planting and cultivating a field (vv 5-9) and then as building a house (vv 10-15).[19]

3:10 like a skilled master builder I laid a foundation. Paul, as the founder of the community, speaks of himself as the master builder but insists that the foundation is Jesus Christ, which is another way of saying: "Let no one say, 'I am for Paul.'" Everything depends on Christ, and him crucified.

3:12-14 if any one builds on the foundation. Different preachers and teachers build on Jesus Christ as the foundation and do so in different ways. Whether they build well or not is something that will be known only in the judgment. But they are warned about the importance of building well and at the same time implicitly reminded that they are only servants of the community.

3:16-17 God's temple. The building metaphor is continued and deepened in these words. The community is God's temple because the Spirit of God dwells among them (cf. 6:19; 2 Cor 6:16). Later Paul will tell them that they are Christ's body (12:12-31). The warning in v 17 is for teachers and preachers who forget their function as servants and instead destroy the temple of God (the community) by causing factions and dissensions.

(b) A reprise of the wisdom-folly of the cross (3:18-20)

3:18-20 If any one among you thinks that he is wise. Paul repeats the gist of his teaching about the wisdom of the cross, first expounded in 1:18-25. It is a second warning and is directed like the warning in 3:16-17 to the divisive teachers in the community. But it is also directed to the groups in the community that have fostered the formation of divisive factions by boasting about their favorite teachers.

(a') A reprise of the function of teachers (3:21-4:21)

3:21 So let no one boast of men. Subsection (a') wraps up in much more specific language almost everything Paul has said in chs 1-3. Specifically, he underlines the function of teachers. They are *servants* and stewards of the mysteries of God, nothing more (4:1). There is an implicit warning here to the teachers to be aware of their status as servants and not to mistakenly consider themselves something more, as they or at least their followers seem to think.

4:2 it is required of stewards that they be found trustworthy. The community is advised to evaluate its teachers for what they are — servants — and judge them on the basis of how faithful they are to the work that the service entails, and not on the basis of eloquence or anything else.

4:3-5 But with me. What the Corinthians think of Paul is unimportant — he leaves the judgment to God. Paul here seems to be defending himself against certain accusations by the Corinthians. But what these accusations are is not clear, unless it be that he is not as eloquent in a rhetorical sense as their favorite teachers. Paul's lack of eloquence is implicitly admitted in 2:1-5 and 4:19-20.

4:6-13 I have applied all this to myself and Apollos. The contrast Paul draws between the exaltation theology of the Corinthians (4:6-8) and the crucifixion theology of the apostles as followers in the way of the cross of Jesus (4:9-13) provides a psychological portrait of Paul's opponents at Corinth and a preview of Paul's argumentation for the charism of true apostleship in 2 Cor 2:14-5:15; 10:1-12:18.

4:14-21 I do not write this to make you ashamed. Paul's concluding remarks are meant to take some of the sting out of his forceful rebuke of the Corinthians. At the same time, he leaves no doubt about his authority as an apostle.

Part II (5:1-6:20): Scandals in the community

Besides information about factions in the community, Paul had information about a man living with his stepmother (5:1-13); about Christians taking other Christians before civil courts (6:1-11); and about Christians indulging in casual fornication with Corinthian prostitutes on the basis that "All things are lawful for me" (6:12-20). Paul treats these problems in his typical A-B-A' format and in each case gives both a judgment expressing his disapproval and, to a limited extent, the reasons for his disapproval. The reasons for his disapproval or, if we may speak of them as such, the principles of his moral theology are more interesting than his disapproval, but we will speak of his disapproval first.

Parallel structure

(a) **Sexual immorality** (5:1-13)
    (b) Lawsuits among Christians (6:1-11)
(a′) **Sexual immorality** (6:12-20)

Text

(a)   5:1 It is actually reported that there is **immorality** among you, and of a kind that is not found even among pagans; for a man is living with his father's wife. ²And you are arrogant! Ought you not rather to mourn? Let him who has done this be removed from among you. ³For though absent in body I am present in spirit, and as if present, I have already pronounced judgment ⁴in the name of the Lord Jesus on the man who has done such a thing. When you are assembled, and my spirit is present, with the power of our Lord Jesus, ⁵you are to deliver this man to Satan for the destruction of the flesh, that his spirit may be saved in the day of the Lord Jesus.

⁶Your boasting is not good. **Do you not know** that a little leaven leavens the whole lump? ⁷Cleanse out the old leaven that you may be a new lump, as you really are unleavened. For Christ, our paschal lamb, has been sacrificed. ⁸Let us, therefore, celebrate the festival, not with the old leaven, the leaven of malice and evil, but with the unleavened bread of sincerity and truth.

⁹I wrote to you in my letter not to associate with **immoral men;** ¹⁰not at all meaning the **immoral** of this world, or the greedy and robbers, or idolaters, since then you would need to go out of the world. ¹¹But rather I wrote to you not to associate with any one who bears the name of brother if he is guilty of **immorality** or greed, or is an idolater, reviler, drunkard, or robber — not even to eat with such a one. ¹²For what have I to do with judging outsiders? Is it not those inside the church whom you are to judge? ¹³God judges those outside. "Drive out the wicked person from among you."

Commentary

5:1 a man is living with his father's wife. Most interpreters presume that this incestuous union refers to cohabitation of stepson and stepmother, either after the father's death or after his divorce from the stepmother. Since both Greek and Roman law condemned such unions, Paul's reason for condemning the union is for all practical purposes an *a fortiori* argument: it is conduct "of a kind that is not found even among pagans." Since even the pagans would condemn such a union, Paul does not find it necessary to give an ethical explanation for his condemnation.

5:2 And you are arrogant! In 5:6, Paul says: "Your boasting is not good." Their arrogant boasting implies that the community is not only not getting rid of the sinner but is even approving his conduct. On what basis Christians could be approving such conduct is difficult to determine precisely. But such approval would not be extraordinary for Christians infected with Gnosticism or filled with the fanaticist enthusiasm of a misguided exaltation theology.

5:3-4 For though absent in body I am present in spirit. Paul does not want to detract from the responsibility of the community to expel the sinner, but at the same time he wants them to know that, absent or present, his vote would be for condemnation. When they are assembled (v 4), therefore, he expects them to take action against the sinner.

5:5 you are to deliver this man to Satan. For the early Christians, to deliver a person to Satan was to ban him or her from the world of the Christian community and put him or her back in the "world" dominated by Satan, the "world" outside the community. In the apocalyptic thinking of the time, humanity was divided into two realms: the kingdom of God and the kingdom of Satan. Paul's purpose is salvific. He bans the sinner "for the destruction of the flesh, that his spirit may be saved in the day of the Lord Jesus." "Flesh" designates the person in weakness without the help of God—in this case as belonging to the realm of Satan. "Spirit" designates the person as under the domination of God—in this case as belonging to the realm of God. What is hoped for is that the excommunication from the love-dominated Christian community will bring the man to repent of his sin and return to the warmth and love of his Christian brethren.

5:6-8 a little leaven leavens the whole lump. Paul's analogy deals with the effect of the individual on the community. Because leaven symbolized evil, it was customary in the Jewish celebration of the Passover to remove all leaven from the house and to eat only unleavened bread. The implication here is that the incestuous man is like leaven and, if permitted to remain, will contaminate the whole community. In Paul's mind, the community is a new creation brought into being by Christ, the paschal lamb (v 7). As a new creation, the community should be unleavened, i.e., uncontaminated by "the old leaven, the leaven of malice and evil."

5:9-11 I wrote to you in my letter not to associate with immoral men. Paul refers here to an earlier (now lost) letter in which he had counseled the Corinthians not to associate with immoral men. Some in Corinth rightly claimed that this was impossible. But they misunderstood Paul. He meant not to associate with immoral *Christians* (v 11). He will not allow them to justify associating with the incestuous man on the basis that he meant they should not associate with any immoral people whatsoever—advice it would be manifestly impossible to follow without leaving society altogether.

5:12-13 For what have I to do with judging outsiders? Christians are to judge other Christians; "God judges those outside." As Christians, the Corinthians are called to live by higher norms of behavior than non-Christians do. It is according to these higher norms that they are to judge one another. Those who do not live up to these norms are to be judged by their fellow Christians. They are "not even to eat with such a one." Since the incestuous man has not lived up to these norms, they are advised to "drive out the wicked person from among you" (v 13).

Paul's failure to give an ethical, i.e., philosophical, explanation for his condemnation is interesting, because it shows that in this case, as in many others, he is content to accept what we would call the common estimation of good men concerning what is right and wrong. It is immorality "of a kind not found even among the pagans" (5:1). Paul is not out to create a new system of ethics, either because he did not consider it necessary or, as we shall see later, because he believed that Christian conduct was to be predicated upon a norm higher than anything ethics could demand.

(b) Lawsuits among Christians

Text

(b) 6:1 When one of you has a grievance against a brother, does he dare go to law before the unrighteous instead of the saints? ²Do you not know that the saints will judge the world? And if the world is to be judged by you, are you incompetent to try trivial cases? ³Do you not know that we are to judge angels? How much more, matters pertaining to this life! ⁴If then you have such cases, why do you lay them before those who are least esteemed by the church? ⁵I say this to your shame. Can it be that there is no man among you wise enough to decide between members of the brotherhood, ⁶but brother goes to law against brother, and that before unbelievers?

⁷To have lawsuits at all with one another is defeat for you. Why not rather suffer wrong? Why not rather be defrauded? ⁸But you yourselves wrong and defraud, and that even your own brethren.

⁹Do you not know that the unrighteous will not inherit the kingdom of God? Do not be deceived; neither the immoral, nor idolaters, nor adulterers, nor homosexuals, ¹⁰nor thieves, nor the greedy, nor drunkards, nor revilers, nor robbers will inherit the kingdom of God. ¹¹And such were some of you. But you were washed, you were sanctified, you were justified in the name of the Lord Jesus Christ and in the Spirit of our God.

Commentary

6:1 When one of you has a grievance against a brother. Paul's remarks about judging in 5:12-13 remind him of another scandal in the community. The Corinthians not only have grievances against each other but they are taking them before civil courts for adjudication. Ideally, there should be no serious disputes between members of the community. Paul, however, is a realist. The Corinthians are far from perfect. But the least they can do is settle their disputes among themselves.

6:2-6 Do you not know that the saints will judge the world? In apocalyptic literature, those (the saints) who belong to the forces of good (God's army) will judge the forces of evil at the last judgment. They will even judge the rebellious angels (v 3). Paul cites this popular apocalyptic concept in order to make his point in vv 4-6 that since they will judge even the angels, there must be someone among them to judge cases of one Christian against another.

6:7-8 To have lawsuits at all with one another is defeat for you. It is defeat because it means that the Corinthians do not understand the wisdom of the cross (1 Cor 1–4); they do not realize that a Christian "repays no one evil for evil" (Rom 12:17), does "not overcome evil by evil, but overcomes evil with good" (Rom 12:21), and lives by Jesus' command: "Love your enemies and pray for those who persecute you" (Mt 5:43). As in 5:1-13, nothing is said about ethics. The norms of behavior for Christians are higher than the norms of ethics, and it is behavior guided by these norms, not mere intellectual acceptance of them, that proves who is the committed Christian.

6:9-10 Do you not know that the unrighteous will not inherit the kingdom of God? Paul's list of unrighteous sinners in vv 9-10 is somewhat similar to his list in 5:11. The conduct he describes is the conduct he considers typical of the "world"—those allied with Satan and the forces of evil. Such sinners can in no way conduct themselves as Satan's followers and at the same time inherit the kingdom of God. The two are irreconcilable. Implicitly, Paul is again reminding his readers that a Christian's commitment to Christ is proved in practice. Practice follows being, and the Corinthians' "being" is a "being" in Christ.

6:11 But you were washed . . . sanctified . . . justified. When the Corinthians accepted baptism ("were washed"), they committed themselves to Christ and to Christ's norms of behavior. Such a commitment separated them from the world (they were "sanctified" in the sense of being separated from the world to belong to God) and put them in the right relationship with God (they were "justified" in the Pauline sense of being justified by faith). It is through such a commitment to Christ that they have been removed from the world and have become members of the people of God.

(a') Sexual immorality (6:12-20)

Text

(a')   6:12 "All things are lawful for me," but not all things are helpful. "All things are lawful for me," but I will not be enslaved by anything. ¹³"Food is meant for the stomach and the stomach for food"—and God will destroy both one and the other. The body is not meant for **immorality,** but for the Lord, and the Lord for the body. ¹⁴And God raised the Lord and will also raise us up by his power. ¹⁵**Do you not know** that your bodies are members of Christ? Shall I therefore take the members of Christ and make them members of a prostitute? Never! ¹⁶**Do you not know** that he who joins himself to a prostitute becomes one body with her? For, as it is written, "The two shall become one." ¹⁷But he who is united to the Lord becomes one spirit with him. ¹⁸Shun **immorality.** Every other sin which a man commits is outside the body; but the **immoral man** sins against his own body. ¹⁹**Do you not know** that your body is a temple of the Holy Spirit within you, which you have from God? You are not your own; ²⁰you were bought with a price. So glorify God in your body.

Commentary

6:12 "All things are lawful for me." These words are in quotation marks, along with the first part of v 13, because almost all commentators accept them as quotations from the Corinthians' letter to Paul used to justify their indulgence in casual fornication.[20] Some consider the words to be the Corinthians' deduction from Paul's preaching that Christians were no longer bound by the Mosaic law (cf. Galatians and Romans). Others explain them as the declaration of Christians infected with Gnosticism's attitude toward the body and sex in general, or as the proud boast of Christians misled by a misguided exaltation theology. Paul agrees with them (6:12b), but not without serious qualifications.

6:13-14 "Food is meant for the stomach and the stomach for food." Presumably this analogy was used by the Corinthians to justify their scandalous conduct. Paul condemns their conduct, not on ethical, i.e., philosophical, grounds, but on the grounds that fornication and eating cannot, as physical functions, be simply equated, as if one were not different from the other. They cannot be simply equated because eating and drinking will cease, but the body (person) will be raised up as Jesus was raised up (v 14). Fornication, moreover, as Paul indicates in vv 15-17, is different from eating because it involves another human being.

6:15-17 Do you not know that your bodies are members of Christ? Paul's second reason for condemning casual fornication is that Christians no longer belong to themselves. They are members of Christ's body, and their bodies belong to Christ (cf. v 20). To make their bodies one with the body of a prostitute would in one sense be to alienate what does not fully belong to them, and in another sense to make the body of Christ one with a prostitute, because they belong to Christ's body, the community. The underlying reason for the condemnation of fornication, therefore, is not because it is unethical (Paul does not bother to speak about the ethics of fornication), but because it is conduct unbecoming a member of Christ's body. The norm, if Paul were to formulate it, seems to be quite simply that Christ would not do such a thing. Since Christians belong to the body of Christ, they should not do such things either. The nearest Paul comes to an ethical argument is in v 16b, where he quotes Gn 2:24, "The two shall become one," implying that intercourse is meant to cement a permanent union of two persons. Fornication with a prostitute would, of course, be an act that ignores and excludes any kind of meaningful union.

6:18 Shun immorality. Every other sin which a man commits is outside the body. J. Murphy-O'Connor rightfully notes that this line should read "Every sin which a man may commit" and not "every *other* sin," as the RSV translates it.[21] He attributes these words to the Corinthians as another attempt on their part to justify their casual fornications. He interprets the Corinthians to mean that physical actions have no moral character whatever and that sin is possible only on the level of motive and intention. Paul's reply to such a misguided notion is: "On the contrary, the immoral man sins against his own body." Paul's argument is that the body and actions performed with the body are morally relevant. Therefore, he who does not use his body as God intended (in this case, as it is intended to be used in marriage according to Gn 2:24) but rather as God did not intend (by indulging in fornication) sins against his own body.

6:19-20 Do you not know that your body is a temple of the Holy Spirit within you? Through Christ's passion (v 20a), Christians share in the life of God and become temples of the Holy Spirit both as individuals and as a community. Since this was brought about by God at the price of Christ's death, Paul can say to them, "You are not your own" (v 19b). He rightfully, therefore, exhorts them to use their bodies to glorify the God who made them his own (v 20b). The Holy Spirit, in other words, has brought about a drastic change in the bodily condition of Christians. As P. Meyer puts it: "The gift of the Holy Spirit claims the realm of bodily existence as its 'temple' just as the 'price' of Jesus' death claims the Christian person as God's. The implication is that what *is* at man's disposal is *to be* placed at God's."[22]

Paul's basic norm for Christian behavior

In his moral argumentation, Paul sometimes appeals to norms of conduct based upon the teaching of the Old Testament and sometimes to the norms of conduct accepted by men of good will. His overarching and transcendent norm, however, is the indicative of the Christian's existence.[23] He expresses it best in Gal 5:25: "If we live by the Spirit, let us also walk by the Spirit," and Gal 2:20: "I have been crucified with Christ; it is no longer I who live, but Christ who lives in me; and the life I now live in the flesh I live by faith in the Son of God, who loved me and gave himself for me." Paul's indicative for the Christian's existence presupposes that the baptized Christian lives by the life-giving power of the Spirit that comes from the Father through the risen Christ and makes all who believe in Christ one with him and with one another in such a way that they are literally a new creation and a new humanity.

Paul's imperatives for Christian behavior flow from this indicative and presuppose a necessary incompatibility between such a principle of activity and any kind of genuinely sinful conduct. As Bornkamm expresses it: "The basis for the incompatibility of sin and grace and therefore of sin and Christian life is not initially a duty, but a fact; not a decision to which we are called, but a decision that has happened to us."[24] In short, it is not a question of striving to be what one is not, but of striving to be what one is.

Paul's indicative of the Christian life underlies not only his imperatives for Christian conduct but also many of his metaphors. It underlies his question in 3:16: "Do you not know that you are God's temple and that God's

Spirit dwells in you?" (cf. also 6:19). It underlies his admonition in 5:7: "Cleanse out the old leaven that you may be a new lump, as you really are unleavened" and his question in 6:15: "Shall I therefore take the members of Christ and make them members of a prostitute?" It is the background concept in most of Paul's statements about the Christian community that is Christ's body (cf. 6:19-20; 10:16-17; 12:12-31). It flows logically and inevitably from Paul's teaching about baptism in Christ (cf. 1 Cor 1:13; Rom 6:3-14).[25]

For Paul, therefore, the overarching and transcendent norm for Christian conduct is determined by the source of Christian vitality or life. Fitzmyer expresses it this way: "The Spirit's law of love is the new inner source and guide of the life by which the *pneumatikos* (spiritual person) lives; it is the ontic principle of vitality, whence springs the love that must interiorize the Christian's entire ethical conduct."[26]

Part III (7:1-14:40): Paul's reply to the Corinthians' letter

Beginning with ch 7, Paul answers questions put to him by the Corinthians in a letter. Paul alludes to these questions in 7:1, 25; 8:1; 12:1; 16:1, and in each case he refers to them with the same opening words, "Now concerning . . ." (*peri de*), e.g. 7:1: "Now concerning the matters about which you wrote . . . ." In dealing with Paul's answers to these questions, the main problem for interpreters is to determine the situational context that provided the background for each of the questions. As always, the one who truly understands the question has already gone a long way toward understanding the answer.

An additional problem lies in determining whether all the material in these chapters was prompted by specific questions put to Paul by the Corinthians' letter or whether some of it was prompted by information received from Chloe's circle (1:11) or from Stephanas, Fortunatus, and Achaicus (16:17). This becomes a problem where Paul introduces new themes without using his customary formula, "Now concerning . . . ." Paul's discussion of hairstyles (11:2-16), the Eucharist (11:17-34), and the resurrection (15:1ff) do not begin with this formula. The problem in this case is to determine what the specific situation was in Corinth that prompted Paul to take up these themes in addition to the themes suggested by the Corinthians' questions. The matter covered in 7:1-14:40 can be divided thematically as follows:

(1) Celibacy and the Christian life (7:1-40).
(2) Freedom, conscience, and idol-meat (8:1-11:1).
(3) On hairstyles at worship (11:2-16).
(4) Community and the Eucharist (11:17-34).
(5) Charismatic gifts and the community (12:1-14:40).

(1) Celibacy and the Christian life (7:1-40)

The two questions that Paul answers in 7:1 and 7:25 are intertwined. In 7:1, the Corinthians ask Paul: "Is it well for a man not to touch a woman?" The Corinthians' implied affirmative answer to their own question and Paul's actual affirmative answer lead naturally to the question about celibacy in 7:25. Unfortunately, Paul does not repeat the exact question in 7:25. One thing, however, is obvious. The Corinthians were confused about the legitimacy of the use of sex in marriage and perhaps about the use of sex at all—they appear to have thought that all should be celibate and that even married persons should live as celibates. This much seems clear both from the nature of the questions asked and from the tone of the answers given.

Throughout the chapter, Paul deals with a variety of situations involved in one way or another with the legitimacy of the use of sex. Paul deals with married persons in 7:1-7; singles and widows in 7:8-11; divorced persons in 7:12-16; with all in 7:17-24; and with committed celibates in 7:25-40. In every instance, the central issue is the use of sex.

Paul's answers, suggestions, and advice, as will be evident, lean definitely to the side of celibacy. He makes it abundantly clear, however, that marriage is good, that sex in marriage is good, and that it is in no way a question of choosing either marriage or celibacy or of choosing what is bad as opposed to what is good, but rather a question of choosing the better over the good. This is evident from his manifest recognition of the legitimacy of the use of sex in marriage (7:2-6) and from his quotation of Jesus' prohibition of divorce (7:10-11), with its implied approbation of marriage duties. Paul, in short, has nothing against marriage and the use of sex in themselves. For Paul, as C. K. Barrett so neatly puts it: "The unmarried state is, for a number of reasons of a pragmatic kind, a very fine thing, and happy are they who can maintain it; but marriage is at worst troublesome, is in no way wrong, and is a divine institution."[27]

The mentality behind the Corinthians' questions about marriage and celibacy is difficult to isolate. The questions imply a preference for celibacy and perhaps even abstinence from the use of sex in marriage. Paul agrees, but only with reservations. The fact that he has to qualify his agreement so much leads to the suspicion that the Corinthians' asceticism with regard to the use of sex was not entirely wholesome and reasonable, was perhaps motivated by the wrong reasons, and was in general unrealistic.

Paul feels that he has to insist upon the mutual sexual rights of married partners (7:2-5). He has to point out that not all have the charismatic gift of celibacy as he does (7:7), and consequently not all have the ability to abstain completely from the use of sex (7:9). He goes out of his way to talk about the obligation of Christians not to divorce (7:10-11) and not even to separate from pagan partners except in extraordinary circumstances (7:12-16). His very realistic advice in 7:36-38 concerning the situation of what appears to be young Christians living together by commitment but not exercising marital rights suggests a certain unrealism and perhaps even fanaticism concerning the whole matter of sex on the part of the Corinthians.

Some authors have suggested that the unreal asceticism was prompted, not by any specifically Christian teaching or principle, but by a Gnostic teaching that held that the flesh was evil because it pertained to the realm of the evil demiurge. If this was so, then they were advocating something good in advocating celibacy, but for the wrong reasons.[28] Paul, as a consequence, whether he realized it or not, was arguing against a fanatical Gnostic mentality.

Other authors associate the Corinthian attitude toward marriage and sex with the slogan Paul quoted them as advocating earlier: "All things are lawful for me" (6:12). Only in this case they would be using the slogan to justify freely terminating marital relations against the will of one partner (7:2-5) or to divorce pagan partners (7:12-16) or to disrupt family life in general (7:17-24).

Whatever their reasons, whether based upon Gnostic ideas or upon an unreal understanding of the slogan "All things are lawful for me," Paul treats the situation with caution and moderation. Where he agrees, he agrees with realistic limitations; where he disagrees, he disagrees delicately but persuasively. His argumentation begins by covering all states of life from marriage to celibacy to widowhood and the situation of divorced persons (7:1-16), then deals with a general rule for all (7:17-24), and concludes with practical advice with regard to the adoption of the celibate state (7:25-40). The mode of argumentation is the same A-B-A' format used in chs 1–4 and 5–6. It runs as follows:

Parallel structure

(a) Marriage, **celibacy,** and divorced Christians (7:1-16)
    (b) A general rule for all (7:17-24)
(a') Practical advice concerning **celibacy** (7:25-40)

Text

(a)   7:1 **Now concerning** the matters about which you wrote. It is well for a man not to touch a woman. ²But because of the temptation to immorality, each man should have his own **wife** and each woman her own **husband.** ³The **husband** should give to his **wife** her conjugal rights, and likewise the **wife** to her **husband.** ⁴For the **wife** does not rule over her own body, but the **husband** does; likewise the **husband** does not rule over his own body, but the **wife** does. ⁵Do not refuse one another except perhaps by agreement for a season, that you may devote yourselves to prayer; but then come together again, lest Satan tempt you through lack of **self-control.** ⁶I say this by way of concession, not of **command.** ⁷I wish that all were as I myself am. But each has his own special gift from God, one of one kind and one of another. ⁸To the **unmarried** and the **widows** I say that it is well for them to remain single as I do. ⁹But if they cannot exercise **self-control,** they should **marry.** For it is better to **marry** than to be aflame with **passion.**

¹⁰To the **married** I give charge, not I but the Lord, that the **wife** should not separate from her **husband** ¹¹(but if she does, let her remain single or else be reconciled to her **husband**)—and that the **husband** should not divorce his **wife.**

¹²To the rest I say, not the Lord, that if any brother has a **wife** who is an unbeliever, and she consents to live with him, he should not divorce her. ¹³If any woman has a **husband** who is an unbeliever, and he consents to live with her, she should not divorce him. ¹⁴For the unbelieving **husband** is consecrated through his **wife,** and the unbelieving **wife** is consecrated through her **husband.** Otherwise, your children would be unclean, but as it is they are **holy.** ¹⁵But if the unbelieving partner desires to separate, let it be so; in such a case the brother or sister is not bound. For God has called us to peace. ¹⁶**Wife,** how do you know whether you will save your **husband? Husband,** how do you know whether you will save your **wife?**

Commentary

7:1-4 It is well for a man not to touch a woman. Paul's advice to the married begins (7:1) and ends (7:7) with the unlikely suggestion that married persons would be better off celibate! The suggestion, however, is quickly qualified. There is a danger of immorality (*porneia*) for the unmarried (7:2). (The Greek word *porneia* means "sexual immorality" and is the same word here as in 6:14, 18, where Paul's subject was the misuse of sex by casual fornication with prostitutes.) Because of the danger of immorality, Paul urges the Corinthians to exercise the legitimate use of sex in marriage with full respect for the mutual rights of both husband and wife (vv 2-4).

7:5 Do not refuse one another except perhaps by agreement for a season. Abstinence, but only temporary abstinence, is recommended for the sake of greater attention to prayer. This probably reveals Paul's rabbinic mentality. The rabbis considered sexual abstinence a help toward undistracted study of the Scriptures. As H. Conzelmann suggests: "Apparently Paul is thinking of continuous prayer carried out with the persistence of a rabbi's study of the Torah."²⁹ The suggestion is utilitarian. There is no intention of saying that the use of sex in marriage is in any way sinful or defiling.

7:6 I say this by way of concession. Paul's concession could refer to the temporary abstinence recommended in v 5, but more likely, in view of the preference for celibacy expressed in vv 1 and 7, it refers to the whole of what he said in vv 2-5. This fits with the second part of v 6, "not of command," and perhaps implies that whereas Paul agrees with the Corinthians that celibacy is preferable to marriage (7:1, 7), unlike them he would not think of commanding celibacy as an obligation for Christians.

7:7 I wish that all were as I myself am. What Paul implied in v 6, he makes explicit in these words. That he means he is a celibate seems evident and can be demonstrated from 1 Cor 9:5, where he asks: "Do we not have the right to be accompanied by a wife, as the other apostles and the brothers of the Lord and Cephas?" His conclusion, "But each has his own special gift from God, one of one kind and one of another" (v 7b), closes his discussion concerning the legitimate use of sex in marriage, reminds the Corinthians that celibacy is a charismatic gift that not all enjoy, and prepares the way for his brief but pointed advice to the unmarried and widows (vv 8-9).

In 7:1-7, Paul has been speaking about marriage and celibacy in a general way and in relation to the general situation of men and women with regard to the use of sex. In 7:8-16, he deals with three specific categories: the unmarried, those Christians married to Christian partners, and finally those Christians married to pagan or Jewish partners.

7:8-9 To the unmarried and the widows. Paul deals here with Christian singles and widows considering the alternatives: marriage or celibacy. His recommendation of celibacy in v 8 is thoroughly consistent with his preference for celibacy expressed in 7:1, 7. What he says in v 9 is equally consistent with what he had said in 7:2-6. If singles or widows cannot live chastely, i.e., if they do not have the gift of celibate continence, "it is better to marry than to be aflame with passion." "To be aflame with passion" is another way of saying "if they cannot exercise self-control."[30] The reference is not necessarily to unchaste acts but to that constant internal itch for active sexual expression that so distracts a person as to make serving the Lord in peace and joy almost impossible. Paul again is consistent. In 7:1-7, he said he preferred celibacy but that it was not for all. Here he says the same. Anyone wishing to impose a general law of celibacy on Christians cannot claim Paul's support. Whether this was the intent of those at Corinth who questioned Paul about whether "it is well for a man not to touch a woman" is debatable; but if it was, Paul has made clear his opposition.

7:10-11 To the married I give charge, not I but the Lord. In vv 10-16, Paul deals with two classes of married people: Christians married to Christians and considering divorce; Christians married to pagans or Jews and considering divorce. Against Christians married to Christians and contemplating divorce for whatever reasons, Paul quotes Jesus' prohibition of divorce (v 10 and cf. Mk 10:9; Mt 5:32; 19:9).

7:12-16 To the rest I say, not the Lord. With regard to Christians married to pagans or Jews and contemplating divorce, Paul is more lenient, or at least it has seemed so to Christian exegetes down through the centuries. His words "I say, not the Lord" seem to imply that Jesus had said nothing about Christian-pagan marriages and that what Jesus actually said to the Pharisees about marriage (Mk 10:9; Mt 19:3-9) pertained only to Christian-Christian marriages (v 12a). This, of course, is very doubtful. On these presumed and very debatable presuppositions, Paul would be speaking on his own authority about Christian-pagan marriages and divorce, putting them beyond the scope of Jesus' prohibition of divorce.

His advice deals with two marriage situations. In the first case, the believing and the unbelieving partner are willing to live together, presumably in peace and without discord concerning their religious differences. In this case, Paul demands that Jesus' prohibition be obeyed, and there is no inconsistency in his demand (vv 12b-14).

In the second case, the unbelieving partner is unwilling to live in peace with the Christian partner (vv 15-16), and Paul allows the believing partner to separate from, and equivalently, to divorce the unbelieving partner. If he only allows separation and divorce but not remarriage, then his leniency is not in absolute contravention of Jesus' prohibition, since the marriage remains a marriage even though the partners no longer live together. If, on the other hand, Paul means that the Christian partner is now free to marry again, as Christian exegetes through the centuries have interpreted him to mean,[31] then his permission to Christians to divorce and remarry, even where it is a case of a Christian divorcing a pagan or a Jew, is patently in contradiction to Jesus' prohibition, unless it can be proved that Jesus' prohibition was not absolute.

The usual exegetical solution to this impasse is to claim that Paul, speaking under the inspiration of the Spirit, gives the true interpretation of Jesus' prohibition of divorce and remarriage, interpreting it to be absolute only in true marriages between baptized persons.[32] Paul, it is claimed, understood Jesus to have prohibited divorce and remarriage absolutely in relation to baptized Christians but only relatively in relation to non-Christians or Christians married to non-Christians.

In proof of this, exegetes and theologians point to the fact that the Church never allows divorce and remarriage in the case of baptized Christians who have entered a true marriage and consummated the marriage. The Church, on the other hand, has relatively frequently permitted divorce and remarriage in cases where one married partner was not baptized. The Pauline Privilege, the Petrine Privilege, and the Monterey-Fresno case all flow from the dissolubility of a marriage in which at least one of the partners was not baptized. The Church has even granted divorce and remarriage in the case of true marriages between baptized Christians, provided the marriages have not been consummated. These cases have been described and discussed in numerous scholarly works.[32]

The possibility that the Western Catholic Church, like the Eastern Orthodox and the Protestant Churches, might eventually grant divorce and remarriage even in the case of true, consummated marriages between baptized Christians has been much discussed by Scripture scholars, theologians, and canon lawyers. It would be beyond the scope of this study to explore this attractive possibility, but the literature on the subject is abundant.[33]

(b) A general rule for all (7:17-24)

Text

(b) 7:17 Only, let every one lead the life which the Lord has assigned to him, and in which God has called him. This is my rule in all the churches. [18]Was any one at the time of his call already circumcised? Let him not seek to remove the marks of circumcision. Was any one at the time of his call uncircumcised? Let him not seek circumcision. [19]For neither circumcision counts for anything nor uncircumcision, but keeping the commandments of God. [20]Every one should remain in the state in which he was called. [21]Were you a slave when called? Never mind. But if you can gain your freedom, avail yourself of the opportunity. [22]For he who was called in the Lord as a slave is a freedman of the Lord. Likewise he who was free when called is a slave of Christ. [23]You were bought with a price; do not become slaves of men. [24]So, brethren, in whatever state each was called, there let him remain with God.

Commentary

7:17b This is my rule in all the churches. Paul's urging of the general rule, "Let every one lead the life which the Lord has assigned to him, and in which God has called him" (7:17a),[34] in the midst of a discussion of marriage, divorce, and celibacy-virginity sounds like a digression. We suggest, however, that it is not a digression but a critical qualification for Paul's whole argumentation and that, rightly understood, it casts much light on the situation in Corinth that gave rise to the questions the Corinthians were asking about sex, marriage, and celibacy. To begin with, Paul's apparent digression here is similar to his apparent digressions in 2:6-16 (section B of 1:10–4:21), 9:1–10:22 (section B of 8:1–11:1), and 13:1-13 (section B of 12:1–14:40). When each of these apparent digressions is looked at in the context of the entire discussion of which it is a part, it is seen to be, not a digression, but an important qualification of the whole discussion. In this case, the emphasis on the Corinthians' remaining as they were when called to the Christian life suggests that there were some in Corinth who were making strenuous efforts to persuade and perhaps even demand that their fellow Christians change their way of life. That they wanted everybody to be celibate is a reasonable conjecture.

7:18-22 Was any one at the time of his call uncircumcised? Here the point Paul makes is that conversion to Christ does not call for disrupting one's ordinary life in the world. Whatever mode of life one lived before conversion, one should continue in the same mode (all things being equal) after conversion. It is not that the way of each one's life is unimportant in itself, but that it is not necessary to change it violently just because one has been converted. What matters, Paul insists, is "keeping the commandments of God" (v 19c), and that can be done in any walk of life. Those who demand that the circumcised become uncircumcised or vice versa, or that slaves must become free (vv 21-23) are demanding a change of life that is simply not required by conversion to Christianity. As Paul concludes, "Every one should remain in the state in which he was called" (v 20).

7:23-24 do not become slaves of men. This is a critical command. Christians have been bought and paid for by Christ (v 23). They are free, therefore, and should not enslave themselves to men. Presumably, in the context of the whole of 7:1-40, these men are teachers or other self-styled authorities who demand that Christians must give up their marriage rights if they are married, or if married to pagans that they must divorce their pagan partners, or if celibate that they must remain celibate.

Seen in this light, the whole section is not only not a digression but is wholly consistent with Paul's repeated teaching about freedom of choice in regard to marriage or celibacy. Paul considers marriage good and celibacy better, but he will not allow anyone to make either one—and especially celibacy—a matter of obligation for Christians or an essential of Christian belief (cf. 7:7b, 9, 26-28, 35b, 36-38, 39). One's state of life is just not that important, and the Christian life can be led in any state of life. Section B, therefore, far from being a digression, serves the important function of preparing the way for Paul's more positive evaluation of celibacy in 7:25-40 by making it clear beforehand that while celibacy may be better than marriage, it is still not in any way essential for a Christian.

(a') Practical advice concerning celibacy (7:25-40)

Text

(a')   7:25 **Now concerning the unmarried,** I have no **command** of the Lord, but I give my opinion as one who by the Lord's mercy is trustworthy. ²⁶I think that in view of the impending distress it is well for a person to remain as he is. ²⁷Are you bound to a **wife?** Do not seek to be free. Are you free from a **wife?** Do not seek **marriage.** ²⁸But if you **marry,** you do not sin, and if a girl **marries** she does not sin. Yet those who **marry** will have worldly troubles, and I would spare you that.

²⁹I mean, brethren, the appointed time has grown very short; from now on, let those who have **wives** live as though they had none, ³⁰and those who mourn as though they were not mourning, and those who rejoice as though they were not rejoicing, and those who buy as though they had no goods, ³¹and those who deal with the world as though they had no dealings with it. For the form of this world is passing away.

³²I want you to be free from anxieties. The **unmarried** man is anxious about the affairs of the Lord, how to please the Lord; ³³but the **married** man is anxious about worldly affairs, how to please his **wife,** ³⁴and his interests are divided. And the **unmarried** woman or girl is anxious about the affairs of the Lord, how to be **holy** in body and spirit; but the **married** woman is anxious about worldly affairs, how to please her **husband.** ³⁵I say this for your own benefit, not to lay any restraint upon you, but to promote good order and to secure your undivided devotion to the Lord.

³⁶If any one thinks that he is not behaving properly toward his betrothed, if his **passions** are strong, and it has to be, let him do as he wishes:

let them **marry**—it is no sin. ³⁷But whoever is firmly established in his heart, being under no necessity but having his **desire under control,** and has determined this in his heart, to keep her as his betrothed, he will do well. ³⁸So that he who **marries** his betrothed does well; and he who refrains from **marriage** will do better.

³⁹A **wife** is bound to her **husband** as long as he lives. If the **husband** dies, she is free to be **married** to whom she wishes, only in the Lord. ⁴⁰But in my judgment she is happier if she remains as she is. And I think that I have the Spirit of God.

Commentary

This section has been entitled "practical advice," because it deals with norms for determining the adoption or non-adoption of a celibate state, and also because in each of the major sections of Paul's letter (chs 1-4; 5-6; 7:1-40; 8:1-11:1; 12-14; and 15:1-58), it is in the final sections that Paul gives his practical solutions to the questions or problems at issue. After dealing with the wider theological perspectives of the problem of celibacy in 7:1-16 and 7:17-24, he is now ready to deal with the more immediate problem, which is the situation of the unmarried: Should they remain unmarried or should they marry, and is there any obligation to do one or the other?

7:25 Now concerning the unmarried. Paul has already given his stringently qualified judgment that celibacy is better than marriage (7:1, 7, 8-9). Now he explains why. He begins by stating that unlike the matter of divorce, concerning which Jesus had spoken, in the matter of celibacy Jesus had said nothing: "Now concerning the unmarried, I have no command of the Lord, but I give my opinion as one who . . . is trustworthy."³⁵ Paul, of course, is not saying that his opinion means nothing; he is quite conscious of his apostolic authority (cf. 1 Cor 5:1-13). But he takes pains to emphasize throughout his discussion not only that there is no "command of the Lord" but that he himself makes no commandment concerning celibacy. Nonetheless, his opinion is that it is good "for a person to remain as he is" (v 26), whether married or unmarried, and, as he will go on to say, it is better, for reasons that he will give, to remain unmarried (vv 28-35).

7:26-31 in view of the impending distress. Paul presents two arguments in favor of celibacy. The first (vv 26-31) is characterized by apocalyptic language and imagery, and appears to be based upon the expectation of an imminent parousia and end of the world. As in the case of Jeremiah, who was commanded by God not to marry because apocalyptic days were coming when Jerusalem would be destroyed by the Babylonians (Jer 16), so Paul counsels the unmarried not to marry because apocalyptic days are coming upon their world. "The appointed time," Paul says, "has grown very short" (v 29). The unmarried will not, like Jeremiah, have to worry about wife and children when the dire time of the parousia with its apocalyptic upheavals arrives.

At first glance, the argument seems irrelevant. We no longer contemplate, as Paul and his contemporaries did, an imminent end of the world. But there is more to Paul's argument than the imminence of the end. He is arguing in the context of one who lives in the last age of the world, who lives an eschatological existence characterized more by its "citizenship in heaven" (Phil 1:27) than by its attachment to the passing things of earthly existence. The apocalyptic language emphasizes the greater concern for the transcendent, along with a genuine detachment from earthly affairs, that should characterize Christians. Celibacy is one way a Christian can show detachment from this passing world (vv 29-31).

7:32-35 I want you to be free from anxieties. Paul's second argument is characterized by such expressions as "free from anxieties," "anxious about the affairs of the Lord" (v 32), "how to be holy in body and spirit" (v 34), "to secure your undivided devotion" (v 35d). The argument asserts (what seems obvious to some but not to others) that the unmarried will have more time to give to the work of preaching the gospel as Paul does (cf. 9:4-5, 12). In 7:5, Paul used a similar argument when he suggested that married couples might refrain from sexual relations by agreement for a while to devote themselves to prayer. The argument seems to be that celibacy is required for total dedication to the work of the Kingdom, a work so great that it calls for sublimating the good of marriage to the greater good of the work of the Kingdom. Paul supports this argument by his own example (cf. 1 Cor 9:5ff); declares it is a charism (7:7b) that not all enjoy (7:9); exhorts those who can take it to take it (7:1, 7, 8-9, 27-28, 32-35, 37-38, 40), but makes it clear that celibacy is neither essential nor obligatory for any Christian. Paul could have cited the celibacy of Jesus, who gave himself totally to the work of the Kingdom and thus became the paradigm of the perfect disciple. He probably did not cite Jesus' example because those advocating celibacy for all would have made too much of it and might well have tried to use it as a trump card for their unreasonable demands. In sum, the Jew in Paul would have subscribed to the words of Gn 2:18: "It is not good that the man should be alone." But the Christian in Paul, inspired by the surpassing magnitude of the work of the Kingdom, did not hesitate to say: "It is well for a man not to touch a woman" (7:1).

7:36-40 If any one thinks that he is not behaving properly toward his betrothed. The peculiar situation Paul deals with here seems to presuppose some kind of chaste living together of a man and a woman, either married or unmarried, but more likely married. The point has been reached in the relationship where the man at least finds sexual self-control difficult if not impossible. Paul counsels him to "do as he wishes: let them marry—it is no sin" (7:36b). On the other hand, if the man can control himself, Paul counsels continuation of the chaste relationship (7:38). The advice is consistent with everything Paul has said about celibacy. The discussion takes into consideration only the male side and reflects the social customs of the time and male domination, leaving the determination of the nature of the marriage to be decided by the husband.

More difficult to explain is the practice of non-sexual marriage among the Corinthians. The Essenes at Qumran practiced celibacy, but so far as we know, they did not practice non-sexual marriage. For the Essenes, who considered themselves to be the new covenant Israel predicted by Jeremiah and Hosea, celibacy was probably seen as a dictate prescribed by the laws of the Holy War. The final apocalyptic holy war between the forces of God and the forces of evil was considered imminent. In preparation, the Essenes went back to the Old Testament accounts of the Holy War (Nm 10:9; Dt 7:21-22; 20:2-5; 23:10-15) and Holy War practices.[36]

The most significant of these practices for our discussion of celibacy in the Corinthian community is the prescription of ritual cleanliness (Ex 19:14-15; Jos 3:5; Jer 6:4; 22:7; Jl 4:9) and chastity (1 Sm 21:6; 2 Sm 11:11). If these Old Testament prescriptions of chastity as preparation for the Holy War against the forces of evil in the end-time induced the Essenes to embrace celibacy at Qumran, could they not have had a similar influence on the Christians at Corinth preparing for the second coming of Christ and the apocalyptic war that coming would bring about? Paul's apocalyptic terminology and images in 7:26-31 leave no doubt that he associated celibacy with the situation of those who lived in the end-time. We can only speculate that the Holy War laws and the prevailing belief in the early Church that the end-time was near (cf. 1 and 2 Thes; 1 Cor 1:8-9; 7:26-31) contributed to an atmosphere in which it was felt that celibacy, virginity, non-sexual marriages, and even refraining from sexual relations in marriage, at least for a time, were considered a fitting preparation for the end-time.

Whatever the underlying reason, apart from Paul's argument for greater freedom in dedicating oneself to the work of the Kingdom, celibacy and its counterpart, the legitimate use of sex, was a problem at Corinth that Paul dealt with skillfully and with consummate good sense. A much better knowledge of the history of celibacy and a more positive theology of marriage in recent times have led to a renewed discussion of the whole question of celibacy.[37] The literature is abundant and generally adequately nuanced.[38] Since some of it was written before Vatican II and before the recent trend toward a more positive appreciation of marriage as a covenant union and matrimony as a sacrament, the reader is well advised to remember that the whole climate of the discussion has changed markedly from what it was before Vatican II.

(2) 8:1–11:1: Freedom, conscience, and meat sacrificed to idols

Paul's opening words, "Now concerning food offered to idols" (8:1a), repeat the formula of 7:1, 25; 12:1; 16:1 and indicate that the Apostle is taking up another question put to him in the letter from the Corinthians (7:1). His answer, however, is so long and so apparently rambling that some critics refuse to believe that all the material in 8:1–11:1 is of one piece.[39] Others, more correctly we think, see a definite unity and continuity in the three sections of 8:1–11:1 and interpret all of it in relation to a recognizable situation in Corinth.[40] An overview of the material shows that it is written in Paul's usual A-B-A' format, with the last part paralleling the first part.

Parallel structure

(a) The problem: eating **food** sacrificed to **idols** (8:1-13)
    (b) Apparent digressions (9:1–10:22)
        a. Paul's rights as an apostle (9:1-23)
        b. Paul does not take his salvation for granted (9:24-27).
        c. The Israelites in the desert fell into idolatry and fornication (10:1-13).
        d. The table of the Lord versus the table of demons (10:14-22)
(a') Practical solution to the **idol food** problem (10:23–11:1)

The reader who compares sections (a) and (a') will readily notice the parallelism of content and even a close parallelism in vocabulary. The problem is to show how section (b) fits in with sections (a) and (a') and contributes to the unity of the whole section. There are three clues. The first is the A-B-A' format. As we have seen in chs 1-4; 5-6; and 7, Paul's mode of argumentation follows a recognizable format. In each of these earlier sections, the problem is presented with some broad theological perspectives in (a). In (b), Paul qualifies or presents another perspective on the problem. In (a') he gives his practical solution to the problem. As the commentary will show, he does the same in 8:1–11:1.

The second clue is provided by the theme of "eating." This theme runs through every section of 8:1–11:1. Section (a) and section (a') deal with "eating" food sacrificed to idols. Section (b), which looks digressive, deals first with Paul's right as an apostle to "eat" and drink at the community's expense (9:1-23); then with Paul's not taking his salvation for granted (9:24-27), a passage that serves as a transition to the reminder that the Israelites in the desert "ate" and drank and thereby participated in idolatry and fornication (10:1-13); and finally with the incongruity and innate opposition between "eating" at the table of the Lord and "eating" at the table of idols-demons (10:14-22).

It must be admitted that the common theme of eating, even when supported by Paul's A-B-A' mode of argumentation, is at best an ambiguous argument, since it would be precisely the theme of eating that would suggest to an interpolator that material dealing with this subject should be interpolated here. The argument is not entirely without weight, but a better argument for the unity and integrity of 8:1–11:1 is the added light that the material in 9:1–10:22 casts on the overall situation in Corinth in relation to eating idol food.

To begin with, 9:1-23, which appears to many to be an interpolation, has two good links to 8:1-13. First, in 8:1-13 Paul concludes his discussion of knowledge, freedom, love, and conscience by saying: "Therefore, if food is a cause of my brother's falling, I will never eat meat, lest I cause my brother to fall" (8:13). In 9:1-23, Paul goes on to give himself as an example of one who certainly has knowledge, certainly is free, but nevertheless does not exercise his rights when relinquishing his freedom to exercise his rights will be helpful to others (9:19-23).

The second link is more subtle. Paul defends himself as a genuine apostle (9:1-18). He does so because there are some in the community who do not want to recognize him as an apostle. As he says: "If to others I am not an apostle, at least I am to you" (9:2a). The statement suggests that there were opponents contesting Paul's credentials as an apostle. The further statement in 9:3, "This is my defense to those who would examine me," suggests that Paul had done something to incur the criticism of his opponents. What was it? J. C. Hurd believes that it was Paul's apparent inconsistency with regard to eating idol food: "Thus it seems probable that the Corinthians have criticized Paul for being indifferent to the dangers of eating idol meat at some times, and at others forbidding its use."[41] If this is the case, then in 8:1–11:1 Paul is not just discussing in a dispassionate way the pros and cons of eating idol food; he is also defending himself against a double charge: first, that he is not a true apostle; second, that he has been inconsistent in his teaching about the eating of idol food. The two charges go together, since theoretically a true apostle would not be inconsistent in a matter of such religious importance.

All things considered—the common theme of eating, Paul's A-B-A′ mode of argumentation, and the links between 8:1-13 and 9:1ff—there is more than sufficient reason to treat 8:1–11:1 as a unified whole. The commentary on each section confirms this unity.

(a) The problem: eating food sacrificed to idols (8:1-13)

Text

(a) 8:1 Now concerning food offered to idols: we know that "all of us possess knowledge." "Knowledge" puffs up, but love **builds up.**" ²If any one imagines that he knows something, he does not yet know as he ought to know. ³But if one loves God, one is known by him.

⁴Hence, as to the **eating** of food offered to idols, we know that "an idol has no real existence," and that "there is no God but one." ⁵For although there may be so-called gods in heaven or on earth—as indeed there are many "gods" and many "lords"—⁶yet for us there is one God, the Father, **from whom are all things** and for whom we exist, and one Lord, Jesus Christ, through whom are all things and through whom we exist.

[7]However, not all possess this knowledge. But some, through being hitherto accustomed to idols, **eat** food as really offered to an idol; and their **conscience**, being weak, is defiled. [8]Food will not commend us to God. We are no worse off if we do not **eat,** and no better off if we do. [9]Only take care lest this **liberty** of yours somehow become a stumbling block to the weak. [10]For if any one sees you, a man of knowledge, at table in an idol's temple, might he not be encouraged, if his **conscience** is weak, to **eat** food offered to idols? [11]And so by your knowledge this weak man is destroyed, the brother for whom Christ died. [12]Thus, sinning against your brethren and wounding their **conscience** when it is weak, you sin against Christ. [13]Therefore, if food is a cause of my brother's falling, I will never eat meat, lest I cause my brother to fall.

Commentary

8:1 "all of us possess knowledge." These words, probably quoted from the Corinthians' letter, serve to identify the error in their thinking and possibly also the faction that is causing the trouble. Those who boast about "knowledge" could be either incipient Gnostics who put too much stock in "knowledge," or fanaticist exaltation-theology Christians who figured that nothing was forbidden and nothing could hurt them in their now achieved state of salvation and exaltation with Christ, or possibly even ordinary Christians whose knowledge was correct but misapplied. In any case, they are Christians who are content with a "loveless knowledge" that is orthodox as knowledge but useless for Christians because it is blind to the importance of love and to the necessity of subordinating knowledge to love when one's neighbor's good requires it.

8:1b "Knowledge" puffs up, but love builds up. Paul's implicit condemnation of knowledge that "puffs up" is central to his argument, because it calls upon the Corinthians to subordinate knowledge to love. (Paul repeats these words in 10:23-24 in such a way that they form an inclusion with 8:1b). In chs 12–14, he does the same thing by exalting love (ch 13) over the charismatic gifts (chs 12 and 14). Such loveless knowledge is not true knowledge because, as he says in 8:11, it brings about the spiritual ruin of those "for whom Christ died." Thus Paul's central argument is that love is more important than knowledge or, more accurately, that knowledge subordinated to love is the true knowledge.

8:4-6 we know that "an idol has no real existence." Paul both agrees and disagrees with his critics. When he says "all of us possess knowledge," he is agreeing with them on the intellectual assessment of idols. There is only one God. Eating meat sacrificed to idols, as a consequence, means nothing. (In passing, it should be noted that in cities such as Corinth, most meat sold in the markets would have been in some way or other dedicated to the gods. If one could easily have purchased meat not so dedicated, there would have been no problem.) Paul agrees, therefore, but quickly qualifies by pointing out that not all are so intellectually secure.

8:7-13 However, not all possess this knowledge. Paul would agree that, all things being equal, those who know that there are no other gods have a perfect right to exercise the freedom this knowledge gives them. But all things are not equal when fellow Christians recently converted from paganism have scruples about eating idol food, for they quite simply do not have this "knowledge."

Paul distinguishes between a right conscience and an erroneous conscience and takes for granted that each must follow his or her conscience, right or wrong. What he asks of those with a right conscience is not that they should give up their rights but that they should give up the use of their right to follow their right conscience when in so doing they may be a source of temptation to their weaker brethren to go against their erroneous conscience and thereby sin (8:8-12). Paul's conclusion, "Therefore, if food is a cause of my brother's falling, I will never eat meat, lest I cause my brother to fall" (v 13), supports his basic principle that "knowledge puffs up, but love builds up" (8:1b). At the same time, his whole argumentation disposes of the criticism that a man (Paul himself, according to his critics) is inconsistent if he eats food sacrificed to idols on some occasions and on others refuses it. It is not the food but the motive that is important (cf. 10:23-30).

(b) Apparent digressions (9:1-10:22)

Each of the following short sections in 9:1-10:22 will seem to be digressive. If the reader keeps in mind, however, what has been said about idol food, idols, freedom, conscience, and rights in 8:1-13, it will become clear that Paul is still discussing the same situation, but from other angles.

a. Paul's right as an apostle (9:1-23)

Text

(b)   9:1 Am I not free? Am I not an apostle? Have I not seen Jesus our Lord? Are you not my workmanship in the Lord? ²If to others I am not an apostle, at least I am to you; for you are the seal of my apostleship in the Lord.

³This is my defense to those who would examine me. ⁴Do we not have the right to our food and drink? ⁵Do we not have the right to be accompanied by a wife, as the other apostles and the brothers of the Lord and Cephas? ⁶Or is it only Barnabas and I who have no right to refrain from working for a living? ⁷Who serves as a soldier at his own expense? Who plants a vineyard without eating any of its fruit? Who tends a flock without getting some of the milk? ⁸Do I say this on human authority? Does not the law say the same? ⁹For it is written in the law of Moses, "You shall not muzzle an ox when it is treading out the grain." Is it for oxen that God is concerned? ¹⁰Does he not speak entirely for our sake? It was written for our sake, because the plowman should plow in hope and the thresher thresh in hope of a share in the crop. ¹¹If we have sown spiritual good among you, is it too much if we reap your material benefits? ¹²If others share this rightful claim upon you, do not we still more?

Nevertheless, we have not made use of this right, but we endure any-thing rather than put an obstacle in the way of the gospel of Christ. [13]Do you not know that those who are employed in the temple service get their food from the temple, and those who serve at the altar share in the sacrificial offerings? [14]In the same way, the Lord commanded that those who proclaim the gospel should get their living by the gospel.

[15]But I have made no use of any of these rights, nor am I writing this to secure any such provision. For I would rather die than have any one deprive me of my ground for boasting. [16]For if I preach the gospel, that gives me no ground for boasting. For necessity is laid upon me. Woe to me if I do not preach the gospel! [17]For if I do this of my own will, I have a reward; but if not of my own will, I am entrusted with a commission. [18]What then is my reward? Just this: that in my preaching I may make the gospel free of charge, not making full use of my right in the gospel.

[19]For though I am free from all men, I have made myself a slave to all, that I might win the more. [20]To the Jews I became as a Jew, in order to win Jews; to those under the law I became as one under the law — though not being myself under the law — that I might win those under the law. [21]To those outside the law I became as one outside the law — not being without law toward God but under the law of Christ — that I might win those out-side the law. [22]To the weak I became weak, that I might win the weak. I have become all things to all men, that I might by all means save some. [23]I do it all for the sake of the gospel, that I may share in its blessings.

Commentary

9:1-2 Am I not free? Am I not an apostle? Paul defends his rights as an apostle and at the same time fortifies his argument for the pre-eminence of love over knowledge and rights by giving himself as an example of one who has given up the exercise of his rights in order to serve others. He begins with a series of rhetorical questions that establish what the Corinthians can-not seriously doubt, namely, that he is free, that he has seen Jesus, and that at least for them — the community he founded — he is certainly an apostle.

9:3-14 This is my defense. Unlike other apostles, Paul has not de-manded the support for his work that he could rightfully have asked from the Corinthians (vv 4-12). In vv 8-12, he shows how his right to support is based upon Scripture. And in v 14, he refers indirectly to what Jesus himself had said about the support owed to missionaries (cf. Mt 10:10). Paul is making the point that there can be good reasons for giving up one's rights — the same point he made about the right to eat idol food in 8:7-13. He may also be making a point against his opponents. It is possible that they argued Paul was not a true apostle because, unlike the other apostles, he did not demand support. Implied would be the reasoning that he did not demand support because he was not in fact a true apostle.

9:15-18 But I have made no use of any of these rights. Paul is still defending himself as an apostle. He has all the rights of an apostle but does not make use of them because he would rather give up his right to support and preach the gospel free of charge (v 18). That Paul did not always preach the gospel free of charge is clear from Phil 4:10-20. He probably did so in Corinth because of the rambunctious disposition of the Corinthian community and because he was able to support himself there by his own labors. He was, as we know from Acts 18:3, a tentmaker by trade and therefore was not always in need of financial support from the communities he preached to.[42]

9:19-21 For though I am free from all men, I have made myself a slave to all, that I might win the more. In 9:1, Paul asked rhetorically: "Am I not free? Am I not an apostle?" He has already answered the second question in 9:3-18. Now he answers the first question by asserting that he is indeed free, but for the sake of the gospel he has given up many of the rights his freedom allowed him. He is once again making the point about freedom and rights that he made in 8:7-13 by reminding the Corinthians that even though he is as free as they are, he has nevertheless given up the use of his rights in order to attain something far more important. He has in fact made himself "a slave to all" so as to win over as many as possible (9:19). "To the Jews," he says, "I became a Jew . . . . To those outside the law [the Gentiles] I became as one outside the law . . . . To the weak I became weak . . . ." Paul, in short, was not jealous of his rights when giving up the use of his rights would advance the work of the gospel. At first sight, Paul's words might seem to be admitting that he was a bit of a chameleon. But such a charge would be unfair. Paul was not compromising principles; he was freely sacrificing his rights—precisely what he was urging the Corinthians to do in 8:7-13.

9:22-23 To the weak I became weak. The reference to the "weak," i.e., the scrupulous in conscience, turns the reader's mind back to 8:1-13, where Paul discussed the problem of idol food in relation to the "weak" who because of a "weak" conscience might be led to eat idol food against the dictates of their conscience as a result of seeing the "strong" in conscience do the same. What Paul does in 9:1-23 is use his own life as an example to confirm his teaching on the pre-eminence of love over knowledge. His knowledge does not "puff up"; his love "builds up."

b. Paul does not take his salvation for granted (9:24-27).

Text

(b) 9:24 Do you not know that in a race all the runners compete, but only one receives the prize? So run that you may obtain it. [25]Every athlete exercises self-control in all things. They do it to receive a perishable wreath, but we an imperishable. [26]Well, I do not run aimlessly, I do not box as one beating the air; [27]but I pommel my body and subdue it, lest after preaching to others I myself should be disqualified.

Commentary

In the last three parts of section (b), Paul turns from defending himself to attacking the soft spots of his critics. He does not indulge in outright accusations and recriminations. He uses examples. His criticism is implicit in the three examples he gives: first, himself (9:24-27); then the Israelites in the desert taking part in idolatry and fornication (10:1-13); and finally the two tables of sacrifice (10:14-22). All three examples remind the Corinthians that salvation is not something they have already achieved (as exaltation theology would have it) but something for which they must strive and even suffer.

9:24-25 in a race . . . only one receives the prize. The Isthmian games were held regularly at Corinth as a sort of a warm-up for the Olympics, and the city was regularly filled with athletes. Paul likens the Christian to an athlete who knows that he has to train if he wants to triumph in the games. The difference is that the athlete competes for a perishable prize, the Christian for an imperishable one. The Christian can no more take victory for granted than an athlete can.

9:26-27 Well, I do not run aimlessly. Paul again, as in 9:1-23, uses himself as an example. Even though he is an apostle and has subordinated his rights and privileges for the sake of the gospel (cf. 9:15-23), he nevertheless does not take *his* salvation for granted. He does not indulge himself as if the time for suffering and striving were over. He runs hard as a runner in the games and trains strictly to prepare himself for victory. Paul's words imply that there are some among the Corinthians who think that *their* salvation is assured, that their race is already won, and that there is no need for the discipline and self-sacrifice called for by the theology of the cross. These would appear to be the same Christians Paul addressed earlier in the letter when he said: "Already you are filled! Already you have become rich! Without us you have become kings! And would that you did reign, so that we might share the rule with you!" (4:8).

What Paul says about himself and by implication about his opponents here in vv 24-27 is only a lead-up and transition to the more trenchant criticism implied in his account of the Israelites in the desert (10:1-13) and his contrast between the table of the Lord and the table of demons (10:14-22).

c. The Israelites in the desert fell into idolatry and fornication (10:1-13).

Text

(b)   10:1 I want you to know, brethren, that our fathers were all under the cloud, and all passed through the sea, ²and all were baptized into Moses in the cloud and in the sea, ³and all ate the same supernatural food ⁴and all drank the same supernatural drink. For they drank from the supernatural Rock which followed them, and the Rock was Christ. ⁵Nevertheless with most of them God was not pleased; for they were overthrown in the wilderness.

⁶Now these things are warnings for us, not to desire evil as they did. ⁷Do not be idolaters as some of them were; as it is written, "The people sat down to eat and drink and rose up to dance." ⁸We must not indulge in immorality as some of them did, and twenty-three thousand fell in a single day. ⁹We must not put the Lord to the test, as some of them did and were destroyed by serpents; ¹⁰nor grumble, as some of them did and were destroyed by the Destroyer.

¹¹Now these things happened to them as a warning, but they were written down for our instruction, upon whom the end of the ages has come. ¹²Therefore let any one who thinks that he stands take heed lest he fall. ¹³No temptation has overtaken you that is not common to man. God is faithful, and he will not let you be tempted beyond your strength, but with the temptation will also provide the way to escape, that you may be able to endure it.

Commentary

10:1-6 our fathers were all under the cloud. The thrust of Paul's recapitulation of what happened to the Israelites in the desert (cf. Ex 13:21; 14:22; 16:4-35; 17:6; Nm 14:29-30; 20:7-11) should have been clear to anyone in Corinth who knew the sad story of Israel in the desert. The Corinthians who were saying "All of us possess knowledge" (8:1) were insisting on their right to eat idol food and probably also to take part in the banquets held in the pagan temples. Paul's comparison implies as much. Since the Israelites at Baal Peor (Nm 25:1-5) not only took part in idol worship but also in the casual fornication that was part of the Canaanite religion, Paul may be insinuating that some of the Corinthians were doing as much. On the food question, Paul can agree. For the rest, he has to disagree and warn them that they are heading for the fall that so frequently comes to those who are overly confident in themselves. "These things," he says, "happened to them [the Israelites] as a warning, but they were written down *for our instruction*" (10:11).

10:7-13 Do not be idolaters as some of them were. What happened to the Israelites? Even though they had been baptized into Moses (as Christians are baptized into Christ) and even though they ate the same spiritual food and drank the same spiritual drink (as Christians partake of the same Eucharistic bread and wine), yet God was not pleased with them (as he is not pleased with certain Corinthians), for they became idolaters and they "sat down to eat and drink and rose up to dance."

Here, as perhaps no place else in 8:1–11:1, Paul gets down to his real theological disagreement with the idol food enthusiasts. His references to baptism and the Eucharist (10:2-4) imply that his opponents attribute an exaggerated importance to these sacraments. They think that because they have been baptized and have partaken of the Eucharist, they are assuredly saved. This is exaltation theology at its worst. Paul refutes it from the experience of the Israelites in the desert. What happened to them can happen to self-satisfied Christians.

d. The table of the Lord and the table of demons (10:14-22)

Text

(b) 10:14 Therefore, my beloved, shun the worship of idols. [15]I speak as to sensible men; judge for yourselves what I say. [16]The cup of blessing which we bless, is it not a participation in the blood of Christ? The bread which we break, is it not a participation in the body of Christ? [17]Because there is one bread, we who are many are one body, for we all partake of the one bread.

[18]Consider the practice of Israel; are not those who eat the sacrifices partners in the altar? [19]What do I imply then? That food offered to idols is anything, or that an idol is anything? [20]No, I imply that what pagans sacrifice they offer to demons and not to God. I do not want you to be partners with demons. [21]You cannot drink the cup of the Lord and the cup of demons. You cannot partake of the table of the Lord and the table of demons. [22]Shall we provoke the Lord to jealousy? Are we stronger than he?

Commentary

10:14-18 Therefore, my beloved, shun the worship of idols. Paul still does not accuse, but the implication of his analogy is obvious. Food sacrificed to idols is associated with pagan sacrifices in a manner similar to the way the bread and wine of the Eucharist are associated with the sacrificial rite of Christians. Eating idol meat is one thing, taking part in idol worship is another. It is not just a matter of being tempted to idolatry and fornication; it is a matter of loyalty to Jesus.

10:20 No, I imply that what pagans sacrifice they offer to demons. Paul is not retracting his denial of existence to pagan gods; he is simply asserting that there are two opposed camps — one on the side of God, the other on the side of those opposed to God. The latter, in the mythological language of the time, he categorizes as demons.

10:21-22 You cannot drink the cup of the Lord and the cup of demons. To eat at table with another was a sign of friendship and loyalty in Semitic culture. (The evangelists all recount Judas' treachery in the context of the Last Supper. That he sat and ate with Jesus and then went out to betray him added a special horror to his treachery.) No matter that idols and demons are non-entities — the man who eats at their table is in danger of withdrawing his loyalty from Christ and giving it to whatever the Gentiles give their loyalty, whether it be non-existent gods or the demons that symbolize them when understood in opposition to God.

(a') Practical solution to the idol food problem (10:23–11:1)

Text

(a') 10:23 "All things are lawful," but not all things are helpful. "All things are lawful," but not all things **build up.** [24]Let no one seek his own good, but the good of his neighbor. [25]**Eat** whatever is sold in the meat market without raising any question on the ground of **conscience.** [26]For **"the earth is the Lord's, and everything in it."** [27]If one of the unbelievers invites you to dinner and you are disposed to go, **eat** whatever is set before you without raising any question on the ground of **conscience.** [28](But if some one says to you, "This has been offered in sacrifice," then out of consideration for the man who informed you, and for **conscience'** sake — [29]I mean his **conscience,** not yours — do not **eat** it.) For why should my **liberty** be determined by another man's scruples? [30]If I partake with thankfulness, why am I denounced because of that for which I give thanks? [31]So, whether you **eat** or drink, or whatever you do, do all to the glory of God. [32]Give no offense to Jews or to Greeks or to the church of God, [33]just as I try to please all men in everything I do, not seeking my own advantage, but that of many, that they may be saved. 11:1 Be imitators of me, as I am of Christ.

Commentary

Paul's final words return to the problem first brought up in 8:1-13. He has laid down the basic principles in 8:1-13. He has made the necessary qualifications in 9:1-10:22. His opponents cannot accuse him of inconsistency. Nor can they claim that taking part in idol worship is as indifferent a matter as eating idol food. When all is said and done, knowledge is one thing, love and concern for one's neighbor are another. What love calls for, Paul demands: "Give no offense to Jews or to Greeks or to the church of God, just as I try to please all men in everything I do, not seeking my own advantage, but that of many, that they may be saved. Be imitators of me, as I am of Christ" (10:32–11:1).

10:23-24 "All things are lawful." As in 6:12, Paul agrees and disagrees with this Corinthian slogan. Yes, all things being equal; no, if doing what is lawful for a person of strong conscience results in leading a person of weak conscience into sin. In such a case, "not all things build up" (v 23b). The rule for all, strong and weak, is: "Let no one seek his own good, but the good of his neighbor."

10:25-26 Eat whatever is sold in the meat market. This practical advice is directed to all, but especially to the weak. They need to reach maturity. Not asking questions (v 25) is the first step (scrupulous persons are notorious for asking questions). Remembering that everything on earth (even idol food) comes from God (and therefore is good in itself) is the second step (v 26).

10:27-28 If one of the unbelievers invites you to dinner. In Corinth, where Christians were in the minority, invitations to dinner might frequently come from friends who were pagans and who served food sacrificed to idols. In this case, Paul advises: "Ask no questions." His ensuing words are meant to safeguard freedom. If, however, someone else has a scruple, do not eat the idol food, Paul advises. But he quickly qualifies: "Do not eat out of consideration for the man who informed you," implying that in such a case they might lead the person to go against his or her conscience.

10:29 For why should my liberty be determined by another man's scruples? One may give up the use of one's liberty for the sake of the weak, but the scruples of the weak do not in any way diminish or curtail liberty itself.

10:31-33 So, whether you eat or drink . . . do all to the glory of God. Doing all for the glory of God (v 31), not seeking one's own advantage (v 33b), but seeking the advantage of others that they may be saved (v 33c) is a good summary of Paul's program as a Christian and justifies him in urging the Corinthians: "Be imitators of me, as I am of Christ (11:1).

(3) 11:2-16: Men's and women's hairstyles

Paul's remarks about the table of the Lord in 10:14-22 bring to his mind the subject of Christian worship. In chs 11–14, he pursues this subject: 11:2-16 deals with hairstyles at worship; 11:17-34 deals with the Eucharistic celebration; and chs 12–14 deal with charismatic gifts and charismatic persons in the community's worship.

In his discussion of hairstyles in 11:2-16, Paul does not begin with his formula "Concerning . . . ," as he did in 7:1, 25; 8:1. It is not clear, therefore, whether he is responding to another question put to him by letter or simply commenting on information he has from friends.[43]

Text

11:2 I commend you because you remember me in everything and maintain the traditions even as I have delivered them to you. [3]But I want you to understand that the head of every man is Christ, the head of a woman is her husband, and the head of Christ is God. [4]Any man who prays or prophesies with his head covered dishonors his head, [5]but any woman who prays or prophesies with her head unveiled dishonors her head—it is the same as if her head were shaven. [6]For if a woman will not veil herself, then she should cut off her hair; but if it is disgraceful for a woman to be shorn or shaven, let her wear a veil. [7]For a man ought not to cover his head, since he is the image and glory of God; but woman is the glory of man. [8](For man was not made from woman, but woman from man. [9]Neither was man created for woman, but woman for man.) [10]That is why a woman ought to have a veil on her head, because of the angels. [11](Nevertheless, in the Lord woman is not independent of man nor man of woman; [12]for as woman was made from man, so man is now born of woman. And all things are from God.)

[13]Judge for yourselves; is it proper for a woman to pray to God with her head uncovered? [14]Does not nature itself teach you that for a man to wear long hair is degrading to him, [15]but if a woman has long hair, it is her

pride? For her hair is given to her for a covering. [16]If any one is disposed to be contentious, we recognize no other practice, nor do the churches of God.

Commentary

11:2 I commend you because you remember me in everything. The words sound like an indirect quotation from the Corinthians' letter. Presumably they had said something like the following: "We always remember you, Paul, and hold fast to the traditions just as you handed them on to us. However, we would like to know whether it is fitting for women to take part in worship with their heads uncovered (or, perhaps more exactly, with their hair cut short like a man's)?"

11:3-15 But I want you to understand. Paul's reply, however one understands it, should be understood against the limited sociological ambitus of the first century. It does not deal with doctrine but with conventionalized ways of dress and deportment — in this case, with the way men and women wore their hair in the Greek and Jewish cultures of the time. Paul does not consider the matter trivial, but neither does he consider it vital. Otherwise he would hardly say: "Judge for yourselves; is it proper for a woman to pray to God with her head uncovered?" (11:13). It certainly was not proper in the Jewish circles from which Paul came. And it seems entirely probable that in the churches founded by him, the Jewish custom was taken for granted. As Paul says, ". . . we recognize no other practice, nor do the churches of God" (11:16).

Paul's labored exegetical justification for hairstyles at worship in vv 3-16 comes, in all probability, from rabbinic discussions about the sexes according to Gn 2-3. For a more detailed explanation, the reader should consult the larger commentaries.[44] Of some importance, perhaps, is the opinion of some exegetes that both 11:2-16 and 14:33b-36 are interpolations by a conservative editor at the end of the first century who wanted to claim Paul's authority for institutionalizing the stringent limitations on women's participation in worship that had become common by that time.[45] Of more importance, however, is the opinion of those who see Paul concerned about something far more important than simple hairstyles. As R. Scroggs suggests, Paul's brusque conclusion, labored argumentation, peevish tone, and pitiful logic may indicate a hidden agenda. His major concern, hidden perhaps even from himself, may have been a fear of the homosexuality so prevalent in Greek society and so catered to by erasing natural distinctions between the sexes.[46] Whatever is to be said for changing hairstyles, it may be accepted as normal for a woman to have long hair and for a man to have short hair. It may even be considered a natural distinction between the sexes. The removal of this natural distinction and its association with homosexuality may well have been at the origin of Paul's disquiet.

(4) Community and the Eucharist (11:17-34)

Paul's displeasure with the way the Corinthians were celebrating the Lord's supper is a subject for which he had already laid down the fundamental principle with his discussion in 10:14-22 about the differences between the table of the Lord and the table of demons: "Because there is one bread, we who are many are one body, for we all partake of the one bread" (10:17). In their celebration of the Eucharist, the Corinthians are forgetting that they are one body, one community, the body of Christ, and that there is no room in such a community for selfish disdain for the poor. The Eucharist commemorates Christ's death, his total giving of himself for others. One cannot truly celebrate the Eucharist in an atmosphere of selfishness. Paul deals with the problem and its solution by using his typical A-B-A' format, and in this case the parallels between section (a) and section (a') are particularly helpful in solving the exegetical problems in interpreting section (a').

Parallel structure

(a) The Lord's supper is ignored (11:17-22).
   (b) The supper is "in remembrance" of Jesus' death (11:23-26).
(a') The solution of the problem (11:27-34)

Text

(a)   11:17 But in the following instructions I do not commend you, because **when you come together** it is not for the better but for the worse. [18]For, in the first place, when you assemble **as a church,** I hear that there are divisions among you; and I partly believe it, [19]for there must be factions among you in order that those who are genuine among you may be recognized. [20]**When you meet together,** it is not the Lord's supper that you **eat.** [21]For in **eating,** each one goes ahead **with his own meal,** and one is **hungry** and another is drunk. [22]What! Do you not have **houses to eat and drink in?** Or do you **despise the church of God** and humiliate those who have nothing? What shall I say to you? Shall I **commend** you in this? No, I will not.

(b)   [23]For I received from the Lord what I also delivered to you, that the Lord Jesus on the night when he was betrayed took bread, [24]and when he had given thanks, he broke it, and said, "This is my body which is for you. Do this in remembrance of me." [25]In the same way also the cup, after supper, saying, "This cup is the new covenant in my blood. Do this, as often as you drink it, in remembrance of me." [26]For as often as you eat this bread and drink the cup, you proclaim the Lord's death until he comes.

(a')   [27]Whoever, therefore, **eats** the bread or **drinks** the cup of the Lord **in an unworthy manner** will be guilty of profaning the body and blood of the Lord. [28]Let a man examine himself, and so **eat** of the bread and **drink** of the cup. [29]For any one who **eats** and **drinks without discerning the body eats** and **drinks** judgment upon himself. [30]That is why many of you are weak and ill, and some have died. [31]But if we judged ourselves truly, we should not be judged. ³²But when we are judged by the Lord, we are chastened so that we may not be condemned along with the world. ³³So then, my brethren, **when you come together to eat,** wait for one another—³⁴if any one is **hungry,** let him **eat at home**—lest **you come together** to be condemned. About the other things I will give directions when I come.

Commentary

(a) The Lord's supper is ignored (11:17-22).

11:17-22 But in the following instructions I do not commend you. Paul's information is that there are not only factions in the community (v 18) but that when the Corinthians meet for the Eucharist, they are not eating the Lord's supper, but rather, in their avid concern for eating the common meal that was part of the Lord's supper, they are ignoring both the poor and the Lord's supper itself (vv 19-22).[47] The fault is twofold: first, the desecration of the Lord's supper; second, a blatant factionalism that gives the lie to the unity the Lord's supper is meant to signify and bring about and at the same time embarrasses the poor who go hungry while the richer members gorge themselves and get drunk.

Before giving a practical solution to the problem (vv 27-34), Paul first deals with the theological significance of the Lord's supper (vv 23-26). If the Corinthians can be brought to appreciate the Lord's supper as done "in remembrance" of his death and of the new covenant (vv 24-26), the problem with the poor will take care of itself.

(b) The supper is "in remembrance" of Jesus' death (11:23-26).

11:23-26 For I received from the Lord what I also delivered to you. Between his criticism of their scandalous behavior at the celebration of the Eucharist (vv 17-22) and his practical solution to the problem (vv 27-34), Paul inserts a reminder to the Corinthians of the tradition concerning the Eucharist that he had passed on to them (vv 23-25). He does so in order to remind them of the significance of this tradition in relation to their conduct (vv 27-34). The exegetical difficulties of the whole section have exercised commentators for centuries. They are dealt with in the major commentaries and in a number of recent studies.[48]

The immediate difficulty is to explain why Paul inserted this section at all. Why did he not simply speak about the problem as he does in vv 17-22 and then give the solution he had arrived at in vv 27-34? Section (b), in other words, must have some relationship with sections (a) and (a'). What is there in the tradition of the Lord's supper that pertains to the problem in vv 17-22? Our contention is that Paul recounts the tradition not just to repeat what he had preached to the Corinthians at an earlier date but to argue that the Eucharist was instituted to emphasize for Christians the significance of the death of Jesus. The Corinthians must take to heart the Eucharist as the remembrance of Jesus' death and what that death signified in relationship to their conduct toward members of the community (body).

In vv 23-25, Paul reminds the Corinthians of the tradition. The Lord's supper took place on the night of the betrayal (v 23c). The significant acts were those Jesus performed in relation to the bread and the wine (vv 23d-24a). Repeating what Jesus did and said is to be done as a remembrance of his death (vv 24b-25) until he comes again (v 26). It follows, therefore, that the Eucharist is centered on the death of Christ for all and is the sacrament of the Church to be celebrated in the in-between time (the time of the Church) that is to elapse between the historical death of Jesus on the cross and the time of his second coming.

This means that Paul is once again invoking the theology of the cross, and in all probability against the same kind of thinking dealt with in chs 1–4, namely, the thinking of the exaltation-theology enthusiasts. He does so to remind them that the Eucharist they celebrate is itself a call to "cross" theology, which is a theology of sacrifice of self for the sake of one's brethren. The Jesus "given" for mankind calls upon Christians, when they celebrate the Eucharist, to give themselves for others as he gave himself. Those who do not are not doing this "in remembrance" of Jesus' death (v 24).

(a') The solution of the problem (11:27-34)

11:27-32 Whoever . . . eats . . . or drinks . . . in an unworthy manner. The opening words of section (a') hark back to section (a) by repeating a number of times such words as *eat, drink, when you come together to eat, hungry,* and *eating at home.* Paul's point in section (a') is that those who eat or drink at the Eucharistic table as if this meal were no different from any other meal are not "discerning" the body and blood of Jesus. Those who eat and drink without any concern for the poorer members of the community are showing that they do not understand the real significance of the Eucharist. The Eucharist calls upon Christians to remember the death of Jesus and to be concerned for the members of Christ's body just as Jesus was concerned for them.

11:28-29 Let a man examine himself. The examination Paul calls for is discernment of the body: "For any one who eats and drinks without discerning the body eats and drinks judgment upon himself." What "body" is Paul talking about? In section (a), the problem was with the community body. There were factions and there was bad treatment of the poor. Here in (a'), the parallel of section (a), there is good reason to believe Paul is again speaking about the community when he speaks about discernment of the "body." Those who participate in the Eucharist without adverting to the members of the community (body) are guilty of breaking up the community and are therefore guilty of eating and drinking to their own damnation.

11:30 That is why many of you are weak and ill, and some have died. The association of disease and death with sin was common in Jewish circles. Disease and death were linked with the forces of evil, and just as to cure a man was to conquer the forces of evil, so to be guilty of sin was to place oneself under the dominion of evil and to be liable to suffer disease and death as a consequence. The sin presupposed here is the sin of ignoring the poorer members of the community, i.e., "not discerning the body."

11:32 that we may not be condemned along with the world. For Paul, the "world" does not consist of all human beings but only of those who are allied with the forces of evil in their warfare against the kingdom of God.

11:33-34 So then, my brethren, when you come together to eat. Paul's regulation—that the Corinthians eat before they come to the Eucharistic meal (v 34a) and then wait until all are gathered to celebrate the Lord's supper (v 33)—aims at only one thing: the celebration of the Eucharist in such a way that it will be *theologically* understood. In view of the fact that many who had worked all day might suffer serious hunger pains while waiting for the whole community to gather for the Eucharistic supper, the regulation makes eminent sense. Hunger pains would not contribute to a "theological" appreciation of the Eucharist. Paul says nothing about sharing with the poor, not because it is unimportant but because it is less important than truly understanding the significance of the Eucharist. He probably took up the problem of sharing with the poor at another time. As he says: "About the other things [and sharing with the poor would probably be one of these "other things"] I will give directions when I come" (v 34c).

(5) 12:1-14:40: Charismatic gifts and the community

Paul's discussion of the charismatic gifts is arranged in an exquisitely balanced chiastic format of three sections: A (ch 12); B (ch 13); and A' (ch 14), each of which is further divided into similarly balanced a-b-a' subsections. Advertence to this format helps to solve many problems in chs 12–14, not the least of which is the contention of some scholars that the sublime hymn to love in ch 13 is a later interpolation by Paul or some other author.

Parallel structure

A (12:1-31): Criteria for evaluating the gifts

    (a) **One** Spirit but **many different gifts** (12:1-11)
        (b) One body but many different members (12:12-26)
    (a') The **many different gifts** in the **one** body (12:27-31)

B (13:1-13): Apparent digression: Love is the fundamental criterion.

    (a) It is love alone that counts (13:1-3).
        (b) It is love alone that triumphs (13:4-7).
    (a') It is love alone that endures (13:8-13).

A' (14:1-40): Practical advice for charismatics

  (a) **Better to prophesy than to speak in tongues** (14:1-5)
    (b) Tongue-speaking does not build up the community (14:6-25).
  (a') **Better to prophesy than to speak in tongues** (14:26-40)

In the whole of Paul's discussion of the gifts in chs 12–14, one major problem stands out: What was the situation in the Corinthian community that prompted the Corinthians to ask Paul a question "concerning spiritual gifts" (12:1)? As we shall see, the clue to both the question and the problem that prompted the question is given by Paul in the A' section of his chiastic format, i.e., in ch 14. In his discussion of divisive teachers in chs 1–4, Paul dealt with the practical solution to the problem in the A' section of the discussion, i.e., 3:1–4:21. In chs 8–10, he gave his practical solution to the problem of eating idol meat in 10:23-33, the A' section. In a similar manner, in chs 12–14, Paul gives his practical solution to the Corinthians' problem in 14:1-40, the A' section of chs 12–14. This leads us to believe that the question the Corinthians asked Paul had something to do with the problem of charismatics who were either making too much of the gift of tongues or were exercising it in such a way that they were disrupting the liturgical gatherings. If this is kept in mind, it will help considerably in clarifying the direction of Paul's argumentation in chs 12–14.

A (12:1-31): Criteria for evaluating the gifts

Text

(a)   12:1 Now concerning spiritual gifts, brethren, I do not want you to be uninformed. [2]You know that when you were heathen, you were led astray to dumb idols, however you may have been moved. [3]Therefore I want you to understand that no one speaking by the Spirit of God ever says "Jesus be cursed!" and no one can say "Jesus is Lord" except by the Holy Spirit.
    [4]Now there are varieties of **gifts,** but the same Spirit; [5]and there are varieties of service, but the same Lord; [6]and there are varieties of working, but it is the same God who inspires them all in every one. [7]To each is given the manifestation of the Spirit for the common good. [8]To one is given through the Spirit the utterance of wisdom, and to another the utterance of knowledge according to the same Spirit, [9]to another faith by the same Spirit, to another gifts of **healing** by the one Spirit, [10]to another the working of **miracles,** to another **prophecy,** to another the ability to distinguish between spirits, to another various kinds of **tongues,** to another the **interpretation** of tongues. [11]All these are inspired by one and the same Spirit, who apportions to each one individually as he wills.

(b)   [12]For just as the body is one and has many members, and all the members of the body, though many, are one body, so it is with Christ. [13]For by one Spirit we were all baptized into one body — Jews or Greeks, slaves or free — and all were made to drink of one Spirit. [14]For the body does not consist of one member but of many. [15]If the foot should say,

"Because I am not a hand, I do not belong to the body," that would not make it any less a part of the body. ¹⁶And if the ear should say, "Because I am not an eye, I do not belong to the body," that would not make it any less a part of the body. ¹⁷If the whole body were an eye, where would be the hearing? If the whole body were an ear, where would be the sense of smell? ¹⁸But as it is, God arranged the organs in the body, each one of them, as he chose. ¹⁹If all were a single organ, where would the body be? ²⁰As it is there are many parts, yet one body. ²¹The eye cannot say to the hand, "I have no need of you," nor again the head to the feet, "I have no need of you." ²²On the contrary, the parts of the body which seem to be weaker are indispensable, ²³and those parts of the body which we think less honorable we invest with the greater honor, and our unpresentable parts are treated with greater modesty, ²⁴which our more presentable parts do not require. But God has so adjusted the body, giving the greater honor to the inferior part, ²⁵that there may be no discord in the body, but that the members may have the same care for one another. ²⁶If one member suffers, all suffer together; if one member is honored, all rejoice together.

(a′) ²⁷Now you are the body of Christ and individually members of it. ²⁸And God has appointed in the church first apostles, second **prophets,** third teachers, then workers of **miracles,** then **healers,** helpers, administrators, speakers in various kinds of **tongues.** ²⁹Are all apostles? Are all **prophets?** Are all teachers? Do all work **miracles?** ³⁰Do all possess gifts of **healing?** Do all speak with **tongues?** Do all **interpret?** ³¹But earnestly desire the higher **gifts.** And I will show you a still more excellent way.

Commentary

(a) One Spirit but many different gifts (12:1-11)

12:1 Now concerning spiritual gifts. Paul's discussion of the gifts begins, as in 7:1, 25; 8:1, with the word "concerning" and suggests that here again he is replying to a question put to him by the Corinthians in their letter. The question is anything but clear here in ch 12, but, as we suggested above, Paul's downgrading of the gift of tongues in ch 14 makes it reasonably certain that the problem had a great deal to do with the gift and use of tongue-speaking in the community.

12:2 when you were heathen. In the mystery cults of the pagans, individuals under the influence of enthusiastic seizures might say almost anything, no matter how wild, nonsensical, and even blasphemous.⁴⁹ Christians, however—and this is Paul's first fundamental principle for understanding the gifts of the Spirit—are led by the Spirit and therefore could never utter such blasphemous words as "Jesus be cursed!"⁵⁰

12:3 "Jesus be cursed!" How any Christian could say this is difficult to understand. Some exegetes think that Paul is using the curse as a simple but totally unreal example to serve as a contrast to the statement "Jesus is Lord." Others suggest that they are the words backsliding Jewish Christians were compelled to pronounce publicly if they wanted to recant and return to the synagogue. Others, like W. Schmithals, claim that the curse is a real example and suggest that the words can be explained as characteristic of a Gnostic attitude toward the humanity of Jesus.[51] No solution is certain.

12:4-11 Now there are varieties of gifts. Paul's second principle deals with the origin and purpose of the gifts. It is succinctly expressed in v 7: "To each is given the manifestation of the Spirit for the common good." The letter as a whole deals with the common good or upbuilding of the community, and the theme of building runs through the letter (cf. 3:5-15; 8:1; 10:23; 14:3-5, 12, 17, 26). Here Paul is stressing both unity and diversity — unity to draw attention to the giver of the gifts and to thereby counter any boasting on the part of self-important charismatics; and diversity to emphasize that many, rather than just a select few, are given gifts by the Spirit for the building up of the community. Paul's adroit use of the words "the same Spirit," "the same Lord," and "the same God" should be noted (vv 4-6). This is one of the earliest references to the Trinity in the New Testament.

(b) One body but many different members (12:12-26)

12:12-16 just as the body is one. Paul's third principle is that the community needs many different charismatics, each with his or her individual gifts, if it is to function well. To drive home his point, Paul uses the metaphor of the body — a metaphor utilized as early as 494 B.C. by Menenius Agrippa, who made use of it to convince the Roman plebeians that their interests were the same as those of the patricians who formed with them part of the same body politic. Seneca, Epictetus, and the Gnostics made use of the same metaphor.[52] Even though Paul uses the metaphor in relation to the community in Corinth and not in relation to the Church as a whole, his underlying postulate for the metaphor is that all Christians are united as one body with Christ, because all of them share in the one life-giving power of the Spirit that comes from the Father through Christ and makes all who believe one with Christ and with one another.[53] This underlying postulate was already implicit in Paul's questions earlier in the letter, e.g.: "Is Christ divided?" (1:13); "Do you not know that you are God's temple and that God's Spirit dwells in you?" (3:16); "Do you not know that your bodies are members of Christ? Shall I take the members of Christ and make them members of a prostitute?" (6:15); and in the statement: "Because there is one bread, we who are many are one body, for we all partake of the one bread" (10:17). It is Paul's teaching about the unity of Christians in Christ.[54] He will take it up again in Rom 12:1-8.

12:17-26 If the whole body were an eye. Paul uses the metaphor of the body in these verses not so much to emphasize the life-principle that unifies the body-community as to emphasize the need in the community for many people with different individual gifts (cf. vv 18-20). Just as all the members of the body have need of one another and work for the common good of the body, so all the different members of the community with their different individual gifts have need of one another and must work for the building up of the one community. There is a strong reprise here of the teaching in chs 3–4 about service – all are servants in some sense, and those with gifts are called to be servants in a special way. Paul goes out of his way in the metaphor to stress the fact that even the humblest members of the community have gifts and must be respected (vv 22-25). This aspect of the metaphor suggests that Paul thinks it needful for some of the Corinthians to recognize and respect the gifts of others. All in all, the situation is not unlike that in chs 1–4, where the community was breaking up into factions on account of different prestigious teachers. Here they seem to be dividing into groups of charismatics with flamboyant gifts such as tongues and prophecy, and charismatics with less obvious and perhaps less easily recognizable gifts. Paul will have no part with those who boast of their own gifts and look down on or deny the gifts of others.

(a') The many different gifts in the one body (12:27-31)

12:28 first apostles, second prophets, third teachers. Section (a') concludes with a reprise of the enumeration of the gifts mentioned in 12:4-11 and with Paul's evaluation of the gifts according to the criterion of their capacity to build up the community (cf. 12:7). Only the first three, pertaining to the ministry of the word, are listed in an order of importance. The others are mentioned in order to emphasize the main point of section (a), namely, that there is a need for a multiplicity of different gifts (cf. 12:4-6). The first – apostles – signified for Paul itinerant evangelists who preached the gospel, founded Christian communities, and manifested in their own life the death and resurrection of Christ (cf. 1 Cor 4:9-13; 2 Cor 10-13).[55] In the Gospels and Acts, an apostle signified one who had witnessed the risen Christ and had been sent by him to preach the gospel.

The second – prophets – meant those who encouraged, edified, comforted, and inspired their fellow Christians by speaking to them during their liturgical celebrations (cf. 14:3, 6). The prophet's gift was properly inspirational preaching.

The third – teachers – meant those who instructed others in the meaning of the gospel and the Old Testament Scriptures. Their gift was one of illuminating interpretation combined with theological insight.

The other gifts are neither enumerated nor, with the exception of tongue-speaking (cf. 14:1ff), described by Paul. They are simply listed. It should be noted that the gift of tongues is given the last place on the list.

12:29-30 Are all apostles? Paul's concluding questions are rhetorical, and the answer to all is a resounding negative. This indicates that Paul's primary purpose in 12:1-31 is to make the Corinthians recognize and realize that many different individual gifts are necessary for the building up of the community. Some charismatics and their gifts may be more necessary for the common good than others, but the community needs many other gifted persons; all in some way contribute to the health and building up of the body.[56] This conclusion, along with Paul's a-b-a' format, proves that his intent is to argue the need for many and different gifted people to work together for the building up of the community.

12:31 And I will show you a still more excellent way. This verse constitutes Paul's transition to ch 13, where he will deal with the ultimate criterion for evaluating the gifts.

B (13:1-13): Apparent digression: Love is the fundamental criterion.

Paul's hymn to love sounds like a digression and looks like an interpolation, but it is actually a critically important part of his whole argumentation in chs 12–14.[57] It looks like an interpolation because 12:31 ("And I will show you a still more excellent way") and 14:1 ("Make love your aim") have all the earmarks of editorial links used to stitch in ch 13 between chs 12 and 14. Also, it is readily noticeable that if one eliminates the stitches in 12:31 and 14:1, the whole of ch 13 could be eliminated without breaking the continuity between chs 12 and 14. This is the principal reason why some authors consider ch 13 to be an interpolation.[58] This is possible but not necessarily true. It is true that chs 12 and 14 go together and that ch 13 could be excluded without breaking the line of thought from ch 12 to ch 14. However, it is equally true that, whether Paul wrote ch 13 for this context or for some other occasion and interpolated it here himself, the hymn fits beautifully between chs 12 and 14 and elucidates magnificently Paul's central argument stated earlier in 8:1: "Knowledge puffs up, but love builds up," which may be paraphrased here to read: "Gifts puff up, but love builds up."

The arguments given for Paul's writing of ch 13 for some other occasion are that the literary quality, the powerful rhythm, and the admirably chosen vocabulary of the chapter are such that they suggest an independent writing in a different, more exalted frame of mind and for a more solemn occasion. But it should be remembered that Paul was quite capable of sudden and brilliant flights of oratory. His glowing description of apostleship earlier in the same letter (4:9-13) is one example among many, and no one denies that Paul wrote 4:9-13 for the context in which it stands. Ch 13, however, fits its context as well or better than 4:9-13 fits its context.[59] It follows Paul's enumeration of the gifts in 12:27-30, and in 13:2-3 Paul deals specifically with the relationship between the gifts and love. Moreover, the last gifts mentioned in 12:30 are the gifts of tongues and the interpretation of tongues, and it is precisely with the gift of tongues that Paul begins when he intones his hymn to love with the words: "If I speak in the tongues of men and of angels, but have not love, I am a noisy gong or a clanging cymbal."[60] Ch 13 sounds like a digression only if one is not aware that Paul frequently makes what appear to be, but are not, digressions in his mode of argumentation. This has been demonstrated for chs 1–4 and 8–10. Ch 13 is to chs 12–14 what 2:6-16 is to chs 1–4 and what 9:1-10:22 is to chs 8–10.

What Paul accomplished in chs 8–10 by contrasting "knowledge [which taken by itself] puffs up" with "love [which] builds up," he accomplishes here by contrasting charismatic gifts, which taken by themselves can puff up (chs 12 and 14), with love (ch 13), which alone can build up the community in Christ. As in chs 8–10, however, it is not a question of one or the other but of both together. Paul did not speak against "knowledge" in 8:1ff; he only insisted that knowledge must be informed with love if it is to help build up the community. Here he is not against the gifts, even the gift of tongues, but is insisting that all the gifts in the world without love amount to nothing.

Literary questions apart, it is the content of ch 13 that is important. Paul had said earlier that "love builds up" (8:1). Here, for all practical purposes, he says that it is love alone that builds up. The argumentation, as K. Barth sees it, follows three steps: vv 1-3: "It is love alone that counts"; vv 4-7: "love alone that triumphs"; vv 8-13: "love alone that endures."[61]

Text

(a) 13:1 If I speak in the **tongues** of men and of angels, but have not **love,** I am a noisy gong or a clanging cymbal. [2]And if I have **prophetic powers,** and understand all mysteries and all **knowledge,** and if I have all **faith,** so as to remove mountains, but have not **love,** I am nothing. [3]If I give away all I have, and if I deliver my body to be burned, but have not **love,** I gain nothing.

(b) [4]Love is patient and kind; love is not jealous or boastful; [5]it is not arrogant or rude. Love does not insist on its own way; it is not irritable or resentful; [6]it does not rejoice at wrong, but rejoices in the right. [7]Love bears all things, believes all things, hopes all things, endures all things.

(a′) [8]**Love** never ends; as for **prophecies,** they will pass away; as for **tongues,** they will cease; as for **knowledge,** it will pass away. [9]For our **knowledge** is imperfect and our **prophecy** is imperfect; [10]but when the perfect comes, the imperfect will pass away. [11]When I was a child, I spoke like a child, I thought like a child, I reasoned like a child; when I became a man, I gave up childish ways. [12]For now we see in a mirror dimly, but then face to face. Now I know in part; then I shall understand fully, even as I have been fully understood. [13]So faith, hope, **love** abide, these three; but the greatest of these is **love.**

Commentary

(a) It is love alone that counts (13:1-3).

13:1 If I speak in the tongues of men and of angels, but have not love.
The gift of tongues, mentioned last in 12:30, is first here because Paul
wishes to downplay it as much as possible (cf. 14:1ff). Love (*agapē*), which
Paul will attempt to describe positively in vv 4-7, is not a virtue, not a
charismatic gift, not even anything one can know on earth by natural
knowledge. Love is God's gift and a share in his love. Life in love is
equivalent to life in Christ. Without it, all the charismatic gifts count for
nothing.

13:2-3 And if I have prophetic powers. Unlike the gift of tongues, the
gift of prophecy is most helpful for building up the community. Nevertheless, even the gift of prophecy without love is nothing. In short, since the
Christian literally lives through love, no gift, not even a multiplicity of gifts,
can substitute for love.

(b) It is love alone that triumphs (13:4-7).

13:4-7 Love is patient and kind. The description of love in these verses
is probably based on Paul's own understanding of Christ as a person and
makes excellent sense if one substitutes the word "Christ" for the word
"love." Thus, Christ is patient and kind; Christ is not jealous or boastful;
Christ is not arrogant or rude. Christ does not insist on his own way; he is
not irritable or resentful; he does not rejoice at wrong but rejoices in the
right. Christ bears all things, believes all things, hopes all things, endures all
things [of us and for us].[62]

For all practical purposes, what Paul says is that "Christ is love." The
statement is equivalent to the Johannine description of God: "God is love"
(1 Jn 4:8).[63] For those in Christ, therefore, love is a life-force, a gift of "being" that is like the "being" of God who is love. Possessing this love and living the new life in Christ by means of this love is for human beings the difference between Plato's man in the cave and man in the sun. Our problem is
that we hardly begin to fathom what love is. As Paul says in v 12, we see
only its reflection in a mirror instead of seeing or grasping love itself. We do
not really know what it is. Paradoxically, we cannot have love until we give
it; yet we cannot give what we do not have. More properly put, love (*agapē*)
cannot exist at all until it is given because its givenness is its being, except in
God, who is by essence and being love itself.

(a') It is love alone that endures (13:8-13).

13:8-12 Love never ends. Paul concludes his hymn to love as he began
it — with references to the gifts. In vv 1-3, he asserted that gifts such as
tongues, prophecy, and knowledge are nothing without love. Here he pro-

claims the enduring existence of love and contrasts it with the ephemeral and passing existence of the gifts (vv 8-10). The contrast between childhood and manhood in v 11, which may be an indirect criticism of the Corinthians' childish delight in their charismatic gifts, is expressed by means of the rhetorical "I" and thus parallels the use of the rhetorical "I" (for "anyone") in vv 1-3.

13:13 So faith, hope, love abide. If this statement is interpreted as referring to the future life, it makes no sense. In the future life there is place for love but not for faith and hope. One does not need faith for what one sees nor hope for what one has. If the statement is interpreted as a contrast between the present childhood stage of the Corinthians' Christian life (cf. vv 8-12 and 3:1) and their potential future Christian life when they fully appreciate the critical importance of love, then the statement makes excellent sense. When they have grown up spiritually, they will realize that the gifts are transitory and that the essence of the Christian life consists in faith, hope, and love. These abide and must abide throughout our lives on earth, and the greatest of the three is love.

A' (14:1-40): Practical advice for charismatics

The position of ch 14, the A' section of chs 12–14, suggests that the problem about which the Corinthians inquired in 12:1 ("Concerning spiritual gifts") had a great deal to do with the gift of tongues. The position of ch 14 is important because, as we have shown for chs 1–4 and 8–10, Paul's mode of argumentation is to deal first with the more theological aspects of a problem and then with the practical solution of the problem. Since ch 14 deals almost exclusively with the misuse of the gift of tongues in the midst of the Christian assembly, we assume that the Corinthians' question in 12:1 had to do with the evaluation and use of this gift.[64] As in 12:1-31 and 13:1-13, the argumentation follows Paul's customary a-b-a' format.

Text

(a) 14:1 Make love your aim, and earnestly desire the spiritual gifts, especially that you may **prophesy.** [2]For one who speaks in a tongue speaks not to men but to God; for no one understands him, but he utters mysteries in the Spirit. [3]On the other hand, he who **prophesies** speaks to men for their **upbuilding** and **encouragement** and consolation. [4]He who speaks in a tongue **edifies** himself, but **he who prophesies edifies the church.** [5]Now I want you all to speak in tongues, but **even more to prophesy. He who prophesies** is greater than he who speaks in **tongues,** unless some one interprets, so that the **church** may be **edified.**

(b) [6]Now, brethren, if I come to you speaking in tongues, how shall I benefit you unless I bring you some revelation or knowledge or prophecy or teaching? [7]If even lifeless instruments, such as the flute or the harp, do not give distinct notes, how will any one know what is played? [8]And if the bugle gives an indistinct sound, who will get ready for battle? [9]So with yourselves; if you in a tongue utter speech that is not intelligible, how will any one know what is said? For you will be speaking into the air. [10]There are doubtless many different languages in the world, and none is without meaning; [11]but if I do not know the meaning of the language, I shall be a foreigner to the speaker and the speaker a foreigner to me. [12]So with yourselves; since you are eager for manifestations of the Spirit, strive to excel in building up the church.

[13]Therefore, he who speaks in a tongue should pray for the power to interpret. [14]For if I pray in a tongue, my spirit prays but my mind is unfruitful. [15]What am I to do? I will pray with the spirit and I will pray with the mind also; I will sing with the spirit and I will sing with the mind also. [16]Otherwise, if you bless with the spirit, how can any one in the position of an outsider say the "Amen" to your thanksgiving when he does not know what you are saying? [17]For you may give thanks well enough, but the other man is not edified. [18]I thank God that I speak in tongues more than you all; [19]nevertheless in church I would rather speak five words with my mind, in order to instruct others, than ten thousand words in a tongue.

(a')   [20]Brethren, do not be children in your thinking; be babes in evil, but in thinking be mature. [21]In the law it is written, "By men of strange tongues and by the lips of foreigners will I speak to this people, and even then they will not listen to me, says the Lord." [22]Thus, tongues are a sign not for believers but for unbelievers, while **prophecy** is not for unbelievers but for believers. [23]If, therefore, the whole **church** assembles and all speak in tongues, and outsiders or unbelievers enter, will they not say that you are mad? [24]But if all **prophesy,** and an unbeliever or outsider enters, he is convicted by all, he is called to account by all, [25]the secrets of his heart are disclosed; and so, falling on his face, he will worship God and declare that God is really among you.

[26]What then, brethren? When you come together, each one has a hymn, a lesson, a revelation, a tongue, or an interpretation. Let all things be done for **edification.** [27]If any speak in a tongue, let there be only two or at most three, and each in turn; and let one **interpret.** [28]But if there is no one to **interpret,** let each of them keep silence in church and speak to himself and to God. [29]Let two or three **prophets** speak, and let the others weigh what is said. [30]If a revelation is made to another sitting by, let the first be silent. [31]For you can all **prophesy** one by one, so that all may learn and all be **encouraged;** [32]and the spirits of **prophets** are subject to **prophets.** [33]For God is not a God of confusion but of peace.

As in all the churches of the saints, [34]the women should keep silence in the churches. For they are not permitted to speak, but should be subordinate, as even the law says. [35]If there is anything they desire to know, let them ask their husbands at home. For it is shameful for a woman to speak in church. [36]What! Did the word of God originate with you, or are you the only ones it has reached? [37]If any one thinks that he is a **prophet,** or spiritual, he should acknowledge that what I am writing to you is a command of the Lord. [38]If any one does not recognize this, he is not recognized.

³⁹So, my brethren, earnestly desire to **prophesy,** and do not forbid speaking in tongues; ⁴⁰but all things should be done decently and in order.

Commentary

(a) Better to prophesy than to speak in tongues (14:1-5)

14:1-5 earnestly desire the spiritual gifts, especially that you may prophesy. Whatever the precise problem with tongues, Paul's practical advice is summed up here in 14:1b: "Earnestly desire . . . especially that you may prophesy," and in 14:5: "Now I want you all to speak in tongues, but even more to prophesy."[65] Almost the whole of Paul's argumentation both here in 14:1-5 and in 14:6-19 is based on the premise that while the gift of tongues is a genuine and commendable gift, it is also the least important of the gifts and the one most prone to misuse and exaggeration. To make these points, Paul compares the gift of tongues with the gift of prophecy and bears down hard on the contrast between the two in relation to the basic criterion for evaluation of gifts — their potential for the building up of the community. Against this criterion, the gift of tongues is almost, but not quite, relegated to the status of a non-gift. Almost but not quite. As G. Montague says: "The fact that Paul is at pains to balance the use of tongues with other gifts has often led interpreters to overlook the positive values he takes for granted in the gift: (1) It is a language of genuine prayer to God (14:2); (2) By it one builds oneself up (14:4); (3) When accompanied by interpretation, its effect is the same as prophecy (14:5); (4) Paul would like all members of the community to speak in tongues (14:5); (5) Paul himself thanks God that he speaks in tongues more than any of the Corinthians (14:18); (6) Tongues are not to be forbidden (14:39); they are one of the gifts to be sought (14:1); (7) Paul is not trying to discourage tongues but merely to regulate their use."[66]

(b) Tongue-speaking does not build up the community (14:6-25).

Paul's argument in vv 6-25 is based on the premise he laid down in 14:3: "He who prophesies speaks to men for their upbuilding and encouragement and consolation." The gift of tongues, as he will show, has the least building potential of all. His advice, consequently, is: "Since you are eager for manifestations of the Spirit, strive to excel in building up the church" (14:12).

14:6 if I come to you speaking in tongues, how shall I benefit you? If Paul had come to Corinth and spoken in tongues, the Corinthians would not have understood him. Intelligibility is essential.

14:7-9 If even lifeless instruments. Musical instruments playing without sense any kind of notes confuse the listeners. So it is with tongue-speaking.

14:10-12 There are doubtless many different languages. We do not speak foreign languages to people if we want to communicate with them. If we do, we will be foreigners to them and they to us.

14:13-19 Therefore, he who speaks in a tongue should pray for the power to interpret. Tongue-speaking is unintelligible because it means nothing to the mind. It should, therefore, be accompanied by an interpretation; otherwise no one will be able to agree with it, i.e., say "Amen" (v 16), nor will anyone be "edified" (v 17).

14:20-25 Brethren, do not be children in your thinking. Paul's last argument, which is based on the reaction of outsiders to the community, begins with an appeal to the words of Isaiah (28:11-12), which insinuate that the Corinthians themselves are the "unbelievers" (vv 21-22). Then the main and obvious point is made that if outsiders hear members of the community speaking in tongues, they will think they are crazy (v 23); but if they hear them prophesy, they will be impressed and edified (vv 24-25).

(a') Better to prophesy than to speak in tongues (14:26-40)

14:26-32 What then, brethren? When you come together, each one. The rule of order in vv 26-32 gives us the earliest information in the New Testament about the manner in which worship was conducted in a primitive Christian community (see also 1 Cor 11:17-34). Nothing is said about a celebrant, whether bishop, priest, or elder. Paul perhaps takes one for granted. Almost everybody seems to take an active part in the celebration. Paul mentions psalm-singing, instructing, speaking in tongues, interpreting (v 26). Again, as in vv 6-25, he goes out of his way to put down tongue-speaking by limiting its use to two or three, and to no one at all if not accompanied by an interpretation (vv 27-28). A limit is also put on the number of prophets allowed to speak (vv 29-31), but it is not as severe as that on tongue-speaking. It does not have to be severe because, as Paul observes, "the spirits of prophets are subject to prophets. For God is not a God of confusion but of peace" (vv 32-33a). Paul may well be intimating that the spirits of the tongue-speakers are not always under their control.

14:33b-36 As in all the churches of the saints, the women should keep silence. H. Conzelmann says of this section: "In content it is in contradiction to 11:2ff, where the active participation of women is presupposed. . . . . This section is accordingly to be regarded as an interpolation . . . . . In this regulation we have a reflection of the bourgeois consolidation of the Church, roughly on the level of the Pastoral Epistles: it binds itself to the general custom."[67]

No interpreter likes to solve problems by postulating interpolations that conveniently do away with the problem. In this case, fortunately, there is a better way. It has been suggested that Paul's words in vv 33b-35 are not actually his words but rather a quotation from the letter the Corinthians wrote to him (cf. 7:1).[68] If this is true, then the words of v 35 contain Paul's outraged response to the demand of those who want women to keep silent in church. In favor of this explanation are the following: (1) Paul quotes other sayings of the Corinthians in his letter (cf. 1:12; 2:15; 6:12-13; 7:1b; 8:1, 4, 8; 10:23; 11:2; 15:12). So many quotations allow one to suspect that the harsh words of vv 33b-35 may also be a quotation. (2) This interpretation agrees with Paul's words about women prophesying in church in 1 Cor 11:5 and with his words about the equality of all in Gal 3:28. (3) An argument from the law such as that in v 34 sounds very strange in the mouth of Paul, but it would not be strange in the mouth of some of the Corinthians. (4) Most significantly, when Paul in v 36 says "are you the only ones," the words "only ones" are *masculine* in the Greek. Therefore, one might translate the whole passage as follows: "As in all the churches of the saints, the women (you say) should keep silence in the churches. For they are not permitted to speak but should be subordinate, as even the law says. If there is anything they desire to know, let them ask their husbands at home. For it is shameful for a woman to speak in church. What! Did the word of God originate with you (men), or are you (men) the only ones it has reached?"

14:37-38 If any one thinks that he is a prophet. Paul asserts his authority in these verses and thus sums up everything he has said in ch 14 about prophecy and tongue-speaking.

14:39-40 So, my brethren, earnestly desire to prophesy. Paul's conclusion reiterates what he said in 14:1-5 about the greater importance of prophecy over speaking in tongues. His last words, "all things should be done decently and in order," might well constitute a principle for all things liturgical.

Part IV (15:1-58): The resurrection and the resurrection body

Theologically speaking, 1 Cor 15 is critically important because it is the earliest apologetic argumentation in the whole of the New Testament for the physical resurrection of Jesus. Writing in the middle fifties, Paul explicitly states what he himself had taught the Corinthians about the resurrection when he first evangelized them around 51 A.D. This would date Paul's own testimony just twenty-one years after the resurrection. But there is more. Paul reminds his readers that what he had handed on to them in the year 51 was the "tradition" he himself had received (15:3). The "tradition," therefore, was even earlier and in all probability went back to the testimony of those like Peter and others mentioned in vv 6-7 who had seen Jesus in the flesh after his resurrection. This tradition, apologetically speaking, is the strongest possible argument for the physical resurrection of Jesus, because at the time Paul preached it, and even at the time when he wrote 1 Corinthians, many of the original witnesses of the resurrected Christ were still alive.

Our purpose, however, in explaining ch 15 is not to provide proofs for the physical resurrection of Christ. The literature on this aspect of the resurrection is abundant.[69] Our purpose is to try to understand how it could be that, despite Paul's own preaching on the physical resurrection of Jesus, there could nevertheless be people in the Corinthian community who denied the resurrection of the dead. At first sight this seems incredible. How could Christians deny the resurrection of the dead? Surprisingly, there are a number of ways in which one can say "I deny the resurrection of the dead" without absolutely denying all resurrection. Since we do not know which of these opinions Paul is attacking in 1 Cor 15, we shall have to look at each of them and then evaluate the argumentation in 1 Cor 15 to determine which of them Paul is against.

1) Under the influence of Greek philosophical teaching, Corinthian Christians may have affirmed the resurrection of the soul and denied the resurrection of the body, arguing that the body is the prison of the soul and that when the person dies, the soul rises but the body remains in the tomb.

2) Under the influence of Gnostic teaching, Corinthian Christians could quite easily have denied a physical resurrection of the dead. As W. Schmithals says: "The denial of the resurrection of the body is for Gnosticism a foundational dogma . . . . The motivation for the Gnostics' denial of the resurrection is the Gnostic dualism whose mythological background is too well known for it to require a detailed presentation here. Man, so far as he is *sarx* (flesh), is for the Gnostic not only perishable but also despicable . . . . The idea that this lifeless prison must first be awakened to life before the man himself attains genuine life appears to the Gnostic self-consciousness as blasphemy."[70] The Gnostics believed that they were saved and resurrected spiritually, not bodily, through *gnosis* (knowledge). In this sense, Gnostics could accept the resurrection of a spiritual element in man but not the resurrection of the materially evil body.

3) Corinthian Christians, who were not influenced either by Greek philosophical thinking or by Gnostic thinking, might still have held there was no resurrection on the grounds that the resurrection had already taken place at the time of baptism or at the time when they accepted Christ in faith. In 1 Cor 4:8, Paul identifies a group in Corinth who might well have claimed to be already risen with the exalted Christ.[71] These would be the followers of a fanaticist exaltation theology, of whom Paul says: "Already you are filled! Already you have become rich! Without us you have become kings! And would that you did reign, so that we might share the rule with you!" (1 Cor 4:8). Thinking similar to this may be behind the warning in 2 Tim 2:17-18: "Among them are Hymenaeus and Philetus, who have swerved from the truth by holding that the resurrection is past already."

4) Some Corinthian Christians may even have denied the resurrection of the dead on the grounds that the parousia would come before their death

and, as a consequence, there would be no need for a resurrection. This is improbable, but the opinion could be deduced from Paul's words in 1 Thes 4:17: "Then we who are alive, who are left, shall be caught up together with them in the clouds to meet the Lord in the air." If there is no death, there is no need for resurrection.

5) There is even a sense in which Paul himself could be said to deny the resurrection of the dead—not the resurrection of the person but the resurrection of the identical, physical body of the dead person. In ch 15:35ff, Paul insists on a bodily resurrection, but he seems also to insist that the resurrection body will be a spiritual body and therefore not identical with the dead body that goes into the grave and decomposes.

Since Paul himself apparently held that there was no resurrection of the identical physical body that went into the grave, it may be presumed that he was not arguing against this view but against one or more of the four other views.

The fourth of these may be dismissed on the grounds that Paul himself would still hold that there was indeed no death for those still alive at the parousia and therefore no resurrection in the strict sense, but that this was true only for those few alive at the parousia and not for the generality of Christians. He intimates as much in 1 Cor 15:51-53: "Lo! I tell you a mystery. We shall not all sleep [die], but we shall all be changed, in a moment, in the twinkling of an eye, at the last trumpet. For the trumpet will sound, and the dead will be raised imperishable, and we shall be changed. For this perishable nature must put on the imperishable, and this mortal nature must put on immortality." Paul's point is quite simply that the resurrection bodies of all will be different, they will be "changed"—both those who have died and who will therefore have to rise at the parousia and those also who are still alive at the parousia, who will not have to die and therefore will not have to rise. In short, it may be presumed that Paul's argumentation in ch 15 is not against those who held the fourth or the fifth view but against opponents who held to one or the other of the first three views.

What Paul's opponents really meant when they said "there is no resurrection of the dead" may never be determined exactly. It may even be that Paul himself did not know what meaning they attached to the statement. Be that as it may, the statement was more than enough to alarm Paul and to elicit from him the earliest argumentation in the New Testament for the historicity of the physical resurrection of Jesus and for the future physical resurrection of Christians from the dead.

The nature of Paul's argumentation in ch 15 should be noted. It is similar to the argumentation in chs 1–4; 8–10; 12–14 and may well be the key clue to Paul's main point in ch 15. In each of these previous sections, Paul first introduced his theme and dealt with it broadly (cf. chs 1–2 on the wisdom of the cross in general; ch 8 on the morality of eating idol meat; and ch 12 on the charismatic gifts). In the final section of his argumentation, he focused in on the main problem and gave his practical conclusions (cf. chs 3–4 on the function of teachers in the community; ch 10:23-33 on the practical solution to the question of eating idol meat; and ch 14 on the practical solution to the problem of overestimating the gift of tongues).

In 15:1-34, Paul looks with a widely focused lens on the basic question of physical resurrection from the dead. In 15:35-58, he looks with a narrowed focus at the real problem concerning the resurrection, namely, the refusal of some, either on philosophical or Gnostic grounds, to accept bodily resurrection of the dead.[72] If this is so — and we think it is — then the argumentation in 15:1-34 is preliminary to the basic issue taken up in 15:35-58, just as chs 1–2 are preliminary to chs 3–4; ch 8 to ch 10:23-33; and ch 12 to ch 14. This appears to be the way Paul's mind worked on problems: first the broad, then the narrow focus. In sum, this would mean that the key to Paul's central point in ch 15 lies not at the beginning of the chapter (the broad focus), but at the end (the narrow focus).

Paul asks two pivotal questions in ch 15: (1) "Now if Christ is preached as raised from the dead, how can some of you say that there is no resurrection of the dead?" (15:12). (2) "But someone will ask, 'How are the dead raised? With what kind of body do they come?'" (15:35).

His argumentation in 15:1-34 establishes the fact of the bodily resurrection of Jesus. However repugnant it may have been either to Greek philosophical thinking or to Gnostic thinking, it follows from the bodily resurrection of Christ that the resurrection of those who believe in him will also be a bodily resurrection. This is the central point of 15:35-58. In all probability, it was this, the resurrection of the body, that the Corinthians denied when they said "there is no resurrection of the dead" (15:12). Paul's argumentation follows his usual A-B-A' format:

Parallel structure

(a) Argumentation for the **bodily resurrection** of Christ (15:1-11); implications of this common preaching and tradition (15:12-19); first **apocalyptic scenario** (15:20-28)

(b) *Ad hominem* arguments for the resurrection (15:29-34)

(a') Argumentation for a **bodily resurrection** (15:35-49) and second **apocalyptic scenario** (15:50-58)

Text

15:1 Now I would remind you, brethren, in what terms I preached to you the gospel, which you received, in which you stand, [2]by which you are saved, if you hold it fast — unless you believed in vain.

[3]For I delivered to you as of first importance what I also received, that Christ **died** for our sins in accordance with the scriptures, [4]that he was

buried, that he was **raised** on the third day in accordance with the scriptures, ⁵and that he appeared to Cephas, then to the twelve. ⁶Then he appeared to more than five hundred brethren at one time, most of whom are still alive, though some have fallen asleep. ⁷Then he appeared to James, then to all the apostles. ⁸Last of all, as to one untimely born, he appeared also to me. ⁹For I am the least of the apostles, unfit to be called an apostle, because I persecuted the church of God. ¹⁰But by the grace of God I am what I am, and his grace toward me was not in vain. On the contrary, I worked harder than any of them, though it was not I, but the grace of God which is with me. ¹¹Whether then it was I or they, so we preach and so you believed.

¹²Now if Christ is preached as **raised from the dead,** how can some of you say that there is no **resurrection of the dead?** ¹³But if there is no **resurrection of the dead,** then Christ has not been raised; ¹⁴if Christ has not been **raised,** then our preaching is in vain and your faith is in vain. ¹⁵We are even found to be misrepresenting God, because we testified of God that he **raised** Christ, whom he did not raise if it is true that the **dead** are not **raised.** ¹⁶For if the dead are not **raised,** then Christ has not been **raised.** ¹⁷If Christ has not been **raised,** your faith is futile and you are still in your sins. ¹⁸Then those also who have fallen asleep in Christ have perished. ¹⁹If for this life only we have hoped in Christ, we are of all men most to be pitied.

²⁰But in fact Christ has been raised from the **dead,** the first fruits of those who have fallen asleep. ²¹For as by **a man** came **death,** by **a man** has come also the resurrection of the dead. ²²For as in **Adam** all die, so also in Christ shall all be made alive. ²³But each in his own order: Christ the first fruits, then at his coming those who belong to Christ. ²⁴Then comes the end, when he delivers the **kingdom to God** the Father after destroying every rule and every authority and power. ²⁵For he must reign until he has put all his enemies under his feet. ²⁶The last enemy to be destroyed is **death.** ²⁷"For God has put all things in subjection under his feet." But when it says, "All things are put in subjection under him," it is plain that he is excepted who put all things under him. ²⁸When all things are subjected to him, then the Son himself will also be subjected to him who put all things under him, that **God** may be everything to every one.

Commentary

(a) Argumentation for the bodily resurrection of Christ (15:1-11)

15:1-11 Now I would remind you, brethren. Paul reminds the Corinthians that at the time when they first became Christians, the gospel they accepted, which was the gospel *handed down by tradition* and preached by Paul and the other apostles, was. "that Christ died for our sins . . . was buried . . . was raised on the third day . . . appeared to Cephas, then to the twelve . . . then to more than five hundred brethren at one time . . . then to James, then to all the apostles" (vv 3-7).⁷³

Paul's argument, which lays the ground for the question in 15:12, is that Christ's bodily resurrection was central not only to what he himself had preached to the Corinthians but to the basic Christian tradition and to the preaching of all the apostles. The argument is terminated by an inclusion

with 15:1: "Whether then it was I or they, so we preach and so you
believed." The words "so you believed" (15:11) provide an inclusion with
"which you received" (15:1).

(a) Implications of this common preaching and tradition (15:12-19)

15:12-14   Now if Christ is preached as raised from the dead. If the Corinthians want to deny the resurrection of the dead as intellectually or
philosophically repugnant, then logically they must deny both what they believed at the time of their conversion and also what Paul and the apostles
still preach, namely, that Christ was raised bodily from the dead in such a
way that he was seen (vv 12-13). Since the resurrection is so central to the
tradition and the preached gospel, a denial of it eviscerates both the gospel
and the content of what the Corinthians believed when they were converted
(v 14).

15:15-19   We are even found to be misrepresenting God. In addition,
such a denial makes liars of the apostles (v 15) and makes a joke of Christian faith (vv 16-17) and of Christian hope (vv 18-19).

(a) First apocalyptic scenario (15:20-28)

15:20-22   But in fact Christ has been raised from the dead. In contrast
to the hopeless situation of mankind without the certainty of resurrection,
described in vv 12-19, Paul presents the wonderful situation of mankind attained as a result of Christ's death and resurrection. The situation is described in apocalyptic terminology. It begins with the triumphant declaration that Christ raised from the dead is the "first fruits" of those who have
died. Since the situation of the "first fruits" is by definition constitutive of
the whole, this means that all like Christ will eventually rise from the dead
(v 20). Using Adam typology,[74] Paul presents the first Adam as symbolic of
the aeon or era of death and Christ as symbolic of the aeon of life (vv
21-22).

15:23-28   But each in his own order. These words lead Paul into his
apocalyptic scenario (vv 23-28). In apocalyptic thought, everything is sim-
plified for the sake of effect. Time is divided into aeons, or ages: the time of
the dominance of evil versus the time of the dominance of good. Historical
events are determined. And the outcome of history—God's victory over the
forces of evil—is certain. Apocalyptic literature, as mentioned earlier (see p.
31), has four primary characteristics: (1) it has an overall concern with
eschatology; (2) it overemphasizes transcendentalism, leaving everything to
God's initiative; (3) it has a deterministic outlook on the events of history
and the outcome of history as a whole; (4) it smacks of a relative or mitigated dualism in that it personifies and tends to personalize the forces of
evil opposed to God. All these characteristics are evident in vv 23-28. Paul
simplifies the whole of history in order to emphasize the future victory and

resurrection of the just in the great day when Christ will come again and complete the work for which he was sent by the Father — the conquest of all evil and the return of all creation to the rule and reign of God the Father.

The text upon which Paul's little apocalypse is based and from which its concepts are educed is the first verse of Ps 110: "The Lord says to my lord: 'Sit at my right hand, till I make your enemies your footstool.'" Christ's own resurrection, Paul points out, is the first and decisive element in the victory of God over the forces of evil. Christ is the first fruits of the victory, and the remainder of the harvest (Paul is using the Old Testament sacrificial language, according to which the first fruits of a crop represent the whole crop offered to God) is technically the same as the first fruits.

There is a time element, however. Christ will sit at the right hand of the Father *until* he has made all his enemies his footstool. Only when Christ has conquered all enemies of God, and especially death, will the time come for the resurrection of all (vv 25-28). The critical verse for Paul's argumentation about the resurrection of the dead is v 23. There Paul differentiates between Christ (the first fruits), who *has been raised* from the dead, and "those who belong to him" (the rest of the crop), who *will be raised* from the dead in the *future*. The argumentation supports Paul's insistence on the resurrection of the dead and may even be intended to emphasize the fact that the resurrection is future, against the fanaticist exaltation-theology enthusiasts who would like to believe that the resurrection has already taken place.

(b) *Ad hominem* arguments for the resurrection (15:29-34)

Text

> 15:29 Otherwise, what do people mean by being baptized on behalf of the dead? If the dead are not raised at all, why are people baptized on their behalf? [30]Why am I in peril every hour? [31]I protest, brethren, by my pride in you which I have in Christ Jesus our Lord, I die every day! [32]What do I gain if, humanly speaking, I fought with beasts at Ephesus? If the dead are not raised, "Let us eat and drink, for tomorrow we die." [33]Do not be deceived: "Bad company ruins good morals." [34]Come to your right mind, and sin no more. For some have no knowledge of God. I say this to your shame.

Commentary

15:29 what do people mean by being baptized on behalf of the dead? In 15:29-34, Paul returns to the *ad hominem* line of argument he pursued in 15:1-19. Just as he forced the Corinthians to admit that the content of the gospel and the tradition that he and the other apostles preached contained the doctrine of the bodily resurrection of Christ and that they had accepted this doctrine when they first accepted the faith, so now he capitalizes on the practice of those who have themselves "baptized on behalf of the dead" (v 29a).

No one is certain what is meant by baptism for the dead. Most interpreters consider it some kind of proxy baptism whereby the dead were thought to benefit from the salvation offered by Christ's death and resurrection. Paul's argument follows ineluctably: "If the dead are not raised at all, why are people baptized on their behalf" (v 29b)?

15:30-34 Why am I in peril every hour? The remainder of the argumentation, except for the reference to fighting with "beasts at Ephesus" (v 32), speaks for itself. Most authors consider the fighting with beasts to be Paul's metaphorical way of describing the mortal dangers he was exposed to in the course of his three years in the city of Ephesus.

(a') Argumentation for a bodily resurrection (15:35-49) and second apocalyptic scenario (15:50-58)

Text

15:35 But some one will ask, "How are **the dead** raised? With what kind of body do they come?" [36]You foolish man! What you sow does not come to life unless it **dies.** [37]And what you sow is not the body which is to be, but a bare kernel, perhaps of wheat or of some other grain. [38]But God gives it a body as he has chosen, and to each kind of seed its own body. [39]For not all flesh is alike, but there is one kind for men, another for animals, another for birds, and another for fish. [40]There are celestial bodies and there are terrestrial bodies; but the glory of the celestial is one, and the glory of the terrestrial is another. [41]There is one glory of the sun, and another glory of the moon, and another glory of the stars; for star differs from star in glory.

[42]So is it with the **resurrection of the dead.** What is sown is perishable, what is **raised** is imperishable. [43]It is sown in dishonor, it is **raised** in glory. It is sown in weakness, it is **raised** in power. [44]It is sown a physical body, it is **raised** a spiritual body. If there is a physical body, there is also a spiritual body. [45]Thus it is written, "The first man **Adam** became a living being"; the last **Adam** became a life-giving spirit. [46]But it is not the spiritual which is first but the physical, and then the spiritual. [47]The **first man** was from the earth, a man of dust; the second man is from heaven. [48]As was the **man** of dust, so are those who are of the dust; and as is the **man** of heaven, so are those who are of heaven. [49]Just as we have borne the image of the **man** of dust, we shall also bear the image of the **man** of heaven.

[50]I tell you this, brethren: flesh and blood cannot inherit the **kingdom of God,** nor does the perishable inherit the imperishable.

[51]Lo! I tell you a mystery. We shall not all sleep, but we shall all be changed, [52]in a moment, in the twinkling of an eye, at the last trumpet. For the trumpet will sound, and the **dead will be raised** imperishable, and we shall be changed. [53]For this perishable nature must put on the imperishable, and this mortal nature must put on immortality. [54]When the perishable puts on the imperishable, and the mortal puts on immortality, then shall come to pass the saying that is written:

"**Death** is swallowed up in victory."
[55]"O **death,** where is thy victory?
O **death,** where is thy sting?"
[56]The sting of **death** is sin, and the power of sin is the law. [57]But thanks be to **God,** who gives us the victory through our Lord Jesus Christ.

⁵⁸Therefore, my beloved brethren, be steadfast, immovable, always abounding in the work of the Lord, knowing that in the Lord your labor is not in vain.

Commentary

(a′) Argumentation for a bodily resurrection (15:35-49)

15:35 But some one will ask, "How are the dead raised?" In the previous section (15:1-34), Paul refuted arguments against the bodily resurrection of the dead. Here he deals with what appears to be the main objection of those who said "there is no resurrection of the dead" (v 12). Whether on philosophical or Gnostic grounds, his opponents cannot bring themselves to accept a bodily resurrection. Paul, in diatribe style, phrases their objection: "But some one will ask: 'How are the dead raised? With what kind of body do they come?'" (v 35).

15:36-49 You foolish man! Paul's answer is that the resurrection body is indeed a physical body, but not the same as the earthly body that is buried. It is a body totally animated by the spirit: "It is sown a physical body, it is raised a spiritual body" (v 44). The Greek terms for physical body (*sōma psychikon*) and spiritual body (*sōma pneumatikon*) emphasize physical bodies but differentiate the two bodies on the basis of the animating or life-giving principle. This is the whole point of the Adam-Christ contrast in vv 45-49. The first Adam had and gave to his descendants a body animated by a natural life-giving principle. The second Adam, Christ, gives the spirit as a life-giving principle for the resurrection body (v 45). The resurrection body is no less a body than the Adam body, but it is infused with and controlled throughout by the spirit. By a spiritual body, therefore, Paul does not mean some kind of immaterial body but a physical body animated by the spirit.⁷⁵

(a′) Second apocalyptic scenario (15:50-58)

15:50-58 I tell you this, brethren. Paul concludes his argument with a second apocalyptic scenario that is parallel to his earlier scenario (vv 23-28). This one, however, deals only with the end-time and the resurrection of the dead in bodies that will be incorruptible, as opposed to earthly corruptible bodies (vv 52-53). As in the earlier scenario (vv 23-28), the final victory, which destroys death, brings resurrection and immortality with Christ (vv 54-57).

No summary can do justice to Paul's sweeping resurrection theology in 1 Cor 15, but two texts indicate the general direction of his thought: (1) "For as in Adam all die, so also in Christ shall all be made alive. But each in his own order: Christ, the first fruits, then at his coming those who belong to Christ" (vv 22-23); and (2) "If there is a physical body, there is also a spiritual body. Thus it is written, 'The first man Adam became a living being'; the last Adam became a life-giving spirit" (vv 44-45). In Paul's mind, the resurrection of Jesus hails the beginning of a new humanity, just as the creation of Adam hailed the beginning of the old humanity. As "first fruits" of the new humanity, Christ already has a new spiritual (*pneumatikon*) body (*sōma*). The faithful, who are the fullness of the harvest of which Christ is the "first fruits," live now with the "life-giving spirit" of Christ ("the last Adam became a life-giving spirit"). This life-giving spirit affects their inner selves now, conforming them to Christ; at the resurrection it will affect their bodies as well. As Paul says in v 44: "It is sown a physical body, it is raised a spiritual body."

The nature of the risen life, according to Paul, is first of all eschatological. It is eschatological because the final age of the world has dawned with the resurrection of Jesus, and with it a new humanity. This new humanity is opposed to the first creation of humanity in Genesis. The resurrection life-force both now and in the future gives to the Christian "real" life as opposed to somatic or physical or pseudo or Adamic life: "The first man Adam became a living being (*psyche*); the last Adam became a life-giving spirit (*pneuma*)."

Secondly, the risen life will be bodily. The resurrection bodies of the faithful in the future will be brought into being by the power of God and patterned on the resurrected body of Christ, the first fruits. As Paul says in Phil 3:21: "He will change our lowly body to be like his glorious body, by the power which enables him even to subject all things to himself."

Since the Christian even in this life lives with the life-force of the resurrected Christ, the "indicative" of his existence is that he is in Christ and lives with and by the life-giving spirit of Christ. From this fact or "indicative" flow the "imperatives" of Paul's moral theology for Christians (see p. 64).

Part V (16:1-24): The collection, travel plans, farewell greetings

Paul concludes his letter with instructions for a collection (vv 1-4), his travel plans (vv 5-12), and his final greetings (vv 13-24).

Text

16:1 Now concerning the contribution for the saints: as I directed the churches of Galatia, so you also are to do. ²On the first day of every week, each of you is to put something aside and store it up, as he may prosper, so that contributions need not be made when I come. ³And when I arrive, I will send those whom you accredit by letter to carry your gift to Jerusalem. ⁴If it seems advisable that I should go also, they will accompany me.

⁵I will visit you after passing through Macedonia, for I intend to pass through Macedonia, ⁶and perhaps I will stay with you or even spend the winter, so that you may speed me on my journey, wherever I go. ⁷For I do not want to see you now just in passing; I hope to spend some time with you, if the Lord permits. ⁸But I will stay in Ephesus until Pentecost, ⁹for a

wide door for effective work has opened to me, and there are many adversaries. ¹⁰When Timothy comes, see that you put him at ease among you, for he is doing the work of the Lord, as I am. ¹¹So let no one despise him. Speed him on his way in peace, that he may return to me; for I am expecting him with the brethren.

¹²As for our brother Apollos, I strongly urged him to visit you with the other brethren, but it was not at all his will to come now. He will come when he has opportunity.

¹³Be watchful, stand firm in your faith, be courageous, be strong. ¹⁴Let all that you do be done in love.

¹⁵Now, brethren, you know that the household of Stephanas were the first converts in Achaia, and they have devoted themselves to the service of the saints; ¹⁶I urge you to be subject to such men and to every fellow worker and laborer. ¹⁷I rejoice at the coming of Stephanas and Fortunatus and Achaicus, because they have made up for your absence; ¹⁸for they refreshed my spirit as well as yours. Give recognition to such men.

¹⁹The churches of Asia send greetings. Aquila and Prisca, together with the church in their house, send you hearty greetings in the Lord. ²⁰All the brethren send greetings. Greet one another with a holy kiss.

²¹I, Paul, write this greeting with my own hand. ²²If any one has no love for the Lord, let him be accursed. Our Lord, come! ²³The grace of the Lord Jesus be with you. ²⁴My love be with you all in Christ Jesus. Amen.

Commentary

16:1-4 Now concerning the contribution for the saints. The chapter begins with the same formula with which Paul opened chs 7, 8, and 12, suggesting that the last question in the Corinthians' letter to Paul concerned how they were to contribute to his collection for the poor of Jerusalem. Paul speaks about the collection in a number of places (Rom 15:25-28; 2 Cor 8-9; Acts 11:27-30). The troubles he endured in taking it up make us suppose that his compassion for the poor was only one reason for the collection. No doubt he also wanted to show his respect for the mother church in Jerusalem and at the same time establish friendlier relations between his own gentile churches and the almost entirely Jewish Christian church of Jerusalem. After much anguish in taking up the collection, he eventually brought it to Jerusalem, where he was arrested and put into prison (Acts 21).⁷⁶

16:5-9 I will visit you after passing through Macedonia. Paul had mentioned his intention to visit Corinth again earlier in the letter (4:18-21). Now, in view of his directions about the collection and his promise to pick it up himself (16:3), he gives more specific details about his travel plans. As we know from 2 Corinthians and Rom 15:25, Paul did visit Corinth again, and it was from there that he began his journey to Jerusalem, which ended with his imprisonment. The letter ends with a few words of advice (vv 13-18) and with greetings from the churches in Asia (Turkey).

16:10-20 When Timothy comes. Paul concludes with some recommendations concerning Timothy (cf. 4:17), Apollos (cf. 1:11; 3:4), and his three friends Stephanas, Fortunatus, and Achaicus. He closes the letter with greetings from members of the Ephesian community to the community at Corinth (vv 19-20).

16:21-24 I, Paul, write this greeting with my own hand. This remark shows that Paul used professional scribes to write his letters (cf. Rom 16:22). By writing the last part in his own hand, Paul authenticates the letter (cf. Gal 6:11; Phlm 19) and thus obviates the possibility of forgery (cf. 2 Thes 2:2). His last words, "My love be with you all in Christ Jesus," express beautifully what lay beneath all his dealings with the rambunctious Corinthians.

Chapter IV

THE
LETTER OF PAUL TO THE
PHILIPPIANS

In the months that intervened between the writing of 1 and 2 Corinthians, Paul suffered a harrowing and critical experience: he was imprisoned and put on trial for his life. He describes the experience in 2 Cor 1:8-10:

> For we do not want you to be ignorant, brethren, of the affliction we experienced in Asia; for we were so utterly, unbearably crushed that we despaired of life itself. Why, we felt that we had received the sentence of death; but that was to make us rely not on ourselves but on God who raises the dead; he delivered us from so deadly a peril, and he will deliver us; on him we have set our hope that he will deliver us again.

Paul's letter to the Philippians was probably written during this imprisonment, at a time when he did not know whether he was going to live or die.[1] It reflects the concentration of a man under sentence of death. Paul testifies to his thinking about death on this occasion in one of the most moving passages in Philippians:

> . . . it is my eager expectation and hope that I shall not be at all ashamed, but that with full courage now as always Christ will be honored in my body, whether by life or by death. For to me to live is Christ, and to die is gain. If it is to be life in the flesh, that means fruitful labor for me. Yet which I shall choose I cannot tell. I am hard pressed between the two. My desire is to depart and be with Christ, for that is far better. But to remain in the flesh is more necessary on your account (1:20-23).

Under the circumstances, one would expect Paul to put aside other matters and concentrate on preparing himself for death. Instead, he writes a theologically profound letter to the Christians at Philippi—a letter that is to the Pauline letters what Moses' farewell address in Deuteronomy is to the Old Testament and what the Johannine Last Supper discourse is to the Gospels. It is concerned with the spread of the gospel, with the "growth in Christ" of his beloved friends at Philippi, and with his deeper insights into the nature of the Christian life between its beginning in faith and baptism and its consummation in the glory of a resurrection patterned upon the resurrection of Christ.

These deeper insights mark a change in Paul's understanding of the nature of Christian existence. He had already taught that Christian existence depends on the crucifixion and resurrection of Christ as its dynamic source (1 Cor 1–4; 15); but in prison he comes to realize a new truth: just as the Christian's resurrection is to be patterned on the resurrection of Christ, so the day-to-day development of a Christian's life is to be patterned on the obedience, suffering, and crucifixion of Christ!

As Paul begins to realize that it is through suffering that he becomes like Christ, he at the same time begins to reflect more about how others as well as he himself can become more and more transformed into Christ through suffering. It may be that he was convinced that *as an apostle* he had a special call to be a living witness of Christ to others through his sufferings. He may have realized as well that suffering had been the lot of such great prophets as Hosea, Jeremiah, Ezekiel, and Deutero-Isaiah. Whatever the reason, it is a turning point in Paul's thinking.

These deeper insights constitute the theological richness of the letter to the Philippians, a richness Paul draws from again and again in 2 Corinthians, Galatians, and Romans. They are certainly the fundamental insights upon which Paul in 2 Corinthians constructs his concept of the true apostle as one who manifests in his life the suffering of Christ. They are the source of Paul's conviction that "we [Christians] do not lose heart, because our inner being is renewed each day even though our body is being destroyed at the same time" (2 Cor 4:16, and *passim* in 2 Cor 1–5). They appear in Galatians when he argues that the Christian's life is built on faith rather than on works (cp. Gal 1–4 and Phil 3:2-11), and in Romans when he combines the insights of Philippians and Galatians to expound his understanding of mankind's condition in history with and without Christ (Rom 1–8).

Many scholars believe that the letter to the Philippians is a collection of three letters edited into one at the end of the first century, when Paul's letters were brought together and published as a collection.[2] However, the continuity of theme, tone, and feeling in all parts of the letter suggests that, despite the abrupt transition at 3:1-2 and the seeming incompatibility of Paul's remarks about Epaphroditus in 2:23-30 and 4:18, the letter is all of one piece.

The letter, in fact, has the typical A-B-A' format used so often by Paul in 1 Thessalonians and 1 Corinthians, and can be divided as follows:

A (1:1–3:1): Spreading the **gospel** and **growth in Christ**
　B (3:2-16): Apparent digression: Growth in Christ depends on faith in Christ and not on observance of the law.
A' (3:17–4:23): Spreading the **gospel** and **growth in Christ**

Parallels between A and A' are numerous and, we believe, intentional. Note in particular: (1) "partnership [*koinōnia*] in the gospel from the first day until now" (1:5 and 4:15); (2) "at the day of Christ" (1:6, 10 and 3:20; 4:5); (3) "Only let your manner of life [*politeuesthe*] be worthy of the gospel of Christ" (1:27 and 3:20, where "our commonwealth" [*politeuma*] reflects the same thought as "manner of life" in 1:27); (4) "Have this mind [*phroneite*] among yourselves" (2:5 and 4:2, where Euodia and Syntyche are entreated to agree in the Lord [*to auto phronein en Kyriō*]; (5) "I have thought it necessary to send to you Epaphroditus" (2:25 and 4:18); (6) the reference to the Philippians as "saints" (1:2 and 4:21-22); (7) the reference to "sacrifice" (2:17 and 4:18b); (8) the frequent exhortations in both sections to "rejoice in the Lord" (*passim*).

While section B (3:2-16) looks like a digression and is even considered by many to be from a different letter, a closer scrutiny shows it to be intimately connected with the central theme of the letter, namely, growth in Christ.

A (1:1-30): Spreading the gospel and growth in Christ

Section A falls into its own A-B-A' format, as so often in Paul's letters (cf. 1 Cor 1-4 and 12-14, where each major section is arranged in the A-B-A' format). Paul will do the same in 2 Corinthians, Galatians, and Romans.

(a) Fighting the good **fight for the sake of the gospel** (1:1-30)
　(b) Life in Christ (2:1-18)
(a') Fighting the good **fight for the sake of the gospel** (2:19–3:1)

[In the text that goes with each subsection of section A (1:1–3:1), words and expressions in bold type not only indicate the parallelism between subsections (a) and (a') but also indicate the parallelism between section A (1:1–3:1) and section A' (3:17–4:23).]

Text

(a)　1:1 Paul and **Timothy,** servants of Christ Jesus, to all the **saints** in Christ Jesus who are at Philippi, with the bishops and deacons: ²Grace to you and peace from God our Father and the Lord Jesus Christ.
　³I thank my God in all my remembrance of you, ⁴always in every prayer of mine for you all making my **prayer** with **joy,** ⁵**thankful for your partnership in the gospel from the first day until now.** ⁶And I am sure that he who began a good work in you will bring it to completion **at the day of Jesus Christ.** ⁷It is right for me to feel thus about you all, because I hold you in my heart, for you are all partakers with me of grace, both in my imprisonment and **in the defense and confirmation of the gospel.** ⁸For God is my

witness, how I yearn for you all with the affection of Christ Jesus. ⁹And it is my **prayer** that your love may abound more and more, with knowledge and all discernment, ¹⁰so that you may approve what is excellent, and may be pure and blameless **for the day of Christ,** ¹¹filled with the fruits of righteousness which come through Jesus Christ, to the glory and praise of God.

¹²I want you to know, brethren, that what has happened to me has really served to advance the gospel, ¹³so that it has become known throughout the whole **praetorian guard** and to all the rest that my imprisonment is for Christ; ¹⁴and most of the brethren have been made confident in the Lord because of my imprisonment, and are much more bold to speak the word of God without fear.

¹⁵Some indeed preach Christ from envy and rivalry, but others from good will. ¹⁶The latter do it out of love, knowing that I am put here for the defense of the gospel; ¹⁷the former proclaim Christ out of partisanship, not sincerely but thinking to afflict me in my imprisonment. ¹⁸What then? Only that in every way, whether in pretense or in truth, Christ is proclaimed; and in that I **rejoice.**

¹⁹Yes, and I shall **rejoice.** For I know that through your **prayers** and the help of the Spirit of Jesus Christ this will turn out for my deliverance, ²⁰as it is my eager expectation and hope that I shall not be at all ashamed, but that with full courage now as always Christ will be honored in my body, whether by life or by death. ²¹For to me to live is Christ, and to die is gain. ²²If it is to be life in the flesh, that means fruitful labor for me. Yet which I shall choose I cannot tell. ²³I am hard pressed between the two. My desire is to depart and be with Christ, for that is far better. ²⁴But to remain in the flesh is more necessary on your account. ²⁵Convinced of this, I know that I shall remain and continue with you all, for your progress and **joy** in the faith, ²⁶so that in me you may have ample cause to glory in Christ Jesus, because of my coming to you again.

²⁷Only **let your manner of life be worthy of the gospel of Christ,** so that whether I come and see you or am absent, I may hear of you that you stand firm in one spirit, with one mind striving side by side **for the faith of the gospel,** ²⁸and not frightened in anything by your opponents. This is a clear omen to them of their destruction, but of your salvation, and that from God. ²⁹For it has been granted to you that **for the sake of Christ** you should not only believe in him but also suffer for his sake, ³⁰engaged in the same **conflict** which you saw and now hear to be mine.

Commentary

1:3-5 I thank my God. Paul usually introduces the themes of his letter in the thanksgiving section. The thanksgiving section in Philippians is no exception. In v 5, Paul introduces the theme of spreading the gospel. He tells the Philippians that he is thankful for their "partnership in the gospel from the first day until now."³ He will speak again in a direct manner about promoting the gospel in 1:12-26 and in an indirect manner throughout the letter.

1:6-11 And I am sure that he who began a good work in you will bring it to completion at the day of Jesus Christ. Paul begins by speaking about the first and the last stages of life in Christ and thus introduces the major theme of his letter: growth in Christ. In vv 9-11, he speaks about the day-to-day growth of Christian life: "It is my prayer that your love may abound more and more, with knowledge and all discernment, so that you may approve what is excellent, and may be pure and blameless for the day of Christ."

In speaking about the theme "growth in Christ," Paul speaks about three stages of life in Christ: the beginning, which is the work of the Father and the Son; the day-to-day growth in Christ, which is the work of the individual Christian in conjunction with the Father, the Son, and the Holy Spirit; and the consummation or resurrection, when Jesus "will change our lowly body to be like his glorious body, by the power which enables him even to subject all things to himself" (3:21).

Paul develops his "growth in Christ" theme, and especially day-to-day growth in Christ, in four ways: (1) by an appeal to his own example (1:12-30; 3:2-16; 3:17-21); (2) by an appeal to the example and attitude of Christ (2:1-13); (3) by an appeal to the manner of life called for from those whose "commonwealth" (*politeuma*) and homeland are in heaven (1:27-30; 2:1-14; 3:20); (4) by a simple but eloquent appeal to the Philippians to do all that any truly good person would do, whether he or she is Christian or pagan (4:8). Of himself, Paul says: "For me to live is Christ (1:21). He wants the Philippians to feel the same way about their lives.

1:12-13 what has happened to me has really served to advance the gospel. Paul's experience of living in the shadow of execution colors everything he says in vv 12-30. To begin with, he understands the propaganda value of his situation. People will talk about a man on trial and in danger of death. Moreover, when they talk about Paul, they will have to talk about why he is in prison and therefore about the gospel, and this helps to promote the gospel.

1:14-18 most of the brethren have been made confident in the Lord because of my imprisonment. Paul's willingness to sacrifice his life for the gospel has emboldened others to "speak the word of God without fear." The motives of some who preach the gospel (vv 15-17) may be suspect (and it is almost impossible for us to understand now what motives Paul had in mind); but, as Paul says, "What then? Only that in every way, whether in pretense or in truth, Christ is proclaimed" (v 18). The spread of the gospel is the important thing.

1:19-26 Yes, and I shall rejoice. Reflection about the spread of the gospel leads Paul to deeper reflection: Suppose he should be executed (vv 20-26)? The thought, as Paul knows, has many implications. For one, it means that Paul will not be present at the parousia, as he seemed to take for granted in his earlier letters (cf. 1 Thes 4:15-17; 1 Cor 15:51-52). For another, death brings up the question of the future life. Paul does not discuss the possibilities. He simply states his conviction that if he dies, he will be "with Christ." "To die," he says, "is gain" (v 21), and he is strongly attracted to the "gain" because, as he says, "My desire is to depart and be with Christ, for that is far better" (v 23).

Although he does not discuss it, dying and being "with Christ" implies on Paul's part a notion concerning how he would be "with Christ." It could be he thinks his "soul" will be "with Christ." It could also be he thinks that his resurrection will be patterned on that of Christ, and therefore will be a bodily resurrection that will enable him to be "with Christ" immediately after death. If he thinks as a Greek, his notion will almost certainly be that death brings about the dissolution of soul and body, with the soul departing to be with Christ and the body relegated to the tomb until the end of the world. If, however, Paul is thinking like a Jew (and this is the more probable supposition), his notion will be that following his death, he will rise bodily and be immediately "with Christ." His notion then would be governed by what he said about the resurrection of the body in 1 Cor 15:35-49.

1:24-26 But to remain in the flesh is more necessary on your account. Even though Paul considers being with Christ to be "far better" (v 23), he has the feeling that he will not die but will be allowed to continue his work of spreading the gospel. We can surmise, on the basis of his assertion here, that he had received some good news about the probable outcome of his trial. If he was not to die as he had expected, he had nevertheless undergone the chilling experience of thinking he would.

1:27 Only let your manner of life be worthy of the gospel of Christ. In 1:12-26, Paul explained how *his* situation and suffering contributed to the spreading of the gospel. In 1:27-30, he urges the Philippians to do *their* part in spreading the gospel. He urges them to "let their manner of life be worthy of the gospel of Christ." The verb (*politeuesthe*) that Paul uses for "manner of life" comes from *polis* (city) and at least in the broad sense carries with it the meaning "conduct yourselves as worthy citizens of the (heavenly) city to which you belong." The best commentary on Paul's meaning here is the parallel appeal to heavenly citizenship in 3:20: "our commonwealth (*politeuma*) is in heaven." If the Philippians act worthily of their heavenly citizenship, they will "stand firm in one spirit, with one mind striving side by side for the faith of the gospel" (v 27b).

1:28 not frightened in anything by your opponents. Besides conducting themselves in a manner worthy of their heavenly citizenship, Paul urges the Philippians not to be "frightened." Whether the opponents are Gentiles or Jews or Judaizing Christians is not clear; nor is there any way to be certain who these opponents were. The only clues to their identification are Paul's other references to opponents in 1:14-17 (it is unclear who they are); in 3:3ff (where the opponents are clearly either Jews of the synagogue or Judaizers, i.e., Jewish Christians who were insisting on the observance of the Mosaic law as necessary for salvation); and in 3:18-19 (where the opponents seem

again to be either synagogue Jews or Judaizers). The one clue that may
identify the opponents of 1:28 with the opponents of 3:18-19 is the parallelism of the two passages: the first (1:28) is in section A (1:1–3:1), and the
second in section A' (3:17–4:23). On this slim basis, they would be identified
as Jews of the synagogue.

1:29-30 not only believe in him but also suffer for his sake. Paul's appeal here is a strange one. He reminds the Philippians that it is their privilege to take Christ's part and not only to believe in him but "also to suffer
for his sake." Moreover, he asserts that their struggle is the same as his
(1:30). Underlying his conviction that it is a privilege to suffer for Jesus is
his realization that Christian existence should be patterned on the life of the
suffering Jesus and that it is precisely in following the suffering Jesus that
the gospel is spread to others. It seems that Paul's experience in the valley of
death at Ephesus led him to reflect on the nature of Christian life as existence patterned on the life of Christ crucified. The theme appears clearly
here for the first time and is repeated in 2:5-11 and 3:10-11. It will appear
again and again in 2 Corinthians and Romans. By the time the Gospels
come to be written (between 75 and 100 A.D.), the theme of "taking up the
cross and following Christ" will become practically axiomatic for Christian
theology (cf. Mk 8:31ff; Mt 16:21ff; Lk 9:18ff; Jn 12:23ff; 13:1-17;
15:18–16:4).

From this reflection on the nature of Christian existence, there will
develop as well, especially in 2 Corinthians, what might be called Paul's
theory of the twofold existence of Christians—the inner man and the outer
man. The inner man, who, according to Paul, is a "new creation" (2 Cor
5:17), patterns his life on the suffering life of Christ and discovers through
the Spirit that his inner nature is being renewed every day, "even though
[his] outer nature [i.e., his body] is wasting away" at the same time (2 Cor
4:16). Paul expresses this insight best in 2 Cor 5:5-21 and encapsulates it in
one glowing line in 2 Cor 4:10: ". . . always carrying in the body the death
of Jesus, so that the life of Jesus may also be manifested in our bodies."
However it is formulated, this insight lies at the heart of Paul's realized
eschatology.

(b) Life in Christ (2:1-18)

Text

(b)   2:1 So if there is any encouragement in Christ, any incentive of love,
any participation in the Spirit, any affection and sympathy, ²complete my
joy by being of the same mind, having the same love, being in full accord
and **of one mind.** ³Do nothing from selfishness or conceit, but in humility
count others better than yourselves. ⁴Let each of you look not only to his
own interests, but also to the interests of others.
      ⁵Have **this mind** among yourselves, which you have in Christ Jesus,
⁶who, though he was in the form of God, did not count equality with God a

thing to be grasped, [7]but emptied himself, taking the form of a servant, being born in the likeness of men. [8]And being found in human form he **humbled himself** and became obedient unto death, even death on a cross. [9]Therefore God has highly exalted him and bestowed on him the name which is above every name, [10]that at the name of Jesus every knee should bow, in heaven and on earth and under the earth, [11]and every tongue confess that Jesus Christ is Lord, to the glory of God the Father.

[12]Therefore, my beloved, as you have always obeyed, so now, not only as in my presence but much more in my absence, work out your own salvation with fear and trembling; [13]for God is at work in you, both to will and to work for his good pleasure. [14]Do all things without grumbling or questioning, [15]that you may be blameless and innocent, children of God without blemish in the midst of a crooked and perverse generation, among whom you shine as lights in the world; [16]holding fast the word of life, so that in the **day of Christ** I may be proud that I did not run in vain or labor in vain. [17]Even if I am to be poured as a libation upon the **sacrificial offering of your faith,** I am glad and **rejoice** with you all. [18]Likewise you also should be glad and **rejoice** with me.

Commentary

2:1   So if there is any encouragement in Christ. There is a change in the direction of Paul's thought in 2:1-18. In 1:12-26, he spoke about himself in relationship to spreading the gospel. In 1:27-30, he spoke about the Philippians' part in spreading the gospel. In 2:1ff, it is not so much the spreading of the gospel that concerns Paul as the unity of the Philippians and their growth in Christ. The whole section deals with unity and growth in Christ. Unfortunately, the attention given to the kenotic hymn in 2:6-11 has overshadowed the pastoral content of the whole section. We will deal first, therefore, with Paul's pastoral concern in 2:1-18 and then with the kenotic hymn in 2:6-11.

2:2-3   complete my joy by being of the same mind. Paul's concern has to do with a lack of unity among the Philippians. Nothing is said about what led to this lack of unity. Names are not named, nor is any specific group singled out. Commentators are at a loss to identify either the problem or the individuals concerned. There is, however, a small clue to the identity of the rival parties. In 4:2, Paul names names and uses similar language: "I entreat Euodia and I entreat Syntyche to agree in the Lord (*to auto phronein en kyriō*)." In 2:5, Paul uses similar language: "Have this mind among yourselves, which you have in Christ Jesus (*touto phroneite en hymin ho kai en Christo Iēsou*)." Adding to this small clue is the import of Paul's parallel structure. The first reference to disunity occurs in 2:1-5, which is in section A (1:1-3:1); the second is in 4:2, which is in section A' (3:17-4:23). As we have already seen in 1 Corinthians, where Paul uses the same A-B-A' structure, it is his practice to treat a problem broadly in section A and then more specifically in section A'.

It may be objected that this explanation trivializes Paul's pastoral problem, since it seems to reduce it to a squabble between two women. But it should be remembered that Paul's communities were small and even two people in a small community were worthy of Paul's attention, that Paul gives high marks to women in his letters, that women probably were far more important in the Pauline churches than we have been accustomed to believe, and that as a consequence disunity between two important women in a small community might well have posed a good-sized pastoral problem for Paul.[4]

2:4 Let each of you. Whatever the cause of the disunity, Paul's advice is straightforward: "Let each of you look not only to his own interests, but also to the interests of others." He goes on then in the kenotic hymn (2:6-11) to urge them to have that disinterestedness in self that was manifested by Jesus, who gave up his own will to be obedient to the will of the Father, even to the death of the cross. They are to have the same mind as Christ, because what makes them one with one another is their being in Christ. (For an explanation of the hymn in 2:6-11, see pp. 124–130.)

2:12-18 Therefore, my beloved. In his closing exhortation, Paul urges the Philippians to work out their own salvation "with fear and trembling," reminding them that "God is at work" in them (v 13) and urging them to "do all things without grumbling or questioning" (v 14).

2:17 Even if I am to be poured as a libation. Paul envisages the possibility of his death and looks upon it as a sacrificial offering to be added to the sacrificial offering of the Philippians' faith, which, like his own, is willing to put up with suffering and death for the sake of the gospel.

2:18 Likewise you also should be glad and rejoice with me. Paul begins again to speak of his joy. He began by saying, "Complete my joy by being of the same mind" (v 2); he ends by saying, "Rejoice with me."

(a') Fighting the good fight for the sake of the gospel (2:19-3:1)

Text

(a')   2:19 I hope in the Lord Jesus to send **Timothy** to you soon, so that I may be cheered by news of you. [20]I have no one like him, who will be genuinely anxious for your welfare. [21]They all look after their own interests, not those of Jesus Christ. [22]But **Timothy's** worth you know, how as a son with a father he has served with me **in the gospel.** [23]I hope therefore to send him just as soon as I see how it will go with me; [24]and I trust in the Lord that shortly I myself shall come also.
        [25]I have thought it necessary to send to you **Epaphroditus** my brother and fellow worker and fellow **soldier,** and your messenger and minister to my need, [26]for he has been longing for you all, and has been distressed because you heard that he was ill. [27]Indeed he was ill, near to **death.** But God had mercy on him, and not only on him but on me also, lest I should have sorrow upon sorrow. [28]I am the more eager to send him, therefore, that you may rejoice at seeing him again, and that I may be less anxious.

²⁹So receive him in the Lord with all **joy;** and honor such men, ³⁰for he nearly died **for the work of Christ,** risking his life to complete **your service to me.**

3:1 Finally, my brethren, **rejoice** in the Lord. To write the same things to you is not irksome to me, and is safe for you.

Commentary

2:19-24 Timothy. Timothy had been mentioned in 1:1 as the co-sender of the letter. Here Paul will take up again the theme of spreading the gospel mentioned so often in section (a), especially in 1:3-7 and 1:12-26, by speaking about Timothy and Epaphroditus (v 25) as his co-workers in spreading the gospel.⁵ Paul perhaps sends Timothy because he is not sure that he will be alive to visit them, even though he hopes he will and says: "I trust in the Lord that shortly I myself shall come also" (v 24).

2:25-30 Epaphroditus my brother and fellow worker and fellow soldier. Like Timothy, Epaphroditus worked with Paul in spreading the gospel and, like Paul, almost suffered death for the sake of the gospel (cp. 2:30 and 1:20-24). We know nothing about Epaphroditus beyond what is told us here and in 4:18. He evidently came from Philippi and not only brought monetary help for Paul from the Philippian Christians but stayed with Paul to help him. Critics cite the second reference to Epaphroditus in 4:18 as incompatible with what is said about him in 2:25-30 and conclude that 4:10-20 must be a separate "thank you" letter sent by the Philippians to Paul at an earlier date. Since Epaphroditus is mentioned in both section A (1:1–3:1) and in section A' (3:17–4:23), we think it far more likely that the parallel references are the result of Paul's typical A-B-A' format. The parallelism explains better Paul's second reference to Epaphroditus in 4:18 and provides a strong argument for the unity and integrity of the letter as a whole.

3:1 rejoice in the Lord. Characteristically, Paul ends on a note of joy, the sentiment that fills the letter from beginning to end.

EXCURSUS: THE KENOTIC HYMN (PHIL 2:6-11)

Few passages in the New Testament have fascinated scholars more than the little hymn to Christ crucified and yet triumphant in Phil 2:6-11, and few have elicited so vast an amount of literature.⁶ This is true for many reasons, but principally because the hymn gives every appearance of providing the earliest testimony to Christ in the New Testament. It certainly existed prior to Paul's letters written in the fifties. It may even have been written as early as the first decade of Christianity. As such, it gives scholars an insight into what the earliest Christians were thinking and saying about

Jesus. It provides, in a sense, the only light shining out of an otherwise totally dark period in the history of early Christianity.

Conscious of the massive literature on the hymn, we shall limit the scope of our treatment to the following questions. First, how does Paul use the hymn in the context of Phil 2? Second, is the hymn Pauline or non-Pauline? Third, is the hymn an expression of Palestinian Jewish Christology or of Hellenistic Christian Christology? Fourth, is the hymn based on an Adamic "image of God" theology? Fifth, is the hymn based on the "Servant theology" of Is 53? Sixth, is there a "name" Christology in the hymn? None of these questions can be answered exhaustively in the limited scope of our treatment. We will suggest what seem the most probable answers in the light of the available literature on the subject.

First, the context in 2:1-5 and especially 2:3, 14 indicates that Paul included the hymn in order to turn the eyes of his readers to the self-sacrificing attitude of Jesus and thus argue for self-denial, unity, and concord among the wrangling Philippians.[7] In 2 Cor 8:9 and Rom 15:5, Paul argues in a similar manner from the attitude and example of Jesus.

Second, the hymn seems to be non-Pauline, i.e., it seems to have been written by someone other than Paul and at a time sufficiently early for it to have become already well known and quotable by the time Paul wrote his letter to the Philippians. It is considered non-Pauline for two reasons. First, it uses a number of expressions not used by Paul, e.g., *kenoun, morphē, einai isa Theō, harpagmos, schēma,* and *hyperyssoun.* Second, it moves from the death of Jesus directly to his exaltation in heaven, whereas Paul usually moves from the death of Jesus to his resurrection. A few commentators, despite these reasons, consider the hymn Pauline.[8]

Third, the hymn is probably better considered the expression of Palestinian rather than Hellenistic Christianity for the following reasons. First, the author uses parallelism that is more characteristic of Jewish literature than of Hellenistic literature. Second, the author seems to be dependent in much that he says about Jesus upon the thought and language of the fourth of the Servant Songs in Is 53, especially in his reference to the servant (*doulos*) and to Is 45:23 in relation to the name "Lord." Third, the author seems to know well the Adamic theology so popular among the first-century rabbinic theologians.

The remaining questions can be answered only by a meticulous exegesis of the passage and by an exact determination of where in the existence of Jesus the author starts when he begins to speak about him. One may ask: Does he start out from Jesus as pre-existent Son of God in the Trinity, as the traditional interpretation holds? Or does he start out from Jesus as the pre-existent "Son of Man" in the "image and likeness of God," as O. Cullmann and others hold? Or does he start out with the incarnation and say nothing either about or against the pre-existence of Jesus, as C. H.

Talbert holds? We shall present the three interpretations that attempt to answer these questions: the traditional interpretation, the Cullmann interpretation, and the Talbert interpretation. None of these, however, provides the final word. The issue is still very much open to scholarly debate and investigation.

In the traditional interpretation,[9] the word "form" (*morphē*) in v 6 is not interpreted to designate Jesus' intrinsic, i.e., divine, nature, but rather that external glory that flows from and manifests his intrinsic divine nature. "Form" in this interpretation would be the equivalent of what is called in the Old Testament God's "glory" (Heb. *chabod*), as the word is used in Is 6:1; Jgs 8:18; Jb 4:16; Is 44:3; Dn 3:19. Paul uses a similar way of speaking in 2 Cor 4:4, where he speaks of "the splendor of the gospel showing forth the glory of Christ." This interpretation, as C. H. Giblin puts it, sees Jesus as experiencing a "transfiguration in reverse." At the transfiguration Jesus let the external glory that flowed from his intrinsic divine nature manifest itself in his body. Here Jesus, upon entering the world, decides to forgo that external glory and enter the world not only as other men but even more in the form (*morphē*) of a slave (*doulos*). The interpretation has much in its favor, including the weight of a centuries-old tradition and the concurrence of many modern authors.

In relation to this interpretation, the difficult word *harpagmos* in v 6 can be translated either as that which is seized or is to be seized as booty, or that booty or prize which one already has but does not cling to. If the *harpagmos* is what is Jesus' right as flowing from his nature, then he can empty himself of it without emptying himself of his intrinsic nature.

With such an interpretation of *morphē* and *harpagmos,* the difficult words "he emptied himself" (*heauton ekenōsen*) can mean, not that Jesus emptied himself of or gave up his divinity, but that he emptied himself of that external glory that flowed from his intrinsic nature as God. The author of the hymn would be saying in vv 6-7 that in becoming man, Jesus chose to empty himself of the rights and glory that flowed from his intrinsic nature and to appear instead as other men, even as a servant. The words "in the likeness of men" (*en homoiōmati anthrōpōn genomenos*) in v 7c would then be synonymous with the words "the form of a slave" (*morphēn doulou*) in v 7b, and the parallel use of the word *morphē* in v 6a and v 7b would indicate that the term cannot refer to the intrinsic nature but rather to the appearance that flows from one's intrinsic nature.

The traditional interpretation may be summarized as follows. Jesus, being truly God, had the right to the glory (*morphē*) of God. But in becoming man, Jesus freely gave up this external glory and instead chose the external appearance and status of a servant. By so giving up the external glory that flowed from his internal divine nature and by subjecting himself entirely to the will of the Father, even to the death of the cross, Jesus as man-God earned for himself exaltation to the position of Lord (*Kyrios*) of the universe and as such now lives with that glory or *morphē* that was always his as true God.

A second interpretation understands the hymn against the popular "Adamic" theology of the rabbis. This interpretation has been championed by many, but especially by O. Cullmann.[10] In Cullmann's interpretation, the form of God (*morphē theou*) in v 6a is to be understood in the sense of Gn 1:26, where God speaks of making man in his own "image and likeness" (Heb. *dᵉmūt wᵉ tselem*).

According to rabbinic speculation, God created two first men—the perfect first man of Gn 1:26 and the sinful first man of Gn 2-3. Understood against this background of Adamic theologizing, Jesus existed at the beginning in the form of the heavenly man of Gn 1:26 and is to be reckoned the true image and likeness of God, unlike the Adam of Gn 2-3, who tried to be equal with God.

In Cullmann's interpretation, the phrase "he did not count equality with God a thing to be grasped" (v 6bc) is explained on the basis of the contrast between the Adamic first man of Gn 2-3, who sought to seize equality with God, and Jesus, the true heavenly first man of Gn 1:26, who had the right to be equal to God but preferred to prove his right to be the true image and likeness of God as man by humble obedience, in contrast to the other Adam who disobeyed. As Cullmann says: "He who by nature was the only God-man, who deserved the designation by bearing the image of God, became man in fallen flesh through obedience, in which he proved himself precisely the Heavenly Man, and by which he accomplished his atoning work."[11] In confirmation of this interpretation, Cullmann cites Paul's use of Adamic theology and somewhat similar terminology in 1 Cor 15:22; Rom 5:12-19; 2 Cor 4:4; Col 1:15; 3:10; Rom 12:2.

Cullmann sees the hymn as concerned not so much with the question of Christ's natures as with Christ's part in salvation history. Christ's part in salvation history is explained in the hymn as the counterpart of Adam's. "Unlike Adam," as Cullmann puts it, "the heavenly Man, who in his pre-existence represented the true image of God, humbled himself in obedience and now receives the equality with God he did not grasp as a 'robbery.' Although he was already *huios* (son), now he becomes, as Rom 1:4 puts it, *huios tou theou en dynamei* (Son of God in power). As Acts 2:36 expresses it, he is 'made' *kyrios* (Lord)."[12] R. P. Martin schematizes the contrast between Adam and Christ as follows:

ADAM	*CHRIST*
Made in the divine image	Being the image of God
thought it a prize to be grasped at	thought it not a prize to be grasped at
to be as God;	to be as God;
and aspired to a reputation	and made himself of no reputation

and spurned being God's servant	and took upon Him the form of a servant
seeking to be in the likeness of God;	and was made in the likeness of men;
and being found in fashion as a man (of dust, now doomed),	and being found in fashion as a man (Rom. viii. 3),
he exalted himself,	He humbled Himself,
and became disobedient unto death.	and became obedient unto death.
He was condemned and disgraced.	God highly exalted Him and gave Him the name and rank of Lord.[13]

A third interpretation, which has much to be said for it, is the interpretation of C. H. Talbert.[14] Talbert disagrees with Lohmeyer's division of the hymn as falling into six strophes of three lines each and with Jeremias' suggested structure of three strophes with four lines each and suggests, on the basis of a more rigid parallelism than Jeremias, that the hymn should be divided into four strophes, the first parallel with the second and the third parallel with the fourth. Thus, in Talbert's structure, strophe 1 consists of 2:6-7b; strophe 2 of 2:7c-8; strophe 3 of 2:9; and strophe 4 of 2:10-11, as follows:

Hos en morphē theou hyparchōn	who, though he was in the form of God,
ouch harpagmon hēgēsato	did not count equality with God
to einai isa theō,	a thing to be grasped,
alla heauton ekenōsen	but emptied himself,
morphēn doulou labōn,	taking the form of a servant,
en homoiōmati anthrōpōn genomenos	being born in the likeness of men.
kai schēmati heuretheis	And being found in human form
hōs anthrōpos	
etapeinōsen heauton	he humbled himself and became
genomenos hypēkoos mechri thanatou,	obedient unto death,
thanatou de staurou.	even death on a cross.
dio kai ho theos auton hyperypsōsen	Therefore God has highly exalted him
kai echarisato autō to onoma	and bestowed on him the name
to hyper pan onoma	which is above every name,
hina en tō onomati Iēsou	that at the name of Jesus
pan gonu kampsē epouraniōn	every knee should bow, in heaven
kai epigeiōn kai katachthoniōn	and on earth and under the earth,
kai pasa glōssa exomologēsētai	and every tongue confess
hoti kyrios Iēsous Christos	that Jesus Christ is Lord,
eis doxan theou patros.	to the glory of God the Father.

What is significant about Talbert's structure is that strophes 1 and 2 turn out to be parallel in expression and in thought. Since the thought of strophe 2 speaks only of Jesus from the time of his incarnation and says nothing about his pre-existence, Talbert would hold that the thought of strophe 1 says the same and therefore cannot be considered as saying anything positive or negative about the pre-existence of Jesus.

In brief, Talbert accepts Adamic theology as the ideological background of the hymn, as do Cullmann and others, but attempts to prove that in the first two strophes of the hymn (2:6-7b and 2:7c-8) the author is speaking about the incarnate, not the pre-existent, Christ, against those who argue that the author is speaking of the pre-existent Christ in v 6 and the incarnate Christ in vv 7-8. As Talbert expresses it: "Parallel structure points to parallel meanings. That the parallelism between the first two strophes is intended to point to a common meaning is significant because there is no question that strophe 2 speaks of the human existence of Jesus. This would mean that strophe 1 also would be a statement, not about the pre-existence of Jesus, but about his earthly life. Strophe 1 says that Jesus, unlike Adam, did not grasp for equality with God but rather surrendered his life to God. Strophe 2 says that Jesus as a son of Adam surrendered his life to God. Both are concerned with the decision of Jesus to be God's servant rather than to repeat the tragedy of Adam and his sons."[15]

Our last two questions deal with the possibility of both an Isaian "Servant" theology for the hymn and a "name" theology based on Is 45:23. The argument for a background for the hymn in the Servant theology of Deutero-Isaiah is based upon what seem to be good parallels between Phil 2:6-11 and Is 52:13-53 and upon the consequent implication that the author of the hymn conceived the salvific activity of Jesus according to the pattern of Is 53. In Pauline theology, the Servant background is used in a number of passages: Rom 4:24-25; 8:3; 1 Cor 11:23-27; 15:3; Eph 5:2. In Phil 2:6-11 and Is 53, the following parallels seem to warrant a background for the hymn in the Servant theology of Isaiah:

Phil 2:6-11	*Is 52:13-53:12*
2:7 emptied himself	53:10 gives his life as an offering
2:8b obedient unto death	53:8 cut off from the land of the living
2:9 God has highly exalted him	53:13 God highly exalted him
2:10 bestowed on him the name which is above every name that at the name of Jesus every knee should bow.	45:23 To me every knee shall bend: by me every tongue shall swear.

In Is 53, the Servant is exalted precisely because he humbled himself to the death for sinners. In Phil 2:6-11, the same concepts are mirrored in the description of him who, being in the form of God, took on the form of a servant and emptied himself even to the death of the cross, and was therefore and thereafter exalted and given the name *kyrios* (Lord).

The name theology of the hymn flows from the name "Lord" (*kyrios*) given to Christ in 2:9-11. The Septuagint *kyrios* is the Hebrew *Adonai,* which was the equivalent substituted in the Hebrew text for the sacred Tetragrammaton YHWH (Yahweh). The author makes an allusion in 2:9-11 to Is 45:23. This allusion clarifies the meaning of the name given to Jesus, because in Is 45:23 it is a question of all beings bending the knee before the name of Yahweh.

It can be argued that the name means only that Christ is Lord in the sense that he now becomes cosmic ruler with power, especially since the passage seems primarily soteriological rather than Christological. Nevertheless, however strong the soteriological intent of the passage, the name "Lord" in 2:9-11 is the equivalent of the name of God in Is 45:23. One may argue, therefore, that the name given to Jesus is the divine name. The argument is not apodictic, however, because New Testament authors regularly apply to Christ texts predicated of Yahweh in the Old Testament.

B (3:2-16): Apparent digression: Growth in Christ depends on faith and not on observance of the law.

Text

3:2 Look out for the dogs, look out for the evil-workers, look out for those who mutilate the flesh. [3]For we are the true circumcision, who worship God in spirit, and glory in Christ Jesus, and put no confidence in the flesh.

[4]Though I myself have reason for confidence in the flesh also. If any other man thinks he has reason for confidence in the flesh, I have more: [5]circumcised on the eighth day, of the people of Israel, of the tribe of Benjamin, a Hebrew born of Hebrews; as to the law a Pharisee, [6]as to zeal a persecutor of the church, as to righteousness under the law blameless. [7]But whatever gain I had, I counted as loss for the sake of Christ. [8]Indeed I count everything as loss because of the surpassing worth of knowing Christ Jesus my Lord. For his sake I have suffered the loss of all things, and count them as refuse, in order that I may gain Christ [9]and be found in him, not having a righteousness of my own, based on law, but that which is through faith in Christ, the righteousness from God that depends on faith; [10]that I may know him and the power of his resurrection, and may share his sufferings, becoming like him in his death, [11]that if possible I may attain the resurrection from the dead. [12]Not that I have already obtained this or am already perfect; but I press on to make it my own, because Christ Jesus has made me his own. [13]Brethren, I do not consider that I have made it my own; but one thing I do, forgetting what lies behind and straining forward to what lies ahead, [14]I press on toward the goal for the prize of the upward call of God in Christ Jesus.

[15]Let those of us who are mature be thus minded; and if in anything you are otherwise minded, God will reveal that also to you. [16]Only let us hold true to what we have attained.

Commentary

In 3:2ff, the harsh tone of the contents so ill fits the joyful tone of the rest of the letter that critics with few exceptions believe this section to be an interpolation of material taken from another letter to the Philippians and inserted here at the end of the first century, when the Pauline letters were edited into a corpus. The harsh tone notwithstanding, we believe this section to be integral to the letter. Paul turns his attention to enemies of the faith in these verses, and his tone is only slightly more harsh than when he spoke about enemies in 1:27-30 and 3:17-19. In addition, as we have already seen in 1 Corinthians, it is Paul's habit to apparently digress in his central section, the B section of his A-B-A' format (cf. 9:1–10:22, the B section of 8:1–11:1, and 13:1ff, the B section of 1 Cor 12–14). These reasons, when added to the theme of 3:2-16 — faith in Christ as the foundation of growth in Christ-life — we find more than sufficient to convince us that 3:2-16 is integral to the letter and, far from being an interpolation or even a digression, contributes significantly to the central theme of the whole letter, which is growth in Christ-life.

The logic of Paul's argumentation in 3:2-16 follows three steps. First, he argues that the Philippians, who "glory in Christ Jesus," rather than their Jewish enemies, who glory "in the flesh," are the true circumcision and therefore the true Israel (vv 2-4).

Second, Paul argues from his own experience as a Jew who sought salvation through the works of the law (vv 4-6) until his conversion to Christ that it is through faith in Jesus and not through the works of the law that a person achieves salvation (vv 7-14).

Third, since salvation comes through faith in Christ rather than through the works of the law, Paul exhorts the Philippians to "hold true to what we have attained," i.e., to remain true to the conviction that salvation comes only through faith in Christ, implying that it would not be holding "true to what we have attained" if they were to regress by returning to Judaism, with its fateful mistake of looking backward to the law instead of looking forward through faith in Christ (vv 15-16).

3:2 Look out for the dogs. Paul's vituperative language expresses his passionate opposition toward those who were trying to draw the Philippians away from Christ and back to the law and the synagogue. The reference to the enemies as those "who mutilate the flesh," i.e., who practice circumcision, indicates that the enemies are those who wish to return to the Jewish law. As such, they could be either Jews of the synagogue or Judaizing Christians, i.e., Christians who believed that it was necessary to observe the law of Moses in order to be saved. The former supposition presupposes that some of the Philippians had been converts to Judaism prior to becoming converts to Christianity and are now being urged by the Jews to return to the synagogue.

Authors disagree on the identity of the enemies, but three arguments incline us to believe that the enemies were Jews of the synagogue rather than Judaizing Christians. First, Paul argues in v 3 that "we are the true circumcision," i.e., the true Israel — an argument that presupposes "a false Israel," which in this context would fit synagogue Jews better than Judaizing Christians, who despite their regressive tendencies were nevertheless truly Christians. Second, Paul's argument from his own life (vv 4-14) contrasts his life as a synagogue Jew (vv 4-6) with his new life as a believer in Jesus (vv 7-14) and suggests that the enemies are those with whom Paul himself had agreed before his conversion to Christianity. Third, Paul's final exhortation in v 16 to "hold true to what we have attained" presupposes a contrast between a "before" and an "after"—the "before" being allegiance to the synagogue; the "after," allegiance to Christ and Christianity. These are far from apodictic arguments, but they are convincing. Moreover, they have the support of Paul's other statements about the enemies: the first in 1:28, where the enemies are implicitly accused of being "enemies of the gospel"; the second, in 3:18-19, where the enemies are accused of being enemies of the cross. These accusations could be leveled against Judaizing Christians, but they are much more appropriate as accusations against the Jews of the synagogue (cf. Rom 9:30-33 and especially 11:28).

3:3 we are the true circumcision. The statement presupposes a "false Israel," presumably the synagogue, and polarizes the distinction by describing the true Israel as those "who worship God in spirit, and glory in Christ Jesus, and put no confidence in the flesh." It would follow that the false Israel does not worship God in spirit, does not glory in Christ Jesus, and puts its confidence in the flesh. To put one's confidence in the flesh, i.e., in human values, rather than "in the spirit," i.e., divine values, means in Pauline terms to seek salvation through one's own efforts by observance of the law rather than through faith in Christ. It is precisely this difference between "confidence in the flesh" and faith in Christ that will be Paul's subject in vv 4-14, where he will speak of reasons for confidence in the flesh (vv 4-6) and faith in Christ (vv 7-14). The difference is the difference between being a Jew and being a Christian!

3:4-6 Though I myself have reason for confidence in the flesh also. Paul's description of himself as a Jew of the Jews (vv 4-5), persecutor of the Church and strict observer of the law (v 6) is preparatory to his denunciation of confidence in the flesh as spiritual bankruptcy in vv 7-11 and to his declaration in vv 12-16 that nothing in his former life as a Jew can be compared with the value of glorying in Christ Jesus. In short, what he used to glory in—his allegiance to the synagogue and its paramount values—he now considers valueless and has given up totally (as should the Philippians).

3:7-8 whatever gain I had. What Paul used to glory in he has given up totally because it is nothing in comparison with "the surpassing worth of knowing Christ Jesus." What Paul has "lost," among other things, is clarified in what follows.

3:9 not having a righteousness of my own, based on law. "Righteousness" (*dikaiosynē*) is the Hebrew way of speaking about one's right relationship with God and the kind of response to God that relationship calls for. As a Jew, Paul depended on his own efforts in keeping the law to bring about a right relationship with God. He now avows that it is through faith in Christ that he finds his righteousness (right relationship with God) and that this righteousness depends on faith in Christ and not on keeping the law through his own efforts. In Gal 1–4 and Rom 1–8, Paul will develop his teaching on this subject. What he will say there at great length, he encapsulates here in 3:9 in one magnificent, insightful declaration.

3:10-11 that I may know him. "The righteousness from God that depends on faith" severs Paul from his former Judaism and focuses his attention for the future on knowing Jesus and "the power of his resurrection" and on sharing "his sufferings" and "becoming like him in his death" (cf. 1:13-20; 1:29). It is by "becoming like him in his death" (cf. 2:16-21) that Paul hopes to attain, as Jesus did, his "resurrection from the dead" (v 11). The center of gravity of Paul's life has shifted totally from a righteousness "based on law" (v 9) to a righteousness based on faith in Christ and conformity to his life.

3:12 Not that I have already obtained this or am already perfect. Growth in Christ, which for Paul began with faith, will be sustained and increased by an even deeper faith. He acknowledges that he still has far to go in attaining the resurrection from the dead, but he presses on to make it his own, in the confident conviction that Jesus has made him "his own" and that his faith, therefore, will not be disappointed. Some see here a reference to Christians of a Gnostic or exaltation-theology mindset (see pp. 41ff) who may have thought they were already saved and needed do nothing more. If that is the case, Paul's words would have to be understood in this sense: "Not that I (unlike some of you) have already obtained this or am already perfect . . . ." This is possible but difficult to prove.

3:13 forgetting what lies behind. This may well refer to Paul's history as a Jew of the synagogue, but the context of growth in Christ, which is uppermost in his mind here, suggests that he is referring to his past life as a Christian.

3:14 I press on. The goal is union with Christ in the resurrection. The "prize" is that perfection called for by the "upward call of God in Christ Jesus"—a call to be like Christ himself (cf. 2:6-11; 3:20-21).

3:16 let us hold true to what we have attained. Paul's appeal appropriately concludes this whole section by expressing in a positive way what he had said in a negative way in 3:2-3. He calls upon the Philippians to remain true to what they have attained, namely, their belief in attaining salvation, not through works of the law, but through faith in Christ (cf. vv 9-11). A return to Judaism and its doctrine of salvation through observance of the law (cf. vv 2-3 and 7-8) would be a regression (cf. Gal 2:15-21).

A′ (3:17–4:23): Spreading the gospel and growth in Christ

Text

> 3:17 Brethren, join in imitating me, and mark those who so live as you have an example in us. [18]For many, of whom I have often told you and now

tell you even with tears, live as enemies of the cross of Christ. [19]Their end is destruction, their god is the belly, and they glory in their shame, with minds set on earthly things. [20]But **our commonwealth** is in heaven, and from it we await a Savior, the Lord Jesus Christ, [21]who will change **our lowly body** to be like his glorious body, by the power which enables him even **to subject all things to himself.** 4:1 Therefore, my brethren, whom I love and long for, my joy and crown, stand firm thus in the Lord, my beloved.

[2]I entreat Euodia and I entreat Syntyche **to agree in the Lord.** [3]And I ask you also, true yokefellow, help these women, for they have **labored side by side with me in the gospel** together with Clement and the rest of my fellow workers, whose names are in the book of life.

[4]**Rejoice** in the Lord always: again I will say, **Rejoice.** [5]Let all men know your forbearance. The Lord is at hand. [6]Have no anxiety about anything, but in everything by prayer and supplication with thanksgiving let your requests be made known to God. [7]And the peace of God, which passes all understanding, will keep your hearts and your minds in Christ Jesus. [8]Finally, brethren, whatever is true, whatever is honorable, whatever is just, whatever is pure, whatever is lovely, whatever is gracious, if there is any excellence, if there is anything worthy of praise, think about these things. [9]What you have learned and received and heard and seen in me, do; and the God of peace will be with you.

[10]I **rejoice** in the Lord greatly that now at length you have revived your concern for me; you were indeed concerned for me, but you had no opportunity. [11]Not that I complain of want; for I have learned, in whatever state I am, to be content. [12]I know how to be abased, and I know how to abound; in any and all circumstances I have learned the secret of facing plenty and hunger, abundance and want. [13]I can do all things in him who strengthens me. [14]Yet it was kind of you to share my trouble.

[15]And you Philippians yourselves know that **in the beginning of the gospel,** when I left Macedonia, no church entered into **partnership** with me in giving and receiving except you only; [16]for even in Thessalonica you sent me help once and again. [17]Not that I seek the gift; but I seek the fruit which increases to your credit. [18]I have received full payment, and more; I am filled, having received from **Epaphroditus** the gifts you sent, **a fragrant offering, a sacrifice** acceptable and pleasing to God. [19]And my God will supply every **need** of yours according to his riches in glory in Christ Jesus. [20]To our God and Father be glory forever and ever. Amen.

[21]Greet every saint in Christ Jesus. The brethren who are with me greet you. [22]All the **saints** greet you, especially those of **Caesar's household.** [23]The **grace** of the Lord Jesus Christ be with your spirit.

Commentary

In 3:17-4:23, Paul returns to the themes of 1:1-3:1 — spreading the gospel and growth in Christ. He urges the Philippians to grow in Christ by imitating him (3:17), reminds them that they are citizens of a heavenly commonwealth (3:20), and presents a list of virtues they are invited to practice (4:8-9). He concludes the letter as he had begun it (cf. 1:3-11), expressing his gratitude for the help the Philippians supplied him through Epaphroditus and commending them for fulfilling their part of their partnership with him in spreading the gospel (4:10-20).

3:17 join in imitating me. Growth in Christ depends ultimately upon imitating Christ. Paul, however, can invite the Philippians to imitate him because he imitates Christ (cf. 1 Cor 4:16; 11:1; 1 Thes 1:6; 2:4) and because he is conscious of his duty as an apostle to serve as an example to his converts (cf. 4:9; 1 Thes 2:10).

3:18-19 many . . . live as enemies of the cross. Who the "many" are is much debated. Some see them as a new group distinct from the enemies in 3:2-3 and 1:28; others, as the same. The language of 3:18-20 is so similar to the language of 1:27-30 that one may easily conclude to a parallel and to the same enemies, but the enemies in 1:28 are not clearly defined. Enemies whose "god is the belly," who "glory in their shame," and whose "minds are set on earthly things" could be identified as synagogue Jews, Judaizing Christians, or even as early Gnostic Christians. We think it more likely that all the enemies mentioned in the letter (1:28; 3:2-3; 3:18-19) are the same and, for reasons already explained under 3:2-3, would opt for the opinion that here as well as there, the enemies are the synagogue Jews.

3:20 But our commonwealth is in heaven. The "our" expresses the contrast between the heavenly commonwealth of the Philippians and the earthly commonwealth of the enemies described in 3:18-19. The Greek for "commonwealth" is *politeuma,* which could be translated as here or as "citizenship." It is the place to which one owes allegiance. In this sense, the key word is "heavenly" (cp. 3:19: ". . . with minds set on *earthly* things"). In 1:27 (the parallel of this verse in section A), Paul uses the verb *politeuesthe* (derived from the noun *politeuma*) to urge the Philippians to conduct themselves in a manner worthy of their heavenly commonwealth or citizenship. Here the same is implied, in the sense that the Philippians' commonwealth is in heaven and in the future, and that therefore they should so conduct themselves in the present that they will show themselves true citizens of that heavenly commonwealth from which they "await a Savior, the Lord Jesus Christ."

3:21 who will change our lowly body to be like his glorious body. The concepts and even the words Paul uses here bear a strong resemblance to the words of the hymn in 2:6-11 and show that Paul still has the hymn on his mind. The Greek word for "change," or better "transform," used here is *metaschēmatisei,* a verb built on the word *schēmati* found in 2:8. The word for "like" is *symmorphon,* from the noun *morphē* found in 2:6. The word "lowly" (*tapeinōseōs*) suggests the words "he humbled himself" in 2:8. And the whole transformation from lowly to glorious recalls the contrast between Jesus' condition before the cross (2:6-8) and after the cross (2:9-11). For the concept of the resurrection body, see the commentary on 1 Cor 15 and cf. Rom 8:29; 1 Cor 15:49; 2 Cor 3:18; Eph 1:19ff.

4:2 I entreat Euodia and I entreat Syntyche to agree in the Lord. Whatever the problem between Euodia and Syntyche, Paul entreats them "to agree in the Lord" and uses for "agree" the same Greek verb (*phronein*) that he used in introducing the kenotic hymn in 2:5. As J. Paul Sampley puts it: "Far from being exhorted to some mystical union, they are called to live with one another as chapter 2 has expressed it in so many ways: in love, in accord, seeking each other's interests, not in self-service or conceit."[16]

4:8 whatever is true, whatever is honorable. The virtues that Paul suggests the Philippians consider practicing are those a Greek philosopher, especially a Stoic, would recommend to his followers. Paul thus shows his appreciation for what was good in paganism. At the same time, it should be remembered that for Paul these virtues are mentioned in a context that speaks of "the Lord" being "at hand" (v 5) and of the "peace of God, which passes all understanding" (v 7). They are virtues, therefore, that are suffused by all that Paul has said about Jesus (2:5-11) and by all that he has said about pressing on "toward the goal for the prize of the upward call of God in Christ Jesus" (3:14). In brief, he or she who practices them will thereby grow in Christ Jesus.

4:10 I rejoice in the Lord greatly that now at length you have revived your concern for me. In what follows in 4:10-20, critics see a separate "thank you" note written by Paul and incorporated here by the editors of Paul's letters. Our contention is that the A-B-A′ format of the letter as a whole indicates that this section is not a separate letter but simply the parallel of things Paul spoke about in section A (1:1-3:1), e.g., the references to "partnership" in the work of the gospel (cp. 4:15 and 1:5), the references to Epaphroditus (cp. 4:18 and 2:25), and numerous other references (see below). J. Paul Sampley supports this contention by his explanation of 4:10-20 as not so much a "thank you" note as Paul's acknowledgment that the Philippians have lived up to their part of the partnership they entered into with him for the work of spreading the gospel.[17] In such a partnership (*koinōnia*), Paul's part was to do the actual work of evangelizing; the Philippians' part was to support him financially while he did this, their mutual work for the kingdom of God. Sampley shows that such a voluntary, paralegal form of partnership was well known in Roman society.[18] What 4:10-20 amounts to, in brief, is Paul's formal receipt for services supplied by the Philippians in fulfillment of their part of the partnership. Significantly, the whole letter is suffused with references to this partnership and with terminology proper to it. What Paul said informally about this partnership in 1:3ff and about Epaphroditus in 2:25 is here repeated in what amounts, in technical terms, to a formal receipt. Everything in 4:10-20 makes excellent sense when interpreted against the background of a partnership entered into between Paul and the Philippians entailing certain specific voluntary obligations.

4:10b you were indeed concerned for me, but you had no opportunity. For whatever reason, it was only with the sending of Epaphroditus that the

Philippians had the opportunity to fulfill their part of the partnership by helping Paul financially (cf. v 18). Presumably this was while he was in prison.

4:11-13 Not that I complain of want. Until Epaphroditus arrived, Paul had been in financial difficulties but did not complain because, as he points out, he had learned by this time to be content (the Greek word *autarkēs* in its popular Stoic sense means "self-sufficient"), whether he abounds (is financially well off) or is abased (is poor). His reason for this contentment is not based upon Stoic philosophy but upon his confidence "in him who strengthens" him (v 13).

4:14-16 Yet it was kind of you to share my trouble. In what follows, Paul refers to several occasions on which the Philippians helped him (v 16). Most important is his reference in v 15 to the fact that it was only the Philippians who "entered into partnership" with him "in giving and receiving." Here it seems Paul refers specifically to the paralegal Roman form of partnership that he entered into with the Philippians to do the work of evangelization called for by the Kingdom (cf. 1:5-7).

4:17 Not that I seek the gift. "Gift" might well be translated in the terms of partnership as "payment," i.e., as the Philippians' fulfillment of their obligation to support Paul in his (their) work of evangelization.

4:18a I have received full payment. The term Paul uses for "I have received" is *apechō,* the technical commercial term commonly found in papyri receipts and equivalent in modern times to a bill stamped "paid." Paul, in short, has been reimbursed for his work in behalf of the partnership and makes this part of his letter a receipt.

4:18b-20 a fragrant offering, a sacrifice acceptable and pleasing to God. Paul's liturgical imagery reminds the Philippians that their partnership with him is not in connection with any merely worldly commercial enterprise but with the work of God. In 1:5ff, the passage parallel to 4:18, Paul had spoken of his ministry as a sacrificial act (cf. also 2:17, 30; 4:15). His liturgical imagery and his concluding remarks in vv 19-20 insinuate quite aptly that in return for the Philippians' material generosity, God will reward them spiritually.

4:21-23 Greet every saint in Christ Jesus. Paul's conclusion is conventional but contains significant parallels to his opening greeting in 1:1ff (cp. 4.21 with 1:1; 4:23 with 1:2; and cp. the reference in 4:22 to "Caesar's household" with the reference to the "praetorian guard" in 1:13). These parallels, along with others in 4:10-20, constitute an inclusion-conclusion for the letter as a whole.

Parallels between section A (1:1-3:1) and section A' (3:17-4:23)

The following parallels are presented in support of the contention that Philippians is one integral letter written according to Paul's favorite A-B-A' format and against the frequently encountered critical view that the letter is a composite of three different letters, variously discerned as 1:1–3:1 plus 4:4-9 and 4:21-23; 3:2–4:3; and 4:10-20.

1:1	saints		4:22	saints
1:2	grace		4:23	grace
1:5	thankful for your partnership in the gospel from the first day until now		4:15	you . . . know that in the beginning of the gospel . . . no church entered into partnership with me . . . except you only
1:13	praetorian guard		4:22	Caesar's household
1:27	labored side by side		4:3	labored side by side with me
1:27	live worthy of the gospel (*politeuesthe*)		3:20	commonwealth (*politeuma*)
2:8	humbling of Jesus		3:21	our lowly body
2:9-11	Lord of all in heaven, on earth, and under the earth		3:21b	Lord with power to "subject all things to himself"
2:17	as a libation upon the sacrificial offering of your faith		4:18	a fragrant offering, a sacrifice acceptable and pleasing to God
2:25	need (*chreia*)		4:16, 19	need (*chreia*)
2:25	Epaphroditus		4:18	Epaphroditus
3:1	rejoice		4:4	rejoice

Chapter V

THE
SECOND LETTER OF PAUL TO THE
CORINTHIANS

When Paul sent off 1 Cor 1–16 toward the beginning of his third year at Ephesus, he probably thought that the situation at Corinth would soon be reasonably well in hand. He could not have been more mistaken. More serious problems arose. There was even the possibility that rival missionaries might completely subvert his work at Corinth. It was in response to this more menacing situation that Paul wrote 2 Cor 1–13.

What happened in Corinth between the writing of 1 and 2 Corinthians is far from clear. In 2 Corinthians, Paul speaks about a second visit he made to Corinth, about a shocking incident that took place during that visit, about a "painful letter" he had written in relation to the incident (1:15–2:12), and about a third visit he intends to make in the near future (cf. 10:2; 12:14; 13:1). The sequence of events is far from clear, and the critics debate it at length.[1] C. K. Barrett, for example, postulates a partition of 2 Corinthians into two letters: the first, 2 Cor 1–9; the second, 2 Cor 10–13.[2]

We prefer to see the letter as a unity with an A-B-A' format (A = 1:1–7:16; B = 8:1–9:15; A' = 10:1–13:14) and a sequence of events as follows. Sometime in the early summer of 55 A.D., Paul left Ephesus and visited Corinth, as he had promised when he wrote 1 Corinthians (cf. 1 Cor 16:1-5). Before this visit, he had told the Corinthians that he would visit them twice—once on his way from Ephesus to Macedonia and again on his return from Macedonia (cf. 2 Cor 1:15–2:4). But on the first of these two planned visits, a distressing incident took place (cf. 2 Cor 2:1-9). Instead of returning from Macedonia to Corinth, Paul decided against revisiting Corinth and went back from Macedonia to Ephesus.

Not long after his return to Ephesus, Paul wrote a letter to Corinth "out of much affliction and anguish of heart and with many tears"—the letter referred to by authors as the "painful letter" (cf. 2 Cor 2:4-9; 7:8). This letter was probably brought to Corinth by Titus. It is unlikely that 2 Cor 10-13 constitutes this "painful letter," as some critics believe.[3]

Later on, Paul left Ephesus and went north to Troas, hoping to meet Titus there on his return from Corinth. When Titus failed to show up, Paul went on to Macedonia and met him there (cf. 2 Cor 2:12-14; 7:4-16). On the basis of Titus' analysis of the situation at Corinth, Paul then wrote 2 Cor 1-13 to express his feelings of comfort and consolation that things were once again straightened out between himself and the Corinthians (chs 1-7), to give instructions for the taking up of a collection for the Christians of Jerusalem (chs 8-9), and to deal with the problem of certain missionaries from Jerusalem whom Paul calls pseudo-apostles (2:14-7:3 and chs 10-13). In 2:14-7:4 and chs 10-13, Paul defends himself and his gospel against these pseudo-apostles and their accusations. The letter follows his typical A-B-A' format.

A (1:1-7:16): The signs of a true apostle

  (a) 1:1-2:13: **Consolation and reconciliation**

    (1) Greetings and thanksgiving: Paul is **comforted** (1:1-11).
    (2) Paul's **boast,** his change of plans, the **"painful letter"** (1:12-2:4)
    (3) Paul forgives **the offender at Corinth** (2:5-11).
    (4) Paul goes to **Macedonia** to meet **Titus** (2:12-13).

  (b) 2:14-7:3: The ministry of the new covenant

    (1) The triumphal march of the gospel (2:14-17)
    (2) The Corinthians are Paul's letter of recommendation (3:1-3).
    (3) Ministers of the new covenant (3:4-18)
    (4) Earthen vessels (4:1-5:10)
    (5) The new creation and Paul's attitude toward others (5:11-21)
    (6) Appeals to the Corinthians to be worthy of their call (6:1-7:3)

  (a') 7:4-16: **Consolation and reconciliation**

    (1) Paul in **Macedonia** is **comforted** by **Titus'** news (7:4-7).
    (2) Again, the **"painful letter"** and **the offender at Corinth** (7:8-13)
    (3) Paul **boasts** about the Corinthians' response (7:14-16).

B (8:1-9:15): The collection

  (a) An **appeal for generosity** (8:1-15)
  (b) A recommendation for Titus and his companions (8:16-24)
  (a') Another **appeal for generosity** (9:1-15)

A' (10:1-13:14): The signs of a true apostle

  (a) **What Paul will be like** when he comes to Corinth again (10:1-18)
  (b) The signs of a true apostle (11:1-12:11)
  (a') **What Paul will be like** when he comes to Corinth again (12:12-13:14)

This outline presupposes that all of 2 Corinthians constitutes one letter rather than the two or three postulated by some commentators. We are convinced that all of 2 Cor 1-13 constitutes a single, well-integrated letter, and the principal, though not the only, reason for this conviction is the fact that the letter as a whole falls so easily into Paul's customary A-B-A' format.

A (1:1-7:16): The signs of a true apostle
    (a) 1:1-2:13: Consolation and reconciliation
        (1) Greetings and thanksgiving: Paul is comforted (1:1-11).

Text

(a)   1:1 Paul, an apostle of Christ Jesus by the will of God, and Timothy our brother. To the church of God which is at Corinth, with all the saints who are in the whole of Achaia: ²Grace to you and peace from God our Father and the Lord Jesus Christ.

³Blessed be the God and Father of our Lord Jesus Christ, the Father of mercies and God of all **comfort,** ⁴who **comforts** us in all our affliction, so that we may be able to **comfort** those who are in any affliction, with the **comfort** with which we ourselves are **comforted** by God. ⁵For as we share abundantly in Christ's sufferings, so through Christ we share abundantly in **comfort** too. ⁶If we are afflicted, it is for your **comfort** and salvation; and if we are **comforted,** it is for your **comfort,** which you experience when you patiently endure the same sufferings that we suffer. ⁷Our hope for you is unshaken; for we know that as you share in our sufferings, you will also share in our **comfort.**

⁸For we do not want you to be ignorant, brethren, of the **affliction** we experienced in Asia; for we were so utterly, unbearably crushed that we despaired of life itself. ⁹Why, we felt that we had received the sentence of death; but that was to make us rely not on ourselves but on God who raises the dead; ¹⁰he delivered us from so deadly a peril, and he will deliver us; on him we have set our hope that he will deliver us again. ¹¹You also must help us by prayer, so that many will give thanks on our behalf for the blessing granted us in answer to many prayers.

Commentary

1:3-7 Blessed be the God and Father of our Lord Jesus Christ. Paul's thanksgiving in vv 3-11 is notable on two counts. First, it is in the form of an Old Testament liturgical benediction—a stylized prayer of thanksgiving phrased as a blessing (*berakah*) in which God is praised and thanked for his innumerable kindnesses (cf. Pss 105, 106, 148, 150; 1 Kgs 8:15f; 1 Pt 1:3-12).⁴ Second, Paul's thanksgiving focuses the tone of the letter as a whole by emphasizing two of the central themes he will be discussing: (1) the comfort and consolation he enjoys as a result of the good news Titus brought from Corinth (cf. 7:5-16); (2) the importance of suffering for him as an apostle and for the Corinthians as Christians (1:4-7). It is noteworthy that the word "comfort" either as a noun (*paraklēsis*) or as a verb (*parakalein*) occurs ten times in vv 4-7, and the word "suffering," in one form or another (e.g. *thlipsis, thlibō, pascō, pathēma*), occurs eight times in vv 4-8, not counting the references to death and despairing of life that follow in vv 9-11. Paul's emphasis on this apparently paradoxical combination of suffering and comfort runs throughout the letter and plays a large part in his definition of the true apostle and the true Christian as opposed to the pseudo-apostle and the pseudo-Christian (cf. 2:14-15; 4:7–5:5; 6:4-10; 11:19-33; 12:7-10; 13:3-5).

1:8-11 For we do not want you to be ignorant, brethren, of the affliction we experienced in Asia. The references to affliction in Asia, even to the point of despairing of life, feeling like men who "had received the sentence of death," and being rescued from "so deadly a peril" (vv 8-10), probably refer to the same danger of death Paul spoke about in Phil 1:12-26. One cannot be certain, however, because Paul was in prison and in danger of death many times (cf. 2 Cor 6:4-10; 11:22-33).

(2) Paul's boast, his change of plans, and the "painful letter" (1:12–2:4)

Text

(a)   1:12 For our **boast** is this, the testimony of our conscience that we have behaved in the world, and still more toward you, with holiness and godly sincerity, not by earthly wisdom but by the grace of God. [13]For we write you nothing but what you can read and understand; I hope you will understand fully, [14]as you have understood in part, that you can be **proud** of us as we can be of you, on the day of the Lord Jesus.

[15]Because I was sure of this, I wanted to come to you first, so that you might have a double pleasure; [16]I wanted to visit you on my way to **Macedonia,** and to come back to you from **Macedonia** and have you send me on my way to Judea. [17]Was I vacillating when I wanted to do this? Do I make my plans like a worldly man, ready to say Yes and No at once? [18]As surely as God is faithful, our word to you has not been Yes and No. [19]For the Son of God, Jesus Christ, whom we preached among you, Silvanus and Timothy and I, was not Yes and No; but in him it is always Yes. [20]For all the promises of God find their Yes in him. That is why we utter the Amen through him, to the glory of God. [21]But it is God who establishes us with you in Christ, and has commissioned us; [22]he has put his seal upon us and given us his Spirit in our hearts as a guarantee.

[23]But I call God to witness against me—it was to spare you that I refrained from coming to Corinth. [24]Not that we lord it over your faith; we work with you for your joy, for you stand firm in your faith. 2:1 For I made up my mind not to make you another **painful visit.** [2]For if I cause you **pain,** who is there to make me glad but the one whom I have pained? [3]And **I wrote as I did,** so that when I came I might not be **pained** by those who should have made me rejoice, for I felt sure of all of you, that my joy would be the joy of you all. [4]For I wrote you out of much **affliction** and anguish of heart and with many tears, not to cause you **pain** but to let you know the abundant love that I have for you.

Commentary

1:12-14 For our boast is this. Paul's boast that he has acted with sincerity toward the Corinthians is prefatory to his explanation of why he told them he would visit them twice (vv 15-17) and then changed his mind about the second visit because he was afraid it would do more harm than good (1:23-2:4). His observation that "we write you nothing but what you can read and understand" (v 13) does not strike a responsive chord in the hearts of Scripture scholars, however much Paul himself felt that it was true.

1:15-22 Because I was sure of this, I wanted to come to you first, so that you might have a double pleasure. Paul's change of plans, eliminating a second visit to Corinth on his return from Macedonia to Ephesus (vv 15-16), left him open to the Corinthians' petulant accusation of acting insincerely and out of self-interest (v 17). His overly defensive explanation of his change of plans, with its claim and appeal to the straightforward yes or no called for by Jesus in the Sermon on the Mount (cf. Mt 5:37) shows that Paul knew only too well the testy character of his easily offended Corinthian converts (vv 18-22).

1:23-2:4 it was to spare you that I refrained from coming to Corinth. We do not know what happened on the first of Paul's two planned visits, but he speaks of the painful circumstances of the visit and of his fear that another visit would have caused more pain (2:1-2). Instead of a second visit, therefore, Paul sent a letter (2:3), in which he expressed his sorrow and anguish, and no doubt discussed with the Corinthians the confrontation that had made the first visit so painful (2:4).

(3) Paul forgives the offender at Corinth (2:5-11).

Text

(a)   2:5 But if **any one** has caused pain, he has caused it not to me, but in some measure—not to put it too severely—to you all. ⁶For **such a one** this punishment by the majority is enough; ⁷so you should rather turn to forgive and comfort **him,** or he may be overwhelmed by excessive sorrow. ⁸So I beg you to reaffirm your love for **him.** ⁹For this is why I **wrote,** that I might test you and know whether you are obedient in everything. ¹⁰Any one whom you forgive, I also forgive. What I have forgiven, if I have forgiven anything, has been for your sake in the presence of Christ, ¹¹to keep Satan from gaining the advantage over us; for we are not ignorant of his designs.

Commentary

2:5 But if any one has caused pain. The reference to a particular individual who had to be punished in some way (perhaps by a temporary excommunication from the community, as in 1 Cor 5:3-5) provides the best clue to the contents of the "painful letter" as well as to the painful circumstances of Paul's first of two planned visits. One may surmise that on this first visit a member of the community, perhaps at the instigation of a visiting evangelist from Jerusalem, had grossly insulted Paul and perhaps even denied his claim to be a true apostle. One may further surmise that the Corinthians did not stand up for Paul in these painful circumstances as he had a right to expect they would. The situation being such, one can understand why Paul would prefer to deal with it by letter, preferring no doubt to give the Corinthians time to think things over more dispassionately, rather than return in person and thus risk further insults and recriminations. The reference to the punishment (perhaps "reproof" would be a better word) inflicted by the community on the individual (v 6) indicates that Paul's "painful letter" had been successful and his change of plans justified.

(4) Paul goes to Macedonia to meet Titus (2:12-13).

Text

(a)   2:12 When I came to Troas to preach the gospel of Christ, a door was opened for me in the Lord; [13]but my mind could not rest because I did not find my brother **Titus** there. So I took leave of them and went on to **Macedonia.**

Commentary

2:12   When I came to Troas to preach the gospel of Christ. Paul's primary reason for leaving Ephesus and visiting Troas, a city in northwestern Asia Minor (modern Turkey), was to preach the gospel. (It is the thought of the gospel, mentioned here, that turns Paul's mind in the section that follows [2:14-7:3] to the triumphal march of Christ and the gospel through the world.) In addition, Paul hoped to meet Titus there on the latter's return from Corinth with news of the Corinthians' reaction to Paul's "painful letter." When Titus did not show up at Troas, Paul crossed over into Macedonia (v 13) and there, as he mentions in 7:4-16, eventually met up with him. Titus brought the good news that the "painful letter" had been successful in effecting a reconciliation between himself and the Corinthians. It is this good news that explains Paul's comfort and consolation (cf. 1:3-7; 7:4ff). In the closing section (a') of the letter, it is interesting to note the following parallels with section (a): the meeting with Titus in Macedonia (cp. 2:12-13 and 7:5-7); the "painful letter" and the offender at Corinth (cp. 2:3-11 and 7:8-13); Paul's comfort and consolation (cp. 7:4 and 1:3-7); Paul's boast (cp. 2:12-14 and 7:14-16). It is on the basis of these obvious parallels that we posit an A-B-A' format for the whole of 1:1-7:16. Our problem will be to show the relevance of section (b) to sections (a) and (a'). It will not be easy, but it is preferable to the postulate of the many critics who consider 2:14-7:3 to be an interpolation, however ill-conceived and carried out.

(b) 2:14-7:3: The ministry of the new covenant

The subject matter, vocabulary, and tone of 1:1-2:13, and especially 2:12-13, are so similar to the contents of 7:4-16 that many authors consider it certain that 7:4-16 is the immediate sequel and continuation of 1:12-2:13, and that as a consequence 2:14-7:3 must be an interpolation. We have already argued that this need not be so and that what looks like an apparent digression (and therefore an interpolation according to many) in 2:14-7:3 can be explained in the same way as the apparent digressions in 1 Cor 1-4; 5-6; 7; 8-11; 12-14 and the letter to the Philippians. Our problem is to discover what it is in the situation at Corinth and in the immediate context of the letter that leads Paul to what appears to be, but is not, a digression in 2:14-7:3.

There are two clues, and they are both related to the two central and associated themes of 2:14-7:3, namely, the gospel and the minister of the gospel. The immediate clue to why Paul turns so suddenly to these associated themes is his remark in 2:12 about coming to Troas to preach the gospel. This leads him to begin his apparent digression in 2:14-7:3 with an outburst of gratitude for the privilege he enjoys of being chosen by Christ to be the minister to others of the saving grace of the gospel (2:14-16). The other clue that helps to understand 2:14-7:3 as only an apparent digression is the reference in the immediate context (2:5-11) to the particular individual at Corinth who had offended Paul. There is good reason to believe that the offense consisted, among other things, in the impugning of Paul's claim to be a true apostle—a subject to which Paul returns regularly, if indirectly, in 2:14-7:3. In brief, the associated themes of the so-called digression in 2:14-7:3 are intimately connected with the subject matter of the immediate context: the preaching of the gospel at Troas (2:12) and the painful confrontation with an individual during Paul's visit to Corinth (2:5-11).[5]

In 2:14-7:3, Paul defends his apostleship and at the same time expounds the gospel as a message of glory manifested first in the lowliness and suffering of Jesus and then in the suffering and lowliness of the true apostle. As Willi Marxsen puts it: "The lowliness of Paul is the paradoxical proof of the validity of his activity as a servant of Christ."[6] Although Paul deals with much in this section that he will take up again in Galatians and Romans, his manner is not methodically theological, as it is in those letters, but personal, lyrical, and at times emotional. He moves from point to point erratically, linking one with the other by means of a chain of key words or particular expressions or even by common scriptural allusions. It will help the reader a great deal to note these key words, expressions, and scriptural allusions.

It will also help the reader to observe throughout this long section that Paul uses one magnificent mixed-up metaphor after another. He uses the metaphors of the triumphal march (2:14), the "aroma of Christ" (2:15), the "letter written on the heart" (3:1-6), the "veil" on Moses' face (3:12), the light shining out of the darkness (4:6), the apostles as "earthen vessels" (4:7), the body as a "tent" (5:1), and the Christian as a "new creation" (5:17). The positive pole of his metaphors is so overpowering that he simply slips from metaphor to metaphor in an almost frenzied attempt to verbalize the glowing reality in his mind. Underlying the metaphors and common to most of them is Paul's basic intuition about the essence of the spiritual life, namely, that the life-giving power or spirit that comes from the Father through the risen Christ is a power that makes all who believe in Christ one with Christ and with one another in such a way that they are literally a new humanity or a new creation. Understood in the light of this basic intuition and in the light of Paul's pastoral thrust toward a Christomorphism, the metaphors yield a great deal toward the understanding of Paul's theology of Christian spirituality and the apostolic ministry.[7]

(1) The triumphal march of the gospel (2:14-17)

Text

(b)   2:14 But thanks be to God, who in Christ always leads us in triumph, and through us spreads the fragrance of the knowledge of him everywhere. [15]For we are the aroma of Christ to God among those who are being saved and among those who are perishing, [16]to one a fragrance from death to death, to the other a fragrance from life to life. Who is sufficient for these things? [17]For we are not, like so many, peddlers of God's word; but as men of sincerity, as commissioned by God, in the sight of God we speak in Christ.

Commentary

2:14 But thanks be to God, who in Christ always leads us in triumph. Paul's remark about coming to Troas to preach the gospel (2:13) provides the springboard for his discussion of ministry and apostleship. He begins with the metaphor of the Roman triumph, likening the acceptance of Christ and the gospel by the pagans to the triumph of a victorious general. As an apostle who spreads the gospel, Paul pictures himself both as a collaborator of Christ and as one of those conquered by Christ and made by him to walk like a conquered slave in his triumphal procession. For Paul, obviously, it is a privilege to have been conquered by Christ. In Col 2:15, the same metaphor is used to dramatize God's victory over the powers of evil, who are paraded as conquered slaves in the triumphal procession: "He disarmed the principalities and powers and made an example of them, triumphing over them in him."

2:15 For we are the aroma of Christ to God. The metaphor of the "aroma of Christ" is based upon the custom of having incense-bearers in the triumphal procession. In 2:14b, Paul uses the Greek word *osmē* (fragrance) for the odor of this incense as a metaphor for the message of the gospel. But in 2:15 he uses a different Greek word — *euōdia* — which is a technical term for the odor of a sacrifice pleasing to God. Paul uses the more technical term to intimate what he will say more clearly later on, namely, that just as Christ offered himself in sacrifice and was accepted by God, so the apostle, who is meant to be the paradigm of Christ for others, will be offered as a sacrifice to God. The thought behind the metaphor is beautifully expressed in 4:10-12: ". . . always carrying in the body the death of Jesus, so that the life of Jesus may also be manifested in our bodies. For while we live we are always being given up to death for Jesus' sake, so that the life of Jesus may be manifested in our mortal flesh. So death is at work in us, but life in you."

2:16b Who is sufficient for these things? The magnitude of the privilege of being an apostle leads Paul to wonder if anyone is qualified for a mission such as this, and the question introduces one of the central themes of this section and the whole epistle, namely, the subject of the minister of the gospel and his qualifications. Paul's answer to the question takes up the major portion of 2:14-7:3 and all of 2 Cor 10-13. Paul's own answer to the question would be that no one, not even he himself, would be "sufficient." But he is probably retorting to the pseudo-apostles in Corinth who were boasting of their own qualifications and denying his.

2:17 For we are not, like so many, peddlers of God's word. His first retort to his opponents is an implied accusation that they are not just seeking support for their apostolic labors but trying to make money from preaching the gospel. In his earlier letter (1 Cor 9:3-18), Paul had defended his right to support from the communities he evangelized, but he had made it his boast that he never had asked and never would ask for such support from the Corinthians (1 Cor 9:15-18).

(2) The Corinthians are Paul's letter of recommendation (3:1-6).

Text

(b)   3:1 Are we beginning to commend ourselves again? Or do we need, as some do, letters of recommendation to you, or from you? [2]You yourselves are our letter of recommendation, written on your hearts, to be known and read by all men; [3]and you show that you are a letter from Christ delivered by us, written not with ink but with the Spirit of the living God, not on tablets of stone but on tablets of human hearts.

Commentary

For the meaning and significance of this most mixed-up of Paul's metaphors, the reader needs to keep in mind three things: first, the conversion of the Corinthians to Christ came about through the preaching of Paul; second, the consequent argument that the Corinthians' very existence as Christians testifies to the authenticity of Paul as an apostle; third, the text of the new covenant promise of Jeremiah (Jer 31:31-34), which provides the background and some of the vocabulary for Paul's metaphor of the "letter" written on the hearts of the Corinthians. The words in bold type are the words Paul plays on in his metaphor:

> Jer 31:31 Behold, the days are coming, says the Lord, when I will make **a new covenant** with the house of Israel and the house of Judah, [32]**not like the covenant which I made with their fathers** when I took them by the hand to bring them out of the land of Egypt, my covenant which they broke, though I was their husband, says the Lord. [33]But this is the covenant which I will make with the house of Israel after those days, says the Lord: **I will put my law within them, and I will write it upon their hearts;** and I will be their God, and they shall be my people. [34]And no longer shall each man teach his neighbor and each his brother, saying, 'Know the Lord,' **for they shall all know me,** from the least of them to the greatest, says the Lord; for I will forgive their iniquity, and I will remember their sin no more.

3:1-2 letters of recommendation. Paul's opponents appear to be men who came to Corinth with letters of recommendation authenticating them as missionaries. Who wrote the letters is not clear. An educated guess would suggest that it was the leaders of the Jerusalem church. Whether Paul's opponents accused him of preaching without a letter of recommendation or simply boasted that there was no doubt about their authenticity as apostles because they could present letters of recommendation from the Jerusalem church is not clear. In any event, Paul simply asserts that he has his own letter of recommendation, and it is the Corinthians themselves: "You yourselves are our letter of recommendation, written on your hearts" (v 2).

3:3 and you show that you are a letter from Christ delivered by us. Paul's argument is that the Corinthians are Christians, and since he was the apostle who originally brought them to accept Christ, it follows that Christ, by making the Corinthians Christians through the work of the Spirit, has written in their hearts his own letter of recommendation for Paul. Three agents are involved in the writing of the letter: Christ, who works through the Spirit, who in turn works through Paul to bring about the implantation of the new covenant in the hearts of the Corinthians. Through this letter written on their hearts by the Spirit, Paul can boast that he is a qualified minister of the new covenant (vv 4-6).

(3) Qualified ministers of the new covenant (3:4-18)

Text

(b)   3:4 Such is the confidence that we have through Christ toward God. [5]Not that we are sufficient of ourselves to claim anything as coming from us; our sufficiency is from God, [6]who has qualified us to be ministers of a new covenant, not in a written code but in the Spirit; for the written code kills, but the Spirit gives life.
        [7]Now if the dispensation of death, carved in letters on stone, came with such splendor that the Israelites could not look at Moses' face because of its

brightness, fading as this was, [8]will not the dispensation of the Spirit be attended with greater splendor? [9]For if there was splendor in the dispensation of condemnation, the dispensation of righteousness must far exceed it in splendor. [10]Indeed, in this case, what once had splendor has come to have no splendor at all, because of the splendor that surpasses it. [11]For if what faded away came with splendor, what is permanent must have much more splendor.

[12]Since we have such a hope, we are very bold, [13]not like Moses, who put a veil over his face so that the Israelites might not see the end of the fading splendor. [14]But their minds were hardened; for to this day, when they read the old covenant, that same veil remains unlifted, because only through Christ is it taken away. [15]Yes, to this day whenever Moses is read a veil lies over their minds; [16]but when a man turns to the Lord the veil is removed. [17]Now the Lord is the Spirit, and where the Spirit of the Lord is, there is freedom. [18]And we all, with unveiled face, beholding the glory of the Lord, are being changed into his likeness from one degree of glory to another; for this comes from the Lord who is the Spirit.

Commentary

The subject matter of 3:4-18 is the ministry of the new covenant message. The link with the previous section of the letter is the new covenant promise of Jeremiah (Jer 31:31-34), which Paul continues to interpret in terms of its fulfillment in Christ. In 3:1-3, the emphasis was on the new covenant written on the hearts of the Corinthians; here the emphasis is on the pre-eminence of the new covenant over the old. In 4:1–5:10, Paul will go on to describe himself and the other apostles as the "earthen vessels" that hold this treasure (4:7).

3:4 Such is the confidence that we have through Christ toward God. In 2:16, Paul, speaking about the ministry of the gospel, had asked: "Who is sufficient for these things?" Here Paul claims that sufficiency, but he goes on in vv 4-5 to attribute that sufficiency, not to himself, but to God, "who has qualified us to be ministers of a new covenant" (v 6).

3:6c for the written code kills, but the Spirit gives life. Paul is not putting down the old covenant as something bad or unspiritual. Indeed, as he will declare in Rom 7:14, it is spiritual and inspired by God. Rather, he is talking about the way the old covenant is interpreted by some Jews and especially some Judaizing Christians, namely, as if it were through the keeping of the law by one's own human efforts that one attained justification and salvation. Understood in this way, the "written code" can kill because it reduces religion and salvation to a human achievement and so denies that in reality it can only be a gift of God gratuitously given and freely accepted by those who accept it on faith. The "Spirit" on the other hand "gives life," because it is through the power of the life-giving Spirit that man believes in Christ and puts his trust in Christ, rather than in himself, to achieve a right relationship with God and the salvation that goes with this right relationship. Paul will deal with this difficult theological distinction at much greater length throughout Romans and especially in Rom 7:1ff.

3:7 Now if the dispensation of death . . . came with such splendor. The metaphor centers on the "splendor" or "glory" (Greek: *doxa;* Hebrew: *chabod)* of God, i.e., the externalized manifestation of God's salvific goodness and love as made known through the revelations of the old and new covenant. In addition to playing on the word "splendor" or "glory," the passage as a whole will play on the text of Exodus that describes the radiance (splendor) of Moses' face after he returned from seeing the "splendor" of Yahweh on Mount Sinai (cf. Ex 34:29-35). Paul uses a midrashic interpretation of this passage to bear out his contention that the new covenant is superior to the old. The text bears quoting:

> When Moses came down from Mount Sinai . . ., [he] did not know that the skin of his face shone because he had been talking with God. And when Aaron and all the people of Israel saw Moses, behold, the skin of his face shone, and they were afraid to come near him. . . . And when Moses had finished speaking with them, he put a veil on his face; but whenever Moses went in before the Lord to speak with him, he took the veil off, until he came out; and when he came out, and told the people of Israel what he was commanded, the people of Israel saw the face of Moses, that the skin of Moses' face shone; and Moses would put the veil upon his face again, until he went in to speak with him.

3:9 For if there was splendor in the dispensation of condemnation. Paul uses an *a fortiori* argument. If the old covenant had such splendor, how much greater the splendor of the new covenant, which surpasses the old (vv 10-11)! In short, Paul's argument is that if the old covenant, which failed, had so great a splendor at its inauguration, how much greater is the splendor of the new covenant. Paul develops this argument because in all likelihood his opponents are Judaizing missionaries who are insisting, as in Phil 3:2-16 and Gal 1–4, that it is necessary for salvation to obey the law of Moses.

3:12-13 Since we have such a hope, we are very bold. By a midrashic twist of interpretation (an interpretation that makes the meaning of a biblical text relevant to the immediate audience), Paul then explains the "veil" on Moses' face as put there to conceal from the Israelites the fact that the "glory" of the old covenant that was reflected on Moses' face was meant by God to fade away and be eclipsed by the "splendor" or "glory" of the new covenant revealed by Christ and preached by the apostles.

3:14-16 But their minds were hardened. By another midrashic twist, Paul argues that the "veil" is still hiding from the Jews the splendor of God because the Jews will not accept Christ, who alone can take away the veil and reveal to the Jews the splendor of God. Paul then accommodates the original text of Ex 34:34, which referred to Moses, to refer to the Jews of his own time. The original text reads: "Whenever Moses went in before the Lord to speak with him, he took the veil off." Paul's rereading of the text has a completely different sense. He reads it to mean: "But when a man (any Jew who heeds the Spirit) turns to the Lord (the Spirit, as v 17 states), the veil is removed."

3:17 Now the Lord is the Spirit. This puzzling statement is best interpreted to mean that "the Lord" mentioned in the previous verse ("when a man turns to the Lord") is the Spirit. Paul concludes by arguing that "we all [i.e., Christians who "turn to the Lord," i.e., the Spirit], with unveiled face, beholding the glory of the Lord, are being changed into his likeness from one degree of glory to another; for this comes from the Lord who is the Spirit" (v 18).

3:18 And we all . . . are being changed into his likeness. "Being changed into his likeness" introduces the theme of Christomorphism, which Paul will pursue in 4:10-18. At the same time, it forms an inclusion-conclusion with 3:7. The whole mixed-up metaphor began in 3:7 with Moses' radiant face reflecting the "splendor" of God seen on Mount Sinai. It ends with the astonishing declaration that Christians "with unveiled face, beholding the glory of the Lord," are not just reflecting that glory but "are being changed into his [Christ's] likeness from one degree of glory to another." The declaration presupposes that Christ is the image of God (cf. Gn 1:26) through whom the glory of the invisible Godhead becomes visible to men (cf. 4:4-6). Paul will develop the theme of Christomorphism in 4:1ff and especially in 4:8-12; 5:16-17.

It should be noted that by the time Paul reaches 3:18, his metaphor has more or less cracked under the impact of his developing thought. He had begun by speaking about the ministry of God's revelation. He continued by deducing that as Moses' face reflected like a mirror the revelation of God's glory to the Israelites (vv 7-11), so the apostles, like mirrors, reflect the glory of God revealed in Christ to all men (vv 12-13). By the time he ends in v 18, it is no longer a matter of reflecting the glory on God's or Christ's face, but "we all . . . beholding the glory of the Lord, are being changed into his likeness . . . ."

Paul's metaphor of Christians as mirrors reflecting the glory of Christ cracks under the impact of his understanding of Christians as "a new creation" (5:17). The "mirrors" are metamorphosed into what they reflect by the power of the Spirit, who brings about in humans the new creation that is the life of Christ (cf. 5:7; Rom 6:4; 8:10; Gal 6:15; Eph 4:23-28; Col 3:10). Although Paul mentions the "new creation" for the first time only in 5:17, he already lyrically anticipates it here and in 4:6, where he says: "For it is the God who said, 'Let light shine out of darkness,' who has shone in our hearts to give the light of the knowledge of the glory of God in the face of Christ." Paul's interpretation of Jeremiah's new covenant promise (Jer 31:31-34) has come to an end, but not before he has given the most profound interpretation of that famous text to be found in Sacred Scripture or anywhere else.[8]

(4) Earthen vessels (4:1–5:10)

Text

(b)   4:1 Therefore, having this ministry by the mercy of God, we do not lose heart. [2]We have renounced disgraceful, underhanded ways; we refuse to practice cunning or to tamper with God's word, but by the open statement of the truth we would commend ourselves to every man's conscience in the sight of God. [3]And even if our gospel is veiled, it is veiled only to those who are perishing. [4]In their case the god of this world has blinded the minds of the unbelievers, to keep them from seeing the light of the gospel of the glory of Christ, who is the likeness of God. [5]For what we preach is not ourselves, but Jesus Christ as Lord, with ourselves as your servants for Jesus' sake. [6]For it is the God who said, "Let light shine out of darkness," who has shone in our hearts to give the light of the knowledge of the glory of God in the face of Christ.

[7]But we have this treasure in earthen vessels, to show that the transcendent power belongs to God and not to us. [8]We are afflicted in every way, but not crushed; perplexed, but not driven to despair; [9]persecuted, but not forsaken; struck down, but not destroyed; [10]always carrying in the body the death of Jesus, so that the life of Jesus may also be manifested in our bodies. [11]For while we live we are always being given up to death for Jesus' sake, so that the life of Jesus may be manifested in our mortal flesh. [12]So death is at work in us, but life in you.

[13]Since we have the same spirit of faith as he had who wrote, "I believed, and so I spoke," we too believe, and so we speak, [14]knowing that he who raised the Lord Jesus will raise us also with Jesus and bring us with you into his presence. [15]For it is all for your sake, so that as grace extends to more and more people it may increase thanksgiving, to the glory of God.

[16]So we do not lose heart. Though our outer nature is wasting away, our inner nature is being renewed every day. [17]For this slight momentary affliction is preparing for us an eternal weight of glory beyond all comparison, [18]because we look not to the things that are seen but to the things that are unseen; for the things that are seen are transient, but the things that are unseen are eternal.

5:1 For we know that if the earthly tent we live in is destroyed, we have a building from God, a house not made with hands, eternal in the heavens. [2]Here indeed we groan, and long to put on our heavenly dwelling, [3]so that by putting it on we may not be found naked. [4]For while we are still in this tent, we sigh with anxiety; not that we would be unclothed, but that we would be further clothed, so that what is mortal may be swallowed up by life. [5]He who has prepared us for this very thing is God, who has given us the Spirit as a guarantee.

[6]So we are always of good courage; we know that while we are at home in the body we are away from the Lord, [7]for we walk by faith, not by sight. [8]We are of good courage, and we would rather be away from the body and at home with the Lord. [9]So whether we are at home or away, we make it our aim to please him. [10]For we must all appear before the judgment seat of Christ, so that each one may receive good or evil, according to what he has done in the body.

Commentary

4:1 Therefore, having this ministry by the mercy of God, we do not lose heart. In 4:1–5:10, Paul returns to the task of answering the question he had asked in 2:16b: "Who is sufficient for these things?" The immediate link with the preceding context is found in the words "Therefore, having *this ministry* . . . ." In 3:4-18, Paul had been discussing the vast difference between Moses' ministry of the message of glory of the old covenant and the Christian apostle's ministry of the message of the glory of Christ; now he speaks about the demands this more glorious ministry makes upon the minister of the gospel.

4:2-3 We have renounced disgraceful, underhanded ways. Paul's words do not imply that he had used such methods before. More likely, he is decrying the methods of his opponents.

4:4 In their case the god of this world has blinded the minds of the unbelievers. The "unbelievers" are those of v 3, for whom the gospel is veiled and who have been blinded by the "god of this world," who in biblical terms is the equivalent of Satan, the symbolic leader of the forces of anti-God. Paul does not mean that they are guiltless. Understood is the presupposition that they have allied themselves with the "god of this world" and as a consequence cannot see "the light of the gospel of the glory of Christ."

4:5-6 For what we preach is not ourselves, but Jesus Christ as Lord. Paul directs everything to Christ and sees himself as the servant of all for the sake of Christ. He who said "Let light shine out of darkness," i.e., God the Father, is the one who has shone in Paul's heart and thus brought him to this ministry of the new covenant, which consists in making known to others "the knowledge of the glory of God in the face of Christ." This knowledge is the gospel message, which in turn is the revelation of the glory of God manifested in and through Jesus. In these words Paul practically defines "gospel" as God's revelation of himself through Jesus.

4:7-12 But we have this treasure in earthen vessels. Whether calculated or not, Paul's descent from the metaphor of the ethereal "glory/splendor" of the new covenant in 3:4-18 to the metaphor of the lowly "earthen vessels," i.e., the ministers of the gospel, provides a dramatic counterpoint to his thought. The message of glory is carried by fragile human messengers. And the fragile human messengers witness to the truth of the gospel in the same manner as Christ himself did—by suffering and dying, by "always carrying in the body the death of Jesus, so that the life of Jesus may also be manifested" in their bodies (v 10). It is thus that the life of Jesus is manifested in the life of the apostle (vv 11-12). The true apostle is a paradigm of Christ! Let the pseudo-apostles reflect on that.

4:12 So death is at work in us, but life in you. The thought of dying as Christ did leads Paul to the thought of the resurrection (4:13-18) and to the thought of the resurrection life already present in the life of Christ's followers.

4:14-15 knowing that he who raised the Lord Jesus will raise us also. Equivalently, Paul is saying: "He who dies with Christ, rises with Christ." As more and more people understand and accept this as the true message of the gospel, their thanksgiving will increase to the glory of God (v 15).

4:16 Though our outer nature is wasting away, our inner nature is being renewed every day. Paul speaks of the resurrection life as the Christian's "inner nature," which, ideally at least, increases in vitality as the "outer nature," the body, decreases in vitality and moves toward bodily death. The "inner nature" or "inner man" is the same as the man of the "new creation" Paul speaks about in 5:17 and the same as the man he speaks about in Gal 2:20: "I have been crucified with Christ; it is no longer I who live, but Christ who lives in me."

4:17-18 For this slight momentary affliction. The thought again is that the person who suffers and dies with Christ also rises with Christ. Paul is not saying that his or anyone else's suffering is not burdensome. Suffering is only slight and momentary when compared with its opposite — "the things that are unseen," the "eternal weight of glory beyond all comparison." The sufferings are transient, but the reward, "the things that are unseen," are eternal (v 18).

5:1 For we know that if the earthly tent we live in is destroyed. Paul's statement in 4:18c about "the things that are unseen" provides the link between his reflections on "our outer . . . and inner nature" (4:16) and his reflections on the resurrection body in 5:1-5. The metaphor of the tent for the body is easy enough to understand. What is difficult to determine is how much light this metaphor throws upon Paul's conception of man's anthropological makeup. Does he conceive man according to the Hebrew anthropology of his time as an animated-body person or, as Greek anthropology saw man, as an incarnated soul? It has been argued that Paul's metaphor of the tent for the body indicates his capitulation to the Greek idea of man dichotomized into soul and body. W. D. Davies, however, more rightly argues that Paul's thought here is dominated by the idea of the exodus pilgrimage of man through life, during which he lives in the body as in a tent until he reaches the promised land and puts on his more lasting abode of a spiritual or pneumatic body.[9] The thought, therefore, would be substantially the same as the thought in 1 Cor 15:35ff.[10] For Paul, the earthly body is as transitory as the tents in which the Israelites lived until they finished their pilgrimage and arrived in the promised land.

5:2-5 Here indeed we groan. Paul is not a pessimist nor a sadist but a realist. When one compares what is with what is to come (cf. 4:18), one is forced to admit that life is often quite difficult and even burdensome.

5:6-9 So we are always of good courage. Still reflecting on the difference between what is and what is to come in the resurrection, Paul admits that he "would rather be away from the body and at home with the Lord" (v 8), but in either case he insists that the important thing is to please the Lord (v 9).

5:10 For we must all appear before the judgment seat of Christ. The remark is not idly made, since throughout this section, beginning with 2:14, Paul has been discussing the question of the qualified minister of the new covenant. Whether he or his opponents (with their letters of recommendation) are truly qualified will ultimately be answered in the judgment. Significantly, the judgment will be rendered according to what each "has done in the body." The qualification may be casual, but there is a good chance it is aimed at opponents who belong to the school of exaltation theology. If so, the remark is far from casual.

(5) The new creation and Paul's attitude toward others (5:11-21)

Text

(b)   5:11 Therefore, knowing the fear of the Lord, we persuade men; but what we are is known to God, and I hope it is known also to your conscience. [12]We are not commending ourselves to you again but giving you cause to be proud of us, so that you may be able to answer those who pride themselves on a man's position and not on his heart. [13]For if we are beside ourselves, it is for God; if we are in our right mind, it is for you. [14]For the love of Christ controls us, because we are convinced that one has died for all; therefore all have died. [15]And he died for all, that those who live might live no longer for themselves but for him who for their sake died and was raised.

[16]From now on, therefore, we regard no one from a human point of view; even though we once regarded Christ from a human point of view, we regard him thus no longer. [17]Therefore, if any one is in Christ, he is a new creation; the old has passed away, behold, the new has come. [18]All this is from God, who through Christ reconciled us to himself and gave us the ministry of reconciliation; [19]that is, God was in Christ reconciling the world to himself, not counting their trespasses against them, and entrusting to us the message of reconciliation. [20]So we are ambassadors for Christ, God making his appeal through us. We beseech you on behalf of Christ, be reconciled to God. [21]For our sake he made him to be sin who knew no sin, so that in him we might become the righteousness of God.

Commentary

5:11 Therefore, knowing the fear of the Lord, we persuade men. Turning from God's judgment (5:6-10) to men's judgment of him (5:11-15), Paul appeals to the consciences of the Corinthians to accept him for what he is. Those he wishes to persuade are the Corinthians, since the point of his whole argumentation and appeal is to establish that he is a true apostle, no matter what his opponents say about him.

5:12-13 We are not commending ourselves to you again. The purpose of Paul's argumentation is not so much to commend himself, but that the Corinthians who read what he has been saying in 2:14–5:10 concerning the "qualified" minister of the gospel versus the unqualified will be able "to answer those who pride themselves on a man's position and not on his heart" (v 12b). His statement in v 13: "For if we are beside ourselves, it is for God" leads into what follows in vv 14-21, which concerns Paul's new-found evaluation of all men as redeemed by Christ and therefore, in every instance, "a new creation."

5:14-15 For the love of Christ controls us. What controls Paul's life and what impels him to do what he does as an apostle is his conviction that Christ loves all men and has died for all. It is this overarching fact of life that conditions the way he regards and esteems all the different people with whom he comes in contact.

5:16 From now on, therefore, we regard no one from a human point of view. Paul's attitude toward others is based upon his understanding of Christ's work of reconciliation and upon his consequent view of all men as virtually or potentially new creations. The link between 5:16-21 and 5:6-15 is found in 5:14, in Paul's realization that since Christ died for all men, it must be that Christ loves all men. It is because of this love that Paul declares: "From now on, therefore, we regard no one from a human point of view." Merely human judgment is incapable of rightly evaluating the true dignity of every human person.

5:17 Therefore, if any one is in Christ, he is a new creation. According to God's judgment (and Paul's as a consequence), anyone "in Christ" is a "new creation." Paul, therefore, no longer regards persons simply as men or women. They are infinitely more because God, in Christ, was reconciling the world to himself, "not counting their trespasses against them" (5:19). The whole passage gives one the impression that behind all that Paul says here, there lies not only his profound understanding of the crucifixion (cf. 1 Cor 1:10-2:5) but also his rereading of Jeremiah's new covenant promise (Jer 31:31-34), especially Jer 31:34b: ". . . for I will forgive their evildoing and remember their sin no more."

5:18-20 All this is from God, who through Christ reconciled us to himself. Paul's concluding remarks about the message of reconciliation and about ambassadors for Christ fittingly summarize his reflections on the central and associated themes of 2:14–5:21, namely, the message of the gospel of the new covenant and the ministers of the new covenant. To reconcile means to restore a relationship to what it was before something damaged or destroyed it. The guilty party should be the reconciler. In this case, it is not the guilty party but the injured party—God—who brings about the reconciliation through Christ. That God has done this is the good news of the gospel that Paul, as God's ambassador, announces to the world.

5:21 For our sake he made him to be sin. The passage speaks of humankind's redemption. What men and women deserved — the penalty of sin — Jesus accepted in their place. What they did not deserve because of sin — reconciliation and righteousness, i.e., a right and warm relationship with God again — came about not because of themselves but because of the love of the Father manifested through his Son.

(6) Appeals to the Corinthians to be worthy of their call (6:1-7:3)

Text

(b)   6:1 Working together with him, then, we entreat you not to accept the grace of God in vain. ²For he says, "At the acceptable time I have listened to you and helped you on the day of salvation." Behold, now is the acceptable time; behold, now is the day of salvation.

³We put no obstacle in any one's way, so that no fault may be found with our ministry, ⁴but as servants of God we commend ourselves in every way: through great endurance, in afflictions, hardships, calamities, ⁵beatings, imprisonments, tumults, labors, watching, hunger; ⁶by purity, knowledge, forbearance, kindness, the Holy Spirit, genuine love, ⁷truthful speech, and the power of God; with the weapons of righteousness for the right hand and for the left; ⁸in honor and dishonor, in ill repute and good repute. We are treated as impostors, and yet are true; ⁹as unknown, and yet well known; as dying, and behold we live; as punished, and yet not killed; ¹⁰as sorrowful, yet always rejoicing; as poor, yet making many rich; as having nothing, and yet possessing everything.

¹¹Our mouth is open to you, Corinthians; our heart is wide. ¹²You are not restricted by us, but you are restricted in your own affections. ¹³In return — I speak as to children — widen your hearts also.

¹⁴Do not be mismated with unbelievers. For what partnership have righteousness and iniquity? Or what fellowship has light with darkness? ¹⁵What accord has Christ with Belial? Or what has a believer in common with an unbeliever? ¹⁶What agreement has the temple of God with idols? For we are the temple of the living God; as God said, "I will live in them and move among them, and I will be their God, and they shall be my people. ¹⁷Therefore come out from them, and be separate from them, says the Lord, and touch nothing unclean; then I will welcome you, ¹⁸and I will be a father to you, and you shall be my sons and daughters, says the Lord Almighty." 7:1 Since we have these promises, beloved, let us cleanse ourselves from every defilement of body and spirit, and make holiness perfect in the fear of God.

²Open your hearts to us; we have wronged no one, we have corrupted no one, we have taken advantage of no one ³I do not say this to condemn you, for I said before that you are in our hearts, to die together and to live together.

Commentary

Paul ends section (b) of his letter (2:14-7:3) with two appeals to the Corinthians: the first, in 6:1-10; the second, in 6:11-7:3. Both come from the heart and evince Paul's intense concern for the religious welfare of his beloved but trouble-prone Corinthian Christians.

6:1-2 Working together with him, then, we entreat you. The first appeal (6:1-10) is intimately connected with what Paul had said in 5:18-21 about God reconciling the world to himself through Christ and about Paul as the ambassador to whom has been entrusted the message of this reconciliation. Speaking as God's co-worker, since he is God's ambassador, Paul begs the Corinthians "not to accept the grace of God in vain." The appeal-warning is probably justified if, as Paul suspects, they are still attracted to the preaching of the Judaizing missionaries from Jerusalem, who are extolling the law and obedience to the law as necessary for salvation.

6:3-10 We put no obstacle in any one's way. Speaking about himself and other missionaries as "servants" (v 4), Paul goes on to speak about his function as ambassador-minister of the message of reconciliation. As a good ambassador, he avoids offending anyone unnecessarily lest his ministry suffer. In vv 4-10, he describes his ministry as one of hardship and sacrifice. The description is not digressive, since Paul is still dealing with the question, "Who is qualified to be a minister of the new covenant?" His answer, as usual, is that the way of the servant is like the way of the Master (cf. 4:8-18; 11:23-29; 1 Cor 4:9-12).

6:11-13 Our mouth is open to you, Corinthians; our heart is wide. Paul's second appeal (6:11-7:3) has an A-B-A' format: (a) 6:11-13; (b) 6:14-7:1; (a') 7:2-3. The parallels between (a) and (a') are obvious.

6:14-7:1 Do not be mismated with unbelievers. Paul's second appeal repeats in a different way his long appeal to the Corinthians in 1 Cor 8:1-11:1 to avoid idolatry (cf. especially 1 Cor 10:6-22). The appeal is linked with the previous appeal as another way of saying what Paul had said at the beginning of his first appeal in 6:1: "We entreat you not to accept the grace of God in vain." The appeal in 6:14-7:1 to avoid idolatry is surprising. But almost everything in 1 Cor 5-11 shows how great the danger was that the Corinthians might revert to the idolatrous religions they had practiced before their conversion. They were consorting again with prostitutes (1 Cor 6:12ff). They were involved in marriages with pagans (1 Cor 7:13ff). And they were again attending pagan temples and perhaps even taking part in pagan sacrifices (1 Cor 10:14-22). The second appeal, therefore, is not without some basis.

For sundry reasons, many critics consider 6:14-7:1 to be an interpolation.[11] But, as we have seen, Paul is capable of sudden digressions, and in this case as well as in 1 Cor 5-11, he probably had good reasons for cautioning the Corinthians, whose attitude toward idolatry was verging beyond the bounds of good sense. The A-B-A' format of 6:11-7:3, which is so typical of Paul's style, together with the inclusion-conclusion formed for the whole passage by 6:11-13 and 7:2-3, provides further evidence for the integrity of 6:14-7:1.

(a') 7:4-16: Consolation and reconciliation

Text

(a')   7:4 I have great confidence in you; I have great **pride** in you; I am filled
with **comfort.** With all our **affliction,** I am overjoyed. ⁵For even when we
came into **Macedonia,** our bodies had no rest but we were **afflicted** at every
turn—fighting without and fear within. ⁶But God, who **comforts** the
downcast, **comforted** us by the **coming of Titus,** ⁷and not only by his coming but also by the **comfort** with which he was **comforted** in you, as he told
us of your longing, your mourning, your zeal for me, so that I rejoiced still
more.

⁸For even if I made you sorry with **my letter,** I do not regret it (though I
did regret it), for I see that the **letter** grieved you, though only for a while.
⁹As it is, I rejoice, not because you were grieved, but because you were
grieved into repenting; for you felt a godly grief, so that you suffered no
loss through us. ¹⁰For godly grief produces a repentance that leads to salvation and brings no regret, but worldly grief produces death. ¹¹For see what
earnestness this godly grief has produced in you, what eagerness to clear
yourselves, what indignation, what alarm, what longing, what zeal, what
punishment! At every point you have proved yourselves guiltless in the
matter. ¹²So although I **wrote** to you, it was not on account **of the one who
did the wrong,** nor on account of the one who suffered the wrong, but in
order that your zeal for us might be revealed to you in the sight of God.
¹³Therefore we are **comforted.**

And besides our own **comfort** we rejoiced still more at the joy of **Titus,**
because his mind has been set at rest by you all. ¹⁴For if I have expressed to
him some **pride** in you, I was not put to shame; but just as everything we
said to you was true, so our **boasting** before **Titus** has proved true. ¹⁵And
his heart goes out all the more to you, as he remembers the obedience of
you all, and the fear and trembling with which you received him. ¹⁶I rejoice, because I have perfect confidence in you.

Commentary

In section (a'), as the reader who is familiar with Paul's A-B-A' format
would suspect, Paul returns to almost all of the themes and even many of
the words of section (a). The parallels are clear. The word "comfort," which
occurs ten times in 1:3-7, recurs here in 7:4, 6, 7, 13. There is mention again
of Paul in Macedonia meeting up with Titus (cp. 7:4-7 with 2:12-13). Again
mentioned are the "painful letter" and the offender at Corinth (cp. 7:8-13
and 2:3-11). And once again Paul boasts about the Corinthians' response
(cp. 7:14-16 and 1:12-14). The whole section speaks for itself and need only
be read in conjunction with its counterpart in 1:1–2:13.

B (8:1–9:15): The collection

In chs 8–9, Paul appeals to the Corinthians to contribute generously to
the collection he was taking up for the benefit of the mother church in
Jerusalem (cf. Gal 2:10; 1 Cor 16:1-4; Rom 15:25-28).

Because of the apparently abrupt change of subject from what precedes in chs 1–7, some critics explain these chapters as an addition made to the letter by editors at the end of the first century. Others break chs 8–9 into two letters, because ch 9 seems to repeat what was said in ch 8. Neither explanation is compelling. Paul's expression of confidence in the Corinthians in 7:14-16 provides an excellent transition to the new subject in chs 8–9, and the A-B-A' format of the chapters explains more than adequately the apparent repetitions. The A-B-A' format of chs 8–9 runs as follows: (a) 8:1-15: a first appeal for a generous contribution; (b) 8:16-24: a recommendation for Titus and his companions; (a') 9:1-15: a second appeal for a generous contribution.

(a) First appeal for a generous contribution (8:1-15)

Text

(a) 8:1 We want you to know, brethren, about the **grace of God** which has been shown in the churches of **Macedonia,** ²for in a severe test of affliction, their **abundance** of joy and their extreme poverty have overflowed in a wealth of **liberality** on their part. ³For they gave according to their means, as I can testify, and beyond their means, of their own **free will,** ⁴begging us earnestly for the favor of taking part in the **relief of the saints** — ⁵and this, not as we expected, but first they gave themselves to the Lord and to us by the will of God. ⁶Accordingly we have urged Titus that as he had already made a beginning, he should also complete among you this gracious work. ⁷Now as you excel in everything — in faith, in utterance, in knowledge, in all earnestness, and in your love for us — see that you excel in this gracious work also.

⁸I say this not as a command, but to prove by the earnestness of others that your love also is genuine. ⁹For you know the grace of our Lord Jesus Christ, that though he was **rich,** yet for your sake he became **poor,** so that by his poverty you might become **rich.** ¹⁰And in this matter I give my advice: it is best for you now to complete what a year ago you began not only to do but to desire, ¹¹so that your readiness in desiring it may be matched by your completing it out of what you have. ¹²For if the readiness is there, it is acceptable according to what a man has, not according to what he has not. ¹³I do not mean that others should be eased and you burdened, ¹⁴but that as a matter of equality your **abundance** at the present time should supply their want, so that their **abundance** may supply your want, that there may be equality. ¹⁵**As it is written,** "He who gathered much had nothing over, and he who gathered little had no lack."

Commentary

8:1-9 We want you to know, brethren, about the grace of God. The "grace of God" probably means the gift of faith, forgiveness, and justification that was given to the Macedonians at the time of their conversion and that subsequently inspired them to give generously to the collection for the church of Jerusalem. It should be noted that the repetition of these words in

9:14 forms an excellent inclusion-conclusion with 8:1. In what follows, Paul uses two examples to encourage the Corinthians to give generously: first, the generosity of the churches of Macedonia (vv 1-5); second, the generosity of Jesus (vv 8-9).

8:10-11 And in this matter I give my advice. Paul reminds the Corinthians that they have already volunteered to contribute to the collection (cp. vv 10-11 with vv 6-7).

8:12-15 For if the readiness is there. Since Paul has already spoken about the overflowing generosity of the Macedonians (vv 1-5) and of Jesus (v 9), one might expect him to call for a similar response on the part of the Corinthians. Instead, he understates — he asks only for a contribution from their abundance and further waters down his appeal by suggesting that the recipients of their largesse might reciprocate if ever the situation were reversed (v 14). He concludes by quoting from Ex 16:8, which speaks about the equality of those in the wilderness brought about by those receiving more manna giving to those who received less (v 15).

(b) A recommendation for Titus and his companions (8:16-24)

Text

(b) 8:16 But thanks be to God who puts the same earnest care for you into the heart of Titus. [17]For he not only accepted our appeal, but being himself very earnest he is going to you of his own accord. [18]With him we are sending the brother who is famous among all the churches for his preaching of the gospel; [19]and not only that, but he has been appointed by the churches to travel with us in this gracious work which we are carrying on, for the glory of the Lord and to show our good will. [20]We intend that no one should blame us about this liberal gift which we are administering, [21]for we aim at what is honorable not only in the Lord's sight but also in the sight of men.
[22]And with them we are sending our brother whom we have often tested and found earnest in many matters, but who is now more earnest than ever because of his great confidence in you. [23]As for Titus, he is my partner and fellow worker in your service; and as for our brethren, they are messengers of the churches, the glory of Christ. [24]So give proof, before the churches, of your love and of our boasting about you to these men.

Commentary

8:16-19 But thanks be to God who puts the same earnest care for you into the heart of Titus. Titus was well known to the Corinthians (2:13; 7:5-7) and would make a trustworthy delegate for Paul. His companion, "the brother who is famous among all the churches" (v 18), is not named but is well known as one of Paul's companions (v 19). These two, in addition to one other (v 22), are here given Paul's recommendation as men to be trusted with the collection (vv 23-24).

8:20-21 We intend that no one should blame us. Paul tries to leave no opening for the testy Corinthians to accuse him of fraud with regard to the collection. He fully realizes how much the stain of dishonesty could hinder the work of a missionary.

(a′) Second appeal for a generous contribution (9:1-15)

Text

(a′)   9:1 Now it is superfluous for me to write to you about **the offering for the saints,** ²for I know your readiness, of which I boast about you to the people of **Macedonia,** saying that Achaia has been ready since last year; and your zeal has stirred up most of them. ³But I am sending the brethren so that our boasting about you may not prove vain in this case, so that you may be ready, as I said you would be; ⁴lest if some **Macedonians** come with me and find that you are not ready, we be humiliated — to say nothing of you — for being so confident. ⁵So I thought it necessary to urge the brethren to go on to you before me, and arrange in advance for this gift you have promised, so that it may be ready not as an exaction but as a **willing gift.**

⁶The point is this: he who sows sparingly will also reap sparingly, and he who sows bountifully will also reap bountifully. ⁷Each one must do as he has made up his mind, not reluctantly or under compulsion, for God loves a cheerful giver. ⁸And God is able to provide you with every blessing in **abundance,** so that you may always have enough of everything and may provide in **abundance** for every good work. ⁹**As it is written,** "He scatters abroad, he gives to the **poor;** his righteousness endures for ever."

¹⁰He who supplies seed to the sower and bread for food will supply and multiply your resources and increase the harvest of your righteousness. ¹¹You will be **enriched** in every way for great **generosity,** which through us will produce thanksgiving to God; ¹²for the rendering of this service not only supplies **the wants of the saints** but also overflows in many thanksgivings to God. ¹³Under the test of this service, you will glorify God by your obedience in acknowledging the gospel of Christ, and by the **generosity** of your contribution for them and for all others; ¹⁴while they long for you and pray for you, because of the surpassing **grace of God** in you. ¹⁵Thanks be to God for his inexpressible gift!

Commentary

9:1-5 Now it is superfluous for me to write to you about the offering for the saints. In 8:1-5, Paul used the example of the Macedonians to stimulate the generosity of the Corinthians. Here in 9:2-4, he uses the Macedonians indirectly by mentioning how he had boasted to them about the generosity of the Corinthians. If the Corinthians do not contribute generously, Paul will be humiliated before the Macedonians (vv 3-4).

9:6-15 he who sows sparingly will also reap sparingly. The proverb contains an implicit appeal for generosity and is followed by a number of other implicit and explicit appeals. The reference to the "grace of God" recalls the same words in 8:1 and thus forms an inclusion for the whole of this part of the letter.

A' (10:1-13:14): The signs of a true apostle

In chs 10-13, Paul returns to a subject he had taken up in a less dramatic manner in chs 1-7, namely, the signs of the true apostle. There he had asked, in speaking about the work of the apostolate, "Who is sufficient for these things?" (2:16). In 3:1-7:3, he answered his question by describing the true apostle as a minister of the new covenant (3:1-4:6), as a weak "earthen vessel" carrying in the body "the death of Jesus" (4:7-5:15), and as an "ambassador for Christ" and co-worker with God (5:16-6:10). In chs 10-13, he returns to the subject of the marks of a true apostle and deals with it by contrasting his apostolate with that of certain missionaries whom he refers to as "false apostles, deceitful workmen, disguising themselves as apostles of Christ" (11:13). It is reasonable to believe that these false apostles are the same as those boasting about their "letters of recommendation" in 3:1. In short, Paul does here in 2 Cor 10-13 what he had done in parts of 1 Corinthians: he deals first with the problem in general (1:1-7:16) and then, after an intervening section (8:1-9:15), with the problem in particular (10:1-13:14). The last section of the letter (A'—10:1-13:14) has its own A-B-A' format: (a) what Paul will be like when he comes to Corinth again (10:1-18); (b) the signs of a true apostle (11:1-12:10); (a') what Paul will be like when he comes to Corinth again (12:11-13:14).

(a) What Paul will be like when he comes to Corinth again (10:1-18)

Text

(a)   10:1 I, Paul, myself entreat you, by the meekness and gentleness of Christ—I who am **humble** when face to face with you, but bold to you **when I am away!**—²I beg of you that **when I am present** I may not have to show boldness with such confidence as I count on showing against some who suspect us of acting in worldly fashion. ³For though we live in the world we are not carrying on a worldly war, ⁴for the weapons of our warfare are not worldly but have divine **power** to destroy strongholds. ⁵We destroy arguments and every proud obstacle to the knowledge of God, and take every thought captive to obey Christ, ⁶being ready to punish every disobedience, when your obedience is complete.

⁷Look at what is before your eyes. If any one is confident that he is Christ's, let him remind himself that as he is Christ's, so are we. ⁸For even if I boast a little too much of our **authority,** which the Lord gave **for building you up** and not for destroying you, I shall not be put to shame. ⁹I would not seem to be frightening you with letters. ¹⁰For they say, "His letters are weighty and strong, but his bodily presence is **weak,** and his speech of no account." ¹¹Let such people understand that what we say by letter when **absent,** we do when **present.**

¹²Not that we venture to class or compare ourselves with some of those who **commend** themselves. But when they measure themselves by one another, and compare themselves with one another, they are without understanding. ¹³But we will not boast beyond limit, but will keep to the limits God has apportioned us, to reach even to you. ¹⁴For we are not over-

extending ourselves, as though we did not reach you; we were the first to come all the way to you with the gospel of Christ. [15]We do not boast beyond limit, in other men's labors; but our hope is that as your faith increases, our field among you may be greatly enlarged, [16]so that we may preach the gospel in lands beyond you, without boasting of work already done in another's field. [17]"Let him who boasts, boast of the Lord." [18]For it is not the man who **commends** himself that is accepted, but the man whom the Lord **commends**.

Commentary

10:1-2   I, Paul, myself entreat you. Paul is about to speak about what he will be like when he comes to Corinth again and wants it known that he would prefer to have that tolerant attitude toward his opponents characteristic of the "meekness and gentleness of Christ." The words "I who am humble when face to face with you, but bold to you when I am away" paraphrase a charge of cowardice his opponents were making against him. The charge that he is bold when away refers in all likelihood to the so-called "painful letter" (cf. 2:4; 7:8). The "absent-present" theme recurs in 12:20-21 and 13:10.

10:3-5   For though we live in the world we are not carrying on a worldly war. Paul here refutes the charge of the "some" in v 2 who "suspect us of acting in worldly fashion." It is not clear whether these opponents are Corinthians or outsiders. From what follows, it seems best to consider them outsiders—missionaries who had come into the Corinthian community and charged Paul with being a false apostle. Paul's weapons are not worldly but spiritual (vv 4-5).

10:6   being ready to punish every disobedience. When the Corinthians as a group are obedient, Paul will punish those among them who have been disobedient. It is not clear who the disobedient are, but the context in 10:12-18 suggests that Paul is speaking about missionaries who have invaded his mission field in Corinth and have tried to discredit him as a true apostle.

10:7   Look at what is before your eyes. Paul invites the Corinthians to look at the facts of the situation.

If any one is confident that he is Christ's. These words sound like a paraphrase of the rival missionaries' charge: "We are Christ's, Paul is not!" Paul denies the charge by declaring "so are we."

10:8   For even if I boast a little too much of our authority. Paul admits that he is not reticent about his authority as an apostle, but insists that it is an authority "which the Lord gave for building you up." He repeats this contention in 13:10 and thereby forms a parallel between section (a) and section (a').

10:9-11   I would not seem to be frightening you with letters. Paul's statement almost certainly refers to his three earlier letters—his first lost letter mentioned in 1 Cor 5:9; his second letter (1 Cor 1–16); and his third letter, the "painful letter" mentioned in 2 Cor 2:3-4 and 7:8. His opponents noticed the difference of tone between Paul's preaching and his letters. They contended that, when present, Paul, according to their norms, was unimpressive and hardly what one would expect of a true apostle. His opponents, as he points out in 11:19-20, had no hesitation about exercising their authority over the Corinthians by making slaves of them, imposing on them, ordering them about, and even slapping them in the face. The irony here is that Paul is like Christ, and his accusers unlike Christ.

10:12 Not that we venture to class or compare ourselves with some of those who commend themselves. In 3:1, Paul mentioned how these missionaries came to Corinth with letters of recommendation (presumably from Jerusalem) and repudiated Paul on the grounds that he had no such letter of recommendation to support his claim to be a true apostle. Paul's remarks here about how these false apostles measure themselves by their own standards are preparatory to what he says in vv 13-14.

10:13-18 But we will not boast beyond limit. Paul boasts only that he kept to the limits God had apportioned him, namely, to preach the gospel in Corinth (v 14). His opponents, who came to Corinth after Paul had evangelized and converted the Corinthians, were guilty of boasting about another man's (Paul's) labors. Paul, on the other hand, did not interfere with the work of other apostles, as his opponents were doing by entering into his territory (v 15). He hoped to continue his apostolic work by going beyond Corinth to other places that had not yet heard the gospel (v 16). He is satisfied to be commended by God (vv 17-18) rather than commend himself, as his opponents do.

(b) The signs of a true apostle (11:1-12:10)

Section (b) contains at the same time a sarcastic refutation of his rivals' claim to be true apostles (11:1-21) and Paul's own understanding of what constitutes a true apostle. For Paul, a true apostle is one who suffers for Christ. He is one who boasts only of his weakness, because it is through his weakness that the power of Christ works (11:22-12:10). He can say, in short, "When I am weak, then I am strong" (12:10).

In order to understand this difficult section, the reader needs to be aware of the unusual stance Paul adopts in relation to both his Corinthian audience and to his rivals. His stance toward the Corinthians is that of a man who pleads his case before them by adopting, with obvious and sarcastic parody, the same boastful and foolish manner of speaking used by his rivals. His stance toward his rivals is one of contrast. He contrasts their idea of a true apostle with his own, and by means of the contrast compels the Corinthians to make a true judgment concerning the righteousness of his claims versus those of his opponents.

Text

(b)   11:1 I wish you would bear with me in a little foolishness. Do bear with me! ²I feel a divine jealousy for you, for I betrothed you to Christ to present you as a pure bride to her one husband. ³But I am afraid that as the serpent deceived Eve by his cunning, your thoughts will be led astray from a sincere and pure devotion to Christ. ⁴For if some one comes and preaches another Jesus than the one we preached, or if you receive a different spirit from the one you received, or if you accept a different gospel from the one you accepted, you submit to it readily enough. ⁵I think that I am not in the least inferior to these superlative apostles. ⁶Even if I am unskilled in speaking, I am not in knowledge; in every way we have made this plain to you in all things.

⁷Did I commit a sin in abasing myself so that you might be exalted, because I preached God's gospel without cost to you? ⁸I robbed other churches by accepting support from them in order to serve you. ⁹And when I was with you and was in want, I did not burden any one, for my needs were supplied by the brethren who came from Macedonia. So I refrained and will refrain from burdening you in any way. ¹⁰As the truth of Christ is in me, this boast of mine shall not be silenced in the regions of Achaia. ¹¹And why? Because I do not love you? God knows I do!

¹²And what I do I will continue to do, in order to undermine the claim of those who would like to claim that in their boasted mission they work on the same terms as we do. ¹³For such men are false apostles, deceitful workmen, disguising themselves as apostles of Christ. ¹⁴And no wonder, for even Satan disguises himself as an angel of light. ¹⁵So it is not strange if his servants also disguise themselves as servants of righteousness. Their end will correspond to their deeds.

¹⁶I repeat, let no one think me foolish; but even if you do, accept me as a fool, so that I too may boast a little. ¹⁷(What I am saying I say not with the Lord's authority but as a fool, in this boastful confidence; ¹⁸since many boast of worldly things, I too will boast.) ¹⁹For you gladly bear with fools, being wise yourselves! ²⁰For you bear it if a man makes slaves of you, or preys upon you, or takes advantage of you, or puts on airs, or strikes you in the face. ²¹To my shame, I must say, we were too weak for that!

But whatever any one dares to boast of — I am speaking as a fool — I also dare to boast of that. ²²Are they Hebrews? So am I. Are they Israelites? So am I. Are they descendants of Abraham? So am I. ²³Are they servants of Christ? I am a better one — I am talking like a madman — with far greater labors, far more imprisonments, with countless beatings, and often near death. ²⁴Five times I have received at the hands of the Jews the forty lashes less one. ²⁵Three times I have been beaten with rods; once I was stoned. Three times I have been shipwrecked; a night and a day I have been adrift at sea; ²⁶on frequent journeys, in danger from rivers, danger from robbers, danger from my own people, danger from Gentiles, danger in the city, danger in the wilderness, danger at sea, danger from false brethren; ²⁷in toil and hardship, through many a sleepless night, in hunger and thirst, often without food, in cold and exposure. ²⁸And, apart from other things, there is the daily pressure upon me of my anxiety for all the churches. ²⁹Who is weak, and I am not weak? Who is made to fall, and I am not indignant?

³⁰If I must boast, I will boast of the things that show my weakness. ³¹The God and Father of the Lord Jesus, he who is blessed for ever, knows that I do not lie. ³²At Damascus, the governor under King Aretas guarded the city of Damascus in order to seize me, ³³but I was let down in a basket through a window in the wall, and escaped his hands.

12:1 I must boast; there is nothing to be gained by it, but I will go on to visions and revelations of the Lord. ²I know a man in Christ who fourteen years ago was caught up to the third heaven — whether in the body or out of the body I do not know, God knows. ³And I know that this man was caught up into Paradise — whether in the body or out of the body I do not know, God knows — ⁴and he heard things that cannot be told, which man may not utter. ⁵On behalf of this man I will boast, but on my own behalf I will not boast except of my weaknesses. ⁶Though if I wish to boast, I shall not be a fool, for I shall be speaking the truth. But I refrain from it, so that no one may think more of me than he sees in me or hears from me. ⁷And to keep me from being too elated by the abundance of revelations, a thorn was given me in the flesh, a messenger of Satan, to harass me, to keep me from being too elated. ⁸Three times I besought the Lord about this, that it should leave me; ⁹but he said to me, "My grace is sufficient for you, for my power is made perfect in weakness." I will all the more gladly boast of my weaknesses, that the power of Christ may rest upon me. ¹⁰For the sake of Christ, then, I am content with weaknesses, insults, hardships, persecutions, and calamities; for when I am weak, then I am strong.

Commentary

11:1 I wish you would bear with me in a little foolishness. The Corinthians have put up with a great deal of foolishness from Paul's rivals. Presumably, it is not too much to ask that they put up with a little foolishness from Paul. The theme of foolishness runs throughout the whole section and helps to unify it (cf. 11:1, 16, 17, 19, 21; 12:6, 11).

11:2-3 I feel a divine jealousy for you. Paul justifies his apparent foolishness by pointing out that his purpose is to prevent the seduction of Christ's bride, the Corinthian church, by a new serpent that is out to seduce them as the old serpent seduced Eve.

11:4 For if some one comes and preaches another Jesus. The seduction of Christ's bride is brought about by those who preach another Christ, a different spirit, and a different gospel from those preached by Paul. That Paul's rivals so preach is clear from vv 13-14, where they are castigated as "false apostles, deceitful workmen, disguising themselves as apostles of Christ," just as "Satan disguises himself as an angel of light."

11:5-6 I think that I am not in the least inferior to these superlative apostles. Paul's rivals boast of their superior oratory and knowledge, but as Paul reminds the Corinthians, they know well from their dealings with him that however unskilled (perhaps an understatement) he is in speaking, there is no question about his theological knowledge. The knowledge obviously has to do with Christ, the spirit, and the gospel mentioned in vv 4-5.

11:7-11   Did I commit a sin in abasing myself so that you might be ex-alted, because I preached God's gospel without cost to you? Paul accepted support from other Christian communities (cf. v 9 and Phil 4:10-20) but not from the Corinthians, even though he argued that he had a right to it (cf. 1 Cor 9:4-18). His opponents evidently argued that the laborer is worthy of his hire, and if Paul did not accept compensation for his preaching, it was because he did not consider himself worthy of it and was not therefore a true apostle. Whatever Paul's reason for not accepting compensation from the Corinthians, it certainly was not because he considered himself un-worthy of it. The Corinthians knew well what Paul thought of himself (cf. 1 Cor 9:1ff). There is, therefore, a biting irony in the words "Did I commit a sin in abasing myself so that you might be exalted?" There is also in these words a subtle allusion to the example of Christ, who, as Paul reminded them in 8:9, "though he was rich, yet for your sake became poor, so that by his poverty you might become rich" (cf. also Phil 2:6-11).

11:12   And what I do I will continue to do. Preaching without compen-sation is something Paul can boast about, and he will continue to so preach in order to undermine the claim of his rivals that they work on the same terms as he does.

11:13-15   For such men are false apostles. Paul's judgment of his rivals is severe. What he says about Satan (v 14) should be read in the context of the serpent deceiving Eve (11:2-4). He is severe in his judgment not only because his rivals have attacked him but because they have taught "another Jesus . . . a different spirit . . . a different gospel" (11:4). In all proba-bility, it is the Judaizers' gospel of the law and works (cf. Phil 3:2-16).

11:16-18   I repeat, let no one think me foolish. Paul is not repeating his exact words but rather what he intimated in 11:1. He is not really foolish—he is only feigning foolishness so that the Corinthians will be able to judge between his "foolishness" and the real foolishness of his rivals.

11:19-20   For you gladly bear with fools. If the Corinthians can put up with the foolishness of Paul's rivals, who make slaves of them, put on airs, and even strike them in the face (v 20), then they certainly can put up with Paul's foolishness.

11:21a   To my shame, I must say, we were too weak for that! The state-ment brims with irony. Paul is neither weak nor ashamed, and the Corin-thians know it. He can glory in the fact that he never made slaves of the Corinthians, never put on airs, and certainly never beat them as a master beats his slaves. If the Corinthians can put up with such an exploitation of ecclesiastical authority on the part of his rivals, then they are as much to be blamed as their exploiters.

11:21b-29   But whatever any one dares to boast of—I am speaking as a fool—I also dare to boast of that. Feigning the fool, Paul compares himself with his rivals and outdoes them in every way, especially in self-sacrifice—

the quintessential mark of a true apostle. His rivals glory in being Hebrews, Israelites, descendants of Abraham, and servants of Christ (vv 22-23). Paul is all that and more (vv 28-29). Here he repeats in a different way much that he had already said about the marks of a true apostle in the (A) section (1:1–7:16) of his letter (cf. 2:14-15; 4:7-12; 6:3-10).

11:30-33 If I must boast, I will boast of the things that show my weakness. Paul's rivals boast of their strength. Paul, on the other hand, knows well that all real power, i.e., especially power that moves people to turn to God, comes from God alone. The less the apostle relies on himself, the more he can count on the power of God. Paul therefore glories in his weakness (cf. 4:7-12; 13:3-9). As an example of his weakness, he tells the story of the humiliating method he had to use to escape arrest by the king's guards in Damascus (vv 32-33). No eye-popping exodus miracles there!

12:1-4 I must boast; there is nothing to be gained by it, but I will go on to visions and revelations. Paul continues his feigned foolishness with another reminder that such foolishness is useless. His rivals have evidently boasted that their visions and revelations prove that they are authentic apostles. But Paul, too, can boast of visions. The date of the vision, "fourteen years ago," sometime in the early forties, would suggest that Paul is talking about a real experience and is not just parodying the stories told by his rivals. Apart from that, Paul does not attempt to analyze the vision. That would appear to be the import of such remarks as "I know a man in Christ," "whether in the body or out of the body I do not know, God knows" (vv 2-3), and "things that cannot be told, which man may not utter" (v 4).

12:5-6 On behalf of this man I will boast, but on my own behalf I will not boast, except of my weaknesses. Paul can equal the boasts of his rivals, but he considers such visions and revelations unimportant. Like the gift of tongues, they do nothing to build up the Church (cf. 1 Cor 14). Paul's real boast has to do with his weakness—a weakness that allows the power of God to be manifested for the benefit of the Church (cf. 13:4).

12:7-10 And to keep me from being too elated by the abundance of revelations, a thorn was given me in the flesh. With these four verses, Paul concludes his defense scenario before the Corinthians by asking them to compare his feigned foolishness with the real foolishness of his rivals. His rivals boasted of their strength, their authority, and their visions and revelations. Paul downplays his visions and revelations, refuses to exploit his authority for his own aggrandizement, and boasts only of his weakness.

Paul's "thorn in the flesh" might have been a speech defect or epilepsy or malaria or some other physical ailment. It is impossible to tell and futile to guess. Paul speaks about it to buttress his argument that God's "power is made perfect in weakness" (v 9) and that the authentic signs of a true apostle are found in a life (like that of Christ) that is filled with "weaknesses, insults, hardships, persecutions, and calamities" (v 10). In short, the true apostle is like his master (cf. Mt 10:24-29; Jn 13:13-17).

(a') What Paul will be like when he comes again to Corinth (12:11-13:14)

Text

(a')   12:11 I have been a fool! You forced me to it, for I ought to have been **commended** by you. For I am not at all inferior to these superlative apostles, even though I am nothing. ¹²The signs of a true apostle were performed among you in all patience, with signs and wonders and mighty works. ¹³For in what were you less favored than the rest of the churches, except that I myself did not burden you? Forgive me this wrong!

¹⁴Here for the third time I am ready to come to you. And I will not be a burden, for I seek not what is yours but you; for children ought not to lay up for their parents, but parents for their children. ¹⁵I will most gladly spend and be spent for your souls. If I love you the more, am I to be loved the less? ¹⁶But granting that I myself did not burden you, I was crafty, you say, and got the better of you by guile. ¹⁷Did I take advantage of you through any of those whom I sent to you? ¹⁸I urged Titus to go, and sent the brother with him. Did Titus take advantage of you? Did we not act in the same spirit? Did we not take the same steps?

¹⁹Have you been thinking all along that we have been defending ourselves before you? It is in the sight of God that we have been speaking in Christ, and all for your **upbuilding,** beloved. ²⁰For I fear that perhaps I may come and find you not what I wish, and that you may find me not what you wish; that perhaps there may be quarreling, jealousy, anger, selfishness, slander, gossip, conceit, and disorder. ²¹I fear that when I come again my God may **humble** me before you, and I may have to mourn over many of those who sinned before and have not repented of the impurity, immorality, and licentiousness which they have practiced.

13:1 This is the third time I am coming to you. Any charge must be sustained by the evidence of two or three witnesses. ²I warned those who sinned before and all the others, and I warn them now **while absent,** as I did **when present** on my second visit, that if I come again I will not spare them— ³since you desire proof that Christ is speaking in me. He is not **weak** in dealing with you, but is **powerful** in you. ⁴For he was crucified in weakness, but lives by the **power** of God. For we are **weak** in him, but in dealing with you we shall live with him by the **power** of God.

⁵Examine yourselves, to see whether you are holding to your faith. Test yourselves. Do you not realize that Jesus Christ is in you?—unless indeed you fail to meet the test! ⁶I hope you will find out that we have not failed. ⁷But we pray God that you may not do wrong—not that we may appear to have met the test, but that you may do what is right, though we may seem to have failed. ⁸For we cannot do anything against the truth, but only for the truth. ⁹For we are glad when we are **weak** and you are strong. What we pray for is your improvement. ¹⁰I write this **while I am away** from you, in order that when I come I may not have to be severe in my use of the **authority** which the Lord has given me **for building up** and not for tearing down.

¹¹Finally, brethren, farewell. Mend your ways, heed my appeal, agree with one another, live in peace, and the God of love and peace will be with

you. ¹²Greet one another with a holy kiss. ¹³All the saints greet you. ¹⁴The grace of the Lord Jesus Christ and the love of God and the fellowship of the Holy Spirit be with you all.

Commentary

12:11 I have been a fool! You forced me to it, for I ought to have been commended by you. Paul has finished his feigned "foolishness" defense of himself (11:1–12:10) and now returns to where he left off in 10:18. The immediate link is the subject of recommendations (cp. 10:18 and 12:11). In 3:1ff, Paul's rivals boasted about the letters of recommendation they had. Paul in reply had claimed that the Corinthians themselves constituted his letter of recommendation. He now reminds the Corinthians that they have forced him to play the fool (11:1–12:10), a distasteful experience they should have spared him by giving him the commendation—recommendation they knew he deserved after seeing manifested in him "the signs of a true apostle" (v 12).

12:13-15 For in what were you less favored than the rest of the churches. As Paul mentioned in 11:7-12, he accepted no compensation from the Corinthians. Now, with ill-concealed irony, he says, "Forgive me this wrong!" (v 13). The irony continues as he likens his care for the Corinthians to that of parents providing for their children (v 14) and asks with bittersweet irony, "If I love you the more, am I to be loved the less?" (v 15).

12:16-18 But granting that I myself did not burden you. The Corinthians knew that Paul accepted no support from them. These verses suggest, however, that either his rivals or others were accusing him of defrauding them by making use of funds given to Titus and his companions. Paul had sent Titus to Corinth earlier (cf. 2:13; 7:6-7) and was sending him again (cf. 8:16-24). Paul can do nothing more than deny the charge and appeal to their knowledge of Titus' good character.

12:19 Have you been thinking all along that we have been defending ourselves before you? Paul's defense of himself (11:1–12:10) was not for his own sake but for the sake of the people and for the upbuilding of the Corinthian community (cf. 10:8). The two go together because there will be no building up of the community if Paul and his gospel are discredited and the Corinthians go over to the false apostles and their false gospel (v 9).

12:20-21 For I fear that perhaps I may come and find you not what I wish. The whole of section (a') deals with what Paul will be like when he comes to visit Corinth again, and he regularly mentions this coming visit (cf. 12:14, 20, 21; 13:1, 2, 10), just as he had earlier (cf. 10:2, 10-11) in section (a). These two verses express indirectly Paul's purpose when he wrote the letter. The letter is meant to wean the Corinthians from the false apostles and restore the situation to what it was before the false apostles arrived. If it does not, Paul will again encounter the usual senseless quarreling and disorder (v 20), and will be humbled before them by having to mourn their failure as Christians (v 21). The references to impurity, immorality, and licentiousness may well be references to the vices Paul attacked in 1 Cor 5-6; 8-10. If the Corinthians have repudiated Paul, they have probably also repudiated what he said about these vices in 1 Corinthians.

13:1-3a   This is the third time I am coming to you. Paul's first visit took place when he founded the community; his second, when he had the bitter confrontation with a member of the community (cf. 2:1-11). On his coming third visit, he will act with the authority of the true apostle (v 3). He will demand that they sustain their accusations with witnesses according to Dt 19:15 (v 1a). He warns the sinners that he will not spare them (v 2).

13:3b-4   He is not weak in dealing with you. Jesus will deal with the Corinthians through Paul his apostle. Just as no one can doubt Jesus' power and authority even though he was "crucified in weakness," so they will not be able to doubt Paul's authority even though he has suffered as Christ has suffered (cf. 12:8-10).

13:5-6   Examine yourselves, to see whether you are holding to your faith. The Corinthians are quick to judge others, especially Paul. Now they are asked to judge themselves. Having Jesus in them and holding to the faith are synonymous for Paul (v 5). Paul hopes that if they really hold to the faith, they will see that he has not failed, i.e., that Christ Jesus is in him. Here again Paul is speaking about the purpose for which he wrote the letter.

13:7-9   But we pray God that you may not do wrong. Paul's prayer is motivated by sincere concern for the Corinthians and not by the vain satisfaction he might get from proving himself right and them wrong (v 7). It is the truth of the gospel that is important (v 8). Paul is perfectly willing to appear wrong (weak, in the sense of suffering) as long as the Corinthians accept what is right (i.e., are strong in the truth of the gospel) and continue to improve (v 9).

13:10   I write this while I am away from you. With these words about absence and presence and the writing of letters, Paul returns to what he had said in 10:1-2 about his absence and presence and what he had said in 10:8 about the authority given to him "for building you up and not for destroying you." With these and other parallels (cp. 10:2 with 12:20 and 13:2; 10:7 with 13:5; 10:8 with 13:10; 10:11 with 13:10), Paul provides an excellent inclusion-conclusion for the whole of 10:1-13:14.

13:11-14   Finally, brethren, farewell. If the Corinthians "heed" Paul's appeal, then "the God of love and peace will be with" them (v 13). This fitting admonition terminates the letter and is followed by the usual greetings and blessing (v 14).

Chapter VI

THE
LETTER OF PAUL TO THE
GALATIANS

The country that is today called Turkey was called Galatia in Paul's time. It acquired its name from the Celtic tribes called the Galloi, who moved into north-central Asia Minor in the third century B.C. The territory they occupied came to be called Galatia. Later the Romans took over the whole of Asia Minor and made it into a Roman province called Galatia. Whether the churches Paul writes to were in the original territorial homeland of the Celtic tribes near modern Ankara or in the southern part of Asia Minor, where the towns of Lystra, Derbe, Iconium, and Antioch in Pisidia (all mentioned in Acts 13:13–14:21; 16:1-5 as places Paul evangelized) are situated, is much debated. Wherever in Asia Minor the Galatian churches were situated, it is clear that Paul had founded them on one of his missionary journeys. It is also clear from Paul's own words (cf. Gal 4:8) that the Galatians had been outright pagans at the time of their conversion to Christianity (3:1-5).

Purpose of the letter

Paul wrote to the Galatians because a serious theological crisis had arisen in the churches he had founded. Sometime in the years following his founding of the churches, Jewish Christian missionaries (probably from Jerusalem) visited the Galatian churches and challenged Paul's gospel of salvation through faith in Jesus. Paul calls these missionaries "the circumcised" (cf. 6:13). The name, along with what he says about them in 1:6-10; 2:4-5; 3:1-5, identifies them as Jewish converts to Christianity who were still so wedded to their old way of life in Judaism that they wanted and even insisted that all Christians, even Gentiles such as the Galatians, should be circumcised and observe the Mosaic law. Paul opposes them not only because he has taught that all Christians are free of the law but because they were trying to convince the Galatians that such observance of the law was necessary for salvation. Paul attacks this thesis regularly throughout the letter.[1]

Date of the letter

It is disputed whether Paul wrote Galatians early or late in his career. We have adopted a late date primarily because of the contrast between Paul's relaxed stance toward the law in his earlier letters (1 Thessalonians, 1 and 2 Corinthians) and his severely critical stance in Galatians, Philippians, and Romans. In 1 Cor 7:18-19, written between 54 and 55 A.D., Paul speaks about circumcision as if it were a matter of total indifference to him. "Was any one," he says, "at the time of his call already circumcised? Let him not seek to remove the marks of circumcision. Was any one at the time of his call uncircumcised? Let him not seek circumcision. For neither circumcision counts for anything nor uncircumcision, but keeping the commandments of God." The same is true for his lengthier statement in 1 Cor 9:19-21: "For though I am free from all men, I have made myself a slave to all, that I might win the more. To the Jews I became as a Jew, in order to win Jews; to those under the law I became as one under the law — though not being myself under the law — that I might win those under the law. To those out-side the law I became as one outside the law — not being without law toward God but under the law of Christ — that I might win those outside the law."

In a later statement in 1 Cor 15:56, Paul says: "The sting of death is sin, and the power of sin is the law," but the statement is not in a context of vehement and even virulent opposition to the law such as he shows in Gala-tians and Romans. Again, in 2 Cor 3:6-18, Paul contrasts the greater glory of the new covenant with the dying glory of the old covenant, but there is no clear-cut evidence that he is overtly attacking the law and those who live ac-cording to its tenets. He is at the most indirectly attacking what he thinks may be the brunt of the false gospel preached by the pseudo-apostles men-tioned later in 2 Cor 10-13. Admittedly, Paul attacks the law in Phil 3:2-9 just as vehemently as he does in Galatians and Romans, but almost all com-mentators consider Philippians a late letter, some dating it to the time of 2 Corinthians (ca. 56), others dating it as late as Paul's Roman imprisonment in 60 to 62 A.D.

In brief, Galatians was written late in Paul's career, at a time when he was no longer indifferent about the Mosaic law and circumcision. When he wrote Galatians, he was out to attack the law and to refute those who in-sisted on its observance as necessary for salvation. His language is a far cry from his more tolerant language in 1 Cor 7:18-19; 9:19-21; 15:56, and 2 Cor 3:6-18. In Galatians, the law has become the rival of Christ and the adver-sary of the true gospel! As R. Fuller says: "The view that it [Gal] was written about the time of the Corinthian correspondence has much to commend it. . . . Another consideration is that such a dating brings Gal much closer to Rom with which again it has marked affinities."[2]

It should be noted in passing that this critical issue of circumcision and the observance of the Mosaic law dominates only a brief period of Paul's life. The issue is dead by the time the Gospels come to be written in the last quarter of the first century.[3] If Paul wrote any letters after Romans, he does not bring up the question of the law. In Col 4:11-13, which may or may not be an authentic Pauline letter but is certainly Pauline in tenor, the question of circumcision and the Mosaic law is no longer a matter of critical concern. The same is true in Ephesians.

Internal evidence, therefore, suggests that Galatians was written shortly after 2 Corinthians, sometime around 57 A.D. from either Ephesus or Macedonia. It is not unlikely that the gibe of Paul's adversaries at Corinth: "His letters are weighty and strong, but his bodily presence is weak, and his speech of no account" (2 Cor 10:10) may have led Paul himself to realize for the first time the impact and effectiveness of his letters. Galatians and Romans reflect this consciousness. They are strong, profound, and self-assured — the writings of a theologian conscious of his powers.

Format and division of Galatians

H. D. Betz claims that Galatians is an example of the Greek literary form known as the "apologetic letter" and outlines it as follows: I. Epistolary prescript (1:1-5); II. Exordium (1:6-11); III. Narratio (1:12–2:14); IV. Propositio (2:15-21); V. Probatio (3:1–4:31); VI. Exhortatio (5:1–6:10); VII. Epistolary postscript (6:11-18).[4]

Whatever acquaintance Paul may have had with the literary form known as the "apologetic letter" (and he may indeed have known it and been influenced by it in writing Galatians), we believe the recognition of Paul's typical chiastic format, already recognized and demonstrated in 1 Thessalonians, 1 and 2 Corinthians, and Philippians, helps more for the interpretation of Galatians than pressing it into the format of the Greek "apologetic letter." The letter falls neatly and convincingly into an A-B-B'-A' chiastic format of four sections, with each section divided into Paul's usual a-b-a' subsections, in which (a) and (a') are broadly parallel and (b) contributes to the understanding of (a) and (a'). The similarity of this format to the format of 1 Cor 1–4 and 12–14 will strike the observant reader immediately. The letter may be divided as follows:

A (1:1-3:5): Freedom from the law and circumcision

    (a) Paul's surprise at the Galatians **leaving the only true gospel** (1:1-2:10)
        (b) Peter at Antioch did not observe the Mosaic food laws (2:11-21).
    (a') "O foolish Galatians"—**leaving the only true gospel** (3:1-5)

B (3:6-29): The true sons of Abraham

  (a) **Sons of Abraham by faith** (3:6-9)
    (b) Faith and the law (3:10-22)
  (a') Sons of God and **the posterity of Abraham by faith** (3:23-29)

B' (4:1-31): The true sons of Abraham

  (a) **Slaves versus sons** (4:1-11)
    (b) The Galatians are Paul's "children" in Christ (4:12-20).
  (a') **Sons of the slave** girl **versus sons** of the freeborn wife (4:21-31)

A' (5:1-6:18): Freedom from the law and circumcision

  (a) Freedom from the **law** and **circumcision** (5:1-12)
    (b) Freedom for the works of love and not for self-indulgence (5:13-6:10)
  (a') Freedom from the **law** and **circumcision** (6:11-18)

In studying each section of the letter, it will help considerably if the reader will note how parallel sections and subsections reinforce and clarify one another, e.g., Christian freedom from the law is central to the whole letter. In the A-B-B'-A' format of the letter, however, freedom, which is only a secondary theme in section A (1:1-3:5), becomes the primary theme in section A' (5:1-6:20), where Paul expounds in depth his concept of Christian freedom. The same can be said for parallel subsections, e.g., sons of Abraham by faith in 3:6-9 (subsection a) and sons of God and the posterity of Abraham by faith in 3:23-29 (subsection a').

A (1:1-3:5): Freedom from the law and circumcision

In section A, Paul defends the truth of his gospel of freedom from the law and circumcision through faith in Jesus as the only source of salvation. His arguments are logical and persuasive, once the Galatians concede what they must concede, namely, that when Paul preached the gospel to them, they received, accepted, and experienced within them the influence of the Spirit of Christ.

The arguments run as follows: (1) Paul received his authority to be an apostle directly from Jesus and God (1:2); (2) his gospel as a consequence must logically be the true gospel (1:6-10); (3) he did not receive his gospel from men (1:11-24); (4) the leaders of the church at Jerusalem agreed with his gospel (2:1-10); (5) Cephas at Antioch, by eating with Gentiles, implicitly corroborated Paul's gospel of freedom from the law (2:11-14); (6) both Peter and Paul himself, like the Galatians, had to become believers in Jesus, with the consequent argument that if the law had been able to save, there would have been no necessity for Peter and Paul to become believers. Acknowledging that the observance of the law was necessary for salvation would then be the equivalent of saying that Christ had died in vain

(2:15-21); (7) the Galatians themselves must admit that at the time they became believers, they had not been observing the Mosaic law. It was not, therefore, because of observance of the law that they received the Spirit, but because they believed in Jesus (3:1-5).

(a) Paul's surprise at the Galatians' leaving the only true gospel (1:1-2:10)

Text

(a)   1:1 Paul an apostle—not from men nor through man, but through Jesus Christ and God the Father, who raised him from the dead— ²and all the brethren who are with me, to the churches of Galatia: ³Grace to you and peace from God the Father and our Lord Jesus Christ, ⁴who gave himself for our sins to deliver us from the present evil age, according to the will of our God and Father; ⁵to whom be the glory for ever and ever. Amen.

⁶I am astonished that you are so quickly deserting him who called you in the grace of Christ and turning to a different gospel— ⁷not that there is another gospel, but there are some who trouble you and want to pervert the gospel of Christ. ⁸But even if we, or an angel from heaven, should preach to you a gospel contrary to that which we preached to you, let him be accursed. ⁹As we have said before, so now I say again, If any one is preaching to you a gospel contrary to that which you received, let him be accursed. ¹⁰Am I now seeking the favor of men, or of God? Or am I trying to please men? If I were still pleasing men, I should not be a servant of Christ.

¹¹For I would have you know, brethren, that the gospel which was preached by me is not man's gospel. ¹²For I did not receive it from man, nor was I taught it, but it came through a revelation of Jesus Christ. ¹³For you have heard of my former life in Judaism, how I persecuted the church of God violently and tried to destroy it; ¹⁴and I advanced in Judaism beyond many of my own age among my people, so extremely zealous was I for the traditions of my fathers. ¹⁵But when he who had set me apart before I was born, and had called me through his grace, ¹⁶was pleased to reveal his Son to me, in order that I might preach him among the Gentiles, I did not confer with flesh and blood, ¹⁷nor did I go up to Jerusalem to those who were apostles before me, but I went away into Arabia; and again I returned to Damascus.

¹⁸Then after three years I went up to Jerusalem to visit Cephas, and remained with him fifteen days. ¹⁹But I saw none of the other apostles except James the Lord's brother. ²⁰(In what I am writing to you, before God, I do not lie!) ²¹Then I went into the regions of Syria and Cilicia. ²²And I was still not known by sight to the churches of Christ in Judea; ²³they only heard it said, "He who once persecuted us is now preaching the faith he once tried to destroy." ²⁴And they glorified God because of me.

2:1 Then after fourteen years I went up again to Jerusalem with Barnabas, taking Titus along with me. ²I went up by revelation; and I laid before them (but privately before those who were of repute) the gospel which I preach among the Gentiles, lest somehow I should be running or had run in vain. ³But even Titus, who was with me, was not compelled to be circumcised, though he was a Greek. ⁴But because of false brethren secretly brought in, who slipped in to spy out our freedom which we have in

Christ Jesus, that they might bring us into bondage— ⁵to them we did not yield submission even for a moment, that the truth of the gospel might be preserved for you.

⁶And from those who were reputed to be something (what they were makes no difference to me; God shows no partiality)—those, I say, who were of repute added nothing to me; ⁷but on the contrary, when they saw that I had been entrusted with the gospel to the uncircumcised, just as Peter had been entrusted with the gospel to the circumcised ⁸(for he who worked through Peter for the mission to the circumcised worked through me also for the Gentiles), ⁹and when they perceived the grace that was given to me, James and Cephas and John, who were reputed to be pillars, gave to me and Barnabas the right hand of fellowship, that we should go to the Gentiles and they to the circumcised; ¹⁰only they would have us remember the poor, which very thing I was eager to do.

Commentary

1:1-5 Paul an apostle—not from men nor through man. Paul makes two additions to his usual address, both related to points stressed in the letter: first, that he is an apostle directly commissioned by Jesus (v 1) and not by men. This gives assurance that his gospel must be the true gospel, a proposition he will argue throughout the whole letter; second, that Jesus has given himself for our sins (v 4), an implicit reference to the cross and death of Jesus, which terminated the era of the Mosaic law and initiated the era of Christian liberty. Paul returns to the subject of the cross in 3:1; 5:11; 6:12, 14. The words "to the churches of Galatia" in v 2b indicate that the letter is meant to be a circular letter that is to be read in each of the Galatian communities.

1:6-7 I am astonished. Omitting the customary thanksgiving section (there is really nothing to be thankful for in this situation), Paul goes immediately to the crisis that occasioned the letter. The Galatians are deserting the gospel he preached to them and turning to a different gospel preached to them by "some who . . . want to pervert the gospel of Christ." In 3:1-5, Paul will again express his astonishment and will again speak about the gospel he preached to them. From this point on, Paul will spend every effort to defend the truth of his gospel. In 2 Cor 10–13, he had defended himself as a true apostle. In Galatians, his concern is not so much to defend himself as to defend the authenticity of the gospel he preaches. His defense of himself is secondary and is directed entirely toward establishing the authenticity of his gospel.

1:8-9 But even if we, or an angel from heaven . . . let him be accursed. The conditional curse indicates the seriousness of the situation and is meant to shock any who would contemplate abandoning the original gospel preached to them by Paul. Interestingly enough, Paul balances off the curse threatened in vv 8-9 with a conditional blessing at the end of the letter (6:16), thus forming a sort of curse-blessing inclusion-conclusion.

1:10 Am I now seeking the favor of men, or of God? Supposedly Paul had been accused of preaching freedom from the law in order to please those who found the law burdensome. If that were so, however, he would be foolish to make himself liable to the curse mentioned in v 10. At the end of the letter, Paul turns this accusation against his opponents by accusing them of preaching the gospel of the law and circumcision out of motives of self-interest (6:12-13).

1:11-12 For I would have you know, brethren. Paul's personal certainty that his gospel is the true gospel comes from his knowledge that he received it directly from Jesus. It must, therefore, be the true gospel. Theoretically, if he had received it from men, it might not be the true gospel, since men are prone to error and deception. However, as Paul will go on to argue, he did not get his gospel from men, even from Peter or any other apostle (cf. 1:18-21). Moreover, when he presented his gospel to the apostles in Jerusalem, they found nothing wrong with it (2:1-10). The point of Paul's thumbnail sketch of his life that follows in 1:12–2:21 is to establish the fact that his gospel came to him directly from Jesus rather than from any human being.

1:13-14 For you have heard of my former life in Judaism. Paul's life as a Jew who persecuted the Church rules out his receiving his gospel from anyone prior to his call by Christ. What he says about himself as a Jew zealous for the law and the traditions is similar to what he says on the same subject in Phil 3:3-9.

1:15 But when he who had set me apart before I was born. Paul uses words from Jer 1:5 and likens his call to the call of Jeremiah, who like himself was appointed a prophet to the nations. It is notable that Paul does not speak of being converted to Christianity. Conversion implies a change from the false to the true. At the time of his call, Paul did not look upon Judaism as false. It was only later, when he saw Judaism as apostatizing from Jesus and the Church, the true Israel, that he became conscious of a real opposition between Judaism and Christianity.

1:16-17 I did not confer with flesh and blood, nor did I go up to Jerusalem. If Paul had conferred with "flesh and blood," i.e., men, or had gone up to Jerusalem, his opponents could perhaps have claimed that he received his gospel from someone other than Christ. Since he had not, his boast remains: he received his gospel directly from Christ without intermediaries. By "Arabia," Paul probably means the small but thriving Nabatean kingdom situated in the southern part of the kingdom of Transjordan. From the words "and again I returned to Damascus," it can be deduced that Paul's call took place in that city (cf. Acts 9; 22; 26).

1:18-20 Then after three years I went up to Jerusalem to visit Cephas. Paul argues from his visit to Jerusalem by pointing out that he only went to Jerusalem three years after his call and Jesus' revelation of the gospel to him and by speaking of his visit to Cephas in such a way that it cannot be construed as any kind of official visit. In other words, he did not receive his gospel from Cephas or any other apostle. The oath in v 20 is meant to fortify this contention and shows how serious Paul is.

1:21-24 Then I went into the regions of Syria and Cilicia. He is probably speaking about his stay in Antioch when he speaks of Syria. The Cilicia he mentions is the southern part of Asia Minor (modern Turkey) near his hometown of Tarsus. As a result, Paul had nothing to do with the churches in Judea, and no one could claim that he received his gospel from any of those churches.

2:1 Then after fourteen years I went up again to Jerusalem. If the fourteen years are added to the three years in 1:18, Paul's call could be dated as early as 32 A.D. (seventeen years before the meeting at Jerusalem, which is usually dated to the year 49). If the fourteen years include the three years in 1:18, then Paul's call can be dated to 35–36 A.D.

2:2 I laid before them . . . the gospel which I preach among the Gentiles. The gospel Paul preached among the Gentiles is the gospel he preached to the Galatians, and, as he will show in 2:3-9, this gospel was accepted by the authorities in Jerusalem as the true gospel.

2:3 But even Titus. Titus was a Gentile. The fact that he was not compelled to be circumcised is another proof that circumcision is not necessary for salvation, as Paul's opponents were claiming (cf 6:12-15). If the Jerusalem authorities had considered it necessary, they would have insisted that Titus be circumcised.

2:4 But because of false brethren. The false brethren may not be the same as Paul's opponents in the Galatian churches, but they are described by Paul in terms he would have used for his opponents: they are "secretly" brought in; they spy out our "freedom" (cf. 5:1ff); and their purpose is to bring us into "bondage" (cf. 3:23-4:31).

2:6-9 And from those who were reputed to be something. Paul's support from the apostolic authorities in Jerusalem was unequivocal. As he says in v 9, "when they perceived the grace that was given to me . . . [they] gave to me and Barnabas the right hand of fellowship."[5]

(b) Peter at Antioch did not observe the Mosaic food laws (2:11-21).

Text

(b)   2:11 But when Cephas came to Antioch I opposed him to his face, because he stood condemned. [12]For before certain men came from James, he ate with the Gentiles; but when they came he drew back and separated himself, fearing the circumcision party. [13]And with him the rest of the Jews acted insincerely, so that even Barnabas was carried away by their insincerity. [14]But when I saw that they were not straightforward about the truth of the gospel, I said to Cephas before them all, "If you, though a Jew, live like a Gentile and not like a Jew, how can you compel the Gentiles to live like Jews?"

¹⁵We ourselves, who are Jews by birth and not Gentile sinners, ¹⁶yet who know that a man is not justified by works of the law but through faith in Jesus Christ, even we have believed in Christ Jesus, in order to be justified by faith in Christ, and not by works of the law, because by works of the law shall no one be justified.

¹⁷But if, in our endeavor to be justified in Christ, we ourselves were found to be sinners, is Christ then an agent of sin? Certainly not! ¹⁸But if I build up again those things which I tore down, then I prove myself a transgressor. ¹⁹For I through the law died to the law, that I might live to God. ²⁰I have been crucified with Christ; it is no longer I who live, but Christ who lives in me; and the life I now live in the flesh I live by faith in the Son of God, who loved me and gave himself for me. ²¹I do not nullify the grace of God; for if justification were through the law, then Christ died to no purpose.

Commentary

2:11-14 But when Cephas came to Antioch I opposed him to his face. Paul gives no indication when this meeting with Peter in Antioch (in northeastern Syria) took place. That, however, is not important. What is important is that Peter, whom the Gospels and Acts recognize as the first and the leader of the apostles, had not observed the Mosaic food laws and by his actions testified to Paul's contention that the law was not necessary for salvation. Peter by his actions, therefore, had testified against the theses of the Judaizing missionaries who were trying to convert the Galatians to their gospel of law and circumcision. The argument is indirect but effective, inasmuch as it testifies to the fact that Peter himself, by eating with the Gentiles, showed that he no longer considered the observance of the Mosaic law to be an absolute requisite.

2:15 We ourselves, who are Jews by birth and not Gentile sinners. In 2:14, Paul quoted what he had said to Cephas at Antioch. In 2:15-21, he is probably, but not certainly, continuing to quote at least the substance of his remaining remarks to Cephas on that occasion. Whether this is so or not (and authors dispute whether it is quotation or not), 2:15-21 contains not only Paul's summary of Jewish Christianity's doctrine of justification by faith in Jesus (2:15-16) but also his total rejection of his opponents' doctrine of justification through works of the law (2:17-21). He establishes justification by faith in Jesus as Jewish-Christian doctrine by distinguishing himself and Cephas and other Jewish Christians from the Gentiles by the words: "We ourselves, who are Jews *by birth* and not Gentile sinners." The non-Jews are called "Gentile sinners" because they live outside the law of Moses and circumcision and, theoretically at least, cannot obtain forgiveness for their sins by the various sacrifices, etc., provided by the law. That justification by faith was the common doctrine of Jewish Christianity may be deduced from Paul's words here and also from what is said in Rom 3:21-31; Mt 12:37; Lk 15:11-32, and Jas 2:14-26.

2:16   a man is not justified by works of the law but through faith in Jesus Christ. To this succinct definition of the doctrine of justification by faith, Paul adds an allusion to Ps 143:2: "No one shall be justified before you." To strengthen the quotation and to make it apply to a denial of justification by works, he adds to the quotation the words "by works of the law." This is not untypical of Paul's use of Scripture, as we shall see in 3:6–4:31, where he departs from his more logical method of argumentation used in 1:1–3:5 and begins to argue in a rabbinic manner.

2:17   But if, in our endeavor to be justified in Christ, we ourselves were found to be sinners, is Christ then an agent of sin? Christ would be an agent of sin if it were true to say that leaving the law to believe in him was to do something sinful. Since this cannot be so, it must be right to leave the law and believe in Christ.

2:18   But if I build up again those things which I tore down. The "I" is rhetorical for "anyone." The logic of the argument is simple. Anyone who builds up again what he had torn down is by that very fact admitting that he had made a mistake in tearing down. It follows, then, that by returning to the law (which they had theoretically left when they came to believe in Christ), the Galatians are saying that they had transgressed, i.e., sinned, by believing in Christ. This is manifestly wrong, since believing in Christ certainly does not make anyone a transgressor.

2:19   For I through the law died to the law. Vv 19 and 20 must be read together. The "I" is not personal but rhetorical, as in v 18, and is equivalent to "anyone." Paul's argument that he died to the law through the law and that he now no longer lives but Christ lives in him is based on his argumentation in 3:19-25. There he argues that the law had an active role only until Christ came. When Christ came, the law's purpose was fulfilled and it died. "I" then died to the law. But having died to the law, "I" then began a new life. This new life is life in Christ, given as a gift by God to all who believe in Christ.

2:20   I have been crucified with Christ. This reference to the cross is paralleled in 5:24 and 6:14 and more fully explained in 3:26-28 and Rom 6:1-10. By believing in Christ, Paul has committed himself to Christ and his values and has thus equivalently died with Christ and now lives a life governed by the values of Christ. It is in this sense that Paul can say, "It is no longer I who live, but Christ who lives in me; and the life I now live in the flesh I live by faith in the Son of God, who loved me and gave himself for me" (v 20bcd). The life that Paul "now lives in the flesh" means his mortal life in this world. It is, however, a life no longer lived according to the values of this world but according to the values of Christ. These values are alluded to in the words "by faith in the Son of God, who loved me and gave himself for me." Paul will speak at length about his life based on the values of love and sacrifice in 5:13-26 and in Rom 5:1-11 and 8:1-39.

2:21 I do not nullify the grace of God. The "grace of God" is God's gift of faith in Jesus who died for us. If, however, "justification were through the law," it would follow that Christ had wasted his time in dying for us, since the law would have already supplied the justification for which Christ died. To believe that the law supplies justification is to say that Christ died in vain. It is also the equivalent of nullifying "the grace of God," i.e., the gift of belief in Jesus, since there would be no reason to seek salvation and justification through Jesus if the law already supplied them.

(a') "O foolish Galatians!"—leaving the only true gospel (3:1-5)

Text

(a')   3:1 **O foolish Galatians!** Who has bewitched you, before whose eyes Jesus Christ was publicly portrayed as crucified? [2]Let me ask you only this: Did you receive the Spirit by works of the law, or by hearing with faith? [3]Are you so foolish? Having begun with the Spirit, are you now ending with the flesh? [4]Did you experience so many things in vain?—if it really is in vain. [5]Does he who supplies the Spirit to you and works miracles among you do so by works of the law, or by hearing with faith?

Commentary

3:1 O foolish Galatians! With these words, Paul returns to the expression of astonishment with which he began the letter (cf. 1:6ff) and thus turns the reader's mind back to the central topic of 1:1-2:10 (a)—his dismay and astonishment that the Galatians should be leaving the gospel he preached to them in order to go over to another gospel. In 3:1-5, Paul's ultimate and undeniable argument for the truth of his gospel is based on a premise (v 2) that the Galatians cannot deny—their own experience at the time of their conversion to Christ and justification through faith in Christ.

3:2 Let me ask you only this. Paul's question forces the Galatians to admit that at the time of their conversion they had been pagans (cf. 4:9) and that as pagans they certainly had not been observing the Mosaic law. They must concede, therefore, that at the time of their conversion they had not been justified by the law but by something else. That something else was clearly their belief in Christ, which came about through their belief in the gospel of justification by faith in Christ preached to them by Paul. Thus, the truth of Paul's gospel is proved from their own experience.

3:3 Are you so foolish? Having begun with the Spirit, as the Galatians did, it is certainly foolish to end with, i.e., go back, to the flesh. In this case, "the flesh" means the law and perhaps by innuendo the rite of circumcision. "Beginning with the Spirit" probably refers to the illumination of mind and heart with which the Galatians first embraced Christianity. It may also refer to charismatic gifts.

3:4 Did you experience so many things in vain? Whatever the charismatic nature of the Galatians' experience of the Spirit at the time of their conversion, it has all been in vain if now they go over to what amounts to another gospel – the gospel of the law and circumcision preached by Paul's opponents (cf. 1:6-9; 2:4, 14; 5:10).

3:5 Does he who supplies the Spirit to you . . . ? The question repeats the question of 3:2 and forces the Galatians to admit that the one who supplied the Spirit to them and worked miracles among them did so, not by works of the law, but by reason of their hearing and responding to Paul's gospel by an act of faith in Jesus. On rational grounds alone, this argument should have been enough to convince the Galatians. It is the best and most compelling of all the rational arguments Paul gives in 1:1–3:5. He will not stop, however, with rational arguments. In 3:6–4:31, he will argue his case theologically by submitting it to the test of the truth of Scripture.

B (3:6-29): Faith and law

Section B, like section A, has an a-b-a' format: (a) 3:6-9: sons of Abraham by faith; (b) 3:10-22: faith and the law; (a') 3:23-29: sons of God and descendants of Abraham by faith. The brunt of the argument for the Galatians who doubt Paul's gospel is found in 3:6-9 and 3:23-29. The brunt of the argument against Paul's opponents in Galatia is found in 3:10-22, where Paul answers the objections of his adversaries and shows the inferiority and inadequacy of the law when compared with faith.

(a) Sons of Abraham by faith (3:6-9)

Text

(a)   3:6 Thus Abraham "believed God, and it was reckoned to him as righteousness." ⁷So you see that it is **men of faith** who are the **sons of Abraham.** ⁸And the scripture, foreseeing that God would justify the Gentiles by faith, preached the gospel beforehand to Abraham, saying, **"In you shall all the nations be blessed."** ⁹So then, those who are men of faith are blessed with Abraham who had faith.

Commentary

3:6-7 Thus Abraham "believed God." Since Gn 15:6 tells us that Abraham was justified by faith, it follows that those are the true sons of Abraham who, like him, find justification through faith rather than through the law. For Paul, faith is a gratuitous divine gift that enables a person who accepts it to commit himself or herself to God in total trust and confidence that God wishes only what is good for him or her. Since faith is a gift, it cannot be earned, and, as a consequence, it removes any basis for boasting that a person might look for. What Paul means by "faith in Christ" means essentially belief-trust in Jesus and in what Jesus has revealed, which, in the words of St. John, is that "God so loved the world that he gave his only Son, that whoever believes in him should not perish but have eternal life" (Jn 3:16). Thus, Jesus is the fulfilment of God's promises and the ultimate revelatory act of God in history whereby he shows his love for humankind. To trust in Jesus and in what Jesus calls for is to trust in God. It is to be a believer, a true son of Abraham.

3:8-9 "In you shall all the nations be blessed." Scripture itself spoke of the Gentiles as receiving the same blessing as Abraham—a blessing they receive who, like Abraham, the man of faith, rely on faith. Paul's argument has special force for the Galatians because it presupposes that Abraham, like the Galatians, was a Gentile when he made his act of faith in God. The promise that "In you shall all the nations be blessed" refers directly to Gentiles like the Galatians, since they by definition belong to the "nations." Circumcision, the sign of a Jew, and the law of Moses, which is the heritage and badge of Judaism, *came later.* The promise is made in Gn 15; circumcision, however, is mentioned for the first time only in Gn 17, and the law of Moses according to the Scriptures came into existence even later. Thus faith and the promise preceded both circumcision and the law. The Galatians, like all Gentiles, have been promised blessings in Abraham—blessings that come to them as they came to Abraham, their father, through faith!

(b) Faith and the law (3:10-22)

Text

(b)   3:10 For all who rely on works of the law are under a curse; for it is written, "Cursed be every one who does not abide by all things written in the book of the law, and do them." ¹¹Now it is evident that no man is justified before God by the law; for "He who through faith is righteous shall live"; ¹²but the law does not rest on faith, for "He who does them shall live by them." ¹³Christ redeemed us from the curse of the law, having become a curse for us—for it is written, "Cursed be every one who hangs on a tree"— ¹⁴that in Christ Jesus the blessing of Abraham might come upon the Gentiles, that we might receive the promise of the Spirit through faith.

¹⁵To give a human example, brethren: no one annuls even a man's will, or adds to it, once it has been ratified. ¹⁶Now the promises were made to Abraham and to his offspring. It does not say, "And to offsprings," referring to many; but, referring to one, "And to your offspring," which is Christ. ¹⁷This is what I mean: the law, which came four hundred and thirty years afterward, does not annul a covenant previously ratified by God, so as to make the promise void. ¹⁸For if the inheritance is by the law, it is no longer by promise; but God gave it to Abraham by a promise.

¹⁹Why then the law? It was added because of transgressions, till the offspring should come to whom the promise had been made; and it was ordained by angels through an intermediary. ²⁰Now an intermediary implies more than one; but God is one.

²¹Is the law then against the promises of God? Certainly not; for if a law had been given which could make alive, then righteousness would indeed be by the law. ²²But the scripture consigned all things to sin, that what was promised to faith in Jesus Christ might be given to those who believe.

Commentary

3:10   under a curse. Almost any law, but especially the Mosaic law (cf. Dt 28), threatens a curse (a penalty or punishment) on those who break it. It follows, therefore, that "all who rely on works of the law are under a curse." Also, since the "men of faith" are blessed in Abraham (cf. 3:9), it may be that Paul wants his readers to conclude logically that those who are not men of faith must be under a curse. As Betz puts it: "The logic behind Paul's words, therefore, is simply that exclusion from 'blessing' (cf. 6:6) equals 'curse.'"[6]

3:11   "He who through faith is righteous shall live." Since Hab 2:4 declares that "the righteous shall live by his faith," it should be obvious that "no man is justified before God by the law." Paul quotes the text as proof from the prophets that his teaching about faith is found not only in Gn 15:6 but also in the prophetic writings. Thus, his gospel is supported by both the Law (the Pentateuch, of which Genesis is a part) and the Prophets.

3:12   the law does not rest on faith. The law functions on the basis of observance or non-observance and not on the basis of faith. Its terms are "he who *does* them shall live by them" (Lv 18:5). It says nothing about faith. Those under the law, therefore, are always in danger of being under a curse if they do not do what the law commands. This is a precarious position, since almost no one can keep the law perfectly.

3:13   Christ redeemed us from the curse of the law. By removing us from the realm of the law, Christ has delivered us from the precarious position of being cursed by the law for non-observance. He has delivered us by himself becoming a curse in the crucifixion. According to the Jewish law, "a hanged man is accursed by God" (Dt 21:23). Since Jesus was hanged on a tree, he has borne the curse of the law. But a law that can curse Jesus, the Son of God, in his very act of dying for us, cannot be absolute. Indeed, in cursing Jesus, the law has brought about its own downfall. It is in this sense that Paul means the words: "For I through the law died to the law, that I might live to God. I have been crucified with Christ . . . ." (2:19).

3:14   that in Christ Jesus the blessing of Abraham might come upon the Gentiles. The upshot of Jesus being cursed by the law is that the law is done away with by Jesus, and thus it becomes clear to all that the blessing bestowed on Abraham now comes to the Gentiles, not by the keeping of the law, which has been done away with by Jesus, but through faith.

3:15-18   a human example. A legal will cannot be invalidated by something that happens after the will has been drawn up. God's will, manifested to Abraham, could not therefore be invalidated by the law of Moses, which came into existence four hundred and thirty years after God had made known his will to Abraham. What God promised was precisely that—a promise that would be fulfilled in the future. But if salvation comes through the law, then it cannot come as the result of a promise—"but God gave it to

Abraham by a promise" (v 18). The argument is based on the distinction between promise and law. A promise is something freely made, and its fulfillment remains free. Law deals with justice and mutual rights, and what comes from observance of the law is something due as a right.

3:19a Why then the law? In diatribe style, Paul answers an obvious objection his opponents would throw up to him. If persons are justified by faith, why did God give the law at all? Paul's reply concentrates on four aspects of the law that demonstrate its inferiority to faith: (1) it was given in view of transgressions; (2) it was promulgated by angels; (3) it was valid only temporarily; (4) it cannot give life.

3:19b It was added because of transgressions. Paul's first reply is surprising. Since there can be no transgression where there is no law, Paul concludes that the purpose of the law is to provide the opportunity for transgressions. Legal commands provoke the resistance of the commanded one's ego. Where the ego resists, the law is transgressed. In this event, since the law itself is good, the transgressor becomes a sinner and at the same time becomes conscious of his helplessness to keep the law. This helplessness before the law, however, has the beneficial aspect of forcing the transgressor to rely on faith. Paul develops this complicated concept at greater length in Rom 7:7-25.

3:19c till the offspring should come. The law was *temporary*. It was valid only "till the offspring should come to whom the promise had been made." Jesus is that offspring (cf. 3:16). The law, therefore, has now lost its validity. Paul will pick up this argument again in 3:23-25, when he speaks of the law as a custodian that served until the coming of Christ.

3:19d ordained by angels. Paul's retort here is based on intricate rabbinic reasoning and is intended to demonstrate further the inferiority of the law to the promise. From the fact that Moses functioned as an intermediary at Sinai, it can be deduced that there must have been two groups at Sinai. This is deduced rabbinically, because it is only where groups are concerned that one needs an intermediary. At Sinai, the Israelites composed one of the two groups. Since God himself is one and cannot therefore be considered the other group, the only other possibility is that angels constituted the other group. This shows the inferior character of the law when compared with the promise. The promise was one-on-one — God and Abraham. The law was group-with-group. The former was direct; the latter, indirect.

3:21-22 Is the law then against the promises of God? Continuing in diatribe style to answer the supposed objections of his opponents in the Galatian churches, Paul takes up the objection that the law, as he speaks about it, could be said to be opposed to the promises made to Abraham. "Certainly not," Paul replies. He then goes on to show that it is not a case of opposition but of a critical difference in the efficaciousness of each. The law simply cannot impart life, i.e., the ability to observe what it commands.

Faith, on the contrary, which is the fulfillment of the promises, has the power to impart life and justification.

(a′) Sons of God and posterity of Abraham by faith (3:23-29)

Text

(a′)   3:23 Now before faith came, we were confined under the law, kept under restraint until faith should be revealed. ²⁴So that the law was our custodian until Christ came, that we might be **justified by faith.** ²⁵But now that faith has come, we are no longer under a custodian; ²⁶for in Christ Jesus you are **all sons of God, through faith.** ²⁷For as many of you as were baptized into Christ have put on Christ. ²⁸There is neither Jew nor Greek, there is neither slave nor free, there is neither male nor female; for **you are all one in Christ Jesus.** ²⁹And if you are Christ's, then you are **Abraham's offspring, heirs according to promise.**

Commentary

3:23-24 Now before faith came, we were confined under the law. Paul takes up again the idea that the law was given "because of transgressions" (3:19), so that it might put men under the constraint of sin or transgression that follows upon law. Since the law cannot give life, i.e., the capacity to keep the law and thus please God, its subjects become conscious of their helplessness and are forced to turn to faith. In so doing, the law functions as a mere custodian leading one to saving faith in Jesus. The means is inferior to the end!

3:25-28 we are no longer under a custodian. Those who, like the Galatians, have believed in Jesus are free of the custodian — free of the law. Indeed, all who believe in Jesus have become sons of God through baptism. In Rom 6:1ff, Paul will say more about the meaning of baptism and its relation to life in Christ. Since all are "sons of God," there are no longer any real distinctions between persons; all have the same dignity (v 28). That is the way Paul views all, and his words here have much in common with what he expressed as his view of people in 2 Cor 5:14ff: "For the love of Christ controls us, because we are convinced that one has died for all; therefore all have died. . . . From now on, therefore, we regard no one from a human point of view . . . . Therefore, if any one is in Christ, he is a new creation; the old has passed away, behold, the new has come."

It is disputed whether Paul understood what he says in 3:28 about no more distinctions between Jew or Greek, slave or free, male or female, etc., to be understood literally as applicable to social conditions or as applicable only in an ideal but unattainable way. Without denying the arguments that can be made against Paul's understanding it as applicable to social conditions, this author believes that that is indeed the way Paul understood it. There is some confirmation for this opinion in the way Paul emphasizes freedom in chs 5-6. A fuller treatment would require a book.

3:29 Abraham's offspring. All who believe inherit the promises concerning faith made to Abraham and are, as a consequence, precisely those faith-descendants promised by God to Abraham. By thus returning to the theme of "sons of Abraham by faith," Paul balances off (a′) with (a) and brings his discussion of faith and the law to a close with a neat inclusion-conclusion (cf. 3:6-9).

B′ (4:1-31): The true sons of Abraham

Section B′, like sections A and B, has an a-b-a′ format: (a) 4:1-11: slaves versus sons; (b) 4:12-20: the Galatians are Paul's "children in Christ"; (a′) 4:21-31: slaveborn sons versus freeborn sons.

It should be noted that section B′, with its emphasis on sons versus slaves, is chiastically parallel to section B, which deals with the same subject, namely, sons by faith versus slaves to the law. Thus, the format of the whole letter turns out to be an A-B-B′-A′ chiasm. As we shall see, section A′ (5:1-6:18) will return to the subject matter treated in section A (1:1-3:5), namely, faith brings freedom from the enslaving law and circumcision.

(a) Slaves versus sons (4:1-11)

Text

(a)   4:1 I mean that the heir, as long as he is a child, is no better than a **slave,** though he is the owner of all the estate; ²but he is under guardians and trustees until the date set by the father. ³So with us; when we were children, we were **slaves** to the elemental spirits of the universe. ⁴But when the time had fully come, God sent forth his Son, born of woman, born **under the law,** ⁵to redeem those who were **under the law,** so that we might receive adoption as **sons.** ⁶And because you are **sons,** God has sent the Spirit of his Son into our hearts, crying, "Abba! Father!" ⁷So through God you are no longer a **slave** but a **son,** and if a **son** then an heir.

⁸Formerly, when you did not know God, you were in **bondage** to beings that by nature are no gods; ⁹but now that you have come to know God, or rather to be known by God, how can you turn back again to the weak and beggarly elemental spirits, whose **slaves** you want to be once more? ¹⁰You observe days, and months, and seasons, and years! ¹¹I am afraid I have labored over you in vain.

Commentary

4:1-3 the heir, as long as he is a child, is no better than a slave. In 3:23-29, Paul likened the Jews under the law to youngsters under the tutelage of a custodian. Here he likens them to heirs who have been under the care of trustees (the law) until the time of adulthood, inheritance, and freedom (the time of Jesus), when the inheritance comes as promised to those who have become true sons by faith in Jesus.

4:4-5 But when the time had fully come. When Jesus came, then and then only could those under the guardianship of the law become free of the "elemental spirits" (the law, which regulated so many activities in Judaism) and become the adopted sons of God in Christ.

4:6-7 And because you are sons. The Galatians' experience until confronted by the Judaizers' demand that they become subject to the law had been an experience of the freedom of the sons of God who could call God "Abba Father." This meant they were no longer slaves to anybody or anything (as the Jews were slaves to the law), but true sons and true heirs who had come into the inheritance promised to all who would become sons of Abraham by faith in Jesus.

4:8 Formerly. Unlike the Jews, who were slaves to the law, the Galatians had been slaves to pagan gods, which was just another kind of slavery.

4:9-10 but now that you have come to know God. Having tasted the freedom of the sons of God, how, Paul asks, can the Galatians go back to another form of slavery, i.e., the slavery of the law, with its ceremonial observance of "days, and months, and seasons, and years!" Giving in to the Judaizers' demands that they obey ritual laws and seasons is only another form of slavery.

(b) The Galatians are Paul's children in Christ (4:12-20).

Text

(b)   4:12 Brethren, I beseech you, become as I am, for I also have become as you are. You did me no wrong; [13]you know it was because of a bodily ailment that I preached the gospel to you at first; [14]and though my condition was a trial to you, you did not scorn or despise me, but received me as an angel of God, as Christ Jesus. [15]What has become of the satisfaction you felt? For I bear you witness that, if possible, you would have plucked out your eyes and given them to me. [16]Have I then become your enemy by telling you the truth? [17]They make much of you, but for no good purpose; they want to shut you out, that you may make much of them. [18]For a good purpose it is always good to be made much of, and not only when I am present with you. [19]My little children, with whom I am again in travail until Christ be formed in you! [20]I could wish to be present with you now and to change my tone, for I am perplexed about you.

Commentary

4:12 become as I am, for I also have become as you are. Paul, in giving up the slavery of the law, had become like the Galatians, who had never been subject to the law. Now he asks them to imitate him by giving up the slavery to the law imposed on them by the Judaizers.

4:13-15 it was because of a bodily ailment. Whatever the ailment Paul suffered, his purpose here is to remind the Galatians, as he did in 3:1-6, of the first days when they became Christians — a time when they did not even know the law and when they accepted joyfully Paul's gospel of salvation through faith and faith alone.[7]

4:16 Have I then become your enemy? What the Galatians accepted so joyfully from Paul as the truth, they are now rejecting in favor of the gospel of the Judaizers. This means that Paul, who rejects the Judaizers' gospel, has become their enemy. If he had not brought them the truth, they would have known only the gospel of the Judaizers and would not have considered him an enemy. Thus, he has become their enemy just because he told them the truth.

4:17-18 They make much of you. Paul attributes to the Judaizers the selfish motive of alienating the Galatians from Paul's gospel of freedom in order to make them dependent on their own gospel of the law and their own interpretation of it. This, as many have observed, is a role for which some religious leaders seem ideally typecast.

4:19 My little children. In an oblique reference back to 4:12-15 and 3:1-5, where he had reminded the Galatians that it was through him alone that they had come to faith in Jesus, Paul asserts in the clearest terms his claim to their loyalty—they are his children in the faith. Without him, they would never have become Christians.

(a') Slaveborn sons versus freeborn sons (4:21-31)

Text

(a')   4:21 Tell me, you who desire to be **under law,** do you not hear the **law?** [22]For it is written that Abraham had two **sons,** one by a **slave** and one by a free woman. [23]But the **son of the slave** was born according to the flesh, the **son of the free woman** through promise. [24]Now this is an allegory: these women are two covenants. One is from Mount Sinai, bearing **children for slavery;** she is Hagar. [25]Now Hagar is Mount Sinai in Arabia; she corresponds to the present Jerusalem, for she is in **slavery** with her children. [26]But the Jerusalem above is free, and she is our mother. [27]For it is written, "Rejoice, O barren one that dost not bear; break forth and shout, thou who are not in travail; for the desolate hath more children than she who hath a husband."

[28]Now we, brethren, like Isaac, are children of promise. [29]But as at that time he who was born according to the flesh persecuted him who was born according to the Spirit, so it is now. [30]But what does the scripture say? "Cast out the **slave and her son;** for the **son of the slave** shall not inherit with the **son of the free woman.**" [31]So, brethren, we are not children of the **slave** but of the **free woman.**

Commentary

4:21-23 Abraham had two sons. Abraham's sons were Ishmael by Hagar, an Egyptian slave (Gn 16:1-6), and Isaac by Sarah, his freeborn wife (Gn 21:8-21).

4:24-28 an allegory.[8] With undisguised rabbinic allegorizing, Paul likens his gospel of the new covenant to Sarah and her son Isaac, and the Judaizers' old covenant gospel to Hagar, the slave, and her slaveborn son Ishmael. The allegory goes as follows:

Sarah = the Jerusalem on high, i.e., those who are free of the law through faith.	Hagar = the present Jerusalem, i.e., those Jews and Judaizers still enslaved to the law.
Isaac = the freeborn sons of Paul's gospel of faith.	Ishmael = the slaveborn sons of the Judaizers' gospel.
New covenant = the realization of the promise and the freedom it brings.	Sinai = the Sinai covenant, which is symbolic of the law and the slavery it brings.

4:27 "Rejoice." Paul recalls here the appeal of Deutero-Isaiah in Is 45:1 to the new Jerusalem of the future, which is likened to a barren woman who is suddenly alive with children. Implicitly, Paul summons to his assistance against his opponents the prophecies of Deutero-Isaiah, which spoke so ecstatically about the new Jerusalem, the new exodus, and the new creation — all fulfilled in the gospel of faith and freedom preached to them by him.

4:29 he who was born according to the flesh. Continuing his allegory, Paul likens his opponents' persecution of himself and his gospel to slaveborn Ishmael's persecution of Isaac, the freeborn son (cf. Gn 21:9).

4:30 "Cast out the slave and her son." As Abraham had cast out Hagar and her son Ishmael, so the Galatians are exhorted to cast out Hagar and her modern sons — the Judaizers and their gospel of law and circumcision (cf. Gn 21:10).

A' (5:1-6:18): Freedom from the law and circumcision

Section A', like sections A, B, and B', has an a-b-a' format: (a) freedom from the law and circumcision (5:1-12); (b) freedom for the works of love and not for self-indulgence (5:13-6:10); (a') freedom from the law and circumcision (6:11-18).

Section A', with its emphasis on the freedom of faith versus the slavery of the law and circumcision, turns the reader's mind back to section A (1:1-3:5), where Paul refuted the gospel of those who "slipped in to spy out our freedom which we have in Christ Jesus, that they might bring us into bondage" (2:4) and insisted that "even Titus . . . was not compelled to be circumcised, though he was a Greek" (2:3). The recurrence in section A' of so many themes and key-words that already appeared in section A suggests that Paul is deliberately throwing the reader's mind back to section A in order to complete and round out his A-B-B'-A' chiastic format.

(a) Freedom from the law and circumcision (5:1-12)

Text

(a)   5:1 For freedom Christ has set us free; stand fast therefore, and do not submit again to a yoke of slavery. ²Now I, Paul, say to you that if you receive **circumcision,** Christ will be of no advantage to you. ³I testify again to every man who receives **circumcision** that he is bound to keep the whole law. ⁴You are severed from Christ, you who would be justified by the **law**; you have fallen away from **grace**. ⁵For through the Spirit, by faith, we wait for the hope of righteousness. ⁶For in Christ Jesus **neither circumcision nor uncircumcision is of any avail**, but faith working through love.

⁷You were running well; who hindered you from obeying the truth? ⁸This persuasion is not from him who called you. ⁹A little leaven leavens the whole lump. ¹⁰I have confidence in the Lord that you will take no other view than mine; and **he who is troubling you** will bear his judgment, whoever he is. ¹¹But if I, brethren, still preach **circumcision,** why am I still persecuted? In that case the stumbling block of **the cross** has been removed. ¹²I wish those who unsettle you would mutilate themselves!

Commentary

5:1   For freedom Christ has set us free. Paul is speaking about freedom from the law (cf. 1:6-10; 2:3-5; 2:12-16), which amounts to freedom from the "yoke of slavery." In 4:8-9, he had reminded the Galatians of their first slavery when they "served" as slaves to gods who were not really gods. To accept the false gospel of the Judaizers would be to enslave themselves a second time — this time to the law of Moses.⁹

5:2-5   if you receive circumcision. Circumcision is the rite whereby a person commits himself to the law of Moses as the way of justification before God. In such a case, Paul says, "Christ will be of no advantage to you," for since the death of Jesus on the cross (2:19-21), justification is only by faith in Christ. Paul sums up here the argument of 2:15-21, which itself is reducible to the words of 2:21: "If justification were through the law, then Christ died to no purpose."

5:6   faith working through love. What is new and different in section A′ (5:1-6:18) is Paul's emphasis on the law of love, which he calls the "law of Christ" (cf. 6:2). Undoubtedly his opponents accused him of catering to license in morals by teaching freedom from the law. Here Paul sounds for the first time his rebuttal of such an accusation. In 5:13-6:10, he will develop at length the argument that Christians, far from being called to a freedom that leads to license, are called to a proper and rigorous use of their freedom, which is a freedom through the Spirit to love their neighbors according to the law of Christ.

5:7-10   You were running well. Again Paul returns to the argument of section A (1:1-3:5). The Galatians were progressing well in their Christian life until the Judaizers, with their false gospel of obedience to the law, diverted them from Paul's gospel of freedom (cf. 1:6-9; 2:12-16). Paul's astonishment here forms a parallel with his astonishment in 1:6-10 and 3:1.

5:11a   But if I, brethren, still preach circumcision. Paul's opponents have evidently argued that Paul himself preached circumcision. Paul does not deny it.¹⁰ When he wrote 1 Cor 7:17-24 and 9:19-23, his attitude toward circumcision was one of indifference. Now that the Judaizers have exalted circumcision and the law and made them the source of justification, the situation has changed drastically. Paul can no longer be indifferent. He is emphatically against circumcision and the law when they are looked upon as necessary for salvation, and it is precisely for this reason that he is being persecuted. His argument: "If I still preach circumcision, why am I still persecuted?" is thus an *ad hominem* argument. He would not be attacked if he were still preaching circumcision!

5:11b In that case the stumbling block of the cross has been removed. As Paul had insisted in section A (1:1–3:5), it was the cross that made the difference and brought it about that Christians were freed from the law (cf. 2:19-21; 3:1). If Paul were still preaching circumcision, the Judaizing Christians would not be disturbed by what he was saying concerning the cross. Paul is persecuted precisely because he contends that the cross does away with circumcision and the law, and that now justification comes through faith in Christ. His preaching about the cross is the "stumbling block" for his opponents!

(b) Freedom for the works of love and not for self-indulgence (5:13–6:10)

Text

(b)   5:13 For you were called to freedom, brethren; only do not use your freedom as an opportunity for the flesh, but through love be servants of one another. [14]For the whole law is fulfilled in one word, "You shall love your neighbor as yourself." [15]But if you bite and devour one another take heed that you are not consumed by one another.

[16]But I say, walk by the Spirit, and do not gratify the desires of the flesh. [17]For the desires of the flesh are against the Spirit, and the desires of the Spirit are against the flesh; for these are opposed to each other, to prevent you from doing what you would. [18]But if you are led by the Spirit you are not under the law.

[19]Now the works of the flesh are plain: immorality, impurity, licentiousness, [20]idolatry, sorcery, enmity, strife, jealousy, anger, selfishness, dissension, party spirit, [21]envy, drunkenness, carousing, and the like. I warn you, as I warned you before, that those who do such things shall not inherit the kingdom of God.

[22]But the fruit of the Spirit is love, joy, peace, patience, kindness, goodness, faithfulness, [23]gentleness, self-control; against such there is no law. [24]And those who belong to Christ Jesus have crucified the flesh with its passions and desires. [25]If we live by the Spirit, let us also walk by the Spirit. [26]Let us have no self-conceit, no provoking of one another, no envy of one another.

6:1 Brethren, if a man is overtaken in any trespass, you who are spiritual should restore him in a spirit of gentleness. Look to yourself, lest you too be tempted. [2]Bear one another's burdens, and so fulfill the law of Christ. [3]For if any one thinks he is something, when he is nothing, he deceives himself. [4]But let each one test his work, and then his reason to boast will be in himself alone and not in his neighbor. [5]For each man will have to bear his own load.

[6]Let him who is taught the word share all good things with him who teaches.

⁷Do not be deceived; God is not mocked, for whatever a man sows, that he will also reap. ⁸For he who sows to his own flesh will from the flesh reap corruption; but he who sows to the Spirit will from the Spirit reap eternal life. ⁹And let us not grow weary in well-doing, for in due season we shall reap, if we do not lose heart. ¹⁰So then, as we have opportunity, let us do good to all men, and especially to those who are of the household of faith.

Commentary

Subsection (b) consists of two exhortations (5:13-26 and 6:1-10) dealing with the proper use of freedom so that it leads to living according to Christ's law of love instead of living a life of self-indulgence. It is the centrality of the law of love that unifies both exhortations. The contrast between a life of self-indulgence and a life dominated by the law of love is brought out in the contrast between the "flesh" and the Spirit.

5:13 do not use your freedom as an opportunity for the flesh. By "flesh" Paul means the merely human, unspiritual values, man in his proneness to sin. In all probability, Paul's opponents had accused him of preaching a freedom from the law that amounted to freedom to live a licentious life. Paul makes it clear that by freedom from the law he does not mean freedom for a life of self-indulgence. On the contrary, he exhorts the Galatians: "through love be servants of one another." Thus, rather than enslaving themselves to the law, they are to become slaves-servants to one another and thus fulfill the law of Christ. In 6:2, he says the same thing in another way: "Bear one another's burdens, and so fulfill the law of Christ." It is through works of love, in short, that one preserves one's freedom!

5:14 fulfilled in one word. Paul agrees with Matthew (22:39) and Mark (12:31) on the centrality of the law of love (cf. also Rom 13:9 and 1 Cor 13). As he points out in 6:2, this law is "the law of Christ," and no one who fulfills this law can be accused of catering to license and self-indulgence. Paul's use of the words "the whole law" is a little surprising in view of the way he has been speaking about the law, but his emphasis is on love as the fulfillment of the law. It is quite possible as well that Paul's enemies accused him of being "lawless" because he opposed the law of Moses. Paul's retort in that case would be, "Not so! I am subject to the law of Christ—the law of love."

5:16-17 do not gratify the desires of the flesh. The cravings of the flesh lead to self-indulgence and are opposed to the Spirit who calls us to be "servants of one another" (5:13b) and to bear one another's burdens and so fulfill the law of Christ.

5:18 But if you are led by the Spirit you are not under the law. The law of Christ and the guidance of the Spirit call for infinitely more than the law does, but the distinction here is not on the basis of what is called for morally but on the basis of the one calling, i.e., the Spirit. As Paul says in 5:25: "If we live by the Spirit, let us also walk by the Spirit." He who lives by the

Spirit does not need the law. Aristippus, the philosopher, claimed pretty much the same for philosophers: "Being once asked, what advantage philosophers have, he replied: 'Should all laws be repealed, we shall go on living as we do now.'"[11]

5:19-23 Now the works of the flesh are plain. One does not need to transgress a law to know evil and the works of the flesh. The flesh itself, i.e., man prone to evil, leads man to indulge in the works of the flesh that Paul lists in vv 19-21. The list is dominated by sins that flow from self-indulgence. The opposite of the flesh is the Spirit, under whose influence man performs the works called for by love of neighbor, "against [which] there is no law" (vv 22-23).

5:24 And those who belong to Christ Jesus have crucified the flesh. This is a fuller development and parallel of what Paul had said in 2:19-20. Those who die with Christ die to the flesh and, with the power of Jesus given through the Spirit, overcome the promptings of the flesh and produce the fruits of the Spirit. Paul will develop this concept at greater length in Rom 6:1ff.

5:25 If we live by the Spirit, let us also walk by the Spirit. Paul's "indicative" for the Christian's existence is that the Christian lives by the power of the Spirit. The "imperative" of the Christian's existence follows: the Christian must walk, i.e., live ethically or behave, by the Spirit. In short, the Christian cannot simply possess the Spirit — the Spirit must be active in his or her life and be allowed to produce the fruits, i.e., works, proper to the Spirit.

6:1-5 if a man is overtaken in any trespass. Paul's first example of how the Galatians can live up to the law of Christ deals with an erring fellow Christian. Since Christians led by the Spirit are not immune to temptation and sin, they should help one another return to God. They should "restore [the sinner] in a spirit of gentleness," always mindful of their own weakness and their own responsibility to God. The qualification "in a spirit of gentleness" might well be in contrast to the severity of the Judaizing proponents of the law of Moses. It is also possible that the Galatians were distressed by finding that they still fell into sin. They may therefore have been looking for the assurance and protection that the law of Moses seemed to provide. Paul takes this into account by pointing out that while they are still subject to sin and temptation and while they still have sinners in the community, this is no reason for distress. Let them simply help one another to return to God and live as Christians should.

6:6 Let him who is taught the word. Paul's second example of how the Galatians can live up to the law of Christ is very practical.[12] The community needs ministers of the word. And ministers of the word need support if they are to give their time and energy to instruction. Paul had said substantially the same thing about support of apostles, preachers, and teachers in 1 Cor

9:4-14. Why he uses this particular example instead of another at this juncture in his letter is difficult to explain. One can only surmise that the Galatians have neglected those appointed by Paul as their teachers, and Paul wants to remind them of their responsibilities according to the law of Christ.

6:7-9 Do not be deceived. There is no reaping without sowing. There is no eternal life without the works of the Spirit. Paul's reminder takes up again the opposition between the flesh and the Spirit that he had spoken about in 5:16-25. If his opponents were saying that Paul was not interested at all in "works," he assures them this is not true. He is against works only as understood as earning salvation. No amount of works can earn salvation, which is a gift from God. But those who receive the gift of faith in Jesus, the manifestation of the Father's love, are expected to manifest in their lives that love for one another that Jesus manifested for all.

6:10 let us do good to all men. Paul is perfectly aware of the universality of redemption and of God's love (cf. 3:28 and 2 Cor 5:14-19). His addition of the words "especially to those who are of the household of faith" is not meant to be in any way restrictive of love to one's immediate neighbors. Paul would have agreed that "love begins at home." His words have a practical bent. It is easy to love in general; true love goes out to those around us, whose needs are palpable.

(a') Freedom from the law and circumcision (6:11-18)

In subsection (a'), Paul returns to the theme of 5:1-11 and to the overall theme of section A (1:1-3:5). In many ways, this last subsection sums up both Paul's argument and his opinion of his opponents. They are "those who receive circumcision" (6:13), who "want to make a good showing in the flesh" (6:12), a showing that "would compel [the Galatians] to be circumcised" (6:12b), and who do so "only in order that they may not be persecuted for the cross of Christ" (6:12c).

Text

(a')   6:11 See with what large letters I am writing to you with my own hand. [12]It is those who want to make a good showing in the flesh that would compel you to be **circumcised,** and only in order that they may not be persecuted for the **cross** of Christ. [13]For even those who receive **circumcision** do not themselves keep the **law,** but they desire to have you **circumcised** that they may glory in your flesh. [14]But far be it from me to glory except in the **cross** of our Lord Jesus Christ, by which the world has been crucified to me, and I to the world. [15]For **neither circumcision counts for anything, nor uncircumcision,** but a new creation. [16]Peace and mercy be upon all who walk by this rule, upon the Israel of God. [17]Henceforth **let no man trouble me;** for I bear on my body the marks of Jesus. [18]The **grace** of our Lord Jesus Christ be with your spirit, brethren. Amen.

Commentary

6:11 See with what large letters I am writing to you with my own hand.
Paul writes his own postscript (6:11-18) to the letter, which was written
down by a professional scribe or by a secretary either from dictation or
from Paul's own draft. The elaborate plan and formulation of the letter
would suggest that Paul had made a very careful first draft of the contents.
A professional scribe would ensure a clear and easy-to-read letter. The
postscript allows Paul to authenticate the letter and at the same time conclude it with a brief résumé of his main points. Writing in "large letters" is
probably Paul's way of emphasizing the importance of his concluding
remarks.

6:12a It is those who want to make a good showing in the flesh. Paul
accuses the Judaizers of acting out of selfish motives in trying to persuade
the Galatians to accept circumcision. "A good showing in the flesh" is
equivalent to boasting (cf. 6:4, 13; Phil 3:3, 17-19; 2 Cor 11:12-13; 12:1-10).

6:12b that they may not be persecuted for the cross of Christ. If the
Judaizers had preached the cross and the freedom from the law that went
with the cross (cf. 5:11; 2:4-5, 11-14), they would have been persecuted as
Paul was persecuted. Rightly or wrongly, Paul interprets their insistence on
circumcision as a way of escaping the persecution they would have encountered if they had preached the cross. It is of course possible that they
were preaching both circumcision and the cross.

6:13 For even those who receive circumcision. The accusation is clear.
For all their emphasis on circumcision and the obedience to the law that it
calls for, Paul's opponents do not themselves keep the law. How Paul
knows this, we cannot know. If the Galatians, however, verify that the
Judaizers do not in fact keep the law, Paul's case will be considerably
strengthened. The accusation that "they desire to have you circumcised that
they may glory in your flesh" (cf. 6:12; 2:4) is equivalent to saying that they
want to take credit for making converts as a meritorious work for which
they can boast before God.

**6:14 But far be it from me to glory except in the cross of our Lord
Jesus Christ.** The difference between Paul's and his opponents' boasting is
that Paul boasts, not about what he himself has done, i.e., about his own
achievements, but about what Jesus has done for him by dying on the cross
(cf. 1 Cor 1:31; 2 Cor 10:17). Properly speaking, man has nothing to boast
about, because all that he has he receives from God (cf. 1 Cor 3:18-21; 4:7).
Boasting about oneself is self-praise; boasting about the cross is praise of
Jesus. Through the cross, Paul can say, "the world has been crucified to me,
and I to the world." The cross has changed the Christian's relationship to
the world from one of being a slave to one of being a free "son of God" (cf.
3:26-28; 4:4-6, 22ff; 5:1, 13).

6:15 For neither circumcision counts for anything, nor uncircumcision, but a new creation. What Christ has accomplished through the cross has so radically changed the status of human beings that they are literally a "new creation," persons "in Christ," members of the body of Christ — in short, persons who now live with a new life through the life-giving Spirit of Christ (cf. 2:19-20; 5:25). In the "old creation," men and women lived according to the "flesh," i.e., as beings apart from the influence and life-giving Spirit of Christ. Through Christ, they live a new existence. Circumcision and uncircumcision belong to the old creation. They no longer have any meaning for anyone who lives in Christ through the Spirit. To go back to circumcision would be for the Galatians to deny the new creation and go back to the old. Here, therefore, Paul repeats in a more trenchant manner what he had already said in 2:15-21.

6:16 Peace and mercy be upon all who walk by this rule. The "rule" refers to what Paul said in v 15: "neither circumcision counts for anything, nor uncircumcision, but a new creation." The blessing implored upon those who "walk by this rule" is conditional and therefore implies a corresponding threat or curse upon those who try to reinstate circumcision and do not, as a consequence, "walk by this rule." Those who have read the letter from beginning to end will remember that Paul had threatened a curse on those who preached a gospel different from his gospel of faith in Jesus (cf. 1:8-9). Thus, everything Paul has said in the letter is framed by the conditional curse in 1:8-9 and the conditional blessing in 6:16. The Galatians who follow the gospel of the Judaizers are put under a curse; those who follow Paul's gospel come under a blessing. They are the Israel of God (v 16b). They are the "true" Israel as opposed to the "false" Israel of the Judaizers. In short, all who follow Paul's gospel, whether Jew or Gentile, constitute the true Israel of God. The others have apostatized. Without using the words "the true Israel," both John (15:1-25) and Matthew (11:20-27; 12:43-50; 13:1-52) make the same point in their Gospels.

6:17 Henceforth let no man trouble me; for I bear on my body the marks of Jesus. Paul's appeal for no trouble is his way of saying "Let this foolishness end!" The expression "the marks of Jesus" has nothing to do with what has been referred to as the stigmata, i.e., the wounds of the crucified Christ. Most likely it has something to do with the custom of religious tatooing in the ancient world. It is possible that Christians had themselves tatooed with the sign of the cross. Paul plays on this custom by referring to the wounds and welts he had accumulated during his missionary life. He may even be referring to the marks left on his body from the frequent scourgings he had received (cf. 2 Cor 11:24-25). Implicit perhaps in his remark is the contention that just as the cross is the true gospel (cf. 2:19-21; 3:1; 6:12), so the true apostle is the one who bears the marks of suffering of the crucified Christ.

Chapter VII

THE
LETTER OF PAUL TO THE
ROMANS

Paul's letter to the Romans, as someone has said, "is the profoundest work in existence; it is the cathedral of Christian faith." For theologians, it is the Mount Everest of the New Testament, dared by many, conquered by few. It forces them to stretch their minds, take only the grand perspectives, and look only at cosmic theological maps. It has spawned theological monstrosities such as Augustine's *massa damnata,* Calvin's chilling predestinarianism, and much that has been coldly inhuman in Jansenism, Puritanism, and Christianity in general.

Pelagius and Augustine failed to conquer it in the fourth and fifth centuries and left a legacy of dead-end trails to generations of Christians up to the present day. Luther and Calvin failed in the sixteenth century and opened up their own misleading trails for Christians of the last four centuries. Modern scholars, as K. Stendahl points out, have not done much better.[1] Despite an avalanche of commentaries, studies, monographs, and dissertations, Romans remains the unconquered peak of New Testament studies. Let the reader beware!

Romans is probably Paul's last letter, written about the year 57, during the three months Paul stayed in Corinth (cf. Acts 19:21; 20:3; and Rom 15:22-23; 16:1), prior to his going to Jerusalem. His intention, as he tells the Romans (15:22ff), was to go to Jerusalem to deliver the money collected for the poor and from there to set out for Spain. His arrest in Jerusalem and his imprisonments in Caesarea and Rome caused a change in plans.

Why Paul wrote to the Christians of Rome has never been satisfactorily explained.[2] His other letters were written to communities that he himself had founded. But he had never been to Rome, and the church at Rome was already flourishing and influential by the time he wrote his letter. One has to wonder why he wrote his most deeply theological letter to a church that he had not founded and did not even know except by hearsay. His own explanation seems almost banal: "For I long to see you, that I may impart to you some spiritual gift to strengthen you, that is, that we may be mutually encouraged by each other's faith, both yours and mine" (1:11-12; see also 15:14-21; 16:25-26). Presumably the letter is a preliminary attempt on Paul's part to share some spiritual gift with them. This explanation has seemed so inadequate that many have suggested, and probably with good reason, that Paul had a hidden agenda.

W. Marxsen interprets the hidden agenda as Paul's attempt to defend Jewish Christians in the Roman church from the contempt of gentile Christians.[3] He argues that the Jewish Christians had become a minority in the Roman church following the decree of Claudius (c. 49 A.D.) expelling Jews from Rome. He finds the main message of the letter in Paul's emphasis on the unity of the body (community) in 12:3ff and his defense of those with weak consciences (14:1-15:13), presumably Jewish Christians scrupulous about many things in pagan society that did not bother those with strong consciences. In brief, the plight of his Jewish Christian compatriots in the Roman church occasioned the letter and gave Paul an opportunity to defend them, explain the enigma of the Jews' rejection of Jesus, and in general give an overall explanation of his gospel in the light of the relationship between Jews and Gentiles in the Church.

While there is much to be said for Marxsen's explanation, Paul's hidden agenda seems to go deeper than a simple defense of his Jewish compatriots. A better explanation would be that Paul understood well the importance and influence of the Roman church and needed both their help and understanding for his project of preaching the gospel in Spain (15:28). He needed their understanding because of accusations made against him by Judaizing Christians and others that he was not a genuine apostle, that his preaching of faith alone as the heart of the gospel was an invitation to license, and that his insistence on Christian liberty was tantamount to espousing an unbridled antinomianism (see especially Paul's spirited refutation of these accusations throughout the letter, but especially in chs 6-7).

If Paul had a hidden agenda, therefore, it seems more likely that it was in the nature of an apologia for himself and his gospel. He used the opportunity the letter afforded him to accomplish several objectives: (1) to prevent the infestation of the Roman church by the Judaizers with their teaching of salvation through works and dependence on the law; (2) to defend himself as an apostle; (3) to defend himself against the accusations of his enemies; (4) to correct misinterpretations of his letter to the Galatians; (5) to give an overall, in-depth explanation of his preaching in relation to faith and the law, the law and liberty, and the relationship of Jews and Gentiles in the Church in the light of God's plan of salvation for all. In short, Paul had warned the Philippians and the Galatians against the Judaizers. Now he does the same for the influential Roman church. One clear sign of this overall purpose is Paul's use of the diatribe. Almost all the objections he brings up from imaginary opponents are actually objections dealt with in Galatians, in which he was forced to oppose the objections of the Judaizers to his gospel of faith.

Concerning the fifth point mentioned above, the relationship of Jews and Gentiles in the Church, it should be observed that by the year 57 A.D., Paul had come to realize that, contrary to all expectations and even contrary to all that the Old Testament promised, the Jews were not accepting the gospel and the Gentiles were. "The first had become last, and the last, first." Theologically, this posed a monumental problem for Paul and others (cf. Mk 4; Mt 13; Jn 12:37ff) concerning God's fidelity to his promises to the Jews. It was a critical event in Paul's life when he realized this and perhaps explains better than anything else why so much space is allotted in Romans to the so-called Jewish question. Paul deals with it throughout the letter, especially in his oft-repeated "Jews first but also Greeks" remarks, but in a special way in chs 9–11, the most difficult and most profound section of the whole letter.

Paul's literary techniques in Romans

Bornkamm says: "Paul's theology resists all efforts to reproduce it as a rounded-off system carefully arranged under headings, as it were, a *Summa theologiae.* . . . The plain fact is that Paul's statements are just not found thus arranged as fundamental doctrines of dogmatics; practically always they are in fragmentation and invariably woven in with others. Admittedly, no exposition, the present one included, can avoid ordering Paul's trains of thought under leading topics and problems. Yet this is makeshift; in actual fact, everything is intertwined."[4]

It is true that "everything is intertwined." It is also true, however, that there is method in Paul's intertwining. Käsemann, more rightly than Bornkamm, says: "Until I have proof to the contrary I proceed on the assumption that the text has a central concern and a remarkable inner logic that may no longer be entirely comprehensible to us."[5] The key to this "remarkable inner logic," we believe, lies in recognizing literary techniques such as the following:

1) The use of a structural format that consists of parts divided into sections according to an A-B-A' or A-B-C-B'-A' chiasm. This format, so prominent in Paul's earlier letters, assumes even greater importance in Romans because of the difficulties commentators have had in determining where one part ends and another begins. As we shall see, recognition of Paul's chiastic formats contributes considerably to a correct interpretation of the letter.

2) The use of concentric-circle presentations to express Paul's fundamental insights. Concentric-circle presentation consists in returning regularly to the same fundamental subject matter and presenting it under

different forms or tableaus, so that under each form substantially the same subject matter is treated but from different aspects and with additional light on matters of detail. The Old Testament presents two classic presentations in concentric-circle form: Is 40–55 (dealing with the new exodus, the new covenant, and the new creation) and Dn 2; 7–12 (dealing with the coming of the messianic kingdom, which is described in four different apocalyptically staged tableaus). In the New Testament, John's Gospel uses concentric-circle presentation by depicting the gift of new life from above as being born again (Jn 3:5), as the water of eternal life (Jn 4:9-15), and as the bread of life (Jn 6:32-58). In Matthew's Gospel, the evangelist in his five great discourses (Mt 5–7; 10; 13; 18; 23–25) repeats in one way or another the same basic concepts concerning discipleship that he summarizes in the missionary mandate of 28:18-20.

In Rom 1–11, the recognition of the following four concentric-circle presentations does much to clarify the substance of Paul's thought.

a) The contrast between failed humanity "without Christ" and successful humanity "with Christ"; for example, in 1:18–3:20, all humanity, pagans (1:18-32) as well as all Jews (2:1–3:20), are under sin's dominion and therefore "without Christ," whereas those who have the faith of Abraham (3:21–4:25) represent successful humanity "with Christ."

b) The contrast between Adamic ("without Christ") and second-Adam ("with Christ") humanity in 5:12-21.

c) The contrast between humanity under the reign of "Lord Sin" ("without Christ") and humanity under the reign of "Lord Christ" ("with Christ") in 6:1-23.

d) The contrast between the "unspiritual" ("without Christ") and the "spiritual" ("with Christ") self in 7:9-25.

3) The use of polarity presentation to highlight the positive pole of his argument. By polarity presentation is meant the contrasting of opposites in such a way that the negative pole is used solely in view of what the author wants to explain about the positive pole, and what he says about the negative pole is to be interpreted only in relation to the positive pole. The notoriously difficult passage dealing with Adam and Christ in Rom 5:12-21 would appear to be a classic case of polarity presentation and when so interpreted makes excellent sense. The same can be said for the contrasts in all of the concentric-circle presentations mentioned above.

Outline and structure of Romans

The structure decided upon here has been determined by the discovery in Romans of Paul's typical and by now adequately demonstrated predilection for an A-B-A′ chiastic format. Each part and section can be divided into lesser A-B-A′ or A-B-C-B′-A′ formats. These will be indicated at the beginning of the commentary on each part and section.

Part I (1:1–4:25): Paul's thesis: Faith in Jesus is the sole source of salvation for all. It is God's system.

   A (1:1-17): Greetings, thanksgiving, and statement of thesis
      B (1:18–3:20): Apparent digression: The Gentiles' system and the Jews' system cannot justify. All need God's justice because all have sinned.
   A' (3:21–4:25): Thesis summarized (3:21-31) and objection concerning the law answered with an argument from Scripture (4:1-25)

Part II (5:1–11:36): Paul's thesis in another form: God's love for humanity is the foundation of man's hope for salvation.

   A (5:1-11): Thesis stated: God loves humanity and has proved his love by sending his Son to die for sinners.
      B (5:12–7:25): Apparent digression: Paul's faith system versus the system of law. Experience proves that all need God's saving love and those who believe have experienced it.
   A' (8:1–11:36): Thesis of 5:1-11 summarized (8:1-39) and concluded by argument from Scripture showing that God's love does not exclude the Jews (9:1–11:36).

Part III (12:1–16:27): Exhortations, Paul's plans, conclusion

   A (12:1–13:14): Exhortations
      B (14:1–15:13): Apparent digression: the strong and the weak
   A' (15:14–16:27): Conclusion, Paul's plans, final greetings

Perspectives for interpreting Romans

Interpreting Romans demands enlarged perspectives. The enlarged perspectives proposed here do not settle categorically any of the major problems in the letter, but they do help to put the letter as a whole into a more realistic context.

First, in Rom 1-11, Paul is theologizing about humanity on a universal, collective, and timeless scale. When he speaks about human beings in relation to God, he is thinking about all humanity—humanity before, at the time of, and for all the ages after Christ. When he speaks about salvation history, he is taking into consideration the dimensions of God's dealing with humanity from the time of creation to the time of the parousia. When he speaks about judgment and salvation, he is speaking about God's final judgment on humanity and humanity's ultimate salvation. Paul, in short, is speaking eschatologically and apocalyptically.

Second, Paul's basic distinction is not between the collectivity and the individual (he has little to say about individuals as individuals) but between humanity "without Christ" and humanity "with Christ."

Third, humanity "without Christ" is the collectivity for which Jesus died (Rom 5:1-11). It is symbolized by Adam, the eponymous ancestor of sinful mankind, the symbolic progenitor, therefore, of that humanity designated by Paul as "unspiritual" man as opposed to Jesus, the eponymous ancestor (the new Adam) of that same humanity designated by Paul as "spiritual" man (cf. Rom 5:12-21; 8:1-39).

Fourth, underlying Paul's conception of humanity "without Christ" is one fundamental assumption that helps considerably to clarify his thought. The assumption is that, at least theoretically, there are three ways in which humanity can approach and please God and thereby achieve justification and salvation.

The first way is the human-centered system of philosophy according to which persons can know God and what pleases him by using their God-given intellectual faculties. This system does not work, as Paul demonstrates in 1:18-32.

The second way is the human-centered system of salvation according to which persons can achieve salvation as payment for accomplishing the works demanded by the law. This system does not work either, as Paul demonstrates in 2:1-3:20.

The third way is God's way. It is the God-given system of justification and salvation through faith in Christ. This system works because it is God's system and because God offers to all the gift of faith and the consequent ability to know and please him. This faith system is stated in 1:16-17 and expounded in 3:21-26. It is demonstrated as true for both Jews and Gentiles in 4:1-25. This third way is further proved by Paul's theses enunciated in 5:1-11 and 8:1-39. It is further expounded by polarity presentation in 5:12-7:25.

There are objections to this third way, however, and Paul deals with these objections throughout the letter. The first major objection is that if this is God's way, how explain the existence of the law? This objection is expressed in 3:27-31 and refuted in 4:1-25. The second major objection is that if this is God's way, then how explain God's apparent failure to keep his promises to Israel, since Israel as a nation has not accepted faith in Christ? This objection is implicit in 9:1ff and is refuted by the overall argumentation of chs 9-11.

Part I (1:1-4:25): Paul's thesis: Faith in Jesus is the source of salvation for all. It is God's system.

    A (1:1-17): Greetings, thanksgiving, and statement of thesis
      B (1:18-3:20): Apparent digression: The Gentiles' system and the Jews' system cannot justify.
    A' (3:21-4:25): Thesis summarized and objection concerning the law answered with an argument from Scripture

It is important whenever consulting a commentary never to become so intent on the details as to lose sight of the context as a whole. In a commentary on Romans, this is doubly important. The reader is advised therefore in doing section A (1:1-17) to keep in mind section A' (3:21-4:25), and in doing each of these to keep in mind section B (1:18-3:20). In Paul's mind, one section complements another, and the reader understands him best only in the context of the whole.

A (1:1-17): Greetings, thanksgiving, and statement of thesis

Text

> 1:1 Paul, a servant of Jesus Christ, called to be an apostle, set apart for the gospel of God ²which he promised beforehand through his prophets in the holy scriptures, ³the gospel concerning his Son, who was descended from David according to the flesh ⁴and designated Son of God in power according to the Spirit of holiness by his resurrection from the dead, Jesus Christ our Lord, ⁵through whom we have received grace and apostleship to bring about the obedience of faith for the sake of his name among all the nations, ⁶including yourselves who are called to belong to Jesus Christ, ⁷to all God's beloved in Rome, who are called to be saints: Grace to you and peace from God our Father and the Lord Jesus Christ.
>
> ⁸First, I thank my God through Jesus Christ for all of you, because your faith is proclaimed in all the world. ⁹For God is my witness, whom I serve with my spirit in the gospel of his Son, that without ceasing I mention you always in my prayers, ¹⁰asking that somehow by God's will I may now at last succeed in coming to you. ¹¹For I long to see you, that I may impart to you some spiritual gift to strengthen you, ¹²that is, that we may be mutually encouraged by each other's faith, both yours and mine.
>
> ¹³I want you to know, brethren, that I have often intended to come to you (but thus far have been prevented), in order that I may reap some harvest among you as well as among the rest of the Gentiles. ¹⁴I am under obligation both to Greeks and to barbarians, both to the wise and to the foolish: ¹⁵so I am eager to preach the gospel to you also who are in Rome.
>
> ¹⁶For I am not ashamed of the gospel: it is the power of God for salvation to every one who has faith, to the Jew first and also to the Greek. ¹⁷For in it the righteousness of God is revealed through faith for faith; as it is written, "He who through faith is righteous shall live."

Commentary

In section A, Paul begins with a long greeting (1:1-7) and follows with his usual thanksgiving section (1:8-15). He then states his thesis concerning faith in Christ as the way of salvation for all (1:16-17). This thesis will be taken up again in detail in section A' (3:21-4:25) and in a completely new way in Part II (5:1-11:36).

1:1 Paul, a servant of Jesus Christ, called to be an apostle. Paul's solemn greeting identifies him first as "a servant of Jesus Christ," i.e., as a Christian, then as one "called to be an apostle." In v 5, he makes it clear that he received his apostleship from Christ himself, and thus differentiates himself from the many other apostles sent out by the different Christian churches. He, like the Twelve, has been sent by Christ himself. He has been "set apart for the gospel of God." Just as the Old Testament prophets were set apart by God, i.e., sanctified (cf. Jer 1:5; Gal 1:15), so Paul is set apart to proclaim the good news.

1:2 which he promised beforehand through his prophets in the holy scriptures. In making the point that the gospel was already foretold by the prophets, Paul could be referring to any number of texts (e.g., Jer 31:31-34, which he develops in 2 Cor 3:1ff), but the point he is making here is the relationship between the Old Testament and the New, which will be one of the major themes of the letter (cf. 4:1-25; 9:1ff).

1:3-4 the gospel concerning his Son. Paul's belief in the dual nature of Jesus, human and divine, is expressed in the words "descended from David according to the flesh" (Jesus' human nature) "and designated Son of God in power according to the Spirit of holiness" (Jesus' divine nature). The addition of the words "in power" to the word "designated" suggests that Paul considers the resurrection to have been the act whereby Jesus as Son of God manifested publicly his divine nature. As Barrett puts it, ". . . behind the Chalcedonian orthodoxy of 'two natures' united in Christ's person lies an earlier belief in the two tenses of his activity."[6]

1:5-6 through whom we have received grace and apostleship. Paul defines the purpose for which Jesus called him to be an apostle as: "to bring about the obedience of faith . . . among all the nations." Faith means to put one's trust in Jesus. Obedience of faith means to obey Jesus on the basis of this trust-faith (cf. 6:15-23). As Paul pointed out in Gal 5–6, Christians were indeed freed from the law, but this freedom was not to degenerate into license. They were expected to live by the "law of Christ," which called for an obedience that included higher standards than any law could demand. The words "among all the nations" define the scope of Paul's apostleship. The words "including yourselves" emphasize that the Roman church is mainly a gentile community. They also imply that since Paul was sent by Christ as an apostle to the Gentiles, he has every right to be addressing the gentile Romans.

1:8-17 First, I thank my God through Jesus Christ for all of you. In the thanksgiving sections of his letters, Paul usually focuses on the themes of his letter. The thanksgiving section here (vv 8-17) is no exception. Two themes are mentioned: his desire to visit Rome (vv 10-13) and his eagerness to preach the gospel to the Romans (vv 14-17). Little more is said about visiting Rome until the end of the letter (15:14-33). There Paul reveals what he does not mention here, namely, that his planned visit to Rome is by way of a stopover on the way to Spain and that he is hoping for the Romans' help in his missionary venture in Spain (15:22-24, 28-29).

Paul's major theme in the thanksgiving section, however, is the gospel, and he proceeds immediately to define the essence of the gospel as he under-

stands it (vv 16-17). What he says about the gospel in these last verses is frequently treated as separate from the thanksgiving section. This cannot be
so, however, since so much that he says in the thanksgiving section is said at
least implicitly in view of what he intends to tell the Romans about his
gospel, e.g., his reference to imparting to them a special gift to strengthen
them (v 11); his reference to his obligation both to Greeks and barbarians (v
14); and his eagerness to preach the gospel in Rome (v 15). Add to these
remarks what Paul had already said about the gospel and his call to be an
apostle in vv 1-6, and it becomes clear that what dominates Paul's mind is
the nature of his gospel. In short, for reasons which are not easy to discern
but which we consider to have been his hidden agenda, Paul intends to explain and defend at length in 1:16–11:36 the precise nature of the gospel as
he understands it.

1:16 For I am not ashamed of the gospel. Paul is proud of his gospel
because it is not just a theoretical message such as a philosopher might
preach but a message imbued with the saving power of God: "it is the power
of God for salvation to every one who has faith." It is a salvific message for
everyone, Jew or Greek. By Greek, Paul means non-Jews, i.e., Gentiles. By
saying "to the Jew first," Paul means that this message, chronologically
speaking, came first to the Jews. He will demonstrate this chronological
priority in 4:1-25, when he deals with the faith of Abraham according to Gn
15:5. He says "Jew first," not because the message of saving faith was given
first to the Jews, but because he intends to explain later (chs 9–11) how it
happened that the Jews who received the message first turned out to be last
in accepting it. The qualification "to every one who has faith" is crucial for
Paul's understanding of the gospel. Without faith, no one can be saved.
What Paul means by faith becomes clearer in v 17.

**1:17a For in it the righteousness of God is revealed through faith for
faith.** Paul is proud of his gospel because "in it," i.e., in what he preaches
about Jesus, there is revealed the "righteousness of God." "Righteousness"
(*dikaiosynē*) is an Old Testament word that can be translated as "virtue,"
"justice," "justification," "uprightness." It comes from covenant theology
and denotes the fidelity of covenant partners in living up to their respective
obligations. Thus, God is just (manifests his righteousness) when he saves,
protects, and cherishes his covenanted people, Israel. And Israel, or any
Israelite, is just when she or he responds to God with loyalty, love, and obedience.

Righteousness is, therefore, a covenant partner's proper and practical
demonstration of loyalty and commitment. God's righteousness, i.e., his
practical demonstration of loyalty and commitment "to the Jew first and
also to the Greek" is manifested in the giving of his Son Jesus to die for
humankind (cf. 5:1-11, where the same is said, not from the aspect of covenant loyalty, but from the more basic aspect of God's love for all human-

kind). For Paul, the performance of his apostolic service, as Bornkamm expresses it, "meant announcing and bringing home to people what God did for the world in Christ to deliver and save it, and proclaiming who were called to lay hold on faith."[7] What God did for the world in Christ to deliver and save it is summed up for Paul in the words "the righteousness of God." Those called to lay hold on faith, the righteousness or righteous response of human beings, are Jew first and also Greek. In the rest of the letter, Paul will deal with the many different aspects of the righteousness of God and the righteousness of human beings. His quotation from Hab 2:4, "He who through faith [loyalty] is righteous shall live," is his way of saying that the way of faith is now and has always been the way to salvation (cf. 3:27-4:25).

B (1:18-3:20): Apparent digression: The Gentiles' system and the Jews' system cannot justify.

In section B, Paul's perspective is from the end-time back. Looking back from the end-time, Paul sees what the history of humanity would have been like without Christ. In (a) he deals with the pagan world (1:18-32); in (b) with God's impartiality in judging all human beings (2:1-19); and in (a') with the Jews (3:1-20).

The reader should remember that this section as a whole describes both something real — the sinful state of all humanity — and something unreal — the situation of humanity "without Christ." This situation is unreal because humanity has never existed "without Christ." Thus, the situation described in 1:18-3:20 is the polar opposite of the real situation of humanity that is described in sections A (1:1-17) and A' (3:21-4:25). The real situation of humanity "with Christ," however, can only be fully appreciated when it is seen as contrasted with the situation of humanity "without Christ" as described in section B (1:18-3:20). Paul uses this same kind of polarity presentation in 5:12-25, the Adamic- versus the Christ-face of mankind; in 6:1-7:5, humanity subject to Lord Sin versus humanity subject to Lord Christ; and in 7:6-25, the unspiritual man versus the spiritual man. In each case, what makes the difference is the fact that God so loved the world of sinful humanity that he sent his Son to die for sinners and thus gave them access through faith to justification and life in Christ (cf 5:1-11; 8:1-39; Jn 3:16).

(a) All Gentiles have sinned. The Gentile system (philosophy) does not work (1:18-32).

Text

(a)   1:18 For the wrath of God is revealed from heaven against all ungodliness and wickedness of men who by their wickedness suppress the truth. [19]For what can be known about God is plain to them, because God has shown it to them. [20]Ever since the creation of the world his invisible nature, namely, his eternal power and deity, has been clearly perceived in the things that have been made. So they are without excuse; ²¹for although they knew God they did not honor him as God or give thanks to him, but they became futile in their thinking and their senseless minds were darkened. ²²Claiming to be wise, they became fools, ²³and exchanged the glory of the immortal God for images resembling mortal man or birds or animals or reptiles.

²⁴Therefore God gave them up in the lusts of their hearts to impurity, to the dishonoring of their bodies among themselves, ²⁵because they exchanged the truth about God for a lie and worshiped and served the creature rather than the Creator, who is blessed for ever! Amen.

²⁶For this reason God gave them up to dishonorable passions. Their women exchanged natural relations for unnatural, ²⁷and the men likewise gave up natural relations with women and were consumed with passion for one another, men committing shameless acts with men and receiving in their own persons the due penalty for their error.

²⁸And since they did not see fit to acknowledge God, God gave them up to a base mind and to improper conduct. ²⁹They were filled with all manner of wickedness, evil, covetousness, malice. Full of envy, murder, strife, deceit, malignity, they are gossips, ³⁰slanderers, haters of God, insolent, haughty, boastful, inventors of evil, disobedient to parents, ³¹foolish, faithless, heartless, ruthless. ³²Though they know God's decree that those who do such things deserve to die, they not only do them but approve those who practice them.

Commentary

1:18 For the wrath of God is revealed from heaven. Paul appears to digress, but a more careful look at his vocabulary in v 17 shows that this section is not a digression but another aspect of what has been "revealed" *(apocalyptetai)* in v 17. In v 17, Paul said, "the righteousness of God is revealed *(apocalyptetai)* through faith for faith," and thus describes the situation of humanity "with Christ." In v 18, he describes how one can see in the saving event the other side of the coin — "the wrath of God" — which "is revealed *(apocalyptetai)* from heaven against all ungodliness and wickedness of men," i.e., the situation of humanity as it is and as it would remain if it were not for God's love in sending his Son to die for such sinful people. God's "wrath" is rarely mentioned by Paul and seems here to be his way of expressing God's aversion to humanity's depravity. It is an apocalyptic word used in the context of the last judgment (cf. Mt 25:31-46) and should not be interpreted literally. All apocalyptic language is metaphorical and should be interpreted figuratively. This case is no exception.

1:19-23 For what can be known about God is plain to them. Gentile humanity has sinned because, despite their ability to know about God through natural philosophy (vv 19-20), they not only failed to honor God (v 21) but went to the other extreme of turning to senseless idols (v 22). The description is obviously broad-brush; nevertheless, it adequately describes the pagan world as it was in Paul's time and as it has been in every time. However one looks at the word "idol" — whether it represents human values, human beings' vaunted image of themselves, or something so endemic to the species as selfishness and self-aggrandizement — it aptly describes what happens to and in humanity in every age when it attempts to live "without Christ."

1:24-32 Therefore God gave them up. The words "gave them up" are repeated three times (vv 24, 26, 28) and in each case signify what in practice occurs more often than not when humanity turns away from God and concentrates instead on its own Godless values and pursuits. Whether by "gave them up" Paul means a direct divine intervention or the ultimate psychological result of Godlessness is not clear. The Hebrew mind considered all causality to be in some way connected with God. Paul, therefore, could speak in such a manner without delving into psychology and without even considering it. His shocking description of pagan immorality in vv 24-32, and especially the list of vices in vv 28-31, would have been seconded by many of the popular moralists of the time.

(b) God is impartial in the eschatological judgment (2:1-29).

Text

(b)   2:1 Therefore you have no excuse, O man, whoever you are, when you judge another; for in passing judgment upon him you condemn yourself, because you, the judge, are doing the very same things. ²We know that the judgment of God rightly falls upon those who do such things. ³Do you suppose, O man, that when you judge those who do such things and yet do them yourself, you will escape the judgment of God? ⁴Or do you presume upon the riches of his kindness and forbearance and patience? Do you not know that God's kindness is meant to lead you to repentance? ⁵But by your hard and impenitent heart you are storing up wrath for yourself on the day of wrath when God's righteous judgment will be revealed. ⁶For he will render to every man according to his works: ⁷to those who by patience in well-doing seek for glory and honor and immortality, he will give eternal life; ⁸but for those who are factious and do not obey the truth, but obey wickedness, there will be wrath and fury. ⁹There will be tribulation and distress for every human being who does evil, the Jew first and also the Greek, ¹⁰but glory and honor and peace for every one who does good, the Jew first and also the Greek. ¹¹For God shows no partiality.

¹²All who have sinned without the law will also perish without the law, and all who have sinned under the law will be judged by the law. ¹³For it is not the hearers of the law who are righteous before God, but the doers of the law who will be justified. ¹⁴When Gentiles who have not the law do by nature what the law requires, they are a law to themselves, even though they do not have the law. ¹⁵They show that what the law requires is written on their hearts, while their conscience also bears witness and their conflicting thoughts accuse or perhaps excuse them ¹⁶on that day when, according to my gospel, God judges the secrets of men by Christ Jesus.

¹⁷But if you call yourself a Jew and rely upon the law and boast of your relation to God ¹⁸and know his will and approve what is excellent, because you are instructed in the law, ¹⁹and if you are sure that you are a guide to the blind, a light to those who are in darkness, ²⁰a corrector of the foolish, a teacher of children, having in the law the embodiment of knowledge and

truth— ²¹you then who teach others, will you not teach yourself? While you preach against stealing, do you steal? ²²You who say that one must not commit adultery, do you commit adultery? You who abhor idols, do you rob temples? ²³You who boast in the law, do you dishonor God by breaking the law? ²⁴For, as it is written, "The name of God is blasphemed among the Gentiles because of you."

²⁵Circumcision indeed is of value if you obey the law; but if you break the law, your circumcision becomes uncircumcision. ²⁶So, if a man who is uncircumcised keeps the precepts of the law, will not his uncircumcision be regarded as circumcision? ²⁷Then those who are physically uncircumcised but keep the law will condemn you who have the written code and circumcision but break the law. ²⁸For he is not a real Jew who is one outwardly, nor is true circumcision something external and physical. ²⁹He is a Jew who is one inwardly, and real circumcision is a matter of the heart, spiritual and not literal. His praise is not from men but from God.

Commentary

In this intermediary section between (a) and (a'), Paul uses the diatribe style, in which an opponent's objection is brought up and then refuted. He supposes that someone objects to his condemnation of the Gentiles by declaring, "They may be sinners, but certainly we are not!" Although the opponent is not named, it seems obvious from what follows in vv 17-29 that Paul is visualizing a Jewish opponent who reacts with horror at being put in the same class as gentile sinners. This section is preliminary and preparatory to Paul's condemnation of the Jews in 3:1-20.

2:1-5 Therefore you have no excuse, O man, whoever you are. The supposed opponent would agree with Paul's judgment of the Gentiles but would deny that he himself would be worthy of such a judgment. Paul asserts the contrary. Those who so self-righteously judge and condemn Gentiles are at the same time judging and condemning themselves, since they are guilty of the same sins. As Käsemann says, "In either Jew or Gentile the reality of mankind in its real alternatives is disclosed in exemplary fashion. . . .. The need for the gospel of God's righteousness does not seem so compelling in relation to the Jew. Hence his illusions must be eradicated."²⁸

2:6-11 For he will render to every man according to his works. God is no respecter of persons. This is the point Paul makes here. In the eschatological judgment, it will not matter whether a person is a Jew or a Gentile. What will matter is the direction and goal of his or her actions.

2:12-16 All who have sinned without the law will also perish without the law. The basis of the salvation of individuals will have nothing to do with the law as law. Again, it is a matter of what one does in response to God's call that makes the difference (vv 12-13). The Gentiles do not have the law (Jewish Old Testament revelation), but they know the will of God from their consciences (v 14) and will be judged on the basis of how they followed their consciences (vv 15-16). Paul is not going back on what he said about justification by faith (rather than by the law). The contrast here is between hearing and doing, not between faith and the law. The justified person is not justified by works but is expected to manifest his or her faith through works of love.

2:17-24 But if you call yourself a Jew. Here Paul both identifies his supposed adversary as a Jew and attacks him again as one who is as guilty as the Gentiles inasmuch as, despite his great religious privileges and boasts (vv 17-20), the Jew nevertheless does not live up to his own teaching (vv 12-24).

2:25-29 Circumcision indeed is of value if you obey the law. Paul takes up another of the vaunted boasts of the Jews, the rite of circumcision, which was a sign of the privileges of the Jews, and shows that it means nothing if it is not accompanied by observance of the law. As in 2:12-15, Paul again judges the Jews on the basis of what they do rather than on the privileges they claim and shows that there is no real difference between Jew and Gentile (vv 26-29).

(a') All Jews have sinned. The Jewish system (the law) does not work either (3:1-20).

Text

(a')   3:1 Then what advantage has the Jew? Or what is the value of circumcision? ²Much in every way. To begin with, the Jews are entrusted with the oracles of God. ³What if some were unfaithful? Does their faithlessness nullify the faithfulness of God? ⁴By no means! Let God be true though every man be false, as it is written, "That thou mayest be justified in thy words, and prevail when thou art judged."

⁵But if our wickedness serves to show the justice of God, what shall we say? That God is unjust to inflict wrath on us? (I speak in a human way.) ⁶By no means! For then how could God judge the world? ⁷But if through my falsehood God's truthfulness abounds to his glory, why am I still being condemned as a sinner? ⁸And why not do evil that good may come? — as some people slanderously charge us with saying. Their condemnation is just.

⁹What then? Are we Jews any better off? No, not at all; for I have already charged that all men, both Jews and Greeks, are under the power of sin, ¹⁰as it is written: "None is righteous, no, not one; ¹¹no one understands, no one seeks for God. ¹²All have turned aside, together they have gone wrong; no one does good, not even one." ¹³"Their throat is an open grave, they use their tongues to deceive." "The venom of asps is under their lips." ¹⁴"Their mouth is full of curses and bitterness." ¹⁵"Their feet are swift to shed blood, ¹⁶in their paths are ruin and misery, ¹⁷and the way of peace they do not know." ¹⁸"There is no fear of God before their eyes."

¹⁹Now we know that whatever the law says it speaks to those who are under the law, so that every mouth may be stopped, and the whole world may be held accountable to God. ²⁰For no human being will be justified in his sight by works of the law, since through the law comes knowledge of sin.

Commentary

Paul is now moving toward the conclusion of section B (1:18–3:20). In 1:18-32, he indicted all Gentiles as sinners. In 2:1-29, he defended the impartiality of God against the unjust claims of the Jews, arguing that God's judgment depends not upon who a person is (e.g., a Jew, with his or her many privileges) but upon what a person does. In 3:1-20, he concludes the basic argumentation of section B (1:18–3:20) by indicting as sinners all Jews as well as all Gentiles. Thus it follows that neither the gentile system (philosophy) nor the Jewish system (the law) has succeeded in saving humanity from its sinfulness. But before proceeding to his indictment of the Jews (3:9-20), Paul first has to deal with two objections (3:1 and 3:5).

3:1-2 Then what advantage has the Jew? As in 2:1ff, Paul's literary form is that of the diatribe, but as Barrett notes, "it is more probable that behind the written matter there lie real debates. . . ."[9] This is probably because Jews hearing Paul's argumentation in 2:1-29 would quite naturally object, "If what you say is true, then Jews are no better off than Gentiles and there is no advantage in being a Jew." Paul denies the validity of this, and indeed must deny it, since the Old Testament insists that God did choose the Jews rather than any other nation in the world and certainly bestowed upon them such privileges as the covenant, the law, circumcision, and the ministry of prophets, priests, and wisdom teachers. Paul, therefore, is obliged to answer: "Much in every way" (v 2). He begins to list advantages by citing the fact that the Jews were entrusted with "the oracles of God," i.e., the Scriptures. He cites no other advantages, however, because his train of thought is suddenly derailed by the reflection that the gift of the Scriptures is something totally dependent on God; man has nothing to do with it. In fact, the gift remains the same even if people (the Jews) do not respond to the message of the Scriptures.

3:3-4 What if some were unfaithful? Despite the infidelity of the Jews, a fact amply documented by the Old Testament Scriptures, God himself remains unfailingly faithful to his promises (in chs 9–11, Paul defends this thesis in depth). "When calling accompanies God's promise," as Käsemann says, "human unfaithfulness cannot nullify God's faithfulness."[10] Paul continues his argument by quoting Pss 115:2 and 50:6, which declare in substance that when the world is put on trial before God and against God, God will always turn out to be the one who is in the right (v 4).

3:5-6 But if our wickedness serves to show the justice of God, what shall we say? Here Paul deals with a new objection. Continuing in the diatribe style, he states the objection he thinks his opponents would make to his argument in v 4. If it is true, they would say, that "our wickedness serves to show the justice of God," then we are doing something good and God should not be angry at us (v 5). Paul's reply is that if this were true, it would be impossible for God to judge the world—a supposition no one would presume to make (v 6).

3:7-8 But if through my falsehood. Here Paul restates the objection of his opponents (v 7) and draws the absurd conclusion they would be compelled to draw if they were consistent, namely, "why not do evil so that good may come?" (v 8a). Some have even claimed that Paul teaches this. He dismisses the charge for the present but takes it up again in 6:1ff (v 8b).

3:9-18 What then? Are we Jews any better off? In relationship to special privileges such as the Scriptures and circumcision, the Jews are better off, as Paul stated in 3:1-2. But in relationship to sinfulness, the Jews are no better off than the Gentiles: ". . . all men, both Jews and Greeks, are under the power of sin" (v 9b). To support this contention, Paul strings together a series of quotes from Pss 14:1-3, 5-9: 140:3; 10:7; 36:1; Is 59:78 (vv 10-18).

3:19-20 Now we know that whatever the law says it speaks to those who are under the law. By "the law" Paul means here the Scriptures as a whole. It follows then that the Scriptures quoted in vv 10-18 establish Paul's contention that all the Jews are sinners (v 19). It also follows that the Jewish system (justification through works of the law) does not work (v 20a). Paul adds to v 20a the observation that "through the law comes knowledge of sin" (v 20b). He will explain what he means by these words when he takes up again the function of the law in 7:7ff. He has now completed his case for universal sinfulness (1:18–3:20). In 3:21–4:25, he will return to the theme of 1:16-17 and argue his case for justification through faith in Christ as opposed to justification through the works of the law.

A' (3:21–4:25): Thesis summarized and the Judaizers' objection answered with scriptural argument

In section A', Paul takes up again the thesis he so briefly stated in 1:16-17 (the conclusion of section A). By means of his apparent digression in section B (1:18–3:20), Paul has indicted the whole human race. Philosophy cannot save the Gentiles, and the law cannot save the Jews. Without Christ, all would be subject to condemnation in God's eschatological judgment. But there is a solution to this impasse. Paul had already revealed the solution in the thesis he enunciated in 1:16-17 at the conclusion of section A (1:1-17). He now develops this thesis in section A ' (3:21–4:25), using again his typical A-B-A' format:

(a) Thesis summarized: Faith alone saves all (3:21-26).
   (b) Judaizers' objection: Are we then abolishing the law by means of faith? (3:27-31).
(a') Objection answered from Scripture: The faith of Abraham proves that the faith system is God's system for all (4:1-25).

Since Paul never defines faith, it is important for an understanding of what he means by faith to compare what he says in 3:21-26 (a) with what he says in 4:1-25 (a'), the parallel of 3:21-26. The two sections are complementary.

(a) Thesis summarized: Faith alone saves all (3:21-26).

Text

(a)   3:21 But now the **righteousness** of God has been manifested **apart from law,** although the law and the prophets bear witness to it, [22]**the righteousness of God through faith** in Jesus Christ for all who **believe.** For there is no distinction; [23]since all have sinned and fall short of the **glory** of God, [24]they are **justified by his grace as a gift,** through the redemption which is in Christ Jesus, [25]whom God put forward as an expiation by his blood, to be received by **faith.** This was to show God's **righteousness,** because in his divine forbearance he had passed over former sins; [26]it was to prove at the present time that he himself is **righteous** and that he **justifies** him who has **faith** in Jesus.

Commentary

3:21   But now the righteousness of God has been manifested apart from law. God's "righteousness," i.e., his saving power, is manifested "apart from law" when the law, i.e., the Old Testament as a whole, is understood only as a means of salvation through works. It is "manifested" (an apocalyptic word, synonymous with the word "revealed" in 1:16-18) through the expiatory death of Christ (cf. vv 24-26). Although manifested apart from the law, this does not mean that there was nothing in the law about faith. As Paul insists, "the law and the prophets bear witness to it." He had already mentioned the witness of the prophets in 1:2 and 1:17. In 4:1-25, he will show how the law also bore witness to the centrality of justification through faith.

3:22-23   the righteousness of God through faith in Jesus Christ for all who believe. The condition for all — Jews and Gentiles — to become justified is to believe in Jesus (v 22), because all have sinned (cf. 1:18–3:20) and all alike have fallen short of God's glory (v 23).

3:24-25a   they are justified by his grace as a gift, through the redemption which is in Christ Jesus. What brings about justification, understood here as reconciliation and renewed friendship with God (cf. 2 Cor 5:14-21), is the act of redemption brought about by Jesus (v 24), "whom God put forward as an expiation by his blood, to be received by faith" (v 25). The important words here are: (1) "as a gift"; (2) "redemption"; (3) "expiation." Paul inserts the words "as a gift" to counter the Judaizers' insistence on works. As he will explain later (cf. 4:4), what is earned as a reward for works cannot be called a gift. The word "redemption" is used in the same sense as in the liberation of the Israelites from Egyptian slavery (Ex 1–19).

All, through the expiatory death of Jesus, have been liberated from their situation of slavery under sin, a situation already described in section B (1:18–3:20). The words "as an expiation by his blood" are important because it is only through the suffering and death of Jesus that humanity can see how abhorrent sin is to God.

3:25b-26 This was to show God's righteousness, because in his divine forbearance he had passed over former sins. In the past, God had as it were overlooked sin, as if it did not matter (v 25b). But the passion and death of Jesus show that God was by no means indifferent to sin. Indeed, Jesus' passion and death prove two things: first, how seriously the all-holy God looks upon sin and therefore how righteous he is (v 26a); and second, how much God loves humanity, a love that can be appreciated only by those who have faith in Jesus' death as God's and Jesus' redemptive act for the salvation of the world. Thus, Jesus' passion and death prove that God intends to justify the one "who has faith in Jesus" (v 26b). "The cross," as Barrett says, "anticipates the results of the last judgment: the Judge of all the earth is seen to do right, and, since he chooses to bear himself, in the person of his Son, the affliction antecedent to the Age to Come, he is able righteously to justify those who believe."[11]

(b) Judaizers' objection: Are we then abolishing the law by means of faith? (3:27-31).

Text

(b) 3:27 Then what becomes of our boasting? It is excluded. On what principle? On the principle of works? No, but on the principle of faith. [28]For we hold that a man is justified by faith apart from works of law. [29]Or is God the God of Jews only? Is he not the God of Gentiles also? Yes, of Gentiles also, [30]since God is one; and he will justify the circumcised on the ground of their faith and the uncircumcised through their faith. [31]Do we then overthrow the law by this faith? By no means! On the contrary, we uphold the law.

Commentary

3:27-28 Then what becomes of our boasting? Paul has expressed the heart of his redemptive theology of faith in 3:21-26. Now he digresses briefly to address once more and in diatribe style the Judaizing adversaries he dealt with in 2:1-29 and 3:1-20. If what he has said about redemption through faith in 3:21-26 is true, it follows that any boasting, i.e., relying on one's works to merit salvation, "is excluded." It is excluded on the principle of faith, because boasting and faith are mutually exclusive (v 27). Our works are our own. If we depend on our works, we do not need faith. But faith is a gift, and "a man is justified by faith apart from works of law" (v 28). In short, Paul's first argument is that the Judaizers' system of salvation is a system that depends on works by which one earns salvation. God's system is a system of faith by which one is justified and saved through belief in Jesus crucified as the manifestation of God's saving power.

3:29-30 Or is God the God of Jews only? Paul's second argument against the Judaizers attacks their boast that God is the God of the Jews only. While it is true that God chose Israel in a special way, it is clear from the Old Testament (cf. Dt *passim;* Jer 9:23f) that his choice was not based on anything Israel could pride herself on but for his own purposes. Moreover, no one can deny that God is the God of the Gentiles also (v 29). Nor can anyone deny that God is one. It follows, therefore, that in matters of justification and salvation, both Jews and Gentiles are in the same position before God. For both, it is only the faith system that justifies (v 30).

3:31 Do we then overthrow the law by this faith? Paul's third argument against the Judaizers is a refutation of their major objection to his faith system. Their objection would run somewhat as follows: "If your system of faith is right, then the law (the whole Old Testament) is wrong and God has been proved to be a deceiver." By "the law" is meant here, as Barrett points out, "not simply the written record of God's revelation of himself to man, but the whole system of religious thought and practice based upon this revelation—in a word, the religion of Judaism."[12] The objection is serious. Paul cannot for a moment agree that his faith system negates the Old Testament. His reply is brilliant. The faith system not only does not negate the law (the religion of the Old Testament) but upholds (in the sense of "confirms") it! Paul will now return, in 4:1-25, section (a'), to the subject of 3:21-26, section (a), namely, the subject of faith. In answer to the pivotal objection of his adversaries in 3:31, at the end of section (b), he will prove from the law itself, i.e., from the Old Testament, that the system of faith is not only the true system but the earliest system according to the Old Testament itself. It is for this reason that in 4:1-25 he turns to Abraham.

(a') Objection answered from Scripture: The faith of Abraham proves that the faith system is God's system (4:1-25).

In what follows, Paul cuts away the ground from under his opponents' feet. They claimed that he was using faith to overthrow the law (3:31). In 4:1-25, he proves just the opposite—namely, the law, understood as God's will manifested in the Old Testament, confirms Paul's thesis of justification through faith and not through the works of the law. To make his point, Paul uses the example of Abraham's faith to prove that, as early as Abraham, faith justified independently of works. He presents three arguments. First, Abraham was justified by faith and not by works (4:1-8). Second, Abraham was justified by faith before the giving of the seal of circumcision (4:9-12). Third, Abraham's faith is the model for all—Jews, Gentiles, and Christians (4:13-25).

Text

(a′)   4:1 What then shall we say about Abraham, our forefather according to the flesh? [2]For if Abraham was **justified** by works, he has something to boast about, but not before God. [3]For what does the scripture say? "Abraham **believed** God, and it was reckoned to him as **righteousness.**" [4]Now to one who works, his wages are not reckoned **as a gift** but as his due. [5]And to one who does not work but trusts him who **justifies** the ungodly, his **faith** is reckoned as **righteousness.** [6]So also David pronounces a blessing upon the man to whom God reckons **righteousness apart from works:** [7]"Blessed are those whose iniquities are forgiven, and whose sins are covered; [8]blessed is the man against whom the Lord will not reckon his sin."

[9]Is this blessing pronounced only upon the circumcised, or also upon the uncircumcised? We say that **faith** was reckoned to Abraham as **righteousness.** [10]How then was it reckoned to him? Was it before or after he had been circumcised? It was not after, but before he was circumcised. [11]He received circumcision as a sign or seal of the **righteousness** which he had by **faith** while he was still uncircumcised. The purpose was to make him the father of all who **believe** without being circumcised and who thus have **righteousness** reckoned to them, [12]and likewise the father of the circumcised who are not merely circumcised but also follow the example of the **faith** which our father Abraham had before he was circumcised.

[13]The promise to Abraham and his descendants, that they should inherit the world, **did not come through the law** but **through the righteousness of faith.** [14]If it is the adherents of the **law** who are to be the heirs, **faith** is null and the promise is void. [15]For the **law** brings wrath, but where there is no **law** there is no transgression. [16]That is why it depends on **faith,** in order that the promise may rest on **grace** and be guaranteed to all his descendants — not only to the adherents of the **law** but also to those who share the **faith** of Abraham, for he is the father of us all, [17]as it is written, "I have made you the father of many nations" — in the presence of the God in whom he **believed,** who gives life to the dead and calls into existence the things that do not exist.

[18]In hope he **believed** against hope, that he should become the father of many nations; as he had been told, "So shall your descendants be." [19]He did not weaken in **faith** when he considered his own body, which was as good as dead because he was about a hundred years old, or when he considered the barrenness of Sarah's womb. [20]No distrust made him waver concerning the promise of God, but he grew strong in his **faith** as he gave **glory** to God, [21]fully convinced that God was able to do what he had promised. [22]That is why his **faith** was "reckoned to him as **righteousness.**" [23]But the words, "it was reckoned to him," were written not for his sake alone, [24]but for ours also. It will be reckoned to us who **believe** in him that raised from the dead Jesus our Lord, [25]who was put to death for our trespasses and raised for our **justification.**

Commentary

4:1-5 What then shall we say about Abraham? Abraham is acknowledged as forefather according to the flesh by all Jews (v 1). But contrary to what Paul's adversaries say about Abraham, namely, that he could boast about his works (v 2), Scripture (Gn 15:6) declares that "Abraham believed God, and it was reckoned to him as righteousness" (v 3). If Abraham's righteousness had been based on works, he would have earned it as his due (v 4). But it was not on the basis of works that Abraham was counted righteous but on the basis of his faith-trust in him who justifies the ungodly (v 5). Therefore, even in the Old Testament, God had already revealed through his treatment of Abraham that righteousness comes through faith and not through works.

4:6-8 So also David. Confirming Paul's argument from the example of Abraham are the words of Ps 32:1-2, where the same verb "reckoned" is used that is used in Gn 15:6, and where the word "blessed" is equivalent to the word "righteous" or "justified." In neither case, Gn 15:6 or Ps 32:1-2, is anything said about works of the law.

4:9-10 Is this blessing pronounced only upon the circumcised, or also upon the uncircumcised? If it were only on the circumcised, Paul's adversaries would have to prove that Abraham was already circumcised at the time he was justified (vv 9-10a). Paul's answer is that it was before and not after (v 10b). His basis for this argument is that the Scriptures speak of Abraham's being justified in Gn 15:6 but only later speak of his being circumcised (Gn 17:10).

4:11a He received circumcision as a sign or seal. Circumcision not only came later, but it came as the seal or confirmation (cf. 1 Cor 9:2, where Paul uses the word "seal" in a similar manner) of what had already taken place, namely, "the righteousness which he [Abraham] had by faith while he was still uncircumcised."

4:11b-12 The purpose was to make him the father of all who believe without being circumcised. Since Abraham was justified before circumcision, it follows that he is the father of all who believe even without being circumcised (v 11b), i.e., he is the father of the Gentiles as well as the Jews. The Gentiles who believe are simply following the example of Abraham (v 12). They do not, therefore, have to be circumcised, as Paul's adversaries would contend.

4:13-15 The promise to Abraham . . . did not come through the law but through the righteousness of faith. The word "promise" is the key word in vv 13-25. By the "promises" Paul means the assurances made by God to Abraham in Gn 12:1-3; 15:5; 17:5; 22:17-18 concerning the blessings that would come in the future to his descendants and through them to all the nations of the world. Paul insists that these promises had nothing to do with the law but were dependent on faith (v 13). The fulfillment of the promise has nothing to do with the law because the law brings wrath; it is concerned with transgressions (vv 14-15). Paul will have more to say about the function of the law in 7:7ff.

4:16-17 That is why it depends on faith. Since the promise is for all, it cannot be dependent on the law, which is only for the Jews, but must be dependent on faith like to that of Abraham, the father of all believers (v 16). This is proved from the Scriptures (Gn 17:5), in which God says of Abraham: "I have made you the father of many nations" (v 17).

4:18-22 In hope he believed against hope. Abraham's hope, humanly speaking, had nothing to stand on. Thus it was hope-trust in God that formed the foundation of his belief (v 18). This was true especially when, at an age when childbearing was humanly impossible for Sarah because of her and Abraham's advanced ages (Gn 17:16-19), Abraham still believed and was rewarded, almost as if it were life out of death, by the birth of Isaac (vv 19-21). It was because of such faith that Abraham's faith was "reckoned to him as righteousness" (Gn 15:6). With these words, Paul returns to his argument in 4:1-8, and by repeating the text of Gn 15:6 forms an inclusion (cp. 4:22 and 4:3). But before he concludes, he has something to say about Christian faith.

4:23-25 But the words . . . were written not for his sake alone, but for ours also. Paul in 4:1-22 gave his scriptural proof for what he contended was God's system of justification through faith and not through the law. Now he applies this thesis to Christians. What was true about Abraham's faith is equally true of Christian faith (v 23). Christians believe in a God who raised Jesus from the dead, just as he gave Abraham a son at a time when Abraham's body was dead as far as generation was concerned (v 24). Christian faith is based upon Jesus because it is through both his death and resurrection that we are justified (v 25).

Part II (5:1-11:36): Paul's thesis in another form: God's love for humanity is the foundation of man's hope for salvation.

In Part I (1:1-4:25), Paul dealt with the thesis of justification by faith in Jesus, using an A-B-A' format that concluded with a long proof from Scripture (4:1-25). In Part II, he deals again with the thesis of justification by faith, this time basing it on the sure foundation of God's love for humanity manifested in the passion and death of Jesus. As in Part I, he uses an A-B-A' format and again concludes with a long proof from Scripture (9:1-11:36). The outline goes as follows:

A (5:1-11): Thesis stated: God loves us and has proved his love by sending his Son to die for sinners.
B (5:12-7:25): Apparent digression: Paul's faith system versus the law system of the Judaizers. Experience proves that all need God's saving love, and those who believe have experienced it.
A' (8:1-11:36): Thesis of 5:1-11 expanded (8:1-39) and concluded with a long argument from Scripture (9:1-11:36).

While Part II is similar in format and basic content to Part I, it differs in a number of ways. First, it speaks more of God's love than of his justice (saving power). Second, it takes up again in diatribe style a number of objections brought up in Part I, but deals with them far more extensively. Third, and perhaps most significant, Part II is more positive than Part I and emphasizes the wonderful consequences for humanity of God's loving act of redemption in and through Jesus. It is no accident that the vast majority of quotations from Romans come from this part of the letter.

A (5:1-11): Thesis stated: God loves us and has proved his love by sending his Son to die for sinners.

Text

5:1 Therefore, since we are **justified** by faith, we have peace with God **through our Lord Jesus Christ.** [2]Through him we have obtained access to this grace in which we stand, and we rejoice in our **hope** of sharing the glory of God. [3]More than that, we rejoice in our **sufferings,** knowing that **suffering** produces endurance, [4]and endurance produces character, and character produces **hope,** [5]and **hope** does not disappoint us, because **God's love** has been poured into our hearts **through the Holy Spirit** which has been given to us.

[6]While we were yet helpless, at the right time **Christ died for the ungodly.** [7]Why, one will hardly die for a righteous man—though perhaps for a good man one will dare even to die. [8]But God shows **his love** for us in that while we were yet sinners **Christ died for us.** [9]Since, therefore, we are now **justified** by his blood, much more shall we be saved by him from the wrath of God. [10]For if while we were enemies we were reconciled to God **by the death of his Son,** much more, now that we are reconciled, shall we be saved by his life. [11]Not only so, but we also rejoice in God **through our Lord Jesus Christ,** through whom we have now received our reconciliation.

Commentary

5:1-2   Therefore, since we are justified by faith, we have peace with God. Paul begins by repeating his thesis from Part I concerning justification by faith in Jesus and by declaring the first consequence of justification to be "peace with God." This peace is the equivalent of the reconciliation of humanity with God. The threat of an apocalyptic judgment so menacingly described in 1:18–3:20 is now over. God has reconciled the world to himself through Jesus (cf. vv 9-10; 2 Cor 5:17-19). This peace is an objective state that, as Barrett observes, "is reflected in the feeling of peace and security which man enjoys when he knows that he is reconciled to God, and peace in biblical and Jewish usage is a comprehensive description of the blessings of salvation."[13] This first consequence of justification is more fully described in v 2 as access through Jesus "to this grace in which we stand," namely, the secure state of peace and reconciliation with God, an access that allows us to "rejoice in our hope of sharing the glory of God." By "the glory of God," Paul probably means that glory lost by Adam's sin, or being in the image and likeness of God (Gn 1:26). The glory of God is further described in 8:13, 21, 29-30.

5:3-5 More than that, we rejoice in our sufferings. The second consequence of justification and reconciliation with God is a changed attitude
toward suffering (vv 3-4). Suffering is now seen as a sharing in the sacrificial love of Jesus for others, a love that "has been poured into our hearts
through the Holy Spirit which has been given to us" (v 5). The best commentary on vv 1-5, and indeed on all that Paul says in vv 1-11, is found in 2 Cor
4:7-5:19, where he describes what it means to him to suffer with Christ. The
Holy Spirit here, as in all of the New Testament, is the agent of God's love,
the one who gives us a share in that love, beginning at baptism and continuing throughout life. Paul says a great deal more about the Holy Spirit in
8:1-39, section (a'), which complements and parallels 5:1-11, section (a).

5:6-9 While we were yet helpless. These verses describe in magnificent
terms the event that proves God's love for humanity. To die for anyone is
certainly a proof of love (v 7). But the death that Jesus suffered out of love
for enemies (sinners in this case) is the ultimate and most convincing proof
that God loves us (v 8). This, more than anything else, assures us that we
will "be saved by him from the wrath of God" (v 9). The wrath of God is the
wrath threatened in the apocalyptic judgment scenario of 1:18-3:20.

5:10-11 For if while we were enemies we were reconciled to God. The
new term used here, reconciliation, is the equivalent of justification and is
just another way of repeating what Paul had said in vv 6-9. To "reconcile"
means to put an end to enmity between God and man considered as a rebel,
just as justification means to put an end to enmity between God and man
considered as a lawbreaker. The best commentary on these verses is contained in what Paul says about reconciliation in 2 Cor 5:13-20.

B (5:12–7:25): Apparent digression: Paul defends his faith system against
the accusations of the Judaizers by proving that all need God's saving
love and that those who believe have experienced it.

Parallel structure

(a) The **Adam-face** of humanity proves that **all need Christ and experience
liberation through him** (5:12-21).

(b) Christians through baptism are **dead** to Lord Sin and alive to serve
Lord **Christ** (6:1-14).

(c) Christians are no longer slaves obedient to sin but slaves obedient to God (6:15-23).

(b') Like a wife whose husband has died, Christians are **dead** to the law
and free to give themselves to another—**Christ** (7:1-6).

(a') The **Adam-face** of humanity shows that **all need Christ and experience
liberation through him** (7:7-25).

Few sections have more difficulties than 5:12-7:25, and few things help more to solve the difficulties than careful attention to Paul's parallel structure. If the reader will read sections (a) and (a') together and then sections (b) and (b') together, he or she will notice how much one is like the other and how much one illuminates the other. Another help toward understanding this difficult section is to realize that in his presentations of the Adam-face of humanity versus the Christ-face of humanity (5:12-25), humanity under the reign of Lord Sin versus humanity under Lord Christ (6:1-23), and the unspiritual versus the spiritual self (7:9-25), Paul is repeating in different ways what he had already said in 1:1-4:25 about humanity without Christ (1:18-3:20) and humanity with Christ (1:16-17; 3:21-4:25). This technique, as mentioned above (p. 203), is known as concentric-circle presentation. It is a great benefit for the reader to realize that in all these concentric-circle presentations Paul is saying substantially the same thing several times over and at the same time nuancing aspects of the basic theme — the situation of humanity with and without Christ — by bringing up and answering in diatribe style the objections of his law-centered opponents to his faith-in-Christ system of justification and salvation.

(a) The Adam-face of humanity proves that all need Christ and experience liberation through him (5:12-21).

Text

(a)   5:12 Therefore as **sin** came into the world through one man and **death** through **sin**, and so **death** spread to all men because all men sinned — [13]**sin** indeed was in the world before the **law** was given, but **sin** is not counted where there is no **law**. [14]Yet **death** reigned from Adam to Moses, even over those whose **sins** were not like the transgression of Adam, who was a type of the one who was to come.
     [15]But the free gift is not like the trespass. For if many **died** through one man's trespass, much more have the grace of God and the free gift in the grace of that one man Jesus Christ abounded for many. [16]And the free gift is not like the effect of that one man's **sin**. For the judgment following one trespass brought condemnation, but the free gift following many trespasses brings justification. [17]If, because of one man's trespass, **death** reigned through that one man, much more will those who receive the abundance of grace and the free gift of righteousness reign in **life** through the one man Jesus Christ.
     [18]Then as one man's trespass led to condemnation for all men, so one man's act of righteousness leads to acquittal and **life** for all men. [19]For as by one man's disobedience many were made sinners, so by one man's obedience many will be made righteous. [20]**Law** came in, to increase the trespass; but where **sin** increased, grace abounded all the more, [21]so that, as **sin** reigned in **death**, grace also might reign through righteousness to eternal **life** through Jesus Christ our Lord.

Commentary

5:12 Therefore as sin came into the world through one man. For Paul, Adam typifies the human person without Christ or, more properly, humanity without Christ. Like Adam, all sinned. This is another way of saying what Paul had already said about all Gentiles and all Jews being sinners in 1:18–3:20. The penalty for Adam's sin, according to Gn 3, was death, and Paul notes that since death has been universal, it follows that sin has been universal. Although Paul probably understood the Adam story historically, it is clear from what he says here that he is interpreting it theologically. Adam, for Paul, represents sinful humanity.

5:13 sin indeed was in the world before the law was given. For Paul, sin in this context is not so much the act of sinning as the disposition to sin, the bent of the ego to assert itself against God (v 13a). Human beings already had this bent even before God decreed that laws be observed. Sin, however, could be counted as sin, i.e., as a transgression of the law, only after a law had been laid down (v 13b). In Adam's case, sin as the bent of the ego to assert itself against God was present even before the fall but was counted as sin only after God had laid down the law (Gn 3:4ff) about not eating from one certain tree in the garden (cf. another version of this in 7:7ff).

5:14a Yet death reigned from Adam to Moses. There was no law, i.e., no Sinai law code, until the time of Moses, but the fact that humans died proves that sin, the cause of death, was always present, even though a law such as that given to Adam had not been given. Death proves, according to Paul, that all, like Adam, had sinned.

5:14b Adam, who was a type of the one who was to come. It is important to note in what way Paul sees Adam as a type of Christ. As will become obvious in vv 15-25, Adam is seen as a type of Christ only in relation to humanity. As Adam is representative of sinful humanity, Christ is representative of redeemed humanity. Christ is, in other words, a second Adam in relationship to humanity looked upon as redeemed. It is the same humanity looked at, on the one hand, as Adam-faced and, on the other, as Christ-faced or, if one prefers, the same humanity seen from the dark side and from the bright side. By "type," therefore, Paul means analogy. As Adam typifies sinful humanity, so analogously Christ typifies redeemed humanity. The analogy, however, is not between equivalents. As Paul will show in vv 15-21, what Christ has done for the good of humanity vastly overbalances the evil effects of Adam-faced humanity.

5:15-21 But the free gift is not like the trespass. Death, which Adam's sin effected, is vastly overbalanced by the gift of redemption effected by Christ (v 15). As sin brought condemnation, Jesus' free gift of grace brought justification (v 16). As through Adam's trespass death reigned, so grace and righteousness reign in life through Christ (v 17). Similarly, as Adam's trespass led to condemnation for all, Christ's act of righteousness leads to acquittal and life for all (v 18). The overbalancing continues with the contrast between the disobedience of Adam and the obedience of Christ (v 19), between the increase of sin and the overabundance of grace brought by Christ (v 20), and finally between the reign of sin, which resulted in death, and the reign of eternal life, which came through Christ (v 21). All the contrasts have one object in view: to set in the starkest possible opposition the bleak situation of Adam-faced humanity with the happy situation of Christ-faced humanity. The two are opposed in this polarity presentation (see p. 203) in such a way that the reader cannot help but marvel at the place and significance of Christ in God's plan of salvation for humanity.

The perplexing problem in 5:12-21 is to explain how "*all* men sinned" (cf. 3:20, 23; 11:32). It is this fact of humanity's solidarity in sin that explains both the first sinful, unredeemed "face" of humanity and the necessity of Christ's death, which gives to mankind a new "face." The comment of Buck-Taylor is all-important here: "For Paul, universal need for salvation, put in juridical terms, is universal guilt."[14] How universal depends on the Pauline concept of "all." According to Paul, a person "without Christ," even though free, does not and probably cannot, equipped only with human power, escape sin. In this sense, at least all adults sin as Adam sinned. And in this sense all are helpless until they are given more than human power to overcome sin—the power, namely, of Christ's life-giving spirit.

It would seem to follow, according to Paul, that Christ has died for all because all, like Adam, have sinned personally and have need of personal redemption. In *each* person, therefore, there is present, though not simultaneously, two "faces." Each person is a sinner (first face) on the one hand prior to Christ's death, and on the other hand redeemed (second face) as a consequence of Christ's death. The "Adam-faced" humanity is the humanity that *would have been* if God had not "so loved the world that he sent his only-begotten Son" to redeem the world and give it the new "Christ-face," which in Pauline terminology is equivalent to the "new creation" and the new "Christ-humanity" (cf. 2 Cor 5:17). In short, all are born "without" Christ and Christ-life. So born into a sinful world, they inevitably but freely sin. Out of this personal complicity in the "sin of the world" (the Johannine terminology for the same situation), they are redeemed by Christ and offered the option of faith. Having received the God-given power to respond to God by the gift of faith, they either respond freely or freely refuse to respond.

(b) Christians through baptism are dead to Lord Sin and alive to serve Lord Christ (6:1-14).

Text

(b)   6:1 What shall we say then? Are we to continue in sin that grace may abound? ²By no means! How can we who **died to sin** still live in it? ³Do you not know that all of us who have been baptized into Christ Jesus were baptized into his **death?** [4]We were buried therefore with him by baptism into **death,** so that as Christ was **raised from the dead** by the glory of the Father, we too might walk in **newness of life.**

[5]For if we have been united with him in a death like his, we shall certainly be united with him in a **resurrection** like his. [6]We know that our old self was crucified with him so that the sinful body might be destroyed, and we might no longer be **enslaved to sin.** [7]For **he who has died is freed from sin.** [8]But if we have **died** with Christ, we believe that we shall also live with him. [9]For we know that Christ being **raised from the dead** will never die again; **death** no longer has dominion over him. [10]The **death** he died he **died to sin,** once for all, but the life he lives he lives to God. [11]So you also must consider yourselves **dead to sin** and **alive** to God in Christ Jesus.

[12]Let not sin therefore reign in your mortal bodies, to make you obey their **passions.** [13]Do not yield your members to sin as instruments of wickedness, but yield yourselves to God as men who have been brought from death to life, and your members to God as instruments of righteousness. [14]For sin will have no dominion over you, since you are **not under law** but under grace.

Commentary

6:1-4 What shall we say then? Are we to continue in sin that grace may abound? Paul deals here in diatribe style with the supposed and probably real objection that his opponents brought against his system of salvation. If, as he claimed in 5:20, "where sin increased, grace abounded all the more," then why not "continue in sin that grace may abound?" (v 1). The objection implies that Christians are not bound by any laws of morality and that they are for all practical purposes antinomians. Paul had dealt briefly with the same objection in 3:5-8. Here he faces it head-on. His reply does not deny the *a fortiori* logic of his opponents but rather the basis of their argument. "How can we who died to sin still live in it?" (v 2). At baptism, Christians die to sin in the sense that they give over to Lord Christ the allegiance they had once paid to Lord Sin (v 3 and cf. vv 12-14). Through baptism, the Christian rises to a new life just as Christ was raised, and the purpose of this spiritual resurrection is to bring about a "newness of life" (v 4).

6:5-7 For if we have been united with him in a death like his, we shall certainly be united with him in a resurrection like his. Baptism anticipates the Christian's resurrection, but that resurrection remains in the future (v 5). What does not lie in the future, however, is the kind of life a Christian is to live as one who anticipates resurrection with Christ. It is the life of one who has been crucified with Christ in such a way that his or her sinful self might be destroyed, that self which was enslaved to (Lord) sin (v 6). It follows, therefore, that the Christian "who has died is freed from sin" (v 7, and cf. 7:1-6, where the same truth is expressed in the little allegory of the woman whose husband has died and who is consequently free to marry again). Free from sin, the Christian is now subject to Christ, and it is this subjection to Christ that determines the kind of life the Christian will lead.

6:8-11 But if we have died with Christ, we believe that we shall also live with him. Here Paul begins to answer in a positive manner the objection raised against him in 6:1. As with Christ, so with the Christian. Death (in this case baptism) leads to a new life, and as a result there can be no question of continuing in sin, as Paul's opponents argued (v 8). As death no longer has dominion over Christ (v 9), and as he now lives to God (v 10), so Christians "must consider [themselves] dead to sin and alive to God in Christ Jesus" (v 11).

6:12-14 Let not sin therefore reign in your mortal bodies. Since Christians are now "alive to God in Christ Jesus" (v 11), it follows that they must not only not continue in sin, as the opponents claimed in 6:1, but must oppose the reign of sin that still tries to impose itself on them (v 12). They should yield themselves, their bodies, to the reign or direction of God (v 13). Being "under grace," the gift of faith in Jesus, the Christian is no longer "under law" (v 14). Being under law means striving to save oneself by one's own efforts; being under grace, Christians live now as Christ would have them live, and such a life is unalterably opposed to sin. The argument has been subtle and involved. Stripped to its bare essentials, it amounts to this: prior to baptism, the Christian was subject to "Lord Sin"; at baptism, the Christian dies to the dominion of "Lord Sin" and becomes subject to the dominion of "Lord Christ."

(c) Christians are no longer slaves obedient to sin but slaves obedient to God (6:15-23).

Text

(c)   6:15 What then? Are we to sin because we are not under law but under grace? By no means! [16]Do you not know that if you yield yourselves to any one as obedient slaves, you are slaves of the one whom you obey, either of sin, which leads to death, or of obedience, which leads to righteousness? [17]But thanks be to God, that you who were once slaves of sin have become obedient from the heart to the standard of teaching to which you were committed, [18]and, having been set free from sin, have become slaves of righteousness. [19]I am speaking in human terms, because of your natural limitations. For just as you once yielded your members to impurity and to greater and greater iniquity, so now yield your members to righteousness for sanctification.
[20]When you were slaves of sin, you were free in regard to righteousness. [21]But then what return did you get from the things of which you are now ashamed? The end of those things is death. [22]But now that you have been set free from sin and have become slaves of God, the return you get is sanctification and its end, eternal life. [23]For the wages of sin is death, but the free gift of God is eternal life in Christ Jesus our Lord.

Commentary

6:15-19 What then? Are we to sin because we are not under law but under grace? Continuing in diatribe style, Paul foresees and answers the objection that might flow from what he had said in 6:14 about Christians not being "under law but under grace." Opponents might gather from the words "not under law" that Christians were not only free from the law but free to do what they pleased. Paul's reply is based on the analogy of a slave-owner and his slave. Christians have indeed been freed from the obedience a slave would owe to the law as a slave-owner (vv 15-16), but they are not free from obedience to God, who is their new owner (vv 17-18). Under the slave-owner sin, they yielded their members "to impurity and to greater and greater iniquity." Under obedience to God, they are expected to yield themselves "to righteousness for sanctification" (v 19). In short, a person cannot serve two masters. Serving God leads to that sanctification which results from righteousness, i.e., conduct commensurate with the response called for from a right relationship with God.

6:20-23 When you were slaves of sin, you were free in regard to righteousness. Pursuing the analogy further, Paul contrasts the end results of slavery to sin, which has no regard for righteousness, with the end results of slavery to God. From the one comes death (vv 20-21); from the other, sanctification and eternal life (vv 22-23).

(b') Like a wife whose husband has died, Christians are dead to the law and free to give themselves to another—Christ (7:1-6).

Text

(b') 7:1 Do you not know, brethren—for I am speaking to those who know the **law**—that the **law** is binding on a person only **during his life?** ²Thus a married woman is bound by **law** to her husband **as long as he lives;** but if her husband **dies** she is discharged from the **law** concerning the husband. ³Accordingly, she will be called an adulteress if she lives with another man while her husband is **alive.** But **if her husband dies she is free from that law,** and if she marries another man she is not an adulteress.

⁴Likewise, my brethren, you have **died to the law** through the body of **Christ,** so that you may belong to another, to him who has been **raised from the dead** in order that we may bear fruit for God. ⁵While we were living in the flesh, our sinful **passions,** aroused by the law, were at work in our members to bear fruit for death. ⁶But now we are **discharged from the law,** dead to that **which held us captive,** so that we serve **not under the old written code** but in the **new life** of the Spirit.

Commentary

7:1-3 Do you not know, brethren . . . that the law is binding on a person only during his life? In perfect parallel with 6:1-14, section (b), which dealt with the Christian being dead to Lord Sin and alive to Lord Christ, Paul now uses another analogy to express the change that comes about when a person becomes a Christian. He first states the obvious: laws are for the living, not for the dead (v 1). He gives as an example a woman whose husband has died; she is free to marry another (vv 2-3).

7:4 Likewise, my brethren, you have died to the law . . . so that you may belong to another. Completing the analogy, Paul likens the Christian to one who is free from the law, which now is dead, and so free to belong to another—Christ. As in 6:1-14, it is like being dead to Lord Sin and alive to Lord Christ.

7:5 While we were living in the flesh, our sinful passions, aroused by the law, were at work in our members to bear fruit for death. Returning to the first husband, equivalent in the analogy to the time when we "were living in the flesh" under the law, Paul describes the work of the law as one of arousing the sinful passions in our members in such a way as to produce death. The words "aroused by the law" signal Paul's intention to deal with the function of the law, a function he will describe more extensively in 7:7-25.

7:6 But now we are discharged from the law . . . so that we serve not under the old written code but in the new life of the Spirit. Freed from the law, the Christian still has to "serve." But now he serves in the "new life of the Spirit," i.e., in freedom from the law but under the influence and direction of the Spirit. For a fuller description of what Paul means by freedom and life under the influence and direction of the Spirit, the reader should consult Gal 5–6.

(a') The Adam-face of humanity shows that all need Christ and experience liberation through him (7:7-25).

Text

(a')   7:7 What then shall we say? That the law is **sin**? By no means! Yet, if it had not been for the law, I should not have known sin. I should not have known what it is to covet if the law had not said, "You shall not covet." [8]But sin, finding opportunity in the commandment, wrought in me all kinds of covetousness. Apart from the law sin lies dead. [9]I was once alive apart from the law, but when the commandment came, **sin** revived and I died; [10]the very commandment which promised life proved to be death to me. [11]For **sin**, finding opportunity in the commandment, deceived me and by it killed me. [12]So the law is holy, and the commandment is holy and just and good. [13]Did that which is good, then, bring death to me? By no means! It was **sin**, working death in me through what is good, in order that **sin** might be shown to be **sin**, and through the commandment might become sinful beyond measure.

[14]We know that the law is spiritual; but I am carnal, sold under sin. [15]I do not understand my own actions. For I do not do what I want, but I do the very thing I hate. [16]Now if I do what I do not want, I agree that the law is good. [17]So then it is no longer I that do it, but **sin** which dwells within me. [18]For I know that nothing good dwells within me, that is, in my flesh. I can will what is right, but I cannot do it. [19]For I do not do the good I want,

but the evil I do not want is what I do. [20]Now if I do what I do not want, it is no longer I that do it, but **sin** which dwells within me.

[21]So I find it to be a law that when I want to do right, evil lies close at hand. [22]For I delight in the law of God, in my inmost self, [23]but I see in my members another law at war with the law of my mind and making me captive to the law of **sin** which dwells in my members. [24]Wretched man that I am! Who will deliver me from this body of death? [25]Thanks be to God through Jesus Christ our Lord! So then, I of myself serve the law of God with my mind, but with my flesh I serve the law of **sin**.

Commentary

7:7a What then shall we say? That the law is sin? By no means! For Paul, as for any Christian and Jew, the law represents God's will. There is no way that the law in itself can be evil. If, however, one distinguishes between the law and the egotism of human beings when confronted by the law, one can see how the law unmasks this egotism and thus allows persons to know what sin is.

7:7b I should not have known what it is to covet if the law had not said: "You shall not covet." It is disputed who Paul means by "I." Is it Paul himself or the average person or someone else? More and more commentators are coming to agree that the "I" represents Adam. As Käsemann says, "There is nothing in the passage which does not fit Adam, and everything fits Adam alone."[15] This solution to the problem is confirmed by the a-b-c-b'-a' format of 6:1–7:25. Just as (b') is parallel to (b), so (a') is parallel to (a), i.e., 7:7-25 is parallel to 5:12-21. In 5:12-21, Paul contrasts the Adam-face of humanity with the Christ-face of humanity and describes graphically the results of Adam's sin. Here in 7:7-25, Paul returns to Adam's sin as the prototypical sin of human beings. Instead of using Adam's name, however, Paul uses the literary "I," putting himself as it were in Adam's place and explaining how it was that the good commandment of God that was meant to lead him to life actually brought about his death. We have, in short, another concentric-circle presentation (cf. 1:18–3:20; 5:12ff) of humanity "without Christ" as opposed to humanity "with Christ" (cf. 3:21–4:25; 5:1-11; 8:1-39).

7:8-12 But sin, finding opportunity in the commandment, wrought in me all kinds of covetousness. It was not until God commanded Adam not to eat of a certain tree in the garden (Gn 3:1ff) that Adam's covetousness was aroused (v 9a). Until God gave the command, sin was as it were dead, and Adam was alive. But once the command was given, sin came alive ("revived"); Adam broke the commandment and suffered the penalty of death (v 9), so that "the very commandment which promised life proved to be death" (v 10). Thus, sin, which for Paul is the egotistical desire of human beings to stand on their own two feet before God and earn their salvation by their own works independently of God, used God's good commandment to deceive Adam and make it the source of his death (v 11). It follows, then, as Paul declared in v 7a, that the law is in no way to be equated with sin but is, on the contrary, "holy and just and good" (v 12).

7:13 Did that which is good, then, bring death to me? By no means! Paul began by asking, "Is the law itself sin?" and proved that it was not (vv 7-12). Still speaking in the name of Adam and still trying to explain the relationship between law and sin, he is forced to ask, in view of his explanation of death resulting from the breaking of the commandment in Gn 2–3, "Did that which is good [God's commandment] bring death to me?" The fault, he declares, was not with the law or the commandment but with sin. By provoking the ego, the commandment, which is good, succeeds in revealing how grossly sinful sin (our propensity to "go it alone" without God) really is.

7:14 We know that the law is spiritual; but I am carnal, sold under sin. In 7:7-13, Paul used verbs in the past tense because he spoke in the name of Adam about what had been Adam's experience in the past. From here to the end of the chapter, he has Adam continue to speak—but in the present tense, thus showing how in his and every person's experience sin is recognized as distinct from God's law. It is taken for granted that everyone agrees the law is spiritual, i.e., it comes from God (v 14a). But at the same time, we always know that we are "carnal," i.e., we have an ego that tends to oppose God's will in such a way that we seem irrevocably committed to the power of sin or, as Paul puts it, "sold under sin" (v 14b).

7:15-16 I do not understand my own actions. This is not meant in the sense that we do not know what we are doing when we sin (v 15a); rather, we cannot explain why we do what we do, since we so often do, not what we want to do, but what we hate (v 15b). From this it follows that there is something in us that tells us that the law, forbidding what we do, is good (v 16). What confirms that the law is good, even when we go ahead and break it, can only be our conscience (cf. 2:15). Thus, our conscience confirms that the law is good, and the fault can only lie elsewhere.

7:17-20 So then it is no longer I that do it, but sin which dwells within me. Paul has exonerated the law from culpability in bringing about Adam's death (vv 7-13). In vv 14-16, he seems to have exonerated Adam as well. Who, then, is to blame? Sin is to blame! But what is sin? (v 17). In vv 18-19, Paul-Adam explains that sin is that propensity of the human being to do the evil he/she does not want to do instead of the good he/she wants to do. This proves that the culprit is sin (v 20).

7:21-23 So I find it to be a law that when I want to do right, evil lies close at hand. Paul repeats what he said in vv 17-20 but adds a new element. He speaks of being "sold under sin" as a law (v 21) that is opposed to the law of God. Since this is so, there can be no doubt that the law is good (the central point in this discussion from 7:7ff). What proves this is the delight he feels in the law of God, at the same time that he experiences in himself this rival law of sin that inclines him to oppose the law of God (vv 22-23).

7:24-25a Wretched man that I am! Who will deliver me from this body of death? The body (person) under the law of sin can only look forward to death. Is this an insurmountable impasse (v 24)? Not at all. Christ provides deliverance from this impasse (cf. 3:21–4:25; 5:1-11, 15-21; 8:1-39).

7:25b So then, I of myself serve the law of God. These words not only are anticlimactic but do not appear to be representative of Paul's thanksgiving in 7:7-25. They are almost certainly a gloss written into the text by one of Paul's earliest commentators.

A' (8:1–11:36): Thesis of 5:1-11 expanded in 8:1-39 and concluded by an argument from Scripture (9:1–11:36)

In dealing with 8:1-39, Käsemann says: "Notwithstanding widespread views to the contrary, the apostle constructed the epistle very carefully and structured it systematically. This section [8:1-39] transcends the context and forms the conclusion to the whole division (chs 5-8)."[16] The reader should not be surprised to discover, therefore, that in 8:1-39 Paul returns to the themes of 5:1-11, section A of Part II (5:1–11:36). In this last section (8:1–11:36) of Part II, he follows the same format as in Part I (1:1–4:25), in which his A' section (3:21–4:25) concluded with an argument from Scripture (4:1-25) in order to refute the objection of his opponents (3:31) that he was doing away with the law.

Parallel structure of section A' (8:1–11:36)

    (a) Triumph through the power of the Spirit (8:1-13)
        (b) Liberation of the world and of the sons of God and brothers of Christ (8:14-30)
    (a') Triumph through the love of God (8:31-39), followed by a long argument from Scripture (9:1–11:36) refuting the objection that God's love does not extend to saving his own chosen people

In following this parallel structure, it will be useful as usual for understanding Paul's thought to compare subsections (a) and (a'). In each, the dominant note can be expressed both positively and negatively: negatively, there is no condemnation for those who are in Christ; positively, those in Christ triumph through the power of the Spirit and the love of God. This was the thesis of 5:1-11 (section A). Here it is developed at length, with many parallels to 5:1-11.

(a) Triumph through the power of the Spirit (8:1-13)

Text

(a) 8:1 There is therefore now **no condemnation** for those who are **in Christ Jesus.** ²For the law of the Spirit of life **in Christ Jesus** has set me free from the law of sin and death. [3]For **God** has done what the law, weakened by the flesh, could not do: **sending his own Son** in the likeness of sinful flesh and for sin, he **condemned** sin in the flesh, [4]in order that the just requirement of the law might be fulfilled in us, who walk not according to the flesh but according to the Spirit.

[5]For those who live according to the flesh set their minds on the things of the flesh, but those who live according to the Spirit set their minds on the things of the Spirit. [6]To set the mind on the flesh is death, but to set the mind on the Spirit is life and peace. [7]For the mind that is set on the flesh is hostile to God; it does not submit to God's law, indeed it cannot; [8]and those who are in the flesh cannot please God.

[9]But you are not in the flesh, you are in the Spirit, if the Spirit of God really dwells in you. Any one who does not have the Spirit of Christ does not belong to him. [10]But **if Christ is in you,** although your bodies are dead because of sin, your spirits are alive because of righteousness. [11]If the Spirit of him who **raised Jesus from the dead** dwells in you, he who **raised Christ Jesus from the dead** will give life to your mortal bodies also through his Spirit which dwells in you.

[12]So then, brethren, we are debtors, not to the flesh, to live according to the flesh — [13]for if you live according to the flesh you will die, but if by the Spirit you put to death the deeds of the body you will live.

Commentary

8:1 There is therefore now no condemnation for those who are in Christ Jesus. Here again, as in 1:18–3:20 and as so often elsewhere in the letter, Paul is speaking from the perspective of the last judgment. The declaration about "no condemnation" sums up the situation of those who are "in Christ" at the judgment. In what follows in the rest of the chapter, Paul will speak of the triumph of those who, being in Christ, allow themselves to be led by the Spirit, which is the power of Christ manifest in the life of the Christian, instead of by the "flesh," which is the propensity of human beings to follow their own egotistical inclinations and values. In speaking from the perspective of the last judgment, Paul is out to accomplish two objectives: first, to emphasize the triumph of Christians in Christ; second, to remind Christians that complete triumph with Christ at the time of the judgment depends on their following him in the present in his way of the cross.

8:2 For the law of the Spirit of life in Christ Jesus has set me free from the law of sin and death. Paul begins to speak of triumph through the Spirit by taking up again the theme he had enunciated in 7:6: "But now we are discharged from the law, dead to that which held us captive, so that we serve not under the old written code but in the new life of the Spirit." By "law" here, Paul means a way of life, a system of religion that succeeds as opposed to the system of the Jews, who put their confidence in themselves and in their obedience to the law of Moses.

8:3-8 For God has done what the law, weakened by the flesh, could not

do. The reason the way of life of the Spirit works is because God did what the law, perverted by the flesh, i.e., by human beings' egotistical propensity to sin, could never do — he sent his own Son to conquer sin and thereby liberate people from their slavery to sin (cf. 5:1, 6-11). God did this "in order that the just requirement of the law," i.e., the righteousness that the law called for but could not on its own produce, "might be fulfilled in us, who walk . . . according to the Spirit" (v 4). In vv 5-8, Paul defines what he means by "flesh" and "Spirit." The flesh means the weakness of human beings prone to sin and focused upon the values of this world. The Spirit, on the other hand, means the power of God by which human beings turn themselves to God and God's values. Flesh in this context does not mean that there is anything intrinsically evil about the body-person as created by God, but refers to that aspect of persons whereby they misuse their God-given gift of freedom to oppose the will of God.

8:9 But you are not in the flesh, you are in the Spirit. Paul is about to give a more positive description of Christian life, but he begins with a warning: "if the Spirit of God really dwells in you" (v 9a). The declaration that "there is therefore now no condemnation for those who are in Christ Jesus" (v 1) is picked up here and qualified by the words, "Any one who does not have the Spirit of Christ does not belong to him" (v 9b). The Spirit of Christ is the same as the Spirit of God, but it is only through Christ that the Spirit is sent and received (cf. Jn 14:25-27; 15:26; 16:7-15).

8:10 But if Christ is in you. Union with Christ is essential. Where there is union with Christ, the body-person that used to be enslaved to sin is dead to that way of life (cf. 6:1-14; 7:1-6). The individual now lives a new life "because of righteousness," i.e., because of the gift of justification through faith in Christ, which renders a person at peace with God (cf. 5:1) and ready, under the influence of the Spirit, to live a life in union with Christ.

8:11 If the Spirit of him who raised Jesus from the dead dwells in you. The warning "if" of v 9 is repeated in relation to the resurrection of Christians. God who raised up Jesus will also raise up Christians, and this too will be brought about by the Spirit. The Spirit is a pledge of our future resurrection, "if" he dwells in us.

8:12-13 So then, brethren, we are debtors, not to the flesh, to live according to the flesh. Since the flesh has done nothing for us, we owe it nothing. Paul should go on to say, "but we are debtors to the Spirit," but he probably takes it for granted, since he has already pointed out how much we should be in debt to the Spirit (v 12). He concludes this section, therefore, with an exhortation and another "if" (cf. vv 9, 11). The "life" mentioned in v 11 is dependent on our living "by the Spirit," letting ourselves be led by the Spirit to lead a life pleasing to God. Baptism is only the beginning. There remain, before the glory of the resurrection, the trials of discipleship.

(b) Liberation of the world and of the children of God and brothers of Christ (8:14-30)

Text

(b)   8:14 For all who are led by the Spirit of God are sons of God. [15]For you did not receive the spirit of slavery to fall back into fear, but you have received the spirit of sonship. When we cry, "Abba! Father!" [16]it is the Spirit himself bearing witness with our spirit that we are children of God, [17]and if children, then heirs, heirs of God and fellow heirs with Christ, provided we suffer with him in order that we may also be glorified with him.

[18]I consider that the sufferings of this present time are not worth comparing with the glory that is to be revealed to us. [19]For the creation waits with eager longing for the revealing of the sons of God; [20]for the creation was subjected to futility, not of its own will but by the will of him who subjected it in hope; [21]because the creation itself will be set free from its bondage to decay and obtain the glorious liberty of the children of God. [22]We know that the whole creation has been groaning in travail together until now; [23]and not only the creation, but we ourselves, who have the first fruits of the Spirit, groan inwardly as we wait for adoption as sons, the redemption of our bodies.

[24]For in this hope we were saved. Now hope that is seen is not hope. For who hopes for what he sees? [25]But if we hope for what we do not see, we wait for it with patience.

[26]Likewise the Spirit helps us in our weakness; for we do not know how to pray as we ought, but the Spirit himself intercedes for us with sighs too deep for words. [27]And he who searches the hearts of men knows what is the mind of the Spirit, because the Spirit intercedes for the saints according to the will of God.

[28]We know that in everything God works for good with those who love him, who are called according to his purpose. [29]For those whom he foreknew he also predestined to be conformed to the image of his Son, in order that he might be the first-born among many brethren. [30]And those whom he predestined he also called; and those whom he called he also justified; and those whom he justified he also glorified.

Commentary

8:14-17 For all who are led by the Spirit of God are sons of God. In v 23, Paul makes it clear that we are sons by adoption. His intent here, as in Gal 4:6-7, is to emphasize the fact that, as sons, Christians are heirs of God and as such inherit eternal life (vv 13-15a). One proof of sonship is the acclamation Christians make during worship when, under the influence of the Spirit, they cry out to God and call him "Abba-Father" (vv 15b-16). They thus testify that we are indeed heirs with Christ, "provided we suffer with him in order that we may also be glorified with him" (v 17).

8:18-23 I consider that the sufferings of this present time are not worth comparing with the glory that is to be revealed to us. The meaning of suffering in v 17 turns Paul's mind to that subject in vv 18-27. He will return to the subject of sonship in vv 28-30. His comparison is between the glory enjoyed by Christians at the time of the parousia and the sufferings that have to be borne in the present. In the time between the present and the parousia, not only the faithful (cf. v 23) but also the whole created universe waits with eager longing for the glorious end-time (v 19). This is so because material creation, which God made subject to his human creation (Gn 1:26-27), has somehow shared in the human fall, and thus, subjected to futility by God, it will only be free from this futility when human creation itself is liberated (vv 20-22). Creation as a consequence joins with humanity in "groaning in travail." Together they long for the parousia, when Christians, "who have the first fruits of the Spirit" as a guarantee of the future, can confidently expect adoption as sons, which will signify their final acceptance into God's family (cf. v 29, where Christians are called brothers of Christ) and the redemption of their bodies, i.e., resurrection (v 29).

8:24-25 For in this hope we were saved. Paul emphasizes in these two verses what he emphasized in vv 9, 11, 13, 18. This is still the time of discipleship, the time of testing. Our hope is for what is unseen and future. We have not arrived, and we must wait with patience for the arrival of the glorious end-time with its wonderful rewards.

8:26-28 Likewise the Spirit helps us in our weakness. Fully recognizing the difficulties of the time of waiting, Paul assures Christians that the Spirit is present to help them. When he says that "we do not know how to pray as we ought, but the Spirit himself intercedes for us with sighs too deep for words," he is probably alluding to the gift of tongues rather than to any lack of knowledge about how to pray (v 26). The Old Testament was full of examples of how to pray, and Paul himself expresses himself regularly in prayers. Those who spoke in tongues — and Paul includes himself among them (cf. 1 Cor 14:18) — expressed their prayer in inarticulate sounds (cf. 1 Cor 15:6-11). Since tongues is a gift of the Spirit, the prayers of those with this gift could be one way he "helps us in our weakness." And God, "who searches the hearts of men" and "knows what is the mind of the Spirit," would therefore readily understand the otherwise inarticulate prayers of those with the gift of tongues (v 27).

8:28-30 We know that in everything God works for good with those who love him. Since God, according to the Jewish way of thinking, is behind everything that happens, it is certainly true that he is behind everything that happens to those who love him (v 28). This line sets the tone for what Paul says in vv 29-30 and especially for what he says about predestination (vv 29a and 30a). Understood as God's arbitrary decision to save some and damn others, independently of how they respond in faith to him, predestination is unworthy of God and categorizes him as a capricious monster. Understood in the sense that God is behind all that happens in the world, but not without taking into account the freedom of human beings, it can be said that God predestined those who he knew would respond to him in faith and love because he was behind everything they did, just as he was behind everything anybody did (v 29). It would be true, then, to attribute to God the call of those predestined, their justification and their glorification (v 30). Their "conformity to the image of his Son" (v 29b) is part of all that God does for those who love him, since it is by such conformity that they become not only children of God (cf. 8:14-17) but brothers of Christ.

(a') Triumph through the love of God (8:31-39)

Text

(a')   8:31 What then shall we say to this? If God is for us, who is against us? [32]He who **did not spare his own Son** but gave him up for us all, will he not also give us all things with him? [33]Who shall bring any charge against God's elect? It is God who justifies; [34]**who is to condemn?** Is it Christ Jesus, who died, yes, **who was raised from the dead,** who is at the right hand of God, who indeed intercedes for us?

[35]Who shall separate us from the love of Christ? Shall tribulation, or distress, or persecution, or famine, or nakedness, or peril, or sword? [36]As it is written, "For thy sake we are being killed all the day long; we are regarded as sheep to be slaughtered." [37]No, in all these things we are more than conquerors through him who loved us. [38]For I am sure that neither death, nor life, nor angels, nor principalities, nor things present, nor things to come, nor powers, [39]nor height, nor depth, nor anything else in all creation, will be able to separate us from the **love of God** in Christ Jesus our Lord.

Commentary

8:31-34   What then shall we say to this? If God is for us, who is against us? The theme of triumph, first sounded in 5:1-11 and resumed in 8:1-13, is concluded in 8:31-39 with a magnificent peroration, still in diatribe style, extolling God's and Christ's love for humanity. The key to the section is contained in the two questions "If God is for us, who is against us?" and "He who did not spare his own Son . . . will he not also give us all things with him?" (8:31-32). With this last question, Paul returns to the central theme of 5:1-11, triumph through God's love, expressed thematically in the words "But God shows his love for us in that while we were yet sinners Christ died for us" (5:8). Under such circumstances, Paul asks two series of questions, the first dealing with the Father's love for humanity (vv 31-34), the second dealing with Christ's love for humanity (vv 35-39).

8:35-39   Who shall separate us from the love of Christ? The second series of questions deals with Christ's love for humanity (v 35). The resounding answer, "Nothing can separate us from the love of Christ," is given in vv 37-39, with the verb "separate" in v 39 forming a subtle inclusion-conclusion with the question in v 35: "Who shall *separate* us from the love of Christ?" The quotation from Ps 44:22 in v 36, which originally spoke of the sufferings of Jews in a time of persecution, follows up the references to persecution, peril, and the sword in v 35b, and applies the words of the psalm to Christians ("For thy [Christ's] sake"), who, as Paul well knew, frequently suffered persecution because of their faith in Christ.

It is interesting, in relation to the whole of 8:31-39, to note that Paul attributes the salvation of humanity not only to God's love for us but also to Christ's love for us. When one notes that 8:31-39 is the (a') section of an a-b-a' format and is balanced by 8:1-13, the (a) section, it becomes readily noticeable that the two sections not only complement each other but, when taken together, constitute a little trinitarian treatise on the work of the Spirit (8:1-13), the work of the Father (8:31-34), and the work of the Son (8:35-39) in effecting the redemption of humanity.

Objection to God's and Christ's love—apparently it does not extend to the Jews—answered from Scripture (9:1-11:36)

In Part I (1:1-4:25), Paul concluded with an argument from Scripture (4:1-25) that proved, against the objection made in 3:31 ("Do we then overthrow the law by this faith?"), that far from the law being overthrown by faith, the law itself testified to the necessity of faith for justification.

The relationship of 9:1-11:36 to what precedes (5:1-8:39 as a whole, but especially 8:1-39, the immediate context for what follows in chs 9-11) has caused a problem for interpreters. We believe that the problem can be resolved by noting that just as Paul concluded Part I (1:1-4:25) with a long argument from Scripture (4:1-25), so in Part II (5:1-11:36) he concludes with a long argument from Scripture (9:1-11:36). In each part, the reason for the argument from Scripture is posed by an obvious objection that would be put to Paul by his opponents.

In Part I, the objection is explicit. After Paul concludes his argumentation for justification through faith in Christ and not through the works of the law (1:1-3:26), he poses the question: "Do we then overthrow the law by faith?" (3:31). His argument from Scripture follows (4:1-25) and proves that far from the law being overthrown by faith, it is rather confirmed, since the law itself testifies from the example of Abraham that it is through faith and not through circumcision or the observance of the Mosaic law that Abraham, the father of the faith, was justified.

In Part II, the objection is implicit. Paul concluded his argumentation for justification based on God's and Christ's love by asking: "If God is for us, who is against us?" (8:31) and "Who shall separate us from the love of Christ?" (8:35). To these triumphant questions any Jew or Judaizer Christian might have responded: "All very well. But if what you say is true, what about the Jews? They have rejected Jesus. Apparently God's and Christ's love does not extend to them. What's more, if what you say is true, then God has not been faithful to the promises he made to his chosen people.

And if that is so, then all that you say about salvation history in the Scriptures is a joke, and what's worse, God is a liar!"

The objection is weighty, and Paul did not need an opponent to verbalize it. His first words in 9:1-5 go from the rhapsodical "Who shall separate us from the love of Christ?" (8:35-39) to the heartrending lament "I have great sorrow and unceasing anguish in my heart" (9:2ff). What follows 8:1-39, therefore, and the implicit objection, is Paul's argumentation from Scripture that God has not been unfaithful to the Jews, that their rejection of Christ has been part of his salvific plan, that this rejection has been only temporary, and that in the end the Jews too will accept Christ and be saved. The format of 9:1-11:36 testifies to the fact that this was indeed Paul's contention and that he had not only theologized in depth to reach these conclusions but had taken care to present his argumentation artistically by arranging it in a well-balanced a-b-c-b'-a' format.

Parallel structure of 9:1-11:36

(a) The Jews' **rejection of the gospel** appears to contradict God's promises to Israel (9:1-5).
  (b) But **God's promises** have been fulfilled through **the remnant** of the Jews who believe (9:6-29).
    (c) The Jews' misguided zeal to achieve justification through the law has led them to reject the gospel (9:30–10:21).
  (b') But **God's promises** have been fulfilled through **the remnant** of the Jews who believe (11:1-10).
(a') The Jews' **rejection of the gospel** is only temporary (11:11-36).

Käsemann recognizes the fivefold division of chs 9-11 but does not advert to the chiastic format. Speaking about 9:1-5, he says: "Already on account of its rhetorical style (Michel) one should recognize in it the introductory counterpart to the conclusion in 11:33-36. If this is so, one can hardly claim that Paul did not know at the outset how his discussion would end. . . . Rather the three chapters are plainly divided into the sections 9:6-29; 9:30-10:21; and 11:1-36, and a thoroughly logical, systematic course of thought corresponds to this."[17]

Here, therefore, more than any other place in the Pauline letters, the chiastic format is critical for a proper understanding of Paul's argumentation. We would even suggest that the reader make a first reading of the text by reading together (a) and (a'), then (b) and (b'), and finally (c).

(a) The Jews' rejection of the gospel appears to contradict God's promises to Israel (9:1-5).

Text

(a)   9:1 I am speaking the truth in Christ, I am not lying; my conscience bears me witness in the Holy Spirit, ²that I have great sorrow and unceasing anguish in my heart. ³For I could wish that I myself were accursed and cut off from Christ for the sake of my brethren, my **kinsmen by race**. ⁴They are **Israelites**, and to them belong the sonship, the glory, **the covenants**, the giving of the law, the worship, and the promises; ⁵to them belong the **patriarchs**, and of their race, according to the flesh, is the Christ. God who is over all be blessed **for ever. Amen**.

Commentary

9:1-3 I am speaking the truth in Christ. In chs 1-8, Paul had been concerned primarily with God and God's system of salvation through faith in Christ. In chs 9-11, his concerns are the same. He has to explain God's apparently unjust way of dealing with Israel. The Gentiles have accepted the gospel, and the Jews have rejected it. "The last have become first, and the first last." How explain this reversal?

Paul begins, for those who might have accused him of indifference, by swearing in the presence of Christ and with the witness of his conscience and the Holy Spirit that this mysterious reversal of expectations (v 1) is a matter of "great sorrow and unceasing anguish" (v 2). So great is his anguish that he would wish, if it were possible, to be cut off from Christ "for the sake of my brethren." This is not possible, of course, but since this is the worst fate Paul could imagine, his willingness to accept it proves indisputably his love for his fellow Jews (v 3). It is possible that Paul is making a reference to Ex 32:31f, where Moses makes a similar offer to sacrifice himself for his Israelite brethren.

9:4-5 They are Israelites, and to them belong the sonship. By citing the great privileges accorded Israel in the course of salvation history, Paul sharpens the apparent paradox of their having rejected the gospel and having ended up last instead of first. In passing, it should be remembered that Israel's rejection of the gospel was a mystery not only for Paul but also for John (12:37ff), Mark (4:1ff), Matthew (13:1ff), and Luke (Acts 28:23ff)—all of whom, like Paul, situated the mystery against the background of salvation history. This latter point is important, because in Paul's solution to the mystery in 9:6-11:36, the reader needs to be aware always that Paul, in his explanation of God's way of acting throughout the course of salvation history, is dealing, not with individuals, but with collectivities. It is this that explains how he can say that Israel has for the present rejected the gospel but in the end will accept it (11:1-36). The same obviously could not be said of individuals.

(b) But God's promises have been fulfilled through the remnant of the Jews who believe (9:6-29).

Text

(b)   9:6 But it is not as though the word of God had **failed**. For not all who are descended from **Israel** belong to **Israel**, ⁷and not all are **children of**

Abraham because they are his **descendants;** but "Through Isaac shall your **descendants** be named." [8]This means that it is not the children of the flesh who are the children of God, but the children of the promise are reckoned as **descendants.** [9]For this is what the promise said, "About this time I will return and Sarah shall have a son." [10]And not only so, but also when Rebecca had conceived children by one man, our forefather Isaac, [11]though they were not yet born and had done nothing either good or bad, in order that God's purpose of **election** might continue, **not because of works** but because of his call, [12]she was told, "The elder will serve the younger." [13]As it is written, "Jacob I loved, but Esau I hated."

[14]What shall we say then? Is there injustice on God's part? By no means! [15]For he says to Moses, "I will have mercy on whom I have mercy, and I will have compassion on whom I have compassion." [16]So it depends not upon man's will or exertion, but upon God's mercy. [17]For the scripture says to Pharaoh, "I have raised you up for the very purpose of showing my power in you, so that my name may be proclaimed in all the earth." [18]So then he has mercy upon whomever he wills, and he **hardens** the heart of whomever he wills.

[19]You will say to me then, "Why does he still find fault? For who can resist his will?" [20]But who are you, a man, to answer back to God? Will what is molded say to its molder, "Why have you made me thus?" [21]Has the potter no right over the clay, to make out of the same lump one vessel for beauty and another for menial use?

[22]What if God, desiring to show his wrath and to make known his power, has endured with much patience the vessels of wrath made for destruction, [23]in order to make known the riches of his glory for the vessels of mercy, which he has prepared beforehand for glory, [24]even us whom he has called, not from the Jews only but also from the Gentiles?

[25]As indeed he says in Hosea, "Those who were not my people I will call 'my people,' and her who was not beloved I will call 'my beloved.'" [26]"And in the very place where it was said to them, 'You are not my people,' they will be called 'sons of the living God.'" [27]And Isaiah cries out concerning **Israel:** "Though the number of the sons of Israel be as the sand of the sea, only a **remnant** of them will be saved; [28]for the Lord will execute his sentence upon the earth with rigor and dispatch." [29]And as Isaiah predicted, "If the Lord of hosts had not left us children, we would have fared like Sodom and been made like Gomorrah."

Commentary

9:6a   But it is not as though the word of God had failed. Here Paul formulates the problem and prepares to give a provisional solution. Appearances are deceiving. Actually, God has not failed, because "a remnant" of Israel, as the Scriptures foretold (9:25-29) and as Paul will argue, has accepted the gospel.

9:6b-7   For not all who are descended from Israel belong to Israel. In preparation for his provisional solution in 9:25-29, Paul begins with a series of arguments from Scripture that deal with two basic points: first, the nature of the true Israel (vv 7-13); and second, the transcendent freedom of God to use Israel for his own purposes in the working out of his plan for the salvation of the world (vv 14-23). He begins with a distinction concerning the promise. The promise was not made to all the children of Abraham (v 7a) but only to those descended through Isaac (v 7b-9) and Jacob (v 10-13).

9:8-10 This means that it is not the children of the flesh who are the children of God, but the children of the promise are reckoned as descendants. By "children of the flesh," Paul means descendants chosen by man as opposed to descendants chosen by God. His point is that God was perfectly free to choose whomever he wanted. Actually he chose Isaac (vv 7b and 9) rather than Ishmael, and Jacob rather than Esau (vv 10-13).

9:11-13 though they were not yet born. The fact that God chose Jacob even before he and Esau were born, and therefore before either one could have done anything to merit election (v 11ab), proves incontrovertibly that God is perfectly free in working out his plan of salvation to choose whomever he pleases. Election clearly is "not because of works but because of his call" (v 11c).

It is of critical importance to recognize that in these verses Paul is not talking about predestination; he is talking only about the election of some rather than others to fulfill functions in the working out of God's plan of salvation history. Those not elected are not rejected. They are quite simply not elected. Nothing more is intended concerning their eventual fate. Actually, those elected are chosen for the sake of the others, since they are chosen in order to bring about the fulfillment of God's promises to Abraham — promises that deal with the fate of all the nations to be "blessed in Abraham" (Gn 12:3). Even the strong statement in v 13, "As it is written, 'Jacob I loved, but Esau I hated,'" taken from Mal 1:2-3, is not to be pressed — first, because the statement deals with two nations, Israel and Edom; second, because the love-hate contrast is simply the Semitic way of opposing opposites to emphasize the positive term, which in this case is the word "love."

9:14-17 What shall we say then? Is there injustice on God's part? In diatribe style, Paul brings up the obvious objection to what he said in vv 7-13 and continues to defend God against the charge of injustice. He begins (v 15) by citing God's description of himself to Moses as a God who is free to have mercy on whomever he wishes (cf. Ex 33:19). From this it follows that it is divine initiative, not human initiative, that is decisive (v 16). A further example follows from Ex 9:16: the way in which God used Pharaoh at the time of the Exodus. Pharaoh considered himself the prime mover of the events surrounding Israel's Exodus. On the contrary, Paul argues. It was God who was using Pharaoh for his own twofold purpose: first, to assert his divine power despite the opposition of Pharaoh (v 17a); second, to make his name proclaimed in all the earth (v 17b). Thus God freely used Pharaoh for his salvation-history purposes. The point is important, for in 11:11, 15, 19, 25, Paul will show that God is using Israel's rejection of Christ in a similar way. It was through Israel's rejection of the gospel that the gospel came to the Gentiles (cf. 11:11, 19, 25).

9:18 So then he has mercy upon whomever he wills, and he hardens the heart of whomever he wills. This apparently harsh statement has elicited swarms of conflicting interpretations. But the context of Paul's argument must be kept in view for a correct understanding of his words. He is talking about God's transcendent freedom to intervene in history to bring about the realization of his plan of salvation. Without Pharaoh's opposition, there would have been no Exodus. Thus, providentially, Pharaoh became involved in God's plan. That Pharaoh opposed God's will was Pharaoh's doing, morally speaking. That God was behind this opposition was true too, but only in the popular Semitic sense that God is behind everything that happens in the world. In that sense, and that sense only, could God be said to have hardened Pharaoh's heart. To whatever degree Pharaoh's actions were morally culpable, they were proper to Pharaoh; to the degree that they contributed to the accomplishment of God's designs for Israel, they were proper to God. Paul is not speaking about either determinism or predestination of individuals. On the contrary, he is talking about God and God's determination to be merciful (vv 15, 16, 23, and cf. 11:32).

9:19-21 You will say to me then, "Why does he still find fault? For who can resist his will?" The objection turns on the presupposition that God was responsible for Pharaoh's sin and that he therefore is at fault. Paul spurns this charge (v 20a) and goes immediately to the more relevant issue of God's transcendent freedom to use for his designs individuals whom he has created. God has the freedom of the potter with his clay. He can mold the clay any way he pleases (v 20b). In the case of Israel and Pharaoh, God has made the one (Israel) "for beauty" and the other (Pharaoh) "for menial use," but that is his inalienable right as divine potter, and no injustice is done.

9:22-24 What if God, desiring to show his wrath and to make known his power. This long, involved question can be understood rightly only if the reader realizes that what Paul has in mind is precisely the central issue under discussion in all of chs 9–11, namely, Israel's rejection of the gospel and the Gentiles' acceptance of it. It is now the Jews rather than Pharaoh who, as vessels of wrath, are being used by the divine potter (v 22) for his own divine purpose (v 23). God's purpose is explained in v 24: to use the Jewish "vessels of wrath" (because they rejected the gospel) "in order to make known the riches of his glory for the vessels of mercy," i.e., those who have accepted the gospel. Who these vessels of mercy are is revealed in v 24: those Jews and Gentiles who have believed in Jesus and now constitute the true Israel.

9:25-29 As indeed he says in Hosea. Paul concludes this section of his argument with a series of quotations from Scripture that support what he had said about Jews and Gentiles in v 24. The words of Hosea (1:10; 2:23) are used to prove that God always intended to call the Gentiles (vv 25-26). The words of Isaiah (10:22f; 1:9) prove that God always intended a "remnant" of the Jews to believe and accept the gospel.

The reference to the "remnant" is important for two reasons. First, it constitutes a refutation of the initial charge that "the word of God has failed" (9:6). God had foretold that a "remnant" would believe, and that remnant was made up precisely of Paul and the many other Jews who had accepted the gospel and now, along with the Gentiles, constituted the true Israel. Second, the theme of the "remnant," explicit in v 27 and implicit in the whole of 9:6-29, will be taken up again in 11:1-10 and treated at more length, thus forming a clear parallel bonding 9:6-29, section (b), and 11:1-10, section (b'). The remnant constitutes the true seed of Abraham (9:6b), and Jewish Christians along with gentile Christians constitute the true children of Abraham (9:7).

(c) The Jews' misguided zeal to achieve justification through the law has led them to reject the gospel (9:30–10:21).

Text

(c)   9:30 What shall we say, then? That Gentiles who did not pursue righteousness have attained it, that is, righteousness through faith; ³¹but that Israel who pursued the righteousness which is based on law did not succeed in fulfilling that law. ³²Why? Because they did not pursue it through faith, but as if it were based on works. They have stumbled over the stumbling stone, ³³as it is written, "Behold, I am laying in Zion a stone that will make men stumble, a rock that will make them fall; and he who believes in him will not be put to shame."

10:1 Brethren, my heart's desire and prayer to God for them is that they may be saved. ²I bear them witness that they have a zeal for God, but it is not enlightened. ³For, being ignorant of the righteousness that comes from God, and seeking to establish their own, they did not submit to God's righteousness. ⁴For Christ is the end of the law, that every one who has faith may be justified.

⁵Moses writes that the man who practices the righteousness which is based on the law shall live by it. ⁶But the righteousness based on faith says, Do not say in your heart, "Who will ascend into heaven?" (that is, to bring Christ down) ⁷or "Who will descend into the abyss?" (that is, to bring Christ up from the dead). ⁸But what does it say? The word is near you, on your lips and in your heart (that is, the word of faith which we preach); ⁹because, if you confess with your lips that Jesus is Lord and believe in your heart that God raised him from the dead, you will be saved. ¹⁰For man believes with his heart and so is justified, and he confesses with his lips and so is saved."

¹¹The scripture says, "No one who believes in him will be put to shame." ¹²For there is no distinction between Jew and Greek; the same Lord is Lord of all and bestows his riches upon all who call upon him. ¹³For, "every one who calls upon the name of the Lord will be saved."

¹⁴But how are men to call upon him in whom they have not believed? And how are they to believe in him of whom they have never heard? And how are they to hear without a preacher? ¹⁵And how can men preach unless they are sent? As it is written, "How beautiful are the feet of those who preach good news!" ¹⁶But they have not all heeded the gospel; for Isaiah says, "Lord, who has believed what he has heard from us?" ¹⁷So faith comes from what is heard, and what is heard comes by the preaching of Christ.

¹⁸But I ask, have they not heard? Indeed they have; for "Their voice has gone out to all the earth, and their words to the ends of the world." ¹⁹Again I ask, did Israel not understand? First Moses says, "I will make you jealous of those who are not a nation; with a foolish nation I will make you angry." ²⁰Then Isaiah is so bold as to say, "I have been found by those who did not seek me; I have shown myself to those who did not ask for me." ²¹But of Israel he says, "All day long I have held out my hands to a disobedient and contrary people."

Commentary

9:30-32a What shall we say, then? Paul turns now to the problem of explaining how Israel came to reject the gospel. In his long answer (all of 9:30-10:21), he begins by underlining Israel's elementary mistake: Israel "pursued the righteousness which is based on law," while the Gentiles, who were not even looking for righteousness, attained it through faith (vv 30-31). The Jews, in short, strove to earn their own righteousness by doing works of the law (v 32). Paul had already explained (3:21-4:25) how righteousness is God's free gift, how it cannot be earned (cf. 4:4), and how it can only be received through faith in Christ. Barrett puts it briefly: ". . . Israel sought the right goal by the wrong means."¹⁸

9:32b-33 They have stumbled over the stumbling stone. Paul combines two texts from Isaiah (8:14 and 28:16) to prove that what happened to Israel was already foretold in the Scriptures. The points he makes from the quoted texts are: first, the stone is Christ; second, those who do not accept him stumble, while those who believe in him are not put to shame. The Jews have not believed; therefore, they have stumbled and have been put to shame.

10:1-4 Brethren, my heart's desire and prayer to God for them is that they may be saved. Despite his personal sorrow over Israel's rejection of the gospel (v 1), and despite the fact that this rejection was part of God's plan of salvation, Paul insists that the Jews were morally responsible for their own fall. They have chosen to follow their own way, the way of works, to achieve righteousness instead of God's way, the way of faith in Christ (vv 2-3), despite the fact that Christ had brought an end to the law (v 4).

It is disputed what is meant by "the end of the law." Most likely Paul means that Christ put an end to the law by accomplishing all that the law hoped to achieve but could not achieve (cf. 3:21; 5:20; 7:1-6: Gal 3:24; Phil

3:2-15) and that as a consequence the Jews from now on were obliged to seek righteousness only through faith in Christ. In 10:5-13, Paul shows that this faith is accessible to all. In 10:14-21, he argues that Israel had the opportunity to hear and accept the gospel but failed to respond. Thus, he continues to make his point that Israel is responsible before God.

10:5-7 Moses writes that the man who practices the righteousness which is based on the law shall live by it. For Paul, the righteousness that is truly based on the law has already been demonstrated to be faith-righteousness (cf. 3:31–4:25). Understood in that sense, Moses' statement (cf. Lv 18:5) supports Paul's argument. The quotations from Deuteronomy that follow are also meant to support Paul's argument. They do so in two ways. First, the author of Deuteronomy, more than most biblical authors, insisted on the gratuity of God's love for Israel and on the fact that Israel had done nothing to deserve or merit that love (cf. Dt 7:6-8; 8:17-18; 9:4-6). In that sense, at least, he was against a theology of righteousness through the works of the law. Second, when the author of Dt 30:12ff spoke of doing God's will, he insisted that it was not difficult. Paul takes these words and applies them to Christ and the gift of faith. In short, as he will insist in vv 6-13, it is not difficult to believe in Christ, and because the Jews do not, they are all the more culpable. To begin with, they do not, in the words of Deuteronomy, have to ask, "Who will ascend into heaven?" i.e., to bring Christ down. Christ has already come (v 6)! Nor do they have to ask, "Who will descend into the abyss?" i.e., to raise Christ from the dead. The resurrection has already taken place (v 7)! In short, the ultimate revelatory acts of God have taken place in Jesus' incarnation and resurrection and call for faith from those who understand the law itself to testify to faith as God's way of achieving righteousness.

10:8-9 But what does it say? The word is near you. Still quoting Deuteronomy (30:14) and referring to faith in Christ ("that is, the word of faith which we preach"), Paul comes to his conclusion: "if you confess with your lips that Jesus is Lord and believe in your heart that God raised him from the dead, you will be saved."

10:10-13 For man believes with his heart and so is justified. This verse summarizes Paul's teaching about faith, righteousness, and salvation (v 10). In support of this teaching, Is 28:16 is quoted (v 11). In 3:22, Paul declared that all, Jews and Gentiles alike, had sinned. Here he makes another universal declaration, but this time concerning salvation rather than sin (v 12). God is the Lord of all, and "every one," as Jl 2:32 had stated, Jew and Gentile alike, "who calls upon the name of the Lord will be saved" (v 13).

10:14-16 But how are men to call upon him in whom they have not believed? In 10:13, Paul quoted Jl 2:32 in the sense that everyone who calls upon the name of the Lord (Jesus) will be saved. Using this quotation as his premise, Paul asks, what steps lead to calling upon the Lord for those who up to the present have not believed in him (v 14a)? Those who have not believed in him are, of course, the Jews, and Paul, like a prosecuting attorney, is preparing an indictment against them. Using questions with self-evident answers, Paul answers his initial question. First, they have to hear (v 14b). Second, to hear, they need a preacher (v 14c). Third, to be a preacher, one must be sent (v 15a), and the necessity for preachers is fortified by a quotation from Is 52:7 (v 15b). Fourth, and most important, they have to obey (v 16a). Paul takes for granted what should logically be his last question, namely, "What must be the response of those whom the preacher calls to faith in Christ?" Instead, he jumps to his conclusion. Not all the Jews (with this qualification Paul leaves room for the "remnant," about which he will speak in 11:1-10) have obeyed (v 16a). And this too was indirectly foretold by Isaiah (v 16b and cf. Is 53:1).

10:17-18 So faith comes from what is heard, and what is heard comes by the preaching of Christ. This verse forms the transition between vv 14-18 and 18-21. If Israel has not heard the gospel, then obviously she is not blameworthy. But she has heard (v 18a). Christian preachers, like Paul and many others, have preached the gospel in the synagogues. In fact, one might say hyperbolically, as Ps 19:5 says about the witness of all created things to God, that the witness of the apostles concerning Jesus has been heard throughout the world (v 18b). Here one must remember that Paul is speaking about Israel as a collectivity. Israel as a nation had heard the gospel, but not every individual in the nation had heard it.

10:19-21 Again I ask, did Israel not understand? Paul does not bother to prove that Israel did indeed understand. He takes it for granted that if the Gentiles understood and accepted the gospel, then certainly Israel should have understood (v 19a). Instead, he goes back to the Scriptures to show that Moses (v 19b and cf. Dt 32:21) and Isaiah (vv 20-21 and cf. Is 55:1f) had already foretold that Israel would be put to shame by the unbelieving Gentiles. This is Paul's way of saying "the first will be last, and the last, first." He had prepared for this paradoxical reversal by repeating a number of times the words "Jew first, then Gentile" (cf. 1:16; 2:9-10; 3:9). In ch 11, he will resolve the paradox by asserting that the Jews remain first in God's love, even though they eventually come to believe only when they have been shamed by the Gentiles (cf. 11:30-32).

(b') But God's promises have been fulfilled through the remnant of the Jews who believe (11:1-10).

Text

(b')   11:1 I ask, then, has God rejected his people? By no means! I myself am an Israelite, **a descendant of Abraham,** a member of the tribe of Benjamin. [2]God has not rejected his people whom he foreknew. Do you not know what the scripture says of Elijah, how he pleads with God against **Israel?**

[3]"Lord, they have killed thy prophets, they have demolished thy altars, and I alone am left, and they seek my life." [4]But what is God's reply to him? "I have kept for myself seven thousand men who have not bowed the knee to Baal." [5]So too at the present time there is a **remnant,** chosen by grace. [6]But if it is by grace, it is **no longer on the basis of works;** otherwise grace would no longer be grace.

[7]What then? **Israel failed** to obtain what it sought. The **elect** obtained it, but the rest were **hardened,** [8]as it is written, "God gave them a spirit of stupor, eyes that should not see and ears that should not hear, down to this very day." [9]And David says, "Let their feast become a snare and a trap, a pitfall and a retribution for them; [10]let their eyes be darkened so that they cannot see, and bend their backs for ever."

Commentary

11:1a I ask, then, has God rejected his people? By no means! This section, (b′), like 9:6-29, section (b), deals with the "remnant." E. Maly rightly groups it with 11:11-36 and entitles the whole chapter "The Mystery Resolved."[19] The mystery has been how God could so love and favor the Jews and at the same time bring it about that at the climax of salvation history they would reject Christ. As Paul will insist in 11:11-36, the first have indeed become last according to God's salvific plan, but they have become last only chronologically. In the end they too will be saved! In the meantime, some Jews—a remnant in comparison with the nation as a whole—have believed (11:1b-10).

11:1b-4 I myself am an Israelite. Paul himself is a Christian Jew. This is proof that not all the Jews have rejected Christ (v 1b). Paul does not bother mentioning what his audience well knows, namely, that there were many other Christian Jews who like himself had accepted Christ (cf. Acts 1-8). This group of believing Jews is the remnant foretold in Scripture when God said to Elijah (1 Kgs 19:18), "I have kept for myself seven thousand men who have not bowed the knee to Baal" (vv 2-4).

11:5-6 So too at the present time there is a remnant, chosen by grace. The Jews who have accepted Christ are small in number, like the seven thousand in the time of Elijah, but they are a true remnant, and their existence proves that God has not been unfaithful to his promises (cp. 9:24, 27-29 and cf. 9:6). Paul throws in the little parenthesis "chosen by grace" (vv 5b-6) in order to emphasize once again his contention that God deals with humanity, not on the basis of works, but on the basis of grace—the gratuitous gift of faith.

11:7-10 What then? Israel failed to obtain what it sought. The remnant, a nation within a nation, obtained what it sought, but Israel as a whole did not. In fact, the nation as a whole was "hardened" (v 7). Here Paul reverts to what he had said about God hardening Pharaoh's heart in 9:18. It is the same with Israel, and the hardening has taken place for the same reason, namely, it is part of God's plan of salvation for the world.

Again, as in 9:18, it is God's freedom of action that is important for Paul and not the question of how God could use Pharaoh, and in this case Israel, without being involved in the possible immorality of what they had done. Paul supports his contention that Israel's rejection of Christ was part of God's plan by quoting from Is 29:10 and Ps 69:22-23. In short, Israel has indeed rejected the gospel, but her rejection has not been total. Moreover, as 11:11-36 will show, this rejection is only temporary. In the end, all Israel will accept the gospel.

(a') The Jews' rejection of the gospel is only temporary (11:11-36).

Text

(a')   11:11 So I ask, have they stumbled so as to fall? By no means! But through their trespass salvation has come to the Gentiles, so as to make **Israel** jealous. [12]Now if their trespass means riches for the world, and if their failure means riches for the Gentiles, how much more will their full inclusion mean!

[13]Now I am speaking to you Gentiles. Inasmuch then as I am an apostle to the Gentiles, I magnify my ministry [14]in order to make **my fellow Jews** jealous, and thus save some of them. [15]For if their rejection means the reconciliation of the world, what will their acceptance mean but life from the dead?

[16]If the dough offered as first fruits is holy, so is the whole lump; and if the root is holy, so are the branches. [17]But if some of the branches were broken off, and you, a wild olive shoot, were grafted in their place to share the richness of the olive tree, [18]do not boast over the branches. If you do boast, remember it is not you that support the root, but the root that supports you.

[19]You will say, "Branches were broken off so that I might be grafted in." [20]That is true. They were broken off because of their unbelief, but you stand fast only through faith. So do not become proud, but stand in awe. [21]For if God did not spare the natural branches, neither will he spare you. [22]Note then the kindness and the severity of God: severity toward those who have fallen, but God's kindness to you, provided you continue in his kindness; otherwise you too will be cut off. [23]And even the others, if they do not persist in their unbelief, will be grafted in, for God has the power to graft them in again. [24]For if you have been cut from what is by nature a wild olive tree, and grafted, contrary to nature, into a cultivated olive tree, how much more will these natural branches be grafted back into their own olive tree.

[25]Lest you be wise in your own conceits, I want you to understand this mystery, brethren: a hardening has come upon part of **Israel,** until the full number of the Gentiles come in, [26]and so all **Israel** will be saved; as it is written, "The Deliverer will come from Zion, he will banish ungodliness from Jacob"; [27]"and this will be my **covenant** with them when I take away their sins." [28]As regards the gospel they are enemies of God, for your sake; but as regards election they are **beloved** for the sake of their **forefathers.** [29]For the gifts and the call of God are irrevocable. [30]Just as you were once disobedient to God but now have received mercy because of their disobedience, [31]so they have now been disobedient in order that by the mercy shown

to you they also may receive mercy. [32]For God has consigned all men to disobedience, that he may have mercy upon all.

[33]O the depth of the riches and wisdom and knowledge of God! How unsearchable are his judgments and how inscrutable his ways! [34]"For who has known the mind of the Lord, or who has been his counselor?" [35]"Or who has given a gift to him that he might be repaid?" [36]For from him and through him and to him are all things. To him be glory **for ever. Amen.**

Commentary

11:11-12 So I ask, have they stumbled so as to fall? By no means! In 11:1-10, Paul spoke about the remnant of the Jews who had accepted Christ. Now he deals with the majority who did not and explains why their rejection of the gospel is only temporary. As Barrett suggests,[20] some Christians might have thought that the Jews were outside the sphere of salvation, in the sense that "they stumbled so as to fall [forever]." Paul denies this vehemently (v 11a). Actually, it was because the Jews rejected the gospel that the apostles turned to the Gentiles (v 11b). This, however, happened so that the Jews would be provoked to jealousy of the Gentiles (cf. Dt 32:21 and Rom 10:19). Implicitly, therefore, it is assumed that this jealousy will lead the Jews to eventually accept the gospel (v 11c). It follows, then, that if the Jews' rejection of the gospel meant so much for the gentile world, the Jews' acceptance will mean even more (v 12). By the Jews' "full inclusion," Paul probably means the addition of the rest of the Jews to the already believing remnant (11:1-10) to form a totality (*plērōma*).

11:13-15 Now I am speaking to you Gentiles. As the apostle commissioned to preach to the Gentiles (cf. Gal 2:7, 9), Paul tells his readers that one reason why he works so hard ("magnify my ministry") is precisely that by converting more Gentiles he may be able to make the Jews jealous and so convert ("save") some of them (cf. 1 Cor 9:22). Under such circumstances, if one compares what their rejection of the gospel had already providentially accomplished, namely, the reconciliation of the Gentiles with God (cf. vv 11-12), with what their acceptance of the gospel will accomplish, it could only be described as "life from the dead" (v 15). By "life from the dead," Paul may mean something miraculous about their conversion, but more likely he means, as Barrett puts it, "that the final return of Israel (v 26) will be the signal for the resurrection, the last stage of the eschatological process initiated by the death and resurrection of Jesus. The full conversion of Israel therefore stands on the boundary of history."[21]

11:16-24 If the dough offered as first fruits is holy, so is the whole lump. This verse signals a new argument for the salvation of the Jews. In offering to God the fruits of the field, the Israelites always gave the first fruits in sacrifice as a token for the totality (cf. Nm 15:18-21). Since Israel, through the remnant, is the first fruits, it follows that the remainder of unconverted Israel constitutes the totality, which, like the first fruits, is holy (v

16a). The same thought is then expressed by the image of the root and the branches (v 16b) and followed by the allegory of the olive tree (vv 17-24). The central point Paul wants to make in the allegory is that Israel remains the "holy root" of the olive tree, which is God's people, despite her temporary rejection of the gospel. If the Gentiles, like branches from a wild olive tree, have been grafted onto the holy root which is Israel, it follows that it will be much easier for God in his own time to graft back onto the holy root the original cut-off branches. Thus, the Gentiles should not gloat over what has happened for the present to the original branches, especially since the same thing can still happen to them (vv 17-22). It will be easy for God, when the original branches give up their unbelief, to graft them back "into their own olive tree" (vv 23-24).

11:25-26a Lest you be wise in your own conceits. Everything in chs 9-11 has been leading up to vv 25-32, and Paul is now ready to express clearly the revelation that makes sense of everything that has happened to Israel (v 25a). The apocalyptic mystery (cf. 1 Cor 15:51), which will become clear in the final judgment, is that Israel's "hardening has come upon part of Israel," i.e., all those apart from the remnant (v 25b), and is temporary. Its ending will come about when the full number of the Gentiles enter the Church (v 25c); then all Israel will be saved (v 26a). Thus, what was hinted at in the allegory of the olive tree will actually take place eventually. The question naturally arises, what does Paul mean by "all Israel"? Everything in chs 9-11 points to a meaning that is representative and not taxative. Israel as a people, but not every Israelite, will be saved. In every group or collectivity there are exceptions.

11:26b-27 as it is written, "The Deliverer will come from Zion." By means of this composite quotation (cf. Is 59:20 and 27:9), Paul makes the point that God always intended to save Israel from her sins and make a new covenant with her.

11:28-32 As regards the gospel they are enemies of God, for your sake. Paul now summarizes the substance of his argumentation in chs 9-11. The Jews are enemies of God for the sake of the Gentiles (v 28a) because, through their rejection of the gospel, the gospel came to the Gentiles (cf. 11:11-12). They are "beloved for the sake of their forefathers" (v 28b), because God can be trusted to fulfill his promises to the patriarchs (cf. 9:4) and because "the gifts and the call of God are irrevocable" (v 29). The thought of vv 28-29 is restated in vv 30-31. Just as the mercy of God brought the Gentiles from disobedience to obedience to the gospel, so the same mercy of God will bring the Jews from rejection of the gospel to ultimate obedience (cf. 9:30-33; 11:11-16). In short, Jews and Gentiles alike have been disobedient (v 32a; cf. 1:18-3:20; 5:12ff). This, however, in the providence of God, has allowed both Jew and Gentile to recognize that, despite deserving God's wrath, they have become the beneficiaries of his mercy. Thus, regardless of what has been said about sin, wrath, and judgment, God's last word is mercy. Humanity's hope is rooted in God's mercy. Ultimate triumph is assured!

11:33-36 O the depth of the riches and wisdom and knowledge of God! Paul had ended ch 8 with a triumphant paean of praise of God's and Christ's love for humanity (8:31-39). In chs 9-11, he refuted a serious objection to the universality of that love by proving that God's love enveloped even his own people who had rejected him. The objection disposed of, Paul now returns to his triumphant paean of praise, closing the circle begun with 8:31-39. Everything Paul has said in chs 9-11 shows forth "the depth of the riches [God's generosity] and wisdom [his salvific plan for Jews and Gentiles] and knowledge [understanding of the human heart] of God" (v 33a). "How unsearchable are his judgments" can be appreciated from an attempt to understand the means he used to bring all humanity under the umbrella of his mercy (v 33b and cf. 11:25-32). Two quotations from the Old Testament (Is 40:13; Jb 41:11) testify to the inscrutability of God's ways (vv 34-35). The last quotation, "who has given a gift to him that he might be repaid?" is given a negative response with the declaration that nothing can be given to God because he is the creator and giver of all to all (v 36a), and therefore deserving of all glory forever (v 36b).

Part III (chs 12–16): Exhortations, Paul's plans, conclusion

In chs 5-8, Paul described in a series of analogies the liberation of humanity through Christ from the sinful self-centeredness that went with subjection to Lord Sin. In chs 12-16, he deals with the conduct befitting those who now serve Lord Christ.

As in Part I (1:1-4:25) and Part II (5:1-11:36), Paul uses an A-B-A' format, but in this case the balance between sections A and A' is minimal. The three sections run as follows: A (12:1-13:14): exhortations; B (14:1-15:13): the strong and the weak in matters of food and feastdays; A' (15:14-16:27): Paul's plans, conclusion. The content of each section is clearly defined and requires little commentary.

A (12:1–13:14): Exhortations

Paul's long series of exhortations breaks down into a neatly balanced A-B-C-B'-A' format: (a) our bodies are for spiritual worship (12:1-2); (b) the community, charismatic gifts, and the love command (12:3-21); (c) submission to civil authority (13:1-7); (b') the love command (13:8-10); (a') our bodies are not for depravity (13:11-14).

Text

(a) 12:1 I appeal to you therefore, brethren, by the mercies of God, to present your bodies as a living sacrifice, holy and acceptable to God, which is your spiritual worship. ²Do not be conformed to this world but be transformed by the renewal of your mind, that you may prove what is the will of God, what is good and acceptable and perfect.

(b)   [3]For by the grace given to me I bid every one among you not to think of himself more highly than he ought to think, but to think with sober judgment, each according to the measure of faith which God has assigned him. [4]For as in one body we have many members, and all the members do not have the same function, [5]so we, though many, are one body in Christ, and individually members one of another. [6]Having gifts that differ according to the grace given to us, let us use them: if prophecy, in proportion to our faith; [7]if service, in our serving; he who teaches, in his teaching; [8]he who exhorts, in his exhortation; he who contributes, in liberality; he who gives aid, with zeal; he who does acts of mercy, with cheerfulness.

[9]Let **love** be genuine; hate what is evil, hold fast to what is good; [10]**love one another** with brotherly affection; outdo one another in showing honor. [11]Never flag in zeal, be aglow with the Spirit, serve the Lord. [12]Rejoice in your hope, be patient in tribulation, be constant in prayer. [13]Contribute to the needs of the saints, practice hospitality.

[14]Bless those who persecute you; bless and do not curse them. [15]Rejoice with those who rejoice, weep with those who weep. [16]Live in harmony with **one another;** do not be haughty, but associate with the lowly; never be conceited. [17]Repay no one evil for evil, but take thought for what is noble in the sight of all. [18]If possible, so far as it depends upon you, live peaceably with all. [19]Beloved, never avenge yourselves, but leave it to the wrath of God; for it is written, "Vengeance is mine, I will repay, says the Lord." [20]No, "if your enemy is hungry, feed him; if he is thirsty, give him drink; for by so doing you will heap burning coals upon his head." [21]Do not be overcome by evil, but overcome evil with good.

(c)   13:1 Let every person be subject to the governing authorities. For there is no authority except from God, and those that exist have been instituted by God. [2]Therefore he who resists the authorities resists what God has appointed, and those who resist will incur judgment. [3]For rulers are not a terror to good conduct, but to bad. Would you have no fear of him who is in authority? Then do what is good, and you will receive his approval, [4]for he is God's servant for your good. But if you do wrong, be afraid, for he does not bear the sword in vain; he is the servant of God to execute his wrath on the wrongdoer. [5]Therefore one must be subject, not only to avoid God's wrath but also for the sake of conscience. [6]For the same reason you also pay taxes, for the authorities are ministers of God, attending to this very thing. [7]Pay all of them their dues, taxes to whom taxes are due, revenue to whom revenue is due, respect to whom respect is due, honor to whom honor is due.

(b')   [8]Owe no one anything, except to **love one another;** for he who **loves** his neighbor has fulfilled the law. [9]The commandments, "You shall not commit adultery, You shall not kill, You shall not steal, You shall not covet," and any other commandment, are summed up in this sentence, "You shall **love** your neighbor as yourself." [10]**Love** does no wrong to a neighbor; therefore **love** is the fulfilling of the law.

(a')   [11]Besides this you know what hour it is, how it is full time now for you to wake from sleep. For salvation is nearer to us now than when we first believed; [12]the night is far gone, the day is at hand. Let us then cast off the works of darkness and put on the armor of light; [13]let us conduct ourselves becomingly as in the day, not in reveling and drunkenness, not in debauchery and licentiousness, not in quarreling and jealousy. [14]But put on the Lord Jesus Christ, and make no provision for the flesh, to gratify its desires.

Commentary

12:1-2 I appeal to you therefore, brethren . . . to present your bodies as a living sacrifice . . . which is your spiritual worship. Paul calls upon members of Christ's kingdom to give visible confirmation of their heavenly citizenship. This is done through our bodies in the way we conduct ourselves in the world so that our actions constitute a living sacrifice and a spiritual worship (v 1). With these words, Paul lays down a general principle for all that the Christian does in daily life. In v 2, he says the same thing negatively by warning Christians: "Do not be conformed to this world but be transformed by the renewal of your mind." In section (a'), he will parallel this exhortation with a warning against the pagan world's use of the body for depravity (cf. 13:11-14).

12:3-8 For by the grace given to me. Paul prefaces his remarks about charismatics and their place in the community, which is the body of Christ, with an exhortation to humility that reminds the reader of what he said about charismatics in 1 Cor 12-14. There the problem had been the pride that certain charismatics took in their individual gifts, particularly the gift of tongues. Here Paul sums up in a general exhortation to the Romans what he had said at much greater length to the Corinthians. First, charismatic gifts call for humility (v 3). Second, charismatic gifts are to the community what the members are to the human body (vv 4-5), and therefore the different gifts are to be used for the good of the community (vv 6-8).

12:9-13 Let love be genuine. In 1 Cor 12-14, Paul spoke first about the gifts (1 Cor 12) and then about love, without which all gifts are useless (1 Cor 13). Here the sequence is the same. Gifts without love are useless (v 9). And love, to be genuine, must be manifested outwardly in one's affection and respect for fellow Christians (v 10), in one's zeal and service (vv 11-12), in one's contributions to the needs of others, and in one's practice of hospitality (v 13). Only in this way will Christians present their "bodies as a living sacrifice" (cf. 12:1).

12:14-21 Bless those who persecute you. Going beyond what he said about love in 1 Cor 13, Paul here restates in his own way what Jesus had said about love of enemies in the Sermon on the Mount (cf. Mt 5:43-48). His remark in v 20b about "burning coals" has puzzled commentators for centuries. "The best that can be said about the 'burning coals,'" as E. Maly puts it, "is that they may suggest the shame experienced by those who are the object of such charitable deeds."[22] Paul's final advice, "Do not be overcome by evil, but overcome evil with good" (v 21), expresses an insight into evil that is rare in the history of human experience.

13:1-7 Let every person be subject to the governing authorities. Paul recommends subjection to civil authority (v 1a) as authority derived from God (v 1b). He does not say it, but one may legitimately infer that Christians are subject to civil authority only to the degree that civil authority actually derives from God. However difficult it is to determine what authority derives from God and what does not, it is upon this basis that Paul warns against resisting civil authorities (vv 2-4), makes it a matter of conscience (v 5), and urges the payment of taxes (vv 6-7). It should seem obvious, as E. Maly remarks, that "what Paul has to say here . . . should not be seen as an absolute statement binding in all details for all times without exception."[23]

13:8-10 Owe no one anything, except to love one another. Paul now returns to the love commandment that underlay all he said in section (b), 12:3-21, about humility, charismatics in relation to the body of Christ, and love of enemies. Here he sees it as the fulfillment of the law (v 8), precisely because the commandments of the law, which are expressed negatively as "You shall not . . ." in order to prevent harm to one's neighbor, are summed up positively in the command "You shall love your neighbor as yourself" (vv 9-10). Paul here elevates love to the supreme position in the daily life of Christians, just as he had in 1 Cor 13. Thus, sections (b), 12:3-21, and (b'), 13:8-10, constitute a summary of what Paul had said in 1 Cor 12-14.

13:11-14 Besides this you know what hour it is. In subsection (a'), vv 11-14, Paul repeats negatively what he had said positively in subsection (a), 12:1-2. In 12:2, he had said, "Do not be conformed to this world but be transformed by the renewal of your mind." Here, in language filled with his feeling that the second coming of Christ is near (v 11), Paul urges the Romans to "cast off the works of darkness" (v 12) and avoid depravity (v 13). They are to "put on the Lord Jesus Christ, and make no provision for the flesh, to gratify its desires" (v 14). Here, as in 12:1-2, Paul contrasts the conduct of Christians who live "in the age to come," i.e., those who live in the messianic end-time age, with the conduct of those who live "in the present age," i.e., the age or time of this world, already described in 1:18-3:20; 5:12ff as the time or age of sin. Those who "make no provision for the flesh" are those who present their "bodies as a living sacrifice" and "spiritual worship" (cf. 12:1). By referring to the body with the negative term *sarx* in 13:14, Paul creates a subtle inclusion-conclusion with his more positive term, *sōma,* for the body in 12:1.

B (14:1-15:13): The strong and the weak in matters of food and feastdays

Paul changes the subject in section B from general exhortations to the consideration of a particular problem—the problem of respect for the consciences of others. This had been a real problem in Corinth (cf. 1 Cor 8-10), the city in which Paul was living when he wrote Romans. Whether it was a real problem in Rome is debated by scholars.[24] However one decides the question, there is no doubt that pagans in general observed "holy" days and practiced fasting from certain foods. Under such circumstances, converts, even at Rome, might have had the same problems with idol food and pagan religious feasts that Paul's converts encountered at Corinth. Paul considers it worth his time, therefore, to deal with the problem of conscience in the context of a situation familiar to any Christian in the pagan world of his time. His A-B-A' format runs as follows: (a) the strong and the weak (14:1-12); (b) conscience and the sacrificing of the use of one's rights for others (14:13-23); (a') the strong and the weak and the example of Christ (15:1-13).

(a) The strong and the weak (14:1-12)

Text

(a) 14:1 As for the man who is **weak** in faith, **welcome** him, but not for disputes over opinions. [2]One believes he may eat anything, while the **weak** man eats only vegetables. [3]Let not him who eats despise him who abstains, and let not him who abstains pass judgment on him who eats; for God has welcomed him. [4]Who are you to pass judgment on the servant of another? It is before his own master that he stands or falls. And he will be upheld, for the Master is able to make him stand.

[5]One man esteems one day as better than another, while another man esteems all days alike. Let every one be fully convinced in his own mind. [6]He who observes the day, observes it in honor of the Lord. He also who eats, eats in honor of the Lord, since he gives thanks to God; while he who abstains, abstains in honor of the Lord and gives thanks to God. [7]None of us lives to himself, and none of us dies to himself. [8]If we live, we live to the Lord, and if we die, we die to the Lord; so then, whether we live or whether we die, we are the Lord's. [9]For to this end Christ died and lived again, that he might be Lord both of the dead and of the living.

[10]Why do you pass judgment on your brother? Or you, why do you despise your brother? For we shall all stand before the judgment seat of God; [11]for it is written, "As I live, says the Lord, every knee shall bow to me, and every tongue shall give praise to God." [12]So each of us shall give account of himself to God.

Commentary

14:1-4 As for the man who is weak in faith, welcome him, but not for disputes over opinions. Paul never identifies the "weak," and it remains debatable whether they are Christian Jews and Gentiles in general or just convert Jews. The parallel "welcome" in 14:1 and 15:7, however, suggests that Paul is thinking of Christian Jews, especially since his "welcome" in 15:8 is followed by the argument that "Christ became a servant to the circumcised." This suggestion is fortified by the appeal from Scripture in 15:9-12 for unity between Jews and Gentiles (v 1a). Welcoming the weak, "but not for disputes over opinions" (v 1b), implies a lack of harmony in the community (cf. 15:5, 13) caused by factions that welcomed only those who agreed with their opinions (strong or weak) concerning food and feastdays. In matters of eating or abstaining, they are to respect each other's opinions (vv 2-3), leaving to God the judgment one way or another (v 4).

14:5-12 One man esteems one day as better than another. In substance, Paul says the same about observance or non-observance of special days (v 5) as he did about eating and abstaining (v 6). He adds, however, as he had in 1 Cor 10:31, that whatever a Christian does should be done "in honor of the Lord" (v 6a) and in praise of the Lord (vv 7-12).

(b) Conscience and sacrificing the use of one's rights for others (14:13-23)

Text

(b)   14:13 Then let us no more pass judgment on one another, but rather decide never to put a stumbling block or hindrance in the way of a brother. [14]I know and am persuaded in the Lord Jesus that nothing is unclean in itself; but it is unclean for any one who thinks it unclean. [15]If your brother is being injured by what you eat, you are no longer walking in love. Do not let what you eat cause the ruin of one for whom Christ died. [16]So do not let what is good to you be spoken of as evil. [17]For the kingdom of God does not mean food and drink but righteousness and peace and joy in the Holy Spirit; [18]he who thus serves Christ is acceptable to God and approved by men.
[19]Let us then pursue what makes for peace and for mutual upbuilding. [20]Do not, for the sake of food, destroy the work of God. Everything is indeed clean, but it is wrong for any one to make others fall by what he eats; [21]it is right not to eat meat or drink wine or do anything that makes your brother stumble. [22]The faith that you have, keep between yourself and God; happy is he who has no reason to judge himself for what he approves. [23]But he who has doubts is condemned, if he eats, because he does not act from faith; for whatever does not proceed from faith is sin.

Commentary

14:13-14 Then let us no more pass judgment on one another. In this section, Paul sums up the advice he had given the Corinthians in 1 Cor 8:1-13 (cf. pp. 78f). His concern is obviously for the "weak," i.e., those whose theological knowledge and conscience formation were so poor that they could not readily perceive that food in itself is neither clean nor unclean but neutral (vv 13-14a). In his reference to Jesus (v 14a), Paul may very well be paraphrasing what Jesus said about food in Mk 7:18-19. His addition of the words "but it is unclean for any one who thinks it unclean" (v 14b) sums up the problem of the "weak." Even though no food is unclean of itself, they mistakenly think it is unclean (probably because of its association with idol worship) and so are bound to follow their erroneous consciences.

14:15-16 If your brother is being injured by what you eat. Paul now turns to the "strong," who with perfectly good consciences eat the food the weak are scrupulous about and thereby, by example, lead some of the weak to go against their consciences and do the same (v 15a). Such conduct Paul labels not "walking in love" (v 15b), causing "the ruin of one for whom Christ died" (v 15c), letting their good (i.e., following their right consciences) "be spoken of as evil" because it has led fellow Christians with weak consciences to follow their example and thus sin (v 16).

14:17-21 For the kingdom of God does not mean food and drink. The drift of vv 17-19 is that food and drink are insignificant when compared with "righteousness and peace and joy in the Holy Spirit" (vv 17-18). Christians should not, therefore, "for the sake of food, destroy the work of God" (v 20a). Although "everything is indeed clean" (v 20b), it is wrong to eat if it makes one's brother stumble (v 21). Paul, in short, is urging the strong to give up, not their right to eat meat, but the use of their right when that use might lead the weak to sin.

14:22-23 The faith that you have, keep between yourself and God. In v 22, Paul addresses the strong and encourages them. In v 23, he addresses the weak and emphasizes the necessity of following their consciences rather than the example of others (cf. 1 Cor 8:7-11; 10:28-29).

(a') The strong and the weak and the example of Christ (15:1-13)

Text

(a')   15:1 We who are strong ought to bear with the failings of the **weak,** and not to please ourselves; [2]let each of us please his neighbor for his good, to edify him. [3]For Christ did not please himself; but, as it is written, "The reproaches of those who reproached thee fell on me." [4]For whatever was written in former days was written for our instruction, that by steadfastness and by the encouragement of the scriptures we might have hope. [5]May the God of steadfastness and encouragement grant you to live in such harmony with one another, in accord with Christ Jesus, [6]that together you may with one voice glorify the God and Father of our Lord Jesus Christ.

[7]**Welcome** one another, therefore, as Christ has **welcomed** you, for the glory of God. [8]For I tell you that Christ became a servant to the circumcised to show God's truthfulness, in order to confirm the promises given to the patriarchs, [9]and in order that the Gentiles might glorify God for his mercy. As it is written, "Therefore I will praise thee among the Gentiles, and sing to thy name"; [10]and again it is said, "Rejoice, O Gentiles, with his people"; [11]and again, "Praise the Lord, all Gentiles, and let all the peoples praise him"; [12]and further Isaiah says, "The root of Jesse shall come, he who rises to rule the Gentiles; in him shall the Gentiles hope."

[13]May the God of hope fill you with all joy and peace in believing, so that by the power of the Holy Spirit you may abound in hope.

Commentary

15:1-6 We who are strong ought to bear with the failings of the weak.
Paul concludes with an exhortation to the strong "to bear with the failings
[already implicitly described in ch 14] of the weak" (v 1) in order to please
and edify them, i.e., build them up. In 1 Cor 8:1, he had laid down the principle: "Knowledge puffs up, love builds up." His thought here is the same (v
2). The thought of pleasing others rather than themselves is so important
for Paul that he reminds them of the way Christ acted and presents him as
their model, just as he did in Phil 2:5ff (v 3a). Using a quotation from Ps
69:10, he speaks of the "reproaches" that Christ bore in his life and passion
for the sake of the weak and the poor. Just so, the strong must be ready to
accept the reproaches that fall upon them because of their association with
the weak (vv 3a-4). This will enable them to "live in harmony with one
another" and thus glorify God (vv 5-6). The call for harmony and unity
reflects the opening of this section, where Paul had urged the Romans to
"welcome" the weak in faith, "but not for disputes over opinions" (cf. 14:1).

15:7-13 Welcome one another, therefore, as Christ has welcomed you.
Again, Christ should be their model (v 7). As he "became a servant to the
circumcised," i.e., the Jews, so the Roman Christians should welcome the
weak (v 8). Christ became a servant to the Jews for two reasons: first, to
fulfill the promises made to the patriarchs (v 8); second, that through them
the promises might be brought to the Gentiles (v 9a) so that, as the Scriptures foretold, Jews and Gentiles might together praise God with united
voice (vv 9b-12). Thus, Paul closes with an appeal for unity, just as he had
begun with an appeal for unity (cf. 14:1). The quotations from the Scriptures (Ps 18:49; Dt 32:43; Ps 117:1; Is 11:10) all deal with the inclusion of
the Gentiles with the chosen people, and this inclusion of the Gentiles, as
Barrett observes, "is not to be regarded as a happy afterthought; it was
foretold in Scripture."[25] Paul concludes with a prayer for his readers (v 13).

A' (15:14-16:27): Paul's plans, greetings, conclusion

The final section of Romans (15:14-16:27) forms more of a parallel with
section A (1:1-17) of Part I than with section A (12:1-13:14) of Part III and
may be intended as an overall inclusion-conclusion. It has the usual three
divisions: (a) 15:14-21; (b) 15:22-33; (a') 16:1-27.

(a) Paul explains his apostolate (15:14-21).

Text

(a)   15:14 I myself am satisfied about you, my brethren, that you yourselves
are full of goodness, filled with all knowledge, and able to instruct one
another. [15]But on some points I have written to you very boldly by way of
reminder, because of the grace given me by God [16]to be a minister of Christ

Jesus to the Gentiles in the priestly service of the gospel of God, so that the offering of the Gentiles may be acceptable, sanctified by the Holy Spirit. [17]In Christ Jesus, then, I have reason to be proud of my work for God. [18]For I will not venture to speak of anything except what Christ has wrought through me to win obedience from the Gentiles, by word and deed, [19]by the power of signs and wonders, by the power of the Holy Spirit, so that from Jerusalem and as far round as Illyricum I have fully preached the gospel of Christ, [20]thus making it my ambition to preach the gospel, not where Christ has already been named, lest I build on another man's foundation, [21]but as it is written, "They shall see who have never been told of him, and they shall understand who have never heard of him."

Commentary

15:14-16 I myself am satisfied about you, my brethren. Paul sounds almost apologetic (v 14), but he has spoken boldly (v 15) and wishes tactfully to lower any hackles he may have raised among intellectually sensitive members of the Roman community. He does so by reminding the Romans that he is only trying to fulfill the mission to the Gentiles for which he was commissioned by Christ (cf. 1:1, 13-14). He likens himself to a priest inasmuch as his conversion of the Gentiles is like a sacrificial offering of praise to God (v 16).

15:17-21 In Christ Jesus, then, I have reason to be proud of my work for God. The "in Christ Jesus" qualification is significant, because the paradoxical point that Paul wishes to make is not so much that he is proud of himself (v 17) as that he is proud of the work that Christ has accomplished through him in the half-circle that extends "from Jerusalem and as far round as Illyricum," i.e., the northern border of Greece (v 19). This has made him ambitious to go on and preach the gospel where it has never been preached before (vv 20-21). With these remarks, Paul is leading up to one of the secondary purposes of his letter: to get help from the Romans for his proposed missionary trip to Spain (cf. 15:28-29). The Scripture quotation in v 21 is from Is 52:15.

(b) Paul's plans (15:22-33)

Text

(b) 15:22 This is the reason why I have so often been hindered from coming to you. [23]But now, since I no longer have any room for work in these regions, and since I have longed for many years to come to you, [24]I hope to see you in passing as I go to Spain, and to be sped on my journey there by you, once I have enjoyed your company for a little. [25]At present, however, I am going to Jerusalem with aid for the saints. [26]For Macedonia and Achaia have been pleased to make some contribution for the poor among the saints at Jerusalem; [27]they were pleased to do it, and indeed they are in debt to them, for if the Gentiles have come to share in their spiritual blessings, they ought also to be of service to them in material blessings. [28]When therefore I have completed this, and have delivered to them what has been

raised, I shall go on by way of you to Spain; [29]and I know that when I come
to you I shall come in the fulness of the blessing of Christ.

[30]I appeal to you, brethren, by our Lord Jesus Christ and by the love of
the Spirit, to strive together with me in your prayers to God on my behalf,
[31]that I may be delivered from the unbelievers in Judea, and that my service
for Jerusalem may be acceptable to the saints, [32]so that by God's will I may
come to you with joy and be refreshed in your company. [33]The God of
peace be with you all. Amen.

Commentary

**15:22-24 This is the reason why I have so often been hindered from
coming to you.** At the beginning of his letter, Paul expressed his desire to
visit the Romans (1:10). What prevented him was his extensive missionary
work mentioned in v 20, which has now been completed (vv 22-23). He is
free, therefore, to move on to new conquests for Christ (cf. 2 Cor 2:14ff).
In fact, his intention is to preach the gospel in Spain, and for this he can use
the Romans' help (v 24). Nothing is known about the outcome of this venture.

**15:25-27 At present, however, I am going to Jerusalem with aid for the
saints.** The "aid for the saints" is the money collected in the Pauline
churches (cf. 2 Cor 8-9). Such a gesture, Paul is convinced, is entirely fitting, since the faith that the Gentiles received had been born in the midst of
the mother church in Jerusalem (v 27).

15:28-29 When therefore I have completed this. Paul's plans were to go
first to Jerusalem and then, via Rome, to Spain. According to Acts 21:15ff,
Paul reached Jerusalem, was arrested, and eventually arrived in Rome — but
as a prisoner on trial for his life. Nothing is known about his activities after
his imprisonment in Rome. He may have been executed, or he may have
been freed, gone on to Spain, returned to Rome, and been executed then.
Nothing can be said for certain. The record is blank.

15:30-33 I appeal to you, brethren. Paul asks for prayers (v 30) because
he knows that he has enemies in Judea, not only synagogue Jews but Christian Jews who did not approve of his teaching about the law (cf. Gal 2:4;
6:11-13) and might therefore refuse the monetary contribution he brought
from his gentile churches (v 31). If all works out well, he will be able to
come to them with joy and be refreshed in their company (v 32).

(a') Greetings and conclusion (16:1-27)

Some scholars believe that ch 16 was added to Romans when a copy of
the letter was sent to Ephesus, where Paul had lived for three years. This
would account for the large number of friends to whom Paul sends
greetings. Other scholars disagree and consider ch 16 the original conclusion
to Romans.[26] We are inclined to hold that it is original.

Text

(a')   16:1 I commend to you our sister Phoebe, a deaconess of the church at Cenchreae, [2]that you may receive her in the Lord as befits the saints, and help her in whatever she may require from you, for she has been a helper of many and of myself as well.

[3]Greet Prisca and Aquila, my fellow workers in Christ Jesus, [4]who risked their necks for my life, to whom not only I but also all the churches of the Gentiles give thanks; [5]greet also the church in their house.

Greet my beloved Epaenetus, who was the first convert in Asia for Christ. [6]Greet Mary, who has worked hard among you. [7]Greet Andronicus and Junias, my kinsmen and my fellow prisoners; they are men of note among the apostles, and they were in Christ before me.

[8]Greet Ampliatus, my beloved in the Lord. [9]Greet Urbanus, our fellow worker in Christ, and my beloved Stachys. [10]Greet Apelles, who is approved in Christ. Greet those who belong to the family of Aristobulus. [11]Greet my kinsman Herodion. Greet those in the Lord who belong to the family of Narcissus. [12]Greet those workers in the Lord, Tryphaena and Tryphosa. Greet the beloved Persis, who has worked hard in the Lord. [13]Greet Rufus, eminent in the Lord, also his mother and mine. [14]Greet Asyncritus, Phlegon, Hermes, Patrobas, Hermas, and the brethren who are with them. [15]Greet Philologus, Julia, Nereus and his sister, and Olympas, and all the saints who are with them. [16]Greet one another with a holy kiss. All the churches of Christ greet you.

[17]I appeal to you, brethren, to take note of those who create dissensions and difficulties, in opposition to the doctrine which you have been taught; avoid them. [18]For such persons do not serve our Lord Christ, but their own appetites, and by fair and flattering words they deceive the hearts of the simple-minded. [19]For while your obedience is known to all, so that I rejoice over you, I would have you wise as to what is good and guileless as to what is evil; [20]then the God of peace will soon crush Satan under your feet. The grace of our Lord Jesus Christ be with you.

[21]Timothy, my fellow worker, greets you; so do Lucius and Jason and Sosipater, my kinsmen. [22]I Tertius, the writer of this letter, greet you in the Lord. [23]Gaius, who is host to me and to the whole church, greets you. Erastus, the city treasurer, and our brother Quartus, greet you.

[25]Now to him who is able to strengthen you according to my gospel and the preaching of Jesus Christ, according to the revelation of the mystery which was kept secret for long ages [26]but is now disclosed and through the prophetic writings is made known to all nations, according to the command of the eternal God, to bring about the obedience of faith — [27]to the only wise God be glory for evermore through Jesus Christ! Amen.

Commentary

16:1-2 I commend to you our sister Phoebe, a deaconess. The Greek word *diakonos,* here rightly translated "deaconess," is used sometimes of one who serves (cf. 2 Cor 11:23) and sometimes in the more technical sense of an ecclesiastical office (cf. 1 Tim 3:8-11). While the office of deaconess is certain at a later date, it is disputed whether it had originated as early as the fifties, when Romans was written. In any case, these few verses serve as a brief letter of recommendation for Phoebe, who had been a helper to many, including Paul himself.

16:3-5a Greet Prisca and Aquila. Paul first met this couple in Corinth, where they were living after being expelled from Rome following an edict of the emperor Claudius against the Jews (cf. Acts 18:1-4). When Claudius died in 54 A.D., they probably returned to Rome and made their home available for Christian meetings (v 51).

16:5b-16 Greet my beloved Epaenetus, who was the first convert in Asia for Christ. By "Asia," Paul means the territory embraced by western Turkey. For "first convert," compare 1 Cor 16:15. The remainder of those mentioned in vv 6-16 would appear to be fellow workers and friends whom Paul met up with in his apostolic travels and who eventually gravitated to Rome and became members of the Christian community there. Paul's memory for names testifies to his gregarious and friendly personality.

16:17-19 I appeal to you, brethren, to take note of those who create dissensions and difficulties. It is possible that this is a general warning. It is equally possible that Paul is referring to the "weak" and "strong" mentioned in 14:1-15:13 (vv 17-18). In either case, he does not want them to spoil the good reputation they have for "obedience"; presumably he means obedience to the faith of the gospel (v 19 and cf. 1:5, 8).

16:20 then the God of peace will soon crush Satan under your feet. Satan is the symbolic leader of the forces of evil arrayed against the kingdom of God. The words "crush . . . under your feet" suggest that Paul is thinking of the famous promise concerning the defeat of the serpent made to the "woman" in Gn 3:15.

16:21-23 Timothy, my fellow worker, greets you. Timothy is mentioned often (cf. Acts 16:1ff and Paul's references to Timothy in many of his letters). All of those mentioned in vv 21-23 are with Paul in Corinth at the time he is writing the letter. Tertius, a professional scribe, may have written the letter from a draft given him by Paul, or he may have taken it down at Paul's dictation (cf. 1 Cor 16:21; Gal 6:11).

16:25-27 Now to him who is able to strengthen you. The style and vocabulary of this closing doxology are not Pauline and lead many scholars to believe that it is a later addition to the letter.[27] In any event, the doxology concentrates on the gospel, which has been the central subject of the letter from the beginning (cf. 1:1ff), on its relationship to the prophets (cf. 1:2), and on the goal of Paul's preaching — "the obedience of faith . . . among all the nations" (cf. 1:5-6). Thus, whether written by Paul or a later writer, the concluding doxology in vv 25-26 aptly sums up the letter. Most fittingly it concludes with a prayer for glory to be given "to the only wise God . . . for evermore through Jesus Christ" (v 27).

Select Bibliography and Notes

CHAPTER I

PAUL AND HIS LETTERS

Select Bibliography

Bornkamm, G. *Paul.* Philadelphia: Fortress Press, 1971.

Davies, W. D. *Paul and Rabbinic Judaism.* London: SPCK, 1965.

Doty, W. G. *Letters in Primitive Christianity.* Philadelphia: Fortress Press, 1973.

Fitzmyer, J. "Pauline Theology," *Jerome Biblical Commentary.* Englewood Cliffs, N.J.: Prentice-Hall, 1968.

Haenchen, E. *The Acts of the Apostles.* Philadelphia: Westminster Press, 1971.

Keck, L. E., and Martyn, J. L. *Studies in Luke-Acts.* Nashville: Abingdon Press, 1966.

Notes for Chapter I: PAUL AND HIS LETTERS

1. Cf. G. Bornkamm, *Paul;* J. Fitzmyer, "A Life of Paul," *JBC* 46:1-45; W. D. Davies, *Paul and Rabbinic Judaism;* C. Buck and G. Taylor, *Saint Paul.*
2. Cf. also Phil 3:2-9; 4:16; 1 Cor 7:7; 9:1-6; 16:5-8; 2 Cor 2:1-13; 11:32-33; 12:2-4, 14, 21; 13:1, 10; Rom 15:22-28.
3. Cf. R. H. Fuller, *The New Testament in Current Studies,* 87-100.
4. Cf. E. Haenchen, *The Acts of the Apostles;* Keck-Martyn, *Studies in Luke-Acts;* G. Bornkamm, *Paul;* C. K. Barrett, *Luke the Historian in Recent Studies.*
5. Cf. Keck-Martyn, *Studies in Luke-Acts,* 258-278.
6. Cf. R. H. Fuller, *New Testament in Current Studies,* 6.
7. For a more critical investigation of Paul's chronology, cf. R. Jewett, *A Chronology of Paul's Life;* Buck-Taylor, *Saint Paul;* P. Parker, "Once More, Acts and Galatians," *JBL* 39 (September 1970) 175-182.
8. Cf. A. Schweitzer, *Paul and His Interpreters.*
9. Cf. C. G. Montefiore, *Judaism and St. Paul.*

10. Cf. J. Bonsirven, *Exégèse rabbinique et exégèse paulinienne.*
11. Cf. W. C. van Unnik, *Tarsus or Jerusalem: The City of Paul's Birth.*
12. Cf. W. D. Davies, *Paul and Rabbinic Judaism.*
13. Cf. W. D. Davies, *op. cit.,* 16.
14. Cf. W. D. Davies, *Introduction to Pharisaeism.*
15. Cf. J. Jeremias, *New Testament Theology,* 308f.
16. Cf. J. L. Houlden, *Paul's Letters from Prison;* J. Fitzmyer, *JBC* 54:1-11; J. Knox, *Philemon Among the Letters of Paul;* M. Getty, *Philippians and Philemon.*
17. For Paul's literary format, cf. W. G. Doty, *Letters in Primitive Christianity;* J. Fitzmyer, *JBC* 47:1-22.
18. J. L. Houlden, *Paul's Letters from Prison,* 259ff, has a fine discussion on the background and development of the thanksgiving section of Paul's letters.
19. Cf. P. Schubert, *Form and Function of the Pauline Thanksgiving,* 180.
20. Cf. F. O. Francis and J. P. Sampley, *Pauline Parallels,* for a comparison of the thanksgiving sections of the Pauline letters.
21. Cf. R. Jewett, *A Chronology of Paul's Life,* and Buck-Taylor, *Saint Paul,* for more exhaustive studies of the chronology of the Pauline letters.
22. Cf. J. L. Houlden, *Paul's Letters from Prison,* 230.
23. Cf. J. Fitzmyer, *JBC* 46:35-42.
24. Cf. P. Feine, J. Behm and W. G. Kümmel, *Introduction to the New Testament,* 246ff.
25. Major commentaries on 1-2 Corinthians deal with the question of the so-called lost letters and parts of letters supposed to have been interpolated into 1-2 Corinthians by editors at the end of the first century.
26. See J. Fitzmyer, *JBC* 46:1-45, for a brief life of Paul, and G. Bornkamm, *Paul,* 3-108, for a longer and more critical biography.
27. Cf. R. Bultmann, *Theology of the New Testament,* 190.

CHAPTER II

FIRST THESSALONIANS

Select Bibliography

Best, E. *A Commentary on the First and Second Epistles to the Thessalonians.* New York: Harper and Row, 1972.

Braaten, C. E. *Christ and Counter-Christ.* New York: Harper and Row, 1972.

Forestell, J. "The Letters to the Thessalonians," *Jerome Biblical Commentary.* Englewood Cliffs, N.J.: Prentice-Hall, 1968.

Morris, L. *Apocalyptic.* Grand Rapids, Mich.: Wm. B. Eerdmans Publishing Co., 1972.

Reese, J. *1 and 2 Thessalonians.* Wilmington, Del.: Michael Glazier, 1979.

Russell, D. S. *The Method and Message of Jewish Apocalyptic.* London: SCM Press, 1964.

Notes for Chapter II: FIRST THESSALONIANS

1. Cf. P. F. Ellis, "Salvation Through the Wisdom of the Cross (1 Cor 1:10–4:21)," *Sin, Salvation, and the Spirit,* ed. D. Durken (Collegeville, Minn.: The Liturgical Press, 1979) 324–333; J. Murphy-O'Connor, *1 Corinthians.*
2. Cf. J. Murphy-O'Connor, *1 Corinthians,* 39.
3. For a description of the cult of Dionysus, see *The Interpreter's Dictionary of the Bible* under "Dionysus" and "Dionysia."
4. Some commentators question the authenticity of 2:13-16. They give two reasons for their doubts: (1) the passage disturbs the ordinary format of a Pauline letter, which begins with an address and one thanksgiving, whereas here there are two thanksgivings. (2) In 2:14-16, there is a bitter attack on the Jews, an attack that seems to reflect the tensions of the period following 80 A.D., when the Jews were excommunicating Christians from the synagogue. But neither of these arguments is persuasive. First, Paul was harsh with the Jews because they hindered others from entering the Church, and this was true long before 80 A.D. Second, the two thanksgivings can be explained as the result of Paul's A-B-A' format, which regularly repeats in the A' section ideas and even exact expressions found in the A section.
5. Paul refers to the parousia frequently in 1 Thes (cf. 1:10; 2:12; 2:19; 3:13; 4:13-17; 5:1-11; 5:23). His reference to waiting for Jesus in 1:10 is particularly significant, since it is Paul's custom to use the thanksgiving section of his letters (here 1:2-10) to anticipate his main topics and thus focus the epistolary situation.
6. *Bella Judaica,* VII, 100–103.
7. *PG* 49:450.
8. The observation of F. C. Grant (*Ancient Judaism and the New Testament,* 93) is right on the mark: "If anything in the New Testament needs to be 'demythologized,' it is surely the apocalyptic hope with its traditional imagery, its strange concepts, figures, symbols, presuppositions, its idea of history and even its conception of God."
9. For a detailed, in-depth study of the *parousia,* see A. L. Moore, *The Parousia in the New Testament.*
10. Paul's frequent exhortations to the Thessalonians to "work" and his reminder of his own efforts and toil (2:9) suggest that the Thessalonians were not only running a parousiac fever but were also indulging in parousiac lethargy, refusing to work and thus making themselves burdensome to others (cf. the references to parousiac lethargy and refusal to work in 2 Thes 3:7-12).
11. Cf. G. Bornkamm, *Paul,* 219–227.
12. See especially: C. Braaten, *Christ and Counter-Christ;* E. Käsemann, *Essays on New Testament Themes,* 169–195; J. A. T. Robinson, *In the End God;* J. Moltmann, *Theology of Hope;* G. Montague, *The Biblical Theology of the Secular;* R. Bultmann, *History and Eschatology;* W. Pannenberg, *Theology and the Kingdom of God;* J. Metz, *Theology of the World.*
13. Cf *The Jerome Biblical Commentary,* 20–24; 64:1-97; 78:62-108; 79:45-51; H. H. Rowley, *The Relevance of Apocalyptic;* D. S. Russell, *The Method and Message of Jewish Apocalyptic;* R. Bultmann, *Kerygma and Myth;* L. Morris, *Apocalyptic;* P. F. Ellis, *The Men and the Message of the Old Testament,* 3rd ed., 533–557; F. Amiot, *The Key Concepts of St. Paul,* 1–190; H. Berkhof, *Christ and the Powers;* L. Hartmann and A. DiLella, *Daniel;* N. Porteous, *Daniel;* H. M. Shires, *The Eschatology of Paul;* O. Plöger, *Theocracy and Eschatology.*

14. This brief section on the apocalyptic literature has already appeared in the author's *Matthew: His Mind and His Message,* 85–86.

15. The apocalyptic tradition and literary form are best understood from a reading of Ez 38–39; Is 24–27; Jl 3–4; Zech 9–14; Dn 7–12; Mt 24; Mk 13; Lk 21:5-36; 1–2 Thes; Rv.

16. W. Lynch, *Images of Hope,* 103, describes well what happens when the apocalyptic imagination loses touch with reality.

17. Cf. *JBC* 20:15-24, and B. Vawter, "Apocalyptic: Its Relation to Prophecy," *CBQ* 22 (1960) 33–46.

18. Cf. G. von Rad, *Wisdom in Israel,* 144–176; 97–110.

19. On the differences between the prophetic and the apocalyptic view of eschatology, cf. J. Moltmann, *The Theology of Hope,* 135ff.

20. We are inclined to believe the apocalyptists took literally their own images and metaphorical language, but the fact that they spoke differently about the same concepts and differ so markedly in their descriptions of apocalyptic scenarios should give us pause. St. Peter's (or Luke's) interpretation of Joel's apocalyptic scenario in Acts 2 indicates a complete lack of concern for the literal fulfillment of Joel's words. And in Daniel, the same concepts are expressed in very different ways in chs 2, 7, 8, 9, 10–12.

21. C. E. Braaten (*Christ and Counter-Christ,* v), expressing his personal opinion, says what many biblical theologians would say today: "The conviction is growing in me that apocalypticism holds the key to a number of problems in theology . . . we can say that the rediscovery of the relevance of apocalyptic is opening up new frontiers of biblical research."

22. C. E. Braaten, *Christ and Counter-Christ,* vi.

23. Cf. L. Gilkey, *Naming the Whirlwind,* 351, regarding the centrality of eschatology for human life.

24. "Eschatology," as H. M. Shires remarks, "deals with things that are final, not only in temporal sequence, but also in truth and value" (*The Eschatology of Paul,* 18).

25. Cf. H. Conzelmann, *An Outline of the Theology of the New Testament,* 307–317; W. Pannenberg, *Jesus: God and Man,* 53–115; H. M. Shires, *The Eschatology of Paul,* 18.

26. Cf. C. H. Dodd, *The Parables of the Kingdom,* 21–59; A. Richardson, *An Introduction to the Theology of the New Testament,* 53f.

27. The attention given to eschatology by Paul is statistically emphasized by H. M. Shires. He finds that "in the generally accepted Pauline corpus there are 1635 verses. Of these 518 or 31½% contain definitely eschatological thought and language" (*The Eschatology of Paul,* 20).

28. Cf. D. E. Nineham, *Saint Mark,* 43f, regarding the "early Christian view of theology."

29. C. H. Dodd, *The Parables of the Kingdom,* 159.

30. J. Jeremias, *The Parables of Jesus,* 230.

31. C. H. Dodd, *The Interpretation of the Fourth Gospel,* 447, n. 1.

32. In German the expression is "sich realisierende Eschatologie," an expression that may be translated as here, "an eschatology that is in process of realization" or as "self-realizing eschatology."

33. Cf. A. L. Moore, *The Parousia in the New Testament,* 175–206.

34. Cf. C. K. Barrett, *Jesus and the Gospel Tradition,* 68.

35. J. Metz (ed.), *The Evolving World and Theology,* 35.

36. Cf. R. Scroggs, *The Last Adam,* 100–111.

37. Cf. J. Moltmann, *Theology of Hope,* 75f; also *Religion, Revolution, and Hope,* 200ff.
38. See P. Teilhard de Chardin, *The Future of Man;* J. Metz, *Theology of the World.*

CHAPTER III

FIRST CORINTHIANS

Select Bibliography

Barrett, C. K. *Commentary on the First Epistle to the Corinthians.* London: Adam and Charles Black, 1971.
Conzelmann, H. *I Corinthians.* Philadelphia: Fortress Press, 1975.
Montague, G. T. *The Spirit and His Gifts.* New York: Paulist Press, 1974.
Murphy-O'Connor, J. *I Corinthians.* Wilmington, Del.: Michael Glazier, 1979.
Schweizer, E. *The Holy Spirit.* Philadelphia: Fortress Press, 1980.

Notes for Chapter III: FIRST CORINTHIANS

1. This is the minimum number agreed upon by all. Some opt for as many as seven.
2. Authors differ on the order and dating of the letters. There was an earlier letter (probably lost) that preceded our present 1 Corinthians (cf. 1 Cor 5:9). 2 Corinthians contains a reference to still another letter (cf. 2 Cor 2:3; 7:8). The following is a working hypothesis: Letter A — the letter mentioned in 1 Cor 5:9; Letter B — 1 Cor 1-16; Letter C — the (lost) painful letter mentioned in 2 Cor 2:3-4:9; 7:8, 12; Letter D — 2 Cor 1-13.
3. Cf. E. Haenchen, *The Acts of the Apostles,* 511.
4. Cf. O. Broneer, "The Apostle Paul and the Isthmian Games," *The Biblical Archaeologist Reader* 2:393-420.
5. For a history and a discussion of the question, see W. Schmithals, *Gnosticism in Corinth,* 113-116; C. K. Barrett, *The Second Letter of Paul to the Corinthians,* 28-30; *The Signs of an Apostle,* passim.
6. Cf. L. Cerfaux, *Christ in the Theology of Saint Paul,* 77f, n. 9.
7. For the history and theory of Gnosticism, see U. Bianchi (ed.), *The Origins of Gnosticism;* W. Schmithals, *Gnosticism in Corinth;* G. MacRae, "Gnosticism and New Testament Studies," *The Bible Today* (November 1968) 2623-2630; R. Mcl. Wilson, *Gnosis and the New Testament.*
8. "Gnosticism," as G. MacRae defines it, "Is a syncretistic, dualistic, anti-cosmic religion of salvation through esoteric knowledge, communicated by a heavenly redeemer, to awaken the dormant spark of divinity in man" (*loc. cit.,* 2625).
9. Cf. U. Bianchi, *The Origins of Gnosticism.*
10. Cf. W. Schmithals, *Gnosticism in Corinth,* 150.
11. But consider the intellectual and emotional bombshell that the preaching of the resurrection provided. At our safe distance of two thousand years, the problems are still great, but nothing resembling the problems of the earliest Christians.

12. Exaltation theology of this kind sounds less strange when it is put side by side with the exaltation theology of John's Gospel. Compare it, for example, with Jn 11:26: ". . . and who ever is alive and believes in me will never die."

13. Cf. H. Conzelmann, *1 Corinthians*, 88.

14. See G. von Rad, *Wisdom in Israel*, 65–70, and especially his comment on p. 67: "The thesis that all human knowledge comes back to the question about commitment to God is a statement of penetrating perspicacity. . . . It contains in a nutshell the whole Israelite theory of knowledge."

15. But see L. Gilkey, *Naming the Whirlwind*, 380ff.

16. Cf. H. Conzelmann, *1 Corinthians*, 59. Explaining the difficulties in this section requires more space than the limited scope of this book allows. The major commentaries should be consulted for a more in-depth explanation.

17. Cf. P. W. Meyer, "The Holy Spirit in the Pauline Letters," *Interpretation* 33 (January 1978) 13–14.

18. Cf. B. A. Pearson, *The Pneumatikos-Psychikos Terminology in 1 Corinthians*.

19. It should be observed that the theme of this section — the "building" of the community, which is the temple (building) of the Holy Spirit — is central to the whole letter (cf. 3:9, 16; 6:19; 8:1; 10:23; 12:12-28; 13:1-13; 14:3, 5, 12, 17, 26).

20. Cf. J. Murphy-O'Connor, "Corinthian Slogans in 1 Cor 6:12-20," *CBQ* 40 (July 1978) 391–396.

21. J. Murphy-O'Connor, *1 Corinthians*, 51–53.

22. Cf. P. W. Meyer, "The Holy Spirit in the Pauline Letters," *Interpretation* 33 (January 1978) 15.

23. See V. P. Furnish, *Theology and Ethics in Paul*, 223–235; *The Love Command in the New Testament;* G. Bornkamm, *Early Christian Experience*, 71–86; J. L. Houlden, *Ethics and the New Testament*, 25–34; R. J. Austgen, *Natural Motivation in the Pauline Epistles;* R. Bultmann, *The Old and New Man; Life and Death; This World and the Beyond.*

24. G. Bornkamm, *Early Christian Experience*, 73.

25. G. Bornkamm (*Early Christian Experience*, 84) makes the point beautifully: "All the imperatives of Paul have their basis in what has happened to us through Christ in baptism — and all imperatives, which are to be obediently laid hold on here and now, can be summarized in the words: 'Seek what is above' (Col 3:1)."

26. Cf. J. Fitzmyer, "Pauline Theology: A Brief Sketch," *JBC* 79.

27. C. K. Barrett, *First Corinthians*, 155.

28. W. Schmithals, *Gnosticism in Corinth*, 234f, takes the opposite tack and believes that it was the Corinthians who thought that Paul, because he forbade intercourse with prostitutes (6:12ff), was also suggesting that they refrain from marital intercourse and even from marriage.

29. H. Conzelmann, *1 Corinthians*, 117.

30. Some interpreters take "being aflame" more literally as the judgment of hellfire for unchaste acts. This would be consistent with Paul's severe words about fornicators in 1 Cor 6:9-10, but not at all with the tenor and tone of his argumentation in ch 7.

31. Not all agree. A number of modern interpreters understand Paul to mean that only separation, not divorce and remarriage, is allowed to the Christian partner in such a marriage.

32. See E. Schillebeeckx, *Marriage: Human Reality and Saving Mystery;* S. Kelleher, "The Problem of the Intolerable Marriage," *America* (September 14, 1968); Q. Quesnell, "Made Themselves Eunuchs for the Kingdom of God," *CBQ* 30 (1968) 335–358; R. A. McCormick, "Notes on Moral Theology," *TS* 32

(March 1971) 107–122 and *TS* 33 (March 1972) 91–100; P. Huizing, "The Indissolubility of Marriage and Church Order" in Concilium 38: *The Sacraments in Theology and Canon Law* (1968) 45–57; R. N. Soulen, "Marriage and Divorce," *Interpretation* 23 (1969) 439–450; W. Harrington, "Jesus' Attitude Towards Divorce," *ITQ* (July 1970); R. J. Taylor, "Divorce in Matthew 5:32; 19:9," *The Clergy Review* (October 1970) 792–800.

33. Cf. J. Fitzmyer, "The Matthaean Divorce Texts and Some New Palestinian Evidence," *TS* 37 (1977) 190–226, and the literature cited in the previous note, especially the reports of R. A. McCormick given in his "Notes on Moral Theology" *TS* 32 (March 1971) 107–122 and *TS* 33 (March 1972) 91–100.
34. Note that Paul terminates this section in v 24 with the words, "So, brethren, in whatever state each was called, there let him remain with God," and thus forms an inclusion-conclusion with v 17.
35. Mt 19:10–12, which is usually invoked in support of Jesus' call for celibacy, more properly deals with the enforced celibacy of those whose married partners have left them. Since they cannot marry again, they must perforce remain celibate. Cf. Q. Quesnell, "Made Themselves Eunuchs for the Kingdom of God," *CBQ* 30 (1968) 29–38.
36. Cf. R. de Vaux, *Ancient Israel,* 258–267.
37. Cf. A. Kosnick, and others, *Human Sexuality: New Directions in American Catholic Thought.*
38. Cf. J. Quinn, "Celibacy and the Ministry in Scripture," *The Bible Today* (February 1970) 3163–3175; Pope Paul VI, encyclical *Sacerdotalis coelibatus* (June 24, 1967); J. G. Gager, Jr., "Functional Diversity in Paul's Use of End-Time Language," *JBL* 89 (September 1970); C. H. Giblin, *In Hope of God's Glory,* 144–174; L. Legrand, *The Biblical Doctrine of Virginity;* J. Blenkinsopp, *Celibacy, Ministry, Church;* C. Freible, "Teilhard, Sexual Love, and Celibacy," *Review for Religious* 26 (1968) 282–294; G. H. Frein (ed.), *Celibacy: The Necessary Option;* E. Kennedy, *The New Sexuality: Myths, Fables, and Hang-ups;* H. Nouwen, *Intimacy;* D. Goergen, *The Sexual Celibate.*
39. W. Schmithals, *Gnosticism in Corinth,* 92ff, is typical of those who consider parts of 8:1–11:1 to be passages taken from a different Pauline letter and inserted here by an editor at the end of the first century.
40. H. Conzelmann, *1 Corinthians,* 137ff; C. K. Barrett, *The First Epistle to the Corinthians,* 16, 199ff; and J. C. Hurd, *The Origin of 1 Corinthians,* 115–149, are typical of those who opt for the unity of everything in 8:1–11:1, despite the harsh transitions between chs 8 and 9 and chs 9 and 10, and despite the apparently digressive nature of the material in 9:1–10:22.
41. Cf. J. C. Hurd, *The Origin of 1 Corinthians,* 127ff.
42. Cf. R. F. Hock, *The Social Context of Paul's Ministry,* 50–65.
43. Cf. J. C. Hurd, *The Origin of 1 Corinthians,* 90f; 182–186; C. K. Barrett, *The First Epistle to the Corinthians,* 247.
44. Cf. H. Conzelmann, *1 Corinthians,* 181–191; C. K. Barrett, *The First Epistle to the Corinthians,* 247–258; J. Murphy-O'Connor, *1 Corinthians,* 104–109.
45. Cf. W. O. Walker, Jr., "1 Corinthians 11:2–16 and Paul's Views Regarding Women," *JBL* 94 (March 1975) 94–110, in favor of the secondary character of 1 Cor 11:2–16; and J. Murphy-O'Connor, "The Non-Pauline Character of 1 Corinthians 11:2–16," *JBL* 95 (December 1967) 615–621, in defense of the authenticity of 1 Cor 11:2–16. See also L. Cope, "1 Cor 11:2–16: One Step Further," *JBL* 97 (September 1978) 435–436; and J. P. Meier, "On the Veiling of Hermeneutics (1 Cor 11:2–16)," *CBQ* 40 (April 1978) 212–226; N. M. Flanagan

and E. H. Snyder, "Did Paul Put Down Women in 1 Cor 14:34-36?" *Biblical Theology Bulletin* 11 (January 1981) 10–12.
46. Cf. R. Scroggs, "Paul and the Eschatological Woman," *JAAR* 40 (1972) 282–303; J. Murphy-O'Connor, "Sex and Logic in 1 Corinthians 11:2-16," *CBQ* 42 (October 1980) 482–500.
47. Cf. J. Murphy-O'Connor, *1 Corinthians,* 111.
48. Cf. J. Murphy-O'Connor, *1 Corinthians,* 109–115; J. Jeremias, *The Eucharistic Words of Jesus;* P. Benoit, R. E. Murphy, and B. van Iersel (eds.), *The Breaking of the Bread,* Concilium 40; W. Marxsen, *The Lord's Supper as a Christological Problem;* E. Schweizer, *The Lord's Supper According to the New Testament;* E. Käsemann, "The Pauline Doctrine of the Last Supper," in *Essays on New Testament Themes,* 108–135; G. Sloyan, "'Primitive' and 'Pauline' Concepts of the Eucharist," *CBQ* 23 (1961) 1–13; H. Conzelmann, *1 Corinthians,* 192–203; C. K. Barrett, *The First Epistle to the Corinthians,* 258–279.
49. Cf. H. Conzelmann, *1 Corinthians,* 205f, for a discussion of the mystery cults.
50. Paul's concluding words about doing everything "decently and in order" in 14:40 may well form an inclusion-conclusion with 12:2-3.
51. Schmithals discusses the problem at length in his *Gnosticism in Corinth,* 124–130, and attributes the words to Gnostic Christians.
52. Cf. C. K. Barrett, *The First Epistle to the Corinthians,* 287ff.
53. C. K. Barrett, *The First Epistle to the Corinthians,* 292, explains the metaphor this way: "The genitive (*Xristou* — of Christ) is not of identity but of possession and authority; not, the body which is Christ, of which Christ consists, but, the body that belongs to Christ, and over which he rules (as Head, as later epistles will say: Col i. 18; ii. 19: Eph i, 22; iv. 15; v. 23; cf. 1 Cor xi. 3), separate from the body even though continuous with it. Since the resurrection (in some anticipated sense, perhaps, before it) Christ has been the new humanity living in the new age. His members have their place in this eschatological entity, and, as members of it, must live accordingly."
54. Cf. R. Schnackenburg, *The Church in the New Testament,* 77–85, 176ff; J. Metz, *Theology of the World,* 81–100, 107–140; *Sacramentum Mundi,* 1:320–323, 332–337.
55. See C. K. Barrett, *The Signs of an Apostle.*
56. The literature on the gifts of the Spirit and the Pentecostal movement is abundant. The following are especially recommended: G. Montague, *The Spirit and His Gifts;* L. J. Suenens, *A New Pentecost;* S. Tugwell, *Did You Receive the Spirit?;* S. Clark, *Spiritual Gifts; Baptized in the Spirit;* K. McDonnell, *Catholic Pentecostalism: Problems in Evaluation;* J. M. Ford, *The Pentecostal Experience;* D. Gelpi, *Pentecostalism: A Theological Viewpoint; Pentecostal Piety;* D. M. Stanley, *Boasting in the Lord;* F. MacNutt, *Healing;* J. Fichter, *The Catholic Cult of the Paraclete;* E. D. O'Connor, *Perspectives on Charismatic Renewal.*
57. Cf. H. Conzelmann, *1 Corinthians,* 217ff; C. K. Barrett, *The First Epistle to the Corinthians,* 298ff; V. Furnish, *Theology and Ethics in Paul; The Love Command in the New Testament;* G. Bornkamm, *Early Christian Experience,* 180–193; J. C. Hurd, *The Origin of 1 Corinthians,* 108–113.
58. J. Hering states categorically: "Chapter 13 did not originally occupy its present place in the Epistle" (*The First Epistle of St. Paul to the Corinthians,* 134).
59. Cf. C. K. Barrett, *The First Epistle to the Corinthians,* 299.
60. Cf. H. Conzelmann, *1 Corinthians,* 221.
61. Quoted from C. K. Barrett, *The First Epistle to the Corinthians,* 299.

62. J. C. Hurd in *The Origin of 1 Corinthians,* 112, observes that if one omits or adds negatives, one gets a description of the Corinthian community; for example, "love is patient and kind" — "The Corinthians are impatient and unkind," etc. This, however, may be reading far too much into Paul's intentions.

63. C. K. Barrett, in *The First Epistle to the Corinthians,* 310, expresses it this way: "As however Paul's description of love proceeds, it becomes apparent not only that the only human model he can have used is Jesus of Nazareth, but that the description is a description of the love of God, who alone loves spontaneously and without motivation (the language is Nygren's)."

64. J. C. Hurd, *The Origin of 1 Corinthians,* 281, reconstructs the correspondence between Paul and the Corinthians (186–195; 226–228) and concludes that "the aspect of the Corinthians' manner of worship which became the major issue between Paul and the Corinthians was their exaggerated emphasis on speaking with tongues."

65. G. Montague gives a good definition of the gifts in his study *The Spirit and His Gifts;* he defines tongues on pp. 27–28; prophecy and the gift of interpretation of tongues on pp. 33–35; see also C. F. D. Moule, *The Holy Spirit;* E. Schweizer, *The Holy Spirit.*

66. G. Montague, *The Spirit and His Gifts.*

67. H. Conzelmann, *1 Corinthians,* 246. See also W. O. Walker, Jr., "1 Corinthians 11:2-16 and Paul's Views Regarding Women," *JBL* 94 (March 1975) 94–110.

68. N. M. Flanagan and E. H. Snyder, "Did Paul Put Down Women in 1 Cor 14:34-36?" *Biblical Theology Bulletin* (January 1981) 10–12.

69. See R. H. Fuller, *The Formation of the Resurrection Narratives;* C. F. Evans, *Resurrection and the New Testament;* E. L. Bode, *The First Easter Morning;* P. Benoit and R. Murphy (eds.), *Immortality and Resurrection;* W. Pannenberg, *Jesus: God and Man,* 66–114; C. F. D. Moule (ed.), *The Significance of the Message of the Resurrection for Faith in Jesus Christ;* J. Moltmann, *The Theology of Hope,* 137–229; R. Bultmann, *Theology of the New Testament,* 1:77–83, 292–313; D. M. Stanley, *Christ's Resurrection in Pauline Soteriology;* W. Künneth, *The Theology of the Resurrection;* R. Jewett, *Paul's Anthropological Terms;* W. Marxsen, *The Resurrection of Jesus of Nazareth;* E. Schillebeeckx, *Jesus.*

70. W. Schmithals, *Gnosticism in Corinth,* 157–158.

71. G. Bornkamm, *Paul,* 73, says: "This is why the great chapter in 1 Cor, ch 15, insists, against those who believe themselves to be already partaking in the life of heaven, that the resurrection of the dead lies still in the future."

72. Cf. B. A. Pearson, *The Pneumatikos-Psychikos Terminology in 1 Corinthians,* 15ff.

73. Some extend the content of the received tradition from vv 3-7; others restrict it to vv 3-5 (cf. C. K. Barrett, *The First Epistle to the Corinthians,* 343; J. Jeremias, *The Eucharistic Words of Jesus,* 101ff; H. Conzelmann, *1 Corinthians,* 257).

74. Cf. O. Cullmann, *The Christology of the New Testament,* 164–181; R. Scroggs, *The Last Adam;* W. Kramer, *Christ, Lord, Son of God,* 65–84.

75. Cf. R. J. Sider, "The Pauline Conception of the Resurrection Body in 1 Corinthians xv.35-54," *New Testament Studies* 21 (1975) 428–439. See also B. A. Pearson, *The Pneumatikos-Psychikos Terminology in 1 Corinthians;* G. W. E. Nickelsburg, Jr., *Resurrection, Immortality, and Eternal Life in Intertestamental Judaism.*

76. For a discussion of the collection and its significance for dating Paul's letters, cf. Buck-Taylor, *Saint Paul,* 23–30.

CHAPTER IV

PHILIPPIANS

Select Bibliography

Getty, M. *Philippians and Philemon.* Wilmington, Del.: Michael Glazier, 1980.
Houlden, J. L. *Paul's Letters from Prison.* The Pelican New Testament Commentaries. Baltimore: Penguin Books, 1970.
Martin, R. P. *Carmen Christi.* London: Cambridge Univ. Press, 1967.
Sampley, J. P. *Pauline Partnership in Christ.* Philadelphia: Fortress Press, 1980.

Notes for Chapter IV: PHILIPPIANS

1. Some authors date Philippians to Paul's Caesarean or Roman imprisonment. Most, however, opt for Ephesus and Paul's imprisonment there as the occasion for the letter (cf. J. Fitzmyer, *JBC* 50:5-6; G. Bornkamm, *Paul,* 80).
2. Cf. J. Fitzmyer, *JBC* 50:7-8; W. Marxsen, *Introduction to the New Testament,* 61; G. Bornkamm, *Paul,* 246-247.
3. For the full significance of the Pauline term "partnership," see J. P. Sampley, *Pauline Partnership in Christ.*
4. Cf. J. P. Sampley, *Pauline Partnership in Christ,* 66-69. As Sampley puts it, Euodia and Syntyche (4:2) "are called to live with one another as chapter 2 has expressed it in so many ways: in love, in accord seeking each other's interests, not in self-service or conceit."
5. Cf. J. P. Sampley, *Pauline Partnership in Christ,* 61-62; 89-91.
6. The most comprehensive treatment of Phil 2:6-11 is R. P. Martin's *Carmen Christi;* see also J. T. Sanders, *The New Testament Christological Hymns;* R. H. Fuller, *The Foundations of New Testament Theology;* O. Cullmann, *The Christology of the New Testament;* R. N. Longenecker, *The Christology of Early Jewish Christianity;* J. L. Houlden, *Paul's Letters from Prison;* R. Scroggs, *The Last Adam;* J. Fitzmyer, *JBC* 50:1ff; J. Jeremias, *Jesus' Promise to the Nations;* C. H. Talbert, "The Problem of Preexistence in Philippians 2:6-11," *JBL* 86 (June 1967) 141-153; G. Howard, "Philippians 2:6-11 and the Human Christ," *CBQ* 40 (July 1978) 368-387; F. Manns, "Philippians 2:6-11: A Judaeo-Christian Hymn," *Theology Digest* (Spring 1978) 4-9; J. P. Sampley, *Pauline Partnership in Christ,* 62-72.
7. Cf. C. H. Giblin, *In Hope of God's Glory,* 109, for a list of terms used in the hymn and in 2:1-18, the context of the hymn.
8. Cf. L. Cerfaux, *Christ in the Theology of St. Paul,* 375ff.
9. Cf. J. Fitzmyer, *JBC* 50:18-19, for a brief explanation of this opinion.
10. Cf. O. Cullmann, *The Christology of the New Testament,* 164-181; also R. P. Martin, *Carmen Christi,* 102ff; 161ff.
11. Cf. O. Cullmann, *Christology,* 178.
12. Cf. O. Cullmann, *Christology,* 181.
13. Cf. R. P. Martin, *Carmen Christi,* 163f.
14. Cf. C. H. Talbert, "The Problem of Preexistence in Philippians 2:6-11," *JBL* 86 (June 1967) 141-153.
15. Cf. C. H. Talbert, *ibid.,* 153.
16. Cf. J. P. Sampley, *Pauline Partnership in Christ,* 68.

17. Cf. J. P. Sampley, *Pauline Partnership in Christ,* 51-72.
18. Cf. J. P. Sampley, *Pauline Partnership in Christ,* 11-17.

CHAPTER V

SECOND CORINTHIANS

Select Bibliography

Barrett, C. K. *The Second Epistle to the Corinthians.* New York: Harper and Row, 1973.
_____. *The Signs of an Apostle.* Philadelphia: Fortress Press, 1972.
O'Curraoin, T. "2 Corinthians," in *A New Catholic Commentary on Holy Scripture.* London: Thomas Nelson and Sons, 1969.
O'Rourke, J. J. "The Second Letter to the Corinthians," *Jerome Biblical Commentary.* Englewood Cliffs, N.J.: Prentice-Hall, 1968.

Notes for Chapter V: SECOND CORINTHIANS

1. Cf. C. K. Barrett, *The Second Epistle to the Corinthians,* 5-21; W. Marxsen, *Introduction to the New Testament,* 77-91; J. J. O'Rourke, in *JBC* 52:1-5; T. O'Curraoin, "2 Corinthians," in *A New Catholic Commentary on Holy Scripture,* 1161-1164.
2. Cf. C. K. Barrett, *The Second Epistle to the Corinthians,* 18-21.
3. Cf. C. K. Barrett, *The Second Epistle to the Corinthians,* 244ff, for a refutation of the view that 2 Cor 10-13 constitutes the "painful letter."
4. Concerning the *berakah,* cf. J. C. Kirby, *Ephesians, Baptism and Pentecost,* 84ff.
5. Concerning the pseudo-apostles and the one in particular who attacked and insulted Paul, Barrett remarks: "They did not accept Paul's apostolic status: he carried no letter of commendation, and his Gospel of justification by faith only apart from the works of the law was suspect. Perhaps not at first, but probably later, they described him as a false apostle . . ., lacking in qualification and authority" (*The Second Epistle to the Corinthians,* 7).
6. Cf. W. Marxsen, *Introduction to the New Testament,* 85.
7. On Christomorphism, see L. Gilkey, *Naming the Whirlwind,* 380f, 408f.
8. Cf. J. Bright, "An Exercise in Hermeneutics (Jer 31:31-34)," *Interpretation* 20 (April 1966) 192-193; G. von Rad, *Message of the Prophets,* 178-186; W. Most, "Biblical Theology of Redemption in a Covenant Framework," *CBQ* 29 (January 1967) 9ff; A. Heschel, *The Prophets,* 128-129; J. Lindblom, *Prophecy in Ancient Israel,* 373; R. Murphy, "Relationship between the Covenants," *CBQ* 26 (October 1964) 351; E. W. Nicholson, *Jeremiah,* 26-52, 180ff.
9. Cf. W. D. Davies, *Paul and Rabbinic Judaism,* 309-320; C. K. Barrett, *The Second Epistle to the Corinthians,* 150-159.
10. Cf. pp. 111f.
11. Cf. N. Perrin, *The New Testament: An Introduction,* 104-105; Feine-Behm-Kümmel, *Introduction to the New Testament,* 211-215; W. Marxsen, *Introduc-*

tion to the New Testament, 77–82; R. H. Fuller, *A Critical Introduction to the New Testament,* 46–49.

CHAPTER VI

GALATIANS

Select Bibliography

Betz, H. D. *Galatians.* Philadelphia: Fortress Press, 1979.
Fitzmyer, J. "Galatians," *The Jerome Biblical Commentary.* Englewood Cliffs, N.J.: Prentice-Hall, 1968.
Osiek, C. *Galatians.* Wilmington, Del.: Michael Glazier, 1980.
Stendahl, K. *Paul Among Jews and Gentiles.* Philadelphia: Fortress Press, 1976.
Taylor, M. J. (ed.). *A Companion to Paul.* New York: Alba House, 1975.

Notes for Chapter VI: GALATIANS

1. Cf. H. D. Betz, *Galatians,* passim.
2. Cf. R. H. Fuller, *A Critical Introduction to the New Testament,* 26; J. N. Sanders, "Galatians," *Peake's Commentary on the Bible,* 973, par 850e.
3. Cf. M. Barth, *Ephesians 1–3,* 34.
4. Cf. H. D. Betz, *Galatians,* 14.
5. On giving "the right hand of fellowship," cf. J. P. Sampley, *Pauline Partnership in Christ,* 29ff.
6. Cf. H. D. Betz, *Galatians,* 144.
7. Cf. C. Osiek, *Galatians,* 49.
8. See Q. Quesnell, *The Gospel of Christian Freedom,* 122ff.
9. Cf. S. Lyonnet, "Law and Liberty," in M. J. Taylor (ed.), *A Companion to Paul.*
10. Cf. C. Osiek, *Galatians,* 64.
11. Cf. H. D. Betz, *Galatians,* 164, n. 27.
12. Cf. C. Osiek, *Galatians,* 79f.

CHAPTER VII

ROMANS

Select Bibliography

Barrett, C. K. *A Commentary on the Epistle to the Romans.* London: Adam and Charles Black, 1957.
Bornkamm, G. *Paul.* New York: Harper and Row, 1971.

Fitzmyer, J. "The Letter to the Romans," *Jerome Biblical Commentary.* Englewood
   Cliffs, N.J.: Prentice-Hall, 1968.
Käsemann, E. *Commentary on Romans.* Grand Rapids, Mich.: Wm. B. Eerdmans,
   1980.
Maly, E. H. *Romans.* Wilmington, Del.: Michael Glazier, 1979.
Munck, J. *Christ and Israel.* Philadelphia: Fortress Press, 1967.
Stendahl, K. *Paul Among Jews and Gentiles.* Philadelphia: Fortress Press, 1976.
Taylor, M. J. (ed.). *A Companion to Paul.* New York: Alba House, 1975.

Notes for Chapter VII: ROMANS

1. Cf. K. Stendahl, *Paul Among Jews and Gentiles,* 1-7.
2. Cf. K. P. Donfried (ed.), *The Romans Debate.*
3. Cf. W. Marxsen, *Introduction to the New Testament,* 95-104.
4. Cf. G. Bornkamm, *Paul,* 117-118.
5. Cf. E. Käsemann, *Romans,* viii.
6. Cf. C. K. Barrett, *Epistle to the Romans,* 21.
7. Cf. G. Bornkamm, *Paul,* 114.
8. Cf. E. Käsemann, *Romans,* 52.
9. Cf. C. K. Barrett, *Epistle to the Romans,* 61.
10. Cf. E. Käsemann, *Romans,* 80.
11. Cf. C. K. Barrett, *Epistle to the Romans,* 80.
12. Cf. C. K. Barrett, *Epistle to the Romans,* 84.
13. Cf. C. K. Barrett, *Epistle to the Romans,* 84.
14. Cf. Buck-Taylor, *Saint Paul,* 244.
15. Cf. E. Käsemann, *Romans,* 196.
16. Cf. E. Käsemann, *Romans,* 246.
17. Cf. E. Käsemann, *Romans,* 257.
18. Cf. C. K. Barrett, *Epistle to the Romans,* 193.
19. Cf. E. Maly, *Romans,* 87.
20. Cf. C. K. Barrett, *Epistle to the Romans,* 212.
21. Cf. C. K. Barrett, *Epistle to the Romans,* 215.
22. Cf. E. Maly, *Romans,* 103.
23. Cf. E. Maly, *Romans,* 105.
24. Cf. K. P. Donfried, *The Romans Debate.*
25. Cf. C. K. Barrett, *Epistle to the Romans,* 272.
26. Cf. C. K. Barrett, *Epistle to the Romans,* 9-13; E. Käsemann, *Romans,* 409-
   422.
27. Cf. E. Käsemann, *Romans,* 422ff.

Bibliography

Allo, E. B. *Saint Paul: Seconde Épître aux Corinthiens.* Paris: Gabalda, 1956.

Amiot, F. *The Key Concepts of St. Paul.* New York: Herder and Herder, 1965.

Audet, J. P. *Celibacy in the Pastoral Service of the Church.* London: Sheed and Ward, 1967.

Austgen, R. J. *Natural Motivation in the Pauline Epistles.* Notre Dame, Ind.: Univ. of Notre Dame Press, 1966.

Banks, R. *Paul's Idea of Community.* Grand Rapids, Mich.: Wm. B. Eerdmans, 1980.

Barrett, C. K. *Commentary on the Epistle to the Romans.* London: Adam and Charles Black, 1967.

_____. *Commentary on the First Epistle to the Corinthians.* New York: Harper and Row, 1968.

_____. *Commentary on the Second Epistle to the Corinthians.* New York: Harper and Row, 1973.

_____. *Luke the Historian in Recent Studies.* Philadelphia: Fortress Press, 1970.

_____. *Jesus and the Gospel Tradition.* Philadelphia: Fortress Press, 1968.

_____. *Signs of an Apostle.* Philadelphia: Fortress Press, 1972.

Benoit, P., and Murphy, R., eds. *Immortality and Resurrection.* Concilium 60. New York: Herder and Herder, 1970.

Benoit, P., and Murphy, R., and van Iersel, B., eds. *The Breaking of Bread.* New York: Paulist Press, 1969.

Berkhof, H. *Christ and the Powers.* Scottdale, Pa.: Herald Press, 1962.

Best, E. *A Commentary on the First and Second Epistles to the Thessalonians.* New York: Harper and Row, 1972.

Betz, H. D. *Galatians.* Hermeneia Commentaries. Philadelphia: Fortress Press, 1979.

Bianchi, U., ed. *The Origins of Gnosticism.* Leiden: Brill, 1967.

Blenkinsopp, J. *The Corinthians' Mirror.* New York: Sheed and Ward, 1964.

_____. *Celibacy, Ministry, Church.* New York: Herder and Herder, 1968.

Bode, E. L. *The First Easter Morning.* Rome: Biblical Institute Press, 1970.

Bonsirven, J. *Exégèse rabbinique et exégèse paulinienne.* Paris: Beauchesne, 1939.

Bornkamm, G. *Paul.* New York: Harper and Row, 1969.

_____. *Early Christian Experience.* New York: Harper and Row, 1969.
Braaten, C. E. *Christ and Counter-Christ.* New York: Harper and Row, 1972.
Buck, C., and Taylor, G. *Saint Paul.* New York: Charles Scribner's Sons, 1969.
Bultmann, R. *The Old and the New Man.* Richmond, Va.: John Knox Press, 1967.
_____. *History and Eschatology.* New York: Harper and Row, 1957.
_____. *Theology of the New Testament.* New York: Charles Scribner's Sons, 1955.
Cerfaux, L. *Christ in the Theology of St. Paul.* New York: Herder and Herder, 1966.
_____. *The Church in the Theology of Saint Paul.* New York: Herder and Herder, 1959.
Conzelmann, H. *1 Corinthians.* Philadelphia: Fortress Press, 1975.
_____. *An Outline of the Theology of the New Testament.* New York: Harper and Row, 1969.
Cullmann, O. *The Christology of the New Testament.* Philadelphia: Westminster Press, 1963.
Davies, W. D. *Paul and Rabbinic Judaism.* London: SPCK, 1955.
_____. *Introduction to Pharisaeism.* Philadelphia: Fortress Press, 1967.
de Vaux, R. *Ancient Israel.* London: Darton, Longman and Todd, 1961.
Dodd, C. H. *The Parables of the Kingdom.* New York: Charles Scribner's Sons, 1961.
_____. *The Interpretation of the Fourth Gospel.* Cambridge: University Press, 1968.
Donfried, K. P., ed. *The Romans Debate.* Minneapolis: Augsburg Press, 1977.
Doty, W. G. *Letters in Primitive Christianity.* Philadelphia: Fortress Press, 1973.
Dungan, D. L. *The Sayings of Jesus in the Churches of Paul.* Philadelphia: Fortress Press, 1971.
Dunn, J. D. G. *Jesus and the Spirit.* Philadelphia: Westminster Press, 1975.
Ellis, P. F. *The Men and the Message of the Old Testament.* Collegeville: Liturgical Press, 1963.
_____. *Matthew: His Mind and His Message.* Collegeville: Liturgical Press, 1974.
Evans, D. F. *Resurrection and the New Testament.* Naperville, Ill.: Alec R. Allenson, 1970.
Fallon, F. T. *2 Corinthians.* Wilmington, Del.: Michael Glazier, 1980.
Feine, P., Behm, J., Kümmel, W. G. *Introduction to the New Testament.* Nashville: Abingdon Press, 1966.
Fichter, J. *The Catholic Cult of the Paraclete.* New York: Sheed and Ward, 1975.
Fitzmyer, J. *Pauline Theology: A Brief Sketch.* Englewood Cliffs, N.J.: Prentice-Hall, 1967.
_____. "The Letter to the Romans," *Jerome Biblical Commentary.* Englewood Cliffs, N.J.: Prentice-Hall, 1968.
Ford, J. M. *The Pentecostal Experience.* Paramus, N.J.: Paulist Press, 1970.
Francis, F. O., and Sampley, J.P. *Pauline Parallels.* Philadelphia: Fortress Press, 1975.
Frein, G. H., ed. *Celibacy: The Necessary Option.* New York: Herder and Herder, 1968.
Fuller, R. H. *The Foundations of New Testament Theology.* New York: Charles Scribner's Sons, 1965.
_____. *The Formation of the Resurrection Narratives.* New York: Macmillan Company, 1971.

————. *The New Testament in Current Studies.* New York: Charles Scribner's Sons, 1962.

Furnish, V. P. *The Love Command in the New Testament.* Nashville: Abingdon Press, 1972.

————. *Theology and Ethics in Paul.* Nashville: Abingdon Press, 1968.

Gelpi, D. *Pentecostalism: A Theological Viewpoint.* New York: Paulist Press, 1971.

Georgi, D. *The Opponents of Paul in 2 Corinthians.* Philadelphia: Fortress Press, 1980.

Getty, M. A. *Philippians and Philemon.* Wilmington, Del.: Michael Glazier, 1960.

Giblin, C. H. *In Hope of God's Glory.* New York: Herder and Herder, 1970.

Gilkey, L. *Naming the Whirlwind.* New York: Bobbs-Merrill, 1969.

Gnilka, J. *The Epistle to the Philippians.* London: Sheed and Ward, 1970.

Goergen, D. *The Sexual Celibate.* New York: Seabury Press, 1975.

Grant, F. C. *Ancient Judaism and the New Testament.* New York: Macmillan Company, 1959.

Guthrie, D. *Galatians.* Century Bible, New Series. London: Nelson, 1969.

Haenchen, E. *The Acts of the Apostles.* Philadelphia: Westminster Press, 1971.

Harrell, P. E. *The Letter of Paul to the Philippians.* Austin, Tex.: R. B. Sweet Co., 1969.

Hartmann, L., and DiLella, A. *Daniel.* The Anchor Bible Series. Garden City, N.Y.: Doubleday, 1976.

Heschel, A. *The Prophets.* New York: Harper and Row, 1962.

Hering, J. *The Second Epistle of Saint Paul to the Corinthians.* London: Epworth, 1967.

Hock, R. F. *The Social Context of Paul's Ministry.* Philadelphia: Fortress Press, 1980.

Holmberg, B. *Paul and Power.* Philadelphia: Fortress Press, 1978.

Houlden, J. L. *Ethics and the New Testament.* Baltimore: Penguin, 1973.

————. *Paul's Letters from Prison.* Baltimore: Penguin, 1970.

Hurd, J. C. *The Origin of 1 Corinthians.* New York: Seabury Press, 1965.

Jeremias, J. *New Testament Theology.* New York: Charles Scribner's Sons, 1971.

————. *The Eucharistic Words of Jesus.* New York: Charles Scribner's Sons, 1966.

————. *The Parables of Jesus.* New York: Charles Scribner's Sons, 1962.

Jerome Biblical Commentary. Edited by R. Brown, J. Fitzmyer, R. Murphy. Englewood Cliffs, N.J.: Prentice-Hall, 1968.

Jewett, R. *Paul's Anthropological Terms.* Leiden: Brill, 1971.

————. *A Chronology of Paul's Life.* Philadelphia: Fortress Press, 1979.

Käsemann, E. *Commentary on Romans.* Grand Rapids, Mich.: Wm. B. Eerdmans, 1980.

————. *Perspectives on Paul.* Philadelphia: Fortress Press, 1971.

————. *New Testament Questions of Today.* Philadelphia: Fortress Press, 1969.

Keck, L., and Martyn, J. L. *Studies in Luke-Acts.* Nashville: Abingdon Press, 1966.

Kennedy, E. *The New Sexuality: Myths, Fables, and Hang-Ups.* Garden City, N.Y.: Doubleday Image Books, 1973.

Kirby, J. *Ephesians, Baptism, and Pentecost.* Montreal: McGill University Press, 1968.

Kosnick, A., and others. *Human Sexuality: New Directions in American Catholic Thought.* New York: Paulist Press, 1977.

Knox, J. *Philemon Among the Letters of Paul.* Nashville: Abingdon Press, 1959.

Kramer, W. *Christ, Lord, Son of God.* Naperville, Ill.: Alec R. Allenson, 1966.
Künneth, W. *The Theology of the Resurrection.* St. Louis: Concordia Publishing House, 1965.
Legrand, L. *The Biblical Doctrine of Virginity.* New York: Sheed and Ward, 1963.
Lindblom, J. *Prophecy in Ancient Israel.* Philadelphia: Fortress Press, 1962.
Longenecker, R. N. *The Christology of Early Jewish Christianity.* Naperville, Ill.: Alec R. Allenson, 1970.
Lynch, W. *Images of Hope.* New York: New American Library, 1966.
MacNutt, F. *Healing.* Notre Dame, Ind.: Ave Maria Press, 1974.
Maly, E. H. *Romans.* Wilmington, Del.: Michael Glazier, 1979.
Martin, R. P. *Philippians.* New Century Bible Commentary. Grand Rapids, Mich.: Wm. B. Eerdmans, 1980.
_____. *Carmen Christi.* Cambridge: University Press, 1967.
Marxsen, W. *Introduction to the New Testament.* Philadelphia: Fortress Press, 1974.
_____. *The Lord's Supper as a Christological Problem.* Philadelphia: Fortress Press, 1970.
_____. *The Resurrection of Jesus of Nazareth.* Philadelphia: Fortress Press, 1970.
Metz, J. *Theology of the World.* New York: Herder and Herder, 1969.
_____., ed. *The Evolving World and Theology.* Concilium 36. New York: Paulist Press, 1967.
Moltmann, J. *Theology of Hope.* New York: Harper and Row, 1965.
_____. *Religion, Revolution, and the Future.* Trans. M. Douglas Meeks. New York: Charles Scribner's Sons, 1969.
Montague, G. T. *The Spirit and His Gifts.* New York: Paulist Press, 1974.
_____. *The Biblical Theology of the Secular.* Milwaukee: Bruce, 1967.
Moore, A. L. *The Parousia in the New Testament.* Leiden: Brill, 1966.
Morris, L. *Apocalyptic.* Grand Rapids, Mich.: Wm. B. Eerdmans, 1972.
Moule, C. D., ed. *The Significance of the Message of the Resurrection for Faith in Jesus Christ.* Naperville, Ill.: Alec R. Allenson, 1968.
Munck, J. *Christ and Israel.* Philadelphia: Fortress Press, 1967.
_____. *Paul and the Salvation of Mankind.* Richmond, Va.: John Knox Press, 1959.
Murphy-O'Connor, J. *1 Corinthians.* Wilmington, Del.: Michael Glazier, 1980.
_____. *Becoming Human Together.* Wilmington, Del.: Michael Glazier, 1977.
Nickelsburg, Jr., G. W. E. *Resurrection, Immortality, and Eternal Life in Intertestamental Judaism.* London: Oxford University Press, 1972.
Nineham, D. E. *Saint Mark.* Baltimore: Penguin, 1963.
Nouwen, H. *Intimacy.* Notre Dame, Ind.: Fides Publishers, 1969.
O'Connor, E. D., ed. *Perspectives on Charismatic Renewal.* Notre Dame, Ind.: University of Notre Dame Press, 1975.
Oraison, M. *The Celibate Condition and Sex.* Trans. Leonard Mayhew. New York: Sheed and Ward, 1967.
Osiek, Carolyn. *Galatians.* Wilmington, Del.: Michael Glazier, 1980.
Pannenberg, W. *Jesus: God and Man.* Philadelphia: Westminster Press, 1968.
_____. *Theology and the Kingdom of God.* Philadelphia: Westminster Press, 1969.
Pearson, B. A. *The Pneumatikos-Psychikos Terminology in 1 Corinthians.* Missoula, Mont.: Scholars Press, 1973.

Perrin, N. *The New Testament: An Introduction.* New York: Harcourt Brace Jovanovich, 1974.

Plöger, O. *Theocracy and Eschatology.* Richmond, Va.: John Knox Press, 1968.

Porteous, N. *Daniel.* Philadelphia: Westminster Press, 1965.

Quesnell, Q. *The Gospel of Christian Freedom.* New York: Herder and Herder, 1969.

Reese, J. M. *1 and 2 Thessalonians.* Wilmington, Del.: Michael Glazier, 1979.

Rigaux, B. *Les Épîtres aux Thessaloniciens.* Paris: Gabalda, 1956.

Robinson, J. A. T. *In the End God.* New York: Harper and Row, 1968.

Rowley, H. H. *The Relevance of Apocalyptic.* New York: Association Press, 1963.

Ruef, J. *Paul's First Letter to Corinth.* London: Penguin, 1971.

Russell, D. S. *The Method and Message of Jewish Apocalyptic.* London: SCM Press, 1964.

Sampley, J. P., and Francis, F. O. *Pauline Parallels.* Philadelphia: Fortress Press, 1975.

_____. *Pauline Partnership in Christ.* Philadelphia: Fortress Press, 1980.

Sanders, J. T. *The New Testament Christological Hymns.* Cambridge: University Press, 1971.

Schillebeeckx, E. *Jesus: An Experiment in Christology.* New York: Seabury Press, 1979.

_____. *Christ: The Experience of Jesus as Lord.* New York: Seabury Press, 1980.

_____. *Marriage: Human Reality and Saving Mystery.* New York: Sheed and Ward, 1965.

Schmithals, W. *Gnosticism in Corinth.* Nashville: Abingdon Press, 1971.

_____. *Paul and the Gnostics.* Nashville: Abingdon Press, 1972.

_____. *The Office of Apostle in the Early Church.* Nashville: Abingdon Press, 1972.

Schnackenburg, R. *The Church in the New Testament.* New York: Herder and Herder, 1965.

Schoeps, H. J. *Paul.* Philadelphia: Westminster Press, 1961.

Schubert, P. *Form and Function of the Pauline Thanksgiving.* Philadelphia: Fortress Press, 1971.

Schweizer, E. *The Holy Spirit.* Philadelphia: Fortress Press, 1980.

_____. *The Lord's Supper According to the New Testament.* Philadelphia: Fortress Press, 1967.

Schweitzer, A. *Paul and His Interpreters.* New York: Schocken Books, 1964.

Scroggs, R. *The Last Adam.* Philadelphia: Fortress Press, 1966.

Shep, J. A. *The Nature of the Resurrection Body.* Grand Rapids, Mich.: W. B. Eerdmans, 1964.

Shires, H. M. *The Eschatology of Paul.* Philadelphia: Westminster Press, 1966.

Stanley, D. M. *Boasting in the Lord.* New York: Paulist Press, 1973.

_____. *Christ's Resurrection in Pauline Soteriology.* Rome: Pontificio Istituto Biblico, 1961.

Stendahl, K. *Paul Among Jews and Gentiles.* Philadelphia: Fortress Press, 1976.

_____. *The Bible and the Role of Women.* Philadelphia: Fortress Press, 1966.

Stoger, A. *The Epistle to Philemon.* London: Sheed and Ward, 1970.

Suenens, L. J. *A New Pentecost.* New York: Seabury Press, 1975.

Taylor, M. J., ed. *A Companion to Paul.* New York: Alba House, 1975.

Teilhard de Chardin, P. *The Future of Man.* New York: Harper and Row, 1955.

Tugwell, S. *Did You Receive the Spirit?* New York: Paulist Press, 1972.

van Unnik, W. C. *Tarsus or Jerusalem: The City of Paul's Birth.* London: Epworth Press, 1962.

von Rad, G. *Wisdom in Israel.* Nashville: Abingdon Press, 1972.

Votaw, C. W. *The Gospels and Contemporary Biographies in the Greco-Roman World.* Philadelphia: Fortress Press, 1970.

West, M., and Francis, R. *Scandal in the Assembly.* New York: W. Morrow, 1970.

Wilson, R. Mcl. *Gnosis and the New Testament.* Philadelphia: Fortress Press, 1968.